PSYCHOLOGY: FIELDS OF APPLICATION

Astrid M. Stec
Douglas A. Bernstein

EDITORS

HOUGHTON MIFFLIN COMPANY
BOSTON   NEW YORK

For my son and my friends who teach me to be loving, patient, and wise.

Astrid M. Stec

For Saul Bernstein, my father. He was the steadfast leader of our little band and the bravest man I have ever known. He lives on in me and in all those whose lives were touched by his kindness and generosity, his humor and his love.

Douglas A. Bernstein

Editor-in-Chief: Kathi Prancan
Senior Associate Editor: Jane Knetzger
Developmental Editor: Pamela Barter
Senior Project Editor: Rosemary R. Jaffe
Senior Production/Design Coordinator: Sarah Ambrose
Senior Manufacturing Coordinator: Priscilla J. Abreu
Marketing Manager: Pamela Laskey

Cover Designer: Harold Burch Design, NYC

Printed in the U.S.A.

Library of Congress Catalog Card Number: 98-71987

ISBN: 0-395-86979-X

1 2 3 4 5 6 7 8 9-QF-02 01 00 99 98

CONTENTS

PREFACE

We got the initial idea for this book when Astrid was preparing to teach a course in the history of psychology. While reviewing textbooks for the course, she was struck by the limited coverage given to applications of psychology. Some texts didn't discuss applications at all, and most included only one chapter. This was a surprise because large numbers of psychologists work in applied areas, and have done so since the beginning of the discipline. Anyone reading a typical history of psychology textbook would get a good understanding of the progress of theories and research in psychology, but would gain little knowledge of how psychologists have applied these to everyday situations. Not only do students sometimes lack information about the connections between academic and applied psychology, but the general public often has a restricted view as well. Many people associate psychology only with assessment and treatment of psychological disorders, and remain unaware that when they, for example, purchase a new computer, take part in a job interview, visit a zoo, serve on a jury, decide to use a condom, travel by plane, or tune their radio, their experiences are influenced by applied psychological research.

Putting these ideas together, we decided to create a book that would introduce undergraduate students to the major areas of applied psychology, while providing a behind-the-scenes look not only at clinical psychology, but other applications as well. We chose to make this an edited book with chapters written by psychologists who specialize in each of the most prominent areas of applied psychology.

We hope that this book is comprehensive enough that it could stand alone as a text for a survey course in applied psychology, and interesting enough that it could be assigned as supplementary reading for introductory, history of psychology, or applied psychology courses. Students will find a wealth of information about research, theories, and applications, as well as an extensive list of references. The book may also introduce students (or career counselors) to the wide range of careers available in applied psychology. In order to appeal to general readers, we have spiced the content with many down-to-earth examples, and have aimed for a readable style and language.

This book reflects the uniqueness of the field of psychology, which, unlike many other disciplines, maintains a close connection between pure, academic science and applications of that knowledge to real-world situations and problems. The contents of the chapters consistently show how scientific research, theories, and practical applications are solidly linked. Another special attribute of this book is that it includes a broad range of applications—everything from how consumers make decisions in choosing products, to what psychologists know about paranormal phenomena. Moreover, readers can choose to focus on various areas of interest. This is a book whose chapters lend themselves to being read in any order, not just from first to last.

The first chapter describes how, when, and why the discipline of psychology and its applications started. It sets the scene and provides some background for the subsequent chapters, each of which focuses on a specific application. In those chapters, the authors give a brief history of their specialty area, examples of research in the area, the theories behind that research, the ways in which the research has been applied, and current challenges in the field. The final chapter provides an overview of the ways in which we are all influenced by applications of psychological research and summarizes some of the work that lies ahead.

The contributors to this book are a diverse group of psychologists from various parts of North America, representing a wide range of specialties. Many have published extensively in their field. Some are employed full time in their area of application; others' chief association is with university departments.

Acknowledgments

First, we would like to express our appreciation to the contributors whose chapters make up the bulk of this book. They were wonderfully cooperative and never seemed to mind when we sent them yet one more request. Secondly, we want to heartily thank those who are close to us for their enthusiastic support of us and this book project. Finally, we wish to extend our sincere gratitude to Jane Knetzger for her wise and ready answers to our numerous questions, to Pam Barter for her diligent work on the manuscript, and to Rosemary Jaffe for ever so carefully and patiently overseeing the production of the book.

Astrid M. Stec
Douglas A. Bernstein

CONTRIBUTORS

Anthony D. Andre, Ph.D., is founder and principal of Interface Analysis Associates, San Jose, California. Interface Analysis Associates is a human factors and ergonomic consulting firm specializing in user interface design, usability evaluation, and workplace ergonomics.

Winfred Arthur, Jr., Ph.D., is an Associate Professor of Psychology at Texas A& M University. His specialty is industrial-organizational psychology, and his research interests include personnel selection, test development and evaluation, and training design, delivery, and evaluation.

Lisa G. Aspinwall, Ph.D., is an Associate Professor of Psychology at the University of Maryland. Her specialties are health and social psychology, and her research interests encompass understanding how people respond to negative events and information, especially how positive beliefs and making comparisons with others influence this process.

Ludy T. Benjamin, Jr., Ph.D., is University Professor of Teaching Excellence at Texas A&M University. His publications focus on the history of American psychology. Currently he is writing a book on the history of psychology in American business.

Douglas A. Bernstein, Ph.D., has been a Professor of Psychology at the University of Illinois at Urbana-Champaign. He now holds visiting appointments at both the University of South Florida and the University of Surrey. He is co-author of several textbooks, including Introductory, Clinical, and Abnormal Psychology, and is chairperson of the Annual National Institute on the Teaching of Psychology.

Stanley Coren, Ph.D., is a Professor of Psychology at the University of British Columbia, Canada. He has researched individual differences, sensory functions, laterality, and human behavior genetics in humans. He has also published books about canine behavior and human-dog interactions.

Ron E. Franco Durán, Ph.D., is an Assistant Professor of Psychology at the University of Miami, Florida. His research interests include the study of group interventions for people living with chronic illness, the effects of help-intended interpersonal communication (such as self-disclosure and empathy), and diversity issues in health psychology.

Frank R. Kardes, Ph.D., is a Professor of Marketing in the College of Business Administration at the University of Cincinnati. His research interests are in consumer psychology; judgment, inference, and decision processes; memory and cognition; social influence; advertising and branding; and experimental methodology.

Michael T. Nietzel, Ph.D., is Professor of Psychology and Dean of the Graduate School at the University of Kentucky. He teaches a seminar on psychology and the law for psychology and law students, and often serves as a consultant to attorneys, judges, and the police on forensic issues.

Glyn C. Roberts, Ph.D., has been a Professor of Kinesiology at the University of Illinois at Urbana-Champaign, and now holds the Chair of Psychology at the Norwegian University of Sport Science in Oslo, Norway. He has published books and chapters on motivational determinants of achievement within the sport context, for both adults and children. He is former president of The North American Society of Sport Psychology.

Leon Segal, Ph.D., is Director of IDEO Design and Product Development in Israel, where he also teaches at the Betzalel Academy of Art and Design. He has designed a variety of products ranging from aircraft cockpits and palmtop computers to medical products and furniture systems.

Robert Sommer, Ph.D., is Professor of Psychology and Chair of the Department of Art at the University of California, Davis. Some of his projects include the design of libraries, airports, classrooms, banks, offices, restaurants, farmers' markets, bicycle paths, mental hospitals, and prisons.

Astrid M. Stec, M.A., is a Professor of Psychology at the University College of the Fraser Valley in Abbotsford, British Columbia, Canada. She is also a registered psychologist in private practice. Her interests lie in the history of psychology, and models of psychotherapy.

Jane Fulton Suri, M.Sc., is Director of Human Factors Design and Research at IDEO in San Francisco. She pioneered the application of psychology to IDEO's design process for products as diverse as toothbrushes and trains. She lectures at Stanford California College of Arts and Crafts and at the University of California, Berkeley, Business School.

Darren C. Treasure, Ph.D., is an Assistant Professor of Kinesiology at Arizona State University, a sport psychology consultant with numerous collegiate programs, and a member of the United States Soccer Federation's National Coaching Staff. His research interests focus on the influence of social psychological variables on behavioral, cognitive, and affective aspects of sport and exercise.

Stuart A. Vyse, Ph.D., is an Associate Professor of Psychology at Connecticut College. His current research is in decision making, choice, superstition, and irrational behavior.

Christopher D. Wickens, Ph.D., is a Professor of Psychology, Head of the Aviation Research Laboratory, and Associate Director of the Institute of Aviation at the University of Illinois at Urbana-Champaign. His research interests focus on the application of human attention, perception, and cognition to operator performance and designs in aviation, air traffic control, and data visualization.

Anita Woolfolk Hoy, Ph.D., is a Professor in the College of Education at Ohio State University. Her research has focused on teachers' knowledge and beliefs, teacher and student motivation, and the application of educational psychology to teaching.

THE SCOPE OF PSYCHOLOGY: MORE THAN MEETS THE EYE

Astrid M. Stec and Douglas A. Bernstein

When you meet someone at a party, on an airplane, or at a dinner and find out that the person is a psychologist, do you think, "Uh-oh, I better watch what I say, or I'll be analyzed"? The stereotype of psychologists as disorder-detecting therapists is no doubt responsible for the fact that, compared to architects, chemists, economists, and engineers, psychologists are far and away the professional group that people "feel most ill at ease with in a social situation."[1] This stereotype is reinforced by our cultural media. Movies and television, for example, almost always portray psychologists as *clinical* psychologists, the subgroup most involved in diagnosing, treating, and studying mental and emotional disorders. Similarly, the psychology sections of most bookstores are devoted mainly to volumes that offer advice, self-help tips, or discussions of treatments for disorders ranging from obesity and bulimia to depression and schizophrenia.

Like most other stereotypes, the one that characterizes all psychologists as mental health professionals is partly true. Clinical psychology *is* the largest single specialty area among members of the American and Canadian Psychological associations. However, clinical psychologists are in the minority in these organizations, accounting for only about 42 percent of their total membership.[2] That percentage is even lower, about 11 percent, in smaller organizations such as the American Psychological Society.[3]

If clinicians are in the minority among psychologists, what do the majority of psychologists do? Does their work have the same relevance to everyday life as the diagnostic, treatment, and research activities of clinicians? If so, why don't most people know about it? These are some of the questions addressed in this book, which describes the evolution of psychology as a scientific discipline that has been applied in ways that affect most people's lives, even if they never seek help from a therapist. By the time you have read the final chapter, we hope you will have a clear understanding of the countless, often surprising, ways in which the work of psychologists touches your everyday life—when you use a computer, prepare to have surgery, drive your car, read an ad, apply for a job, serve on a jury, donate to a cause, or travel by plane. Indeed, we hope that this book helps you to discover how few areas of human life are *not* affected by psychology, and why the twentieth century has been called the "Psychological Century."[4]

In this opening chapter, we briefly describe when, how, and why the discipline of psychology began, and we sketch some of the ways in which psychologists' research results came to be applied in an ever-increasing number of domains. In the next twelve chapters, psychologists who have been deeply involved in a dozen of these domains describe in detail how the application of psychological research affects us all. Finally, in a closing chapter, we summarize the ways in which we are all influenced by applications of psychological research and take a look at how it is likely to affect our everyday lives in the twenty-first century.

The Historical Background of Psychology

Psychology has been accurately described as having a long past but a short history.[5] The word *psychology* was first used about four hundred years ago, but there were few references to it until the nineteenth century.[6] Further, many of the questions that interest psychologists—How does the mind function? How do the mind and body affect each other? What is consciousness, and are there different states of consciousness? Why do people think, feel, and behave as they do?—have been around much longer than there has been a discipline called psychology. These questions were once addressed mainly by philosophers, mystics, and the clergy. Psychology emerged as a separate discipline in the late nineteenth century only when those who would become known as psychologists began to seek answers to these questions using scientific methods instead of relying on intuition, personal experience, speculation about what others experience, or answers passed down from authority figures or tradition.

Scientific methods—which emphasize empirical observation over speculation, logic over intuition, experimentation over tradition, and skeptical inquiry over acceptance of established belief—were by no means new in the nineteenth century. For two hundred years, these methods had been employed in the exploration of natural laws governing biological, chemical, and physical processes—laws that would supplant the idea that the world and the universe are controlled by gods, demons, or other supernatural forces. It took two hundred years, though, before anyone began to use scientific methods to study human behavior and mental processes, thus giving birth to psychology, the *science* of behavior and mental processes. Why did it take so long to recognize that questions about how people think, feel, and behave could be investigated logically and objectively? One reason is that doing so required a major shift in the way people think about themselves. It was not easy for humans to think about behavior, especially their own behavior, as a part of the natural world and that, like the growth of plants or the movement of planets, it might be governed by natural laws that can be described and understood. Second, it took a long time to recognize that our mental experience of the world is not a perfect reflection of that world, that our subjective perceptions, our internal awareness of reality, may differ from what is objectively "out there." Third, it took a while to accept the notion that the goings on in the human mind could be objectively measured like other bodily functions.

It was no coincidence that these revolutionary changes in the way people think about themselves and their behavior appeared in the nineteenth century. In his introduction to nineteenth century thought, historian Richard Schoenwald wrote, "The eighteenth century speculated about whether change was possible. The nineteenth knew deliriously that it was. Men and nations expected to rebuild their lives entirely: more and more people claimed the right to change as the only birthright worth having." The emphasis on change meant that traditions needed to be re-evaluated because old answers were no longer considered adequate. Skepticism became the order of the day. Friedrich Nietzsche, one of the greatest philosophers of the nineteenth century, wrote that "great spirits are skeptics. . . . Convictions are prisons. . . . Freedom from all kinds of convictions, to be able to see freely, is part of strength," and "a very popular error: having the courage of one's convictions; rather it is a matter of having the courage for an *attack* on one's convictions!!!"[7]

As people began to depend less on external traditions as guides for how to be, there was a gradual turning inward, a transition that is evident if we look at changes in art, music, and literature. The paintings of the Old Masters, for example, had focused on reproducing reality, but the painters of the nineteenth century became impressionists: they painted what they *subjectively* perceived, not what they *objectively* saw. (This trend would continue among the abstract artists of the early twentieth century, who gave up any attempt to reproduce what was on the outside and painted what they felt inside.) In music, the harmonies of melody gave way to the dissonances of emotion; in literature, describing an internal stream of consciousness replaced the organized presentation of plot in many novels.

At the same time, the Industrial Revolution fostered growing confidence in science and technology. By the end of the nineteenth century, physics, chemistry, and biology had contributed so many significant discoveries, including evidence for Darwin's theory of evolution, that faith in the sciences began to replace faith in the church; reverence for the scientist as a source of knowledge began to replace reverence for the priest, and the laboratory became ". . . the sacred place where scientific knowledge was created."[8] Scientists, it seemed, could explain and predict things, make new discoveries and inventions, and bring order out of chaos. To many, the blessings of science promised improvements that would create a better life on earth, if not in heaven.

The growth of faith in science and a sharpening focus on internal states laid the groundwork for scientific psychology, but even in the nineteenth century there were those who doubted that the objective, logical methods of science that served chemistry and physics so well could also unlock the secrets of the human mind. Skeptics argued that it was no more possible for the human mind to study itself than it would be for a needle to see its own eye. The breakthrough that dispelled this notion came when physiologist Ernst Weber (1795–1878), and Gustav Fechner (1801–1887), a physiologist and physicist, showed that human perceptions could be quantified. They showed, for example, that people's judgments of how heavy something is can be represented by a mathematical formula that precisely describes the relationship between the object's *physical* weight and a person's *psychological* perception of that weight. Their work in what became known as *psychophysics* set the stage for a new field in which scientists called "psychologists" took on "the awesome mission of scientifically illuminating human nature."[9]

Psychology's Formal Beginnings

The first character to walk on that stage was Wilhelm Wundt (1832–1920), a German physician, philosopher, and physiologist at the University of Leipzig, Germany, who is usually credited as the founder of psychology. Wundt had no intentions of being the first psychologist—he preferred to be known as a philosopher—but he gets the credit because he was the first to establish a laboratory in which he could experimentally investigate phenomena of the mind. The university's allocation of this laboratory space in 1879 provided concrete evidence that psychology could be a science, and established that year as the one most historians mark as the formal beginning of psychology. Within a few years, psychology laboratories were also established in North America—by William James at Harvard University, by G. Stanley Hall at Johns Hopkins University, and James Mark Baldwin at the University of Toronto. By 1900, there were forty-two such labs in North America, and psychology, officially founded in Germany, quickly became largely a North American enterprise.[10] Today, there are approximately 500,000 psychologists worldwide; over half of those who do research live in the United States.[11]

So, contrary to what many people assume, psychology didn't start with Freud, or with efforts to delve into the unconscious, or with concern for helping people through psychotherapy. It began in university laboratories where researchers used scientific methods to answer questions about the human mind, especially those relating to the measurement of conscious mental processes such as sensation, perception, and thinking. That was not how the public viewed psychology, however; most people believed that psychology labs were places for "mental healing, or telepathic mysteries, or spiritistic performances."[12] This belief has been slow to change. It wasn't until 1986 that most people "strongly agreed or somewhat agreed that psychology is a science."[13] Public perceptions notwithstanding, the scientific approach and scientific research methods have always been the mainstay of psychology, even as psychologists' areas of interest have gone beyond the study of consciousness to include efforts to understand all aspects of behavior and mental processes and to apply that knowledge in the numerous arenas represented in this book.

Today, psychology has expanded to the point that it has been described as an "intellectual zoo" in which psychologists can explore almost any topic.[14] Such diversity, combined with long-standing public misperceptions of psychology, has no doubt contributed to some of the confusion that still surrounds the question of what psychology is and what psychologists do.[15] Still, there are advantages to the sometimes confusing complexity within psychology. One such advantage is that, as Robert MacLeod put it, "no psychologist should ever be bored because the very experience of being bored should be sufficiently interesting to relieve [the] boredom."[16] Perhaps it is the wide range of topics that psychologists can address in their research, and the even wider range of activities they can pursue in applying that research, that explains why so few psychologists leave the field, why so few are either unemployed or underemployed,[17] and why psychology remains one of the most popular academic majors in colleges and universities today.[18]

The Promise and Problems of Applied Psychology

Scientific research in psychology has its roots in both North America and Europe, but efforts to apply the knowledge flowing from the psychology laboratory are most closely associated with psychologists in North America. The interest that North American psychologists had in finding practical applications for their work was consistent with the "can-do" pioneering spirit and the seemingly unlimited possibilities for expansion in land, wealth, and social status that flourished in America in the late nineteenth and early twentieth centuries. While European psychologists tended to think about their work in philosophical terms, such as what it contributed to our understanding of consciousness and mind, many American psychologists tended to be concerned with how psychological research could be put to use. Unlike their European colleagues, Americans wanted psychology to be a "science with pragmatic 'cash value.'"[19] And as shown by the contents of this book, this perspective has led North American psychologists to work in areas such as athletic performance, product design, advertising, jury selection, disease prevention, animal training, aviation, architectural design, and the like.

Of course, seeing the practical potential of psychological research is one thing; scientifically demonstrating its value in applied settings is quite another. Conducting high-quality research outside the laboratory presents special challenges. Psychologists working in laboratories can isolate, manipulate, or control for all the factors that might affect the outcome of a study, but practical and ethical restrictions make it difficult or impossible to do the same in nonlaboratory situations. For example, an experimenter can test a particular theory of memory in a laboratory by randomly assigning volunteer research participants to conditions that the theory says should make it either easier or harder to recall new information. However, it would be unethical to test the applied value of memory-improvement methods based on that theory by randomly assigning customers of a memory course to receive either the training program they paid for or, instead, to receive a placebo program, or no program at all. Testing the program in real-life settings is important, though, because it is often difficult to duplicate in the laboratory the variables and conditions that psychologists want to study. Will research volunteers be as motivated as paying customers to learn and practice using the memory-enhancement program being evaluated? Probably not, and that difference in motivation could create an underestimate of the program's value when tested in the laboratory (and perhaps an overestimate in an applied setting).

In short, the differences that usually exist between laboratory and nonlaboratory conditions make it difficult to (1) know how well laboratory-based conclusions about behavior and mental processes will generalize to other settings, and (2) accurately assess the value of those conclusions outside the laboratory. Accordingly, researchers are always looking for ways to increase the similarity between laboratory and field settings by introducing greater control in the field, bringing more relevant versions of subject matter into the lab, or both.

Psychologists who seek to apply psychological research also face challenges that go beyond those posed by the less controlled, often uncontrollable, circumstances in which they choose to work. One of these challenges is dealing with a level of public scrutiny that is usually much higher than that faced by their laboratory-based colleagues. Indeed, laboratory researchers in psychology have traditionally remained out of the public eye, typically working in protected settings at universities and publishing their findings in academic journals that are read mainly by fellow researchers. When these researchers do attract public attention, they risk criticism from their academic colleagues within psychology. Early in this century, for example, Harvard University psychology professor Hugo Münsterberg published some popular articles in which he discussed the application of psychological research to everyday behavior; one piece, for example, promoted moderation in the use of alcohol.[20] Shortly thereafter, the president of Harvard wrote a disapproving letter to Münsterberg in which he noted that "your high standing as a scholar would be more appreciated if you never allowed your name to appear in the press."[21] This letter reflects a view still held by many psychologists today: working in an academic setting on "pure" research is more worthy and prestigious than applying knowledge in the "real world," where commercial or other base considerations might taint one's scientific objectivity. Ironically, this long-standing reluctance among academic psychologists to publish "popular" articles about the nature, meaning, and value of their research underlies much of the public's lack of knowledge about that research, the importance of funding it, who the key figures are in mainstream psychology, or even the many subfields that exist within the discipline.

When the work of academic psychologists does get wide publicity, it is usually not because they have chosen to present it for public consumption, but because reporters in the mass media have taken it upon themselves to interpret (or, more commonly, misinterpret) the work. One example of such uncontrolled popularization of psychological research occurred in relation to the work of James V. McConnell.[22] During the 1960s, McConnell studied planaria (a type of flatworm) and was the first to show that invertebrates can learn by association. What captured headlines, however, was his report that planaria mastered a learning task faster after having eaten parts of another planarium that had already learned the task. These results were never replicated by other researchers and are no longer taken seriously, but in covering these "cannibalism studies," the press exaggerated the implications of what the worms had learned. For example, the *Saturday Evening Post* reported that "uneducated worms can acquire the wisdom of more intellectual ones by eating them."[23] And although McConnell never directly suggested that his work had any implications for humans, he did speculate that it showed that memory has a chemical basis and, thus, that memory-enhancement drugs might someday be possible. The media loved this, and seized on McConnell's comments as suggesting he had found a quick and easy way to improve human intelligence.

When psychologists themselves write for the public, the long-term results may be no better. For example, B. F. Skinner, the famous behaviorist whose laboratory research with pigeons and rats (see Chapters 4 and 12) established many of the basic principles of learning, was widely misinterpreted by the media. After he wrote an article in *Good Housekeeping* magazine about how these principles could be applied through a special temperature-controlled "air-crib" that eliminated the need for babies to wear diapers,[24] the press described him as advocating keeping children in cages. Similarly, *Walden Two* (1948), Skinner's fictional account of a utopian society governed by reward and cooperation, was seen as promoting the use of learning principles to destroy individuality and shape mindless conformity. None of these interpretations was correct. In fact, Skinner advocated that people should become more aware of how they are controlled by their environment, and believed that the use of punishment was the *least* desirable way of changing behavior. Nevertheless, many people incorrectly associate his name with authoritarianism.

These examples, and others, have hardened the resolve of many academic psychologists to seek only the attention of colleagues, journal editors, and funding agencies for their research. Although some are adventurous, most leave it to skilled popularizers of psychological research to inform the public about what they are finding and what it means for the promotion of human welfare.[25]

THE GROWTH OF APPLIED PSYCHOLOGY

Given the risks of being scorned by academic colleagues and misunderstood by the public, it might seem odd that psychologists ever chose to work on applying psychological knowledge in the real world. Why did they do so? It was partly because Americans tend to want to put knowledge to practical use in the service of human welfare, but it was also because the keen competition that has always existed for research jobs in academic settings caused many psychologists to look beyond academe for employment.

During the first half of this century, psychologists who were interested in applying their knowledge of psychology found that schools, mental health clinics, and business and industry, for example, offered many more (and better-paying) employment opportunities than universities did. This was especially true for women. For decades, women were either not admitted to doctoral programs in psychology (or other fields), or were not given degrees when they completed their work. Nor were they considered eligible for university research positions. Their only choice was to work in the "less prestigious" applied areas, so it is no wonder that in the early decades of this century, though more than two-thirds of American psychologists were men, most *applied* psychologists were women.[26] When men did enter applied areas, it was often because they could not make enough money by conducting laboratory-based research in academia.

Consider, for example, the case of Harry Hollingworth, a young professor at Columbia University.[27] His wife, Leta, had also been trained in psychology, but she was ineligible for a faculty position because at that time many educational institutions did not allow married women to teach. To help make ends meet, Harry accepted an offer from the Coca-Cola Company to investigate the effects of caffeine (an ingredient in Coke), on human behavior and mental processes. Working together in their Manhattan apartment, Harry and Leta conducted an excellent controlled experiment in which they gave sixteen people varying doses of caffeine (or a placebo), after which they measured the people's alertness, fatigue, sleep patterns, and performance on a variety of mental and physical tasks. Their research showed that caffeine did not have any harmful effects. This application of psychological research design in the service of a corporation helped pay the bills, but Harry had reason to be apprehensive about the reaction it might bring from his colleagues at Columbia. Indeed, they had already chastised him for having applied psychological principles in the world of advertising, and they were no less unhappy with the fact that Coca Cola had paid him to do research. It was no wonder that early academic psychologists who wished to apply their knowledge and expertise outside the laboratory, for scholarly or financial reasons, tended to follow the lead of Walter Dill Scott and Harlow Gale. These two psychologists carried out their early work in the field of advertising in secret, to avoid the disdain of academics who considered such activity to be intellectual prostitution.[28]

This view was reflected in the policies of the American Psychological Association (APA), which treated applied psychologists as unwanted stepchildren. For about four decades, full membership in the APA required not only a Ph.D., but two publications in "acceptable" scientific journals, a rule that, in effect, meant that most psychologists in applied areas did not qualify. It was not until 1941 that psychologists could attain full APA membership through either publications or five years of service in psychology.[29] In 1943, the official aim of the APA was expanded from its focus on advancing psychology as a science alone, to also advancing it "as a profession and to promote human welfare." This expanded mission provided a place within the APA for the activities and goals of applied psychologists. In fact, that place became so well established that, by 1950, the number of psychologists working in clinical, industrial, and other applied fields outnumbered those working in basic research areas. Indeed, there were so many APA members working in applied specialty areas that academic psychologists began to feel that their interests and needs were being neglected by the APA. After several unsuccessful attempts by representatives of both groups to resolve the differences in their priorities, a group of academics who saw these differences as irreconcilable broke away from APA in 1988 to form their own organization, the American Psychological Society (APS).[30]

Applied psychology did not grow as it did simply because the APA allowed applied psychologists to be full members. It grew also because people in the school systems, business, industry, government, the military, and the general public welcomed, even demanded, the availability of applied psychological research and services. The popularity of applied psychology was such that, even in 1924, humorist Stephen Leacock could write that the United States was suffering from "an outbreak of psychology. In all our great cities there are already, or soon will be, signs that read 'Psychologist—Open Day and Night.'"[31]

Why was applied psychology so well received in society at large? Just as in ancient times, when the need to steer ships by the stars led to the growth of astronomy and the need to irrigate the Nile valley stimulated the development of applied geometry, the remarkable demand for applied psychology in the twentieth century was fueled by the changing needs of society, due in large measure to the industrialization and urbanization of North American culture.

For example, the rapid growth of schools, hospitals, factories, and other large institutions in the early twentieth century separated family members from one another, and from their traditional communities. Where most children had once learned virtually all of their life skills from their parents, it now became more common for children to learn things in school—advanced mathematics, scientific methods, and foreign languages, for example—that their parents did not know. As a result, these children also began to have access to occupational and social positions to which their parents, who may not have had a formal education, could never have aspired. More and more of these young people were moving farther away from their parents, often leaving their home towns altogether, to pursue career opportunities. For many, these educational differences and geographical separations sowed the seeds of family conflicts, undermined the parents' status as primary role models, and negated the traditional role of the family in providing social support, advice, and reminders of cherished values during times of stress. Increasingly, people began to rely on experts outside the family for help with such things.

The goals that people had in mind when consulting with experts also reflected changing values that helped create demands for applied psychology. In nineteenth century North America, people tended to emphasize the importance of having good "character"—especially conscientiousness, honor, integrity, restraint, and the like. In the twentieth century, it began to be important to also have a healthy "personality," a concept that placed increased emphasis on the self.[32] As the importance of self-fulfillment began to rival that of self-discipline or self-sacrifice, and as personal happiness became the ultimate goal for more and more people, psychology, with its focus on the individual, became increasingly relevant. People began to turn to psychologists for "recipes by which they might find fulfillment, sex, and the right job, things without which the modern person would be greatly disturbed."[33] Indeed, many psychological treatment methods are based on the importance of understanding, valuing, and expressing the needs of the self, and one of the most influential psychological theories of human motivation placed self-actualization (personal fulfillment) at the top of a hierarchy of needs.[34]

By the 1940s, psychologists had become extensively involved in providing therapy to adults (see Chapter 3), but they were active much earlier than that in helping parents and teachers deal with the problems of children. Some even wrote "how-to" books on child rearing. These books told parents what to do and what not to do, and some also told them that they couldn't possibly raise their children without the help of experts. For example, in his popular 1928 book *Psychological Care of the Infant and Child*, John B. Watson, noted, "It is a serious question in my mind whether there should be individual homes for children—or even whether children should know their own parents. There are undoubtedly much more scientific ways of bringing up children which will probably mean finer and happier children."[35] He also told parents, "Above all when anything does happen don't let your children see your own trepidation, handle the situation as a trained nurse or doctor would and, finally, learn not to talk in endearing and coddling terms."[36] Watson said that "the world would be considerably better off if it were to stop having children for twenty years (except those reared for experimental purposes) and were then to start again with enough facts to do the job with some degree of skill and accuracy. Parenthood, instead of being an instinctive art, is a science, the details of which must be worked out by patient laboratory methods."[37] Thus, just as some religions had promised hell and damnation if children weren't reared according to the doctrines of the religion, Watson threatened that improper, unscientific child rearing would produce "crippled personalities."[38]

Watson's emphasis on the proper raising of children reflected a major shift at the turn of the century in how children and parents were perceived. In the nineteenth century, parents were perceived as wise and worthy of respect, and children were to be "seen and not heard." But where nineteenth-century children were viewed as merely "redeemable," twentieth-century children came to be seen as "redeemers,"[39] and today—if the money spent on children's gifts, birthday parties, clothes, and lessons is any indication—they have become more important in our culture than the adults who nurture them. The turn of the twentieth century brought changes, too, in views about the value of education, especially early education. In the nineteenth century, it was still believed that children could be harmed, even driven insane, if their "delicate" brains were forced into too much educational activity too soon.* In the twentieth century, the reverse was claimed: that education could prevent insanity and provide for new opportunities.[41]

As compulsory education for children took hold in North America in the early twentieth century, schools became the first arena in which psychologists began applying knowledge gained in psychological laboratories. When the *Journal of Applied Psychology* was founded in 1917, most of its articles concerned the role of psychology in educational issues and settings. Psychologists with expertise in using tests to measure children's mental capacities were welcome in the schools. Their tests of mental functioning became vital in the era of mass education because the schools were faced with trying to educate large numbers of students who varied widely in mental abilities. "Mental testing" was seen as a valuable guide to placing students in various instructional programs depending on what the tests revealed about their abilities. By 1918, over one hundred tests had been constructed to measure specific skills in arithmetic, reading, and spelling. By 1932, 60 percent of schools with over five hundred pupils used general intelligence tests to place students into differing educational tracks.[42] There was little concern then that students could be stigmatized or otherwise harmed by being placed in a "slow" group because it was assumed that intelligence was largely inherited and fixed. It was considered wiser, therefore, to place children "where they belonged."† As described in Chapter 4, psychologists

---

*It was also believed that education could divert people from the occupations to which they are "by nature" adapted.[40]

†Belief in the immutability of mental abilities was so strong at this time that many people advocated controlled breeding of humans, and some were even in favor of forced sterilization. One psychologist offered each of his children one thousand dollars if they would marry the son or daughter of a professor![43]

began to realize that the environment, including the educational environment, could affect academic performance as well as test scores.

Like schools, turn-of-the-century industries were also faced with the task of assessing people's abilities, and here, too, psychologists' expertise in testing had practical applications. Many of them were hired by Ford Motor Company, Goodrich Tire and Rubber, Westinghouse Electric, Heinz Foods, Prudential Insurance, Carnegie Steel, and other major corporations to measure the mental and physical capabilities of potential employees, and then to make recommendations about which individuals should be hired and about which job each new worker could best perform.[44] As with school children, workers were assumed to have a fixed set of abilities, so employment testing was concerned mainly with determining how well, and where, each new employee would fit into the job environment.* The goal, of course, was to help management increase the company's profits and the efficiency of the organization. It was no wonder, then, that *Psychology and Industrial Efficiency*, a 1913 book by Hugo Münsterberg, became a best seller; it was based on a survey in which the author asked manufacturers to describe the mental traits that they considered most desirable in their workers. It wasn't until the late 1920s that research in industrial psychology showed that social factors, such as peer-group pressure to produce at a certain level, were more important for accurately predicting workers' efficiency than either workers' personal characteristics or the physical conditions in which they work.[46] Accordingly, the applied specialty that had originally been called industrial psychology eventually became *industrial-organizational psychology,* in recognition of the importance of organizational patterns in business and industry, including patterns of communication among workers and between workers and managers.[47] This emphasis is even stronger today, as described in Chapter 6.

Early applied psychologists were also active in the field of advertising, an enterprise that began nearly five thousand years ago when Babylonian tradesmen advertised their wares by imprinting signs and symbols on bricks and pottery, and later, when town criers announced not only the time of day but also good places to eat and drink.[48] Psychologists initially offered advertisers effective ways to survey consumer attitudes about their products. The first such survey was conducted in 1895 by Harlow Gale; by 1916 psychologists had written six textbooks on advertising, with titles such as *Advertising and Its Mental Laws*.[49] Later, psychologists' contributions went beyond data-gathering to help change the nature of advertising itself. They pointed out that the impact of advertising would be increased if, instead of using the traditional method of simply describing a product, the advertiser could persuade, cajole, and even subtly manipulate consumers into buying that product. John B. Watson was particularly influential in this regard. Watson began applying behavioral principles to advertising in the late 1920s, after a sex scandal ended his academic research career in the psychology department at Johns Hopkins University. Watson believed that humans are "organic machines" that "we could control . . .

---

*This view is nicely summarized in the motto of the 1933 World's Fair: "Science Finds, Industry Adapts, Man Conforms."[45]

as we do other machines. . . . Love, fear and rage are the same in Italy, Abyssinia and Canada," he said, and advertising should appeal to these emotions.[50] In designing ads for Johnson and Johnson's baby powder, for example, Watson played on new mothers' anxieties and feelings of incompetence about properly caring for their children. He recognized and exploited not only the power of emotional appeals in advertising, but also the impact of experts who recommend products, and the presentation of products as new or improved (for more on psychology in advertising, see Chapter 5).

Psychology has also long been applied in the legal system, especially in the courts and prisons. This specialty, originally called "penal psychology," is now known as *forensic psychology*. Early on, the role of psychologists in prisons was—as in schools, offices, and factories—to give mental tests, though in this case it was for the purpose of classifying prisoners. In the courts, psychologists offered expert testimony as well as testing services. In 1907, for example, Hugo Münsterberg tested the only eyewitness in the trial of a labor leader accused of conspiring to kill an ex-governor of Idaho.[51] The credibility of the witness, a man named Harry Orchard, was in doubt because he also happened to be a convicted mass-murderer. To determine whether Orchard was telling the truth, Münsterberg designed the first modern lie detector. He gave Orchard a word association test, which involved reading a list of words, one at a time, and asking him to say the first word that came to mind. In addition to noting *what* Orchard said, Münsterberg also used a chronoscope to measure how long it took for each response to occur, and other instruments to measure signs of any emotional arousal that accompanied the responses. (This procedure was based on psychological theories of emotion suggesting that such arousal should be especially likely to occur when someone feels guilty about lying. This theory remains the basis for most modern lie detection efforts.) The year after the trial, Münsterberg published a book called *On the Witness Stand*, in which he raised concerns about the potential inaccuracy of eyewitness reports, and the unreliability (and brutality) of forced confessions.[52] These concerns, still relevant today, represented an enlightened view in 1908, given that most people at the time believed that criminals could be identified by certain facial features and other physical characteristics (see Chapter 8 for more discussion about psychologists' contributions to the legal system).

Thus, the early part of the twentieth century saw a number of psychologists put to practical use their expertise in learning, motivation and emotion, mental testing, and research methodology. However, the scale of these initial efforts paled in comparison to what was to come when the demand for applied psychological services expanded during and after World War I, and then exploded during and after World War II. In both wars, the U.S. military employed psychologists to develop and administer the mass testing programs needed to assess the mental abilities of recruits and then assign them to duties commensurate with those abilities. It would have taken far too long to test each of thousands of recruits individually, so to save time and effort, psychologists designed mental tests that could be administered to large groups. During World War I a million recruits took either the Army Alpha Test (which required literacy), or the Army Beta Test (which did not). During World War II, the mental abilities of 9 million men were assessed with a newer instrument, the Army General Classification Test.[53]

Not all of the fifteen hundred psychologists who served in World War II were engaged in testing, selecting, and classifying military personnel, however. It soon became apparent to psychologists and military leaders that human efficiency could be affected not just by the match between individuals and their jobs, but also by the match between individuals and the tools they used to do those jobs. Accordingly, psychologists were asked to assist in improving the design of weapons and other machinery in order to make them, and those who operated them, more efficient and effective. According to Lybrand Palmer Smith, the U.S. Navy's representative on the National Defense Research Committee, this work "did more to help this war than any other single intellectual activity."[54] As described in Chapters 10 and 11, psychologists have continued to apply their knowledge of human performance to improve not only the design and utility of military equipment, but also of civilian products ranging from telephones and computer keyboards to automobile instrument panels and nuclear power plant control systems.

The greatest impact of the world wars on the growth of applied psychology was based on the need to deal with the emotional trauma suffered by its veterans. As World War II drew to a close in the mid-1940s, it became clear that although psychologists' work in mental and personality testing, in matching people to jobs, and in improving the design of military equipment helped win the war, their efforts had not protected many of its combatants, even those who were physically unscathed, from suffering the severe, and often permanent, psychological scars seen in veterans of other wars. Dealing with these emotional casualties took on a high priority in 1944 when President Roosevelt declared that no one suffering from a combat-related disorder would be discharged from the military without receiving treatment.[55] With so many people requiring treatment—forty thousand veterans were in psychiatric hospitals at the end of the war, and countless others needed help as well—psychologists finally began to do what the public had long assumed they did: administer adult psychotherapy. In 1946, the U.S. Veterans Administration (VA) set up university-based programs to train psychologists in clinical work, and VA hospitals soon became the largest employer of clinical psychologists.[56] As described in Chapter 3, laws were eventually passed in all fifty states and all ten Canadian provinces allowing clinical psychologists, like their physician colleagues in psychiatry,* to perform psychotherapy on their own with veteran and non-veteran clients alike.

Combat veterans were not the only psychological casualties of World War II. Those who had lost loved ones in the war were also devastated, and while some grieved in private and others sought professional help, many coped by trying to contact the spirit of their dead relatives. With this interest in spiritism came the

---

*Psychiatrists are medical doctors who have received special training in the causes and treatment of mental disorders.

resurgence of yet another form of applied psychology, that of investigating so-called psychic phenomena. Psychic, or, more properly, *paranormal* phenomena include claims of spiritism (contact or communication with the dead), telepathy (sending or receiving information without using the five known senses), precognition (knowledge of future events), clairvoyance (the ability to perceive objects or events that are not visible or audible), and psychokinesis (moving objects by mental effort alone). Whether they like it or not (and most do not), psychologists have long been associated with paranormal phenomena. For example, until about 1920 the word *psychical* was used to refer to anything that was mental rather than physical, so *psychical* and *psychological* were used interchangeably.[57] And since the term *psychology* is made up of *psyche* (referring to the soul) and *logos* (referring to study or knowledge), it was no wonder that psychical and psychological phenomena were closely associated in the public mind and that psychologists were widely assumed to deal, at least part-time, with matters of spiritism and the soul. In fact, funding for some of the earliest psychology laboratories (including those at Stanford and Harvard universities) was provided on the assumption that research on psychic phenomena would be conducted there.[58] Even today, many people assume that psychologists are interested in paranormal experiences, in spite of the fact that most psychologists (William James being a notable exception) have long sought to establish themselves as scientists who study natural, not supernatural, phenomena. Those who do study claims of the paranormal have been careful to adopt the same objective, scientific methods of evaluation that have always been the hallmark of psychological research. As described in Chapter 13, this research typically reveals claims of the paranormal to be either unfounded, fraudulent, or the result of misinterpretations of natural events.[59]

Psychologists' work in evaluating paranormal phenomena has been a mere footnote in comparison to their far more extensive involvement in the other applied areas mentioned so far. And they have entered new areas of application as well, one of the most significant of which is promoting health and preventing illness through a specialty known as *health psychology*.[60] This field has seen phenomenal growth in the past thirty years as a result of the growing awareness among physicians and psychologists of the connection between physical and psychological states. This "holistic" perspective, which sees people as integrated systems whose psychological and physical components are always interdependent, is reminiscent of nineteenth-century ideas that physical and mental illness were not only linked, but that one could produce the other. Accordingly, it was believed that the psychological comfort a doctor offered was more important than any specific medical treatment. It was also believed that God had done a perfect job in creating people, and that it is up to us to behave in ways that prevent physical and mental diseases.[61] Modern scientific research has provided an empirical basis for many of these beliefs. Scientists have documented not only the causal links between physical and psychological health, but also the importance of behavior (such as regular exercise, a low-fat diet, and nonsmoking) in maintaining health and preventing illness. As described in Chapter 2, health psychologists have applied this research by designing smoking cessation courses, methods for improving compliance with medication regimens, breast cancer screening campaigns, and a wide variety of other health promotion and disease prevention programs. The importance of mind-body connections has also appeared in the work of sports psychologists, who apply research on these links to the improvement of athletic performance (see Chapter 7).

Just as psychologists have expanded our understanding of the reciprocal influence of mind and body, they have also shown how the physical environment and individuals within that environment influence each other. Recognition of this two-way relationship between people and their surroundings is relatively recent. For decades, psychologists had been measuring people's mental characteristics, then helped to assign those people to the educational or work environments where they best "fit." It was presumed that people must adapt to environments, not the other way around. The field of environmental psychology, described in Chapter 9, has transformed this view into one that recognizes that physical surroundings can have significant effects on people, and that it is possible to shape environments so as to maximize the physical and psychological comfort—and thus the performance—of the people who live, work, and study in them.

APPLIED PSYCHOLOGY AND HUMAN VALUES

Applications of psychology, like applications of any other science, are guided not just by the facts, principles, phenomena, and relationships that are discovered in the research laboratory, but also by the values held by those who put such knowledge to practical use, and by society at large. So although there is no doubt that psychologists *can* use their expertise to, say, help attorneys select sympathetic jurors or promote safer sex practices, the question of whether these are things they *should* do raises larger issues. Neither psychology nor any other science can tell us how things ought to be, or what choices we ought to make. Psychologists may be able to predict, and sometimes even control, the relationship between behavior and its consequences, but they are no better equipped than anyone else to make decisions about which consequences are preferable. In other words, psychological research has helped us understand *how* we make moral choices, but not which ones we *ought* to make. As one observer put it, ". . . psychology may help me control my child's behavior, but it can't tell me how my child should behave. [It] may help me construct lessons that my students remember, but it cannot tell me what my students should learn."[62] So although the American Psychological Association's *Ethical Standards for Psychologists and Code of Conduct* states that psychologists should strive to advance human welfare, no one can define precisely just what that means. Applications of psychological knowledge that promote the welfare of one person or group (such as preventing the spread of AIDS by influencing heroin addicts to avoid sharing injection needles) might have negative effects on another person or group (such as the victims of crimes that addicts' continued drug use might cause). Further, actions that promote human welfare today might jeopardize it tomorrow. For example, in the 1970s psychologists worked to have thousands of mental patients released into community-based care from the mind-numbing boredom, neglect, and even abuse associated with long-term confinement in psychiatric hospital wards. They did not foresee, however, that changes in mental health funding policies would condemn many of these patients to lives of homelessness and danger on big-city streets.

So it is incumbent on all of us, psychologists included, to recognize the role of values in applying scientific knowledge, to keep in mind the social forces that are constantly shaping those values, and to listen to voices representing all points of view about what those values should be.

The following chapters describe the ways in which psychologists have chosen to apply what research in psychology has revealed about behavior and mental processes. Taken together, those chapters show how psychology has come to influence, and will continue to influence, our daily lives.

PSYCHOLOGY APPLIED TO HEALTH

Lisa G. Aspinwall and Ron E. Franco Durán

I n the past ten years or so, we have all become more conscious of our health. We watch what we eat, we are concerned about the air we breathe, and we are more determined to exercise our bodies. Psychologists have developed a whole new field, called *health psychology*, to address questions related to health—for example: What is the best way to promote health and prevent disease? Why do people often fail to take important disease-preventive measures? How do people react psychologically to physical illness? What effect does personality have on health?

In fact, health psychology has become so popular that medical centers have become the major employers of psychologists. One recent literature review noted that over a third of the articles published in four prominent psychology journals from 1990 to 1992 dealt in some way with physical health and illness.[1] To understand what has caused this general shift in interest in health and why so many psychologists have become involved in this area, we will take a look at the history of changing views on health.

OLD AND NEW PERSPECTIVES ON HEALTH AND ILLNESS

For the past one hundred years, the predominant approach to health and illness has been a *biomedical* one, which assumes that illness is the consequence of biological pathogenesis (such as the infection of the body by disease-causing microorganisms) or the malfunction of major organ systems. Health was considered to be little more than the absence of disease. According to this view, health could be regained by removing disease-causing microbes or altering or replacing dysfunctional body parts. This rather mechanistic approach made sense given that mechanical improvements (such as refrigeration, pasteurization, and improved drainage systems), new medications (such as sulfa drugs in the 1930s and penicillin in the 1940s), immunizations, and modern surgical techniques greatly reduced death rates, provided immediate cures for once-life-threatening conditions, and helped to prevent some diseases altogether.

Deaths due to acute infectious diseases such as polio, cholera, and influenza declined in industrialized nations as a result of improvements in medical treatment.

However, deaths due to chronic disorders, such as heart disease, cancer, lung diseases, and complications from substance abuse, have continued to rise during the second half of the twentieth century. Such illnesses are now among the leading causes of death in the United States. It has become clear that many of these chronic health conditions are preventable, or at least manageable, not through mechanical interventions, but through modifications in behavior. For example, one government report estimates that 25 percent of all cancer deaths and approximately 350,000 heart attack deaths could be prevented *each year* through the cessation of cigarette smoking alone. Other controllable behaviors such as poor diet and lack of regular exercise similarly contribute to the onset and maintenance of these disorders.[2]

Not only does behavior have an impact on chronic diseases; it also seems that psychological attitudes and social factors maintain the unhealthy behaviors that lead to chronic "preventable" conditions in industrialized societies. Consequently, the biomedical model, with its focus on biological causes and cures through symptom reduction, has recently been replaced by a *biopsychosocial* model.* This model guides the work of health psychologists. It says that health and illness are products of biological factors (such as hormones or viruses, or deficient body systems or parts), psychological factors (such as attitudes or emotions), and social factors (such as culture or group identity).[3] In the biopsychosocial model, each of these three factors is considered and may be differentially weighted in terms of importance when thinking about any given problem related to health and illness.

For example, it is widely accepted that acquired immunodeficiency syndrome (AIDS) is a result of becoming infected with the human immunodeficiency virus (HIV); however, not everyone who comes in contact with HIV becomes infected, and the time between becoming infected with HIV and developing a clinical diagnosis of AIDS varies greatly among individuals. How can this be? According to the biomedical model, one would think a biological pathogen such as HIV would work similarly in every person. But the biopsychosocial model suggests that one needs to consider that some people simply have stronger biological systems than others. This model also raises such questions as these: What beliefs or attitudes influence individuals to maintain health-promoting and, thereby, potentially immune-enhancing behaviors? What kinds of behaviors are associated with longer periods between infection and symptom development? What is the effect of social support on the longevity of persons who have developed AIDS?

The holistic approach embodied in health psychology's biopsychosocial model of health and illness is in many ways old wine in a new bottle. Early models of health and illness traditionally included psychological and social factors. For example, Hippocrates, a physician in ancient Greece, explained links between human personality and disease processes in terms of the balance (or imbalance) among four bodily fluids called "humors": black bile, yellow bile, blood, and phlegm. When describing the dispositions of certain individuals today, we still use some of Hip-

---

*Until the mid-1980s, the medical field vehemently denied the role of psychosocial factors in the onset and maintenance of disease, much less their potential role in achieving health.

pocrates' terms: "melancholic" (too much black bile), "choleric" (an excess of yellow bile), "sanguine" (too great a blood flow), and "phlegmatic" (too much phlegm). Still, no modern health psychologist believes that the treatment of disease involves adding or subtracting these bodily fluids to create a healthy balance. Thus, although the ideas behind the biopsychosocial model may be very old, the discipline of health psychology has incorporated modern methods to test scientifically the quality and complexity of those ideas.

Health psychology has contributed to our understanding of health and illness in numerous areas, including: (1) psychological adjustment to serious illnesses and other negative life events, (2) health beliefs and their influence on behaviors intended to prevent or detect illness, (3) mind-body connections in the causes and treatment of serious illness, (4) psychosocial factors related to health and illness, and (5) measurements of the quality of life. After we discuss the general findings and research in these five areas, we will focus on three specific examples of health behavior: safer sexual behavior, breast cancer detection, and compliance with medication regimens for high blood pressure. Finally, we will describe some general lessons that health psychologists have learned in their exploration of health issues and conclude with a brief discussion of issues at the forefront of the field.

PSYCHOLOGICAL ADJUSTMENT TO SERIOUS ILLNESS AND OTHER NEGATIVE LIFE EVENTS

How do people's lives change following a diagnosis of cancer or spinal cord injury or other events such as the death of a child, partner, or spouse? Health psychology has revealed some surprising findings about how people who have experienced serious illness and other misfortunes see themselves and various aspects of their lives following the illness or event. This research has guided the development of interventions to assist people in coping with such events.

Adjusting Emotional Reactions

In a groundbreaking study, Philip Brickman and his colleagues interviewed three groups of people who might be expected to have very different life experiences: Group 1 consisted of twenty-two adults who had won major state lottery prizes, Group 2 consisted of twenty-nine young adults who had recently been paralyzed in accidents, and Group 3 (the control group) contained twenty-two adults who had had neither experience.[4] Among other questions, respondents were asked to rate how good or bad their recent experience (lottery win or disabling accident) had been, their general happiness in their current stage of life, how happy they were before winning the lottery or before the accident, how happy they expected to be in a couple of years, and how much pleasure they took in everyday activities, such as talking with friends or eating breakfast.

The results of this study were strikingly different from what most people would expect. Although they had recently won hundreds of thousands of dollars, the lottery winners were not different from the control respondents on most measures;

they were not happier, and they reported significantly *less* enjoyment of everyday activities. Even more surprising was that the recently paralyzed individuals, although currently less happy than the controls, did not differ from the controls in expectations of *future* happiness. Interestingly, their current happiness ratings, although lower than those of the control group, were still above the midpoint of the scale, indicating that they did not rate themselves as unhappy. Nor did they rate their accident as the worst thing that could have happened to them. Similarly, the lottery winners did not rate their win as the best thing that could have happened to them.

Equally surprising findings come from a study of emotional experience following a disabling accident. Roxane Cohen Silver interviewed 125 hospitalized patients (mostly young adult men, ages twenty-one to twenty-five) who were physically disabled by accidents.[5] They were interviewed one, three, and eight weeks after their accidents and were asked to indicate how often in the previous week they had experienced anxiety, depression, anger, and happiness.* They reported both positive and negative emotions, with positive emotions increasing over time while negative emotions decreased. It is important to note that these patients were far from overwhelmingly cheerful, but they were much happier than most people would expect. Similar results were found among parents who had lost a child to sudden infant death syndrome.[6]

The results of these studies suggest that people who experience very good fortune are not happier than those who do not, and that people who experience severe misfortune are not as unhappy as most people think. How can this be? One explanation involves *habituation* or *adaptation* to a new *comparison standard*.[7] The lottery winners may find it easy to disregard their past standard of living and take their new affluence as the baseline against which they make all judgments. However, this new standard may make mundane activities, like eating breakfast, seem less exciting. The same shift in comparison standard may be true for the disabled patients; judged against their non-disabled past, the present may not look as good, but if their future is judged with reference to their present, it has the potential to improve. In this way, people may adapt to severe negative life events and illnesses.

Adjusting Beliefs

Illness and adversity may affect not only our emotions, but also the core beliefs we have about ourselves and the world. For example, we may generally believe that the world is a benevolent place where good things happen, that other people are basically good, and that there is meaning in what happens in the world. Similarly, we may believe that we are worthy and personally lucky somehow. Such beliefs support an illusion of invulnerability: if the world is a good place where bad things happen only to bad people and we ourselves are good or lucky, nothing bad will happen to

---

*The researchers reported encountering great resistance from hospital personnel in the conduct of this study. The very idea of asking newly paralyzed people if they were happy seemed cruel at worst and ill advised at best.

us. But negative life events challenge or even shatter such beliefs. In a study of 338 college students, the 83 students who had experienced negative life events—such as the death of a parent or sibling, incest, rape, a fire that destroyed their home, or a disabling accident—scored lower on beliefs about the benevolence of the world and saw themselves as lower in self-worth than the 255 students who had not experienced such events.[8]

How do people cope with such assaults on their beliefs? One response, shown by the college students surveyed, is to change one's beliefs. Another option is to reinterpret the negative experience to fit one's existing beliefs. For example, in order to avoid seeing the world as a place in which bad things happen to good people, some people may assume responsibility or see themselves as having somehow caused the negative event. Taking responsibility means that one can do better next time or take additional precautions. This strategy seems to work as long as people blame changeable parts of themselves, such as their behavior, and not unchangeable parts of themselves, such as their character. If the event cannot be reinterpreted to match their beliefs, people may cope by blocking out disturbing thoughts about the event.

Searching for Meaning

Finding meaning in a negative event is another common adaptive response to serious illness. For example, interviews with breast cancer patients found that 95 percent of them generated some explanation for why their cancer occurred: 41 percent attributed it to stress, 32 percent to particular carcinogens, 17 percent to diet, and 10 percent to accident or injury.[9] No specific explanation was linked to better psychological adjustment, but the large number of patients who found some sort of explanation suggests that the process of finding some meaning is important, perhaps because it changes attitudes and priorities. Consider two examples.[10] One woman said, "I have much more enjoyment of each day, each moment. I am not so worried about what is and what isn't or what I wish I had. All those things you get entangled with don't seem to be part of my life right now." Another said, "I was very happy to find out I am a very strong person. I have no time for game playing any more. I want to get on with life. And I have become more introspective and also let others fend for their own responsibilities. And now almost five years later, I have become a very different person."

Regaining a Sense of Mastery

Good adjustment to chronic illness and other stressors may also be linked to increased attempts to gain control over one's health.[11] In the study of the breast cancer patients, two-thirds believed they had at least some personal control over the recurrence of their cancer, while others believed that their doctor or continued treatment would control the cancer. Many reported active attempts to control their cancer and its treatment by psychological means, such as positive thinking and visualization, as well as dietary changes and obtaining information about cancer and its treatment.

Enhancing the Sense of Self

Illnesses and other negative life events often make people feel bad about themselves. However, a striking finding from the interviews with breast cancer patients was that most patients saw themselves as better adjusted than before their cancer and as better adjusted than other women with breast cancer. In fact, all but two of the patients interviewed thought they were doing as well as or better than other women with breast cancer. How can this be? One mechanism identified is that of *selective evaluation*. This means that one can compare oneself on the basis of one particular characteristic that makes one seem better off than others. For example, one older woman focused on her age and said, "The people I really feel sorry for are these young gals. To lose a breast when you're so young must be awful. I'm 73; what do I need a breast for?" A younger woman, on the other hand, made herself feel better by focusing on her married status saying, "If I hadn't been married, I think this would have really gotten to me. I can't imagine dating or whatever knowing you have this thing and not knowing how to tell the man about it."[12]

In each of these examples, the woman identified some aspect of her illness that could have been worse or that made her situation seem better relative to others, a process called *downward social comparison*. There is now ample evidence to suggest that selective evaluation, making downward comparisons, changing one's comparison standards, and imagining hypothetical worse worlds play an important role in adjustment to many illnesses and stressors, including arthritis, physical decline in aging, and academic pressure.[13]

Individual Differences

There is tremendous variability in people's responses to negative life events. However, many people believe that everyone experiencing a trauma follows the same patterns or stages of reactions. For example, one theory states that there are five stages in reacting to one's own impending death or the impending death of a loved one: denial, anger, bargaining, depression, and acceptance. It is thought that if people do not go through all of the stages or progress from one to the next, they are not grieving the "right" way. Other widely held beliefs are that positive emotions should be absent in the weeks following the loss of a loved one, that failure to exhibit distress after loss creates future mental distress because the person has not "worked through" the loss, that it is necessary for the bereaved person to break down psychological attachments to the lost person in order to recover, and that people will recover only after a certain period of time as they reach a final state of acceptance of the loss.[14] Consequently, we might believe that a man who remarries six months after his wife has died, or a woman who enjoys time with friends after her child has died, or that Bill Cosby, who performed a comedy act weeks after his son was murdered, are not grieving "properly."

However, research has shown that none of these beliefs and assumptions about the "normal" way to react is correct.[15] For example, depression does occur after a loss, but it is far from a universal reaction. When researchers studied people who had experienced bereavement, spinal cord injury, the loss of a child in an auto accident, or other severe negative life events, they found that only 12 to 35 percent of these people met diagnostic criteria for depression. Moreover, there is no evidence that people who do not display depression following loss are at risk for later psychological problems. Similarly, the presence of positive reactions (such as having fun with friends) was not associated with subsequent problems. Finally, research on traumatic stress reveals that people continue to think often about past negative events, including those that happened decades earlier.[16] So the notion that people "get over" events may be simplistic, and efforts to get people to stop thinking about their loss may be unsuccessful and even counterproductive. Instead, it may be better to educate people about the variability in responses to negative life events. This may not only help the person affected, but may also help members of their social network to respond in more useful ways.

We have outlined a variety of positive and negative reactions to distressing events. In describing reports of positive reactions, we do not mean to trivialize the pain, disability, and stress that often result. We simply wish to note that negative effects do not tell the whole story. Documenting both positive and negative changes in response to serious illness and other distressing life events puts the research focus on understanding how people adapt and helps psychologists to develop appropriate interventions to assist people in managing negative changes and cultivating positive ones.

HEALTH BELIEFS AND THEIR INFLUENCE ON PREVENTION AND ILLNESS-DETECTION BEHAVIORS

A second major area of research in health psychology concerns psychological and social factors involved in preventive health behaviors (such as exercise, seat belt use, safer sex, and following a healthy diet) and in illness-detection behaviors (such as breast self-exams, mammography, and HIV testing). There is ample evidence that all of these behaviors reduce one's risk of illness or injury or provide other benefits, yet surprisingly few people practice such behaviors. For more than thirty years, researchers have tried to understand why this is, and their work has yielded several related theories. A consistent aspect of these theories is that failure to adopt important health behaviors cannot be explained by people's lack of knowledge. Considerable evidence suggests instead that several core health beliefs explain whether people will engage in particular health behaviors.[17]

One such set of beliefs involves *perceived barriers* to taking action: These barriers can be physical, psychological, financial, or other costs associated with initiating or continuing a behavior. For example, barriers to obtaining a mammogram may be the cost of the procedure, the fear that cancer may be detected, and the anticipated pain of the procedure. Barriers to simpler preventive actions, like flossing teeth or improving diet, may include a belief that they are inconvenient and time-consuming. Thus, the short-term inconvenience may outweigh the long-term health benefits, especially for people who feel generally healthy. An added challenge is that many preventive behaviors require continuous rather than one-time action. Using sunscreen or seat belts, exercising, and flossing, for example, require that one adhere to the precautionary behavior regularly for it to be effective. Other health behaviors may have to be performed monthly (self-exams), every six months (dental visits), or annually (gynecological exams, mammograms after a certain age, and other checkups).

The effects of perceived barriers may be counteracted by the *perceived benefits* of taking action, such as gains in physical health or psychological well-being. For example, the benefits of a mammogram would be early detection of any cancer and the reduction of worry if none is found.

Perceived susceptibility to illness reflects how much at *risk* people think they are for getting a particular illness. Presumably, people who perceive themselves to be at greatest risk are more likely to act to reduce their risk. But the problem is that many people are unrealistically optimistic with regard to calculating their own susceptibility. In dozens of studies, most people— usually about 70 percent—say they are at less risk than the average person for illness or accident. These findings hold true not just for teenagers, to whom such an illusion of invulnerability is usually attributed, but also for their parents![18] There are many reasons that people think they are at less risk than others.[19] They may (1) simply deny their own risk, (2) focus on their own risk-reducing actions but overlook the fact that other people also engage in such actions, (3) concentrate on other people's risk-increasing actions, or (4) have unrealistic images of people who are at risk (such as thinking that heart disease strikes only heavy-set males around the age of fifty who spend their days eating cheeseburgers in front of the TV set, when, in fact, heart disease is a major killer of women in the United States).

Finally, perceived *severity* of illness is also important. If the illness is perceived to be mild, people may not be motivated to protect themselves.

Although the factors listed have been very useful in predicting health behaviors, they do not provide a complete account of whether people will adopt or maintain a particular health behavior. For example, people who smoke may believe that they are at risk for lung cancer, that the benefits of quitting smoking outweigh the costs of doing so, and that lung cancer is severe, but may feel personally unable to quit. Additionally, people may believe that it is too late to quit if they have smoked for several years because the damage has already been done. These two beliefs— about one's personal ability to carry out a recommended action, termed *self-efficacy*, and about the effectiveness of the recommended action, termed *treatment* or *response efficacy*, have been found to play a substantial role in initiating and maintaining many different kinds of behavior.[20] Yet even when both perceived risk and response efficacy are high, the percentage of people who actually decide to change their behavior to reduce their risk is still quite low.[21]

Finally, many of the major health belief theories also take into account *social norms*, that is, whether one's peers or other important people are perceived to practice healthy behavior. If you smoke but all your friends have quit and find your smoking repulsive, the social pressure may be a potent stimulus for quitting. On the other hand, the perception that other people are not changing their behavior may exert a strong negative influence on behavior change. Many successful interventions have taken advantage of the power of social norms to produce behavior change. For example, HIV risk-reduction interventions for college students and gay men have employed popular opinion leaders, such as peer educators and people nominated by bartenders, to provide information about safer sex. Such interventions have been conducted in groups so that people can see that similar others are learning about safer sexual behavior.[22]

MIND-BODY CONNECTIONS IN THE CAUSES AND TREATMENT OF ILLNESS

It has been estimated that up to one-third of hospitalized medical patients with chronic medical conditions also suffer from psychological disorders such as depression or anxiety, as compared to 2 percent to 4 percent of the general population. Amazingly, however, psychological components of medical illnesses are still understudied, often overlooked, and generally left untreated under the traditional biomedical model.[23] Reasons for this lack of attention include physicians' lack of familiarity with psychological issues, the stigma associated with having emotional (versus "purely physical") problems, and the decreased time physicians spend with their patients due to the constraints of systems such as managed care.

Like the proverbial problem of the chicken and the egg, the answer to what comes first—the physical distress or the psychological disturbance—is not clear. We do know that physical disorders can affect psychological states, and vice versa.[24] For example, pain associated with physical disorders may cause sleep disturbance and alter one's usual routines and ways of coping, produce distortions in thinking and appraisal of problems, and reduce confidence that one can manage problems. Further, people who experience severe pain may not want to interact with other people, or others may avoid them. All of these factors can result in depression or anxiety. Similarly, psychological states such as depression or anxiety can alter immune function and other biological processes, lead to poor health practices and less use of health care, bias people's interpretations of potential symptoms, and interfere with social functioning. Any or all of these factors can create or exacerbate a physical disorder. Consequently, health psychologists stress the importance of identifying and treating psychological distress in patients with physical diseases and have become involved in educating the medical community to pay more attention to the mind-body connection.

One key area that health psychologists have addressed is that of communication between physicians and their patients.* No matter how much physicians value the psychological aspects of health, they will not be able to determine the social, emotional, and psychological status of their patients without first establishing good rapport. One way of establishing good rapport is through clear communication. Doctors have frequently been described as overusing "Medspeak," jargon-filled technical language that health professionals have developed to communicate quickly and efficiently with each other.[25] When doctors use Medspeak with patients,

---

*Health Communication, a professional journal dedicated to this subfield, began publication in 1989.

much of the information they need to communicate—including diagnosis, cause of disease, treatment plan, and medication instructions—may become lost in a rapid-fire jumble of complex terms and abbreviations. Because many patients do not want to appear ignorant or troublesome, they may refrain from asking important questions and thus have a poor understanding of the details of their illness.

Health psychologists train physicians to refrain from using Medspeak, and they also help patients to take more personal control of their health care by asking their doctors for clarification when needed. One recent intervention study that focused on physician training demonstrated that cancer patients whose oncologists took a brief seminar on improving doctor-patient communication reported feeling less depressed and more in control than patients whose physicians had no such training.[26] In another study, cancer patients who attended a ten-minute session intended to help them prepare questions for their doctors asked more questions than those who did not receive the brief intervention, although patients in both groups reported that they would have liked to have had more time with their doctor to ask even more questions.[27] Similar interventions with diabetes patients have resulted in improved treatment compliance and fewer lost workdays.[28]

Educating physicians about effective communication and encouraging patients to ask more questions does not always guarantee that the patient will hear the doctor's message. It has long been known that anxiety can interfere with learning,[29] and people are typically given quite a bit of information about their medical condition and its treatment immediately following diagnosis. Under such conditions, the anxiety associated with receiving the diagnosis may interfere with hearing and remembering what the doctor or nurse said. Therefore, recognizing and treating anxiety may be an important first step in the care of people with serious illness. It may be well worthwhile for the physician to take extra time to assess patients' concerns and attend to nonverbal as well as verbal communication. Efforts to listen closely to patients may ultimately save money by reducing unnecessary doctor visits, especially because it has been estimated that up to 60 percent of doctor visits are made by the "worried well," persons who do not have any evident physical disorder.[30]

PSYCHOSOCIAL FACTORS RELATED TO HEALTH AND ILLNESS

The ways in which people perceive the world, process information, handle strong emotions, and are connected socially may be linked to health-related behaviors and outcomes. By studying how people cope with adversity, researchers have identified several characteristics associated with health and illness.

Hardiness

People who are psychologically hardy are committed to important goals, believe they can control events in their lives, and appraise problems as challenges. A number of studies have found hardiness—alone and in combination with various other factors, such as social support—related to self-reports of good physical and mental health.[31]

Proving that any personality factor causes changes in health is a difficult task. In the case of hardiness, many researchers have pointed out that self-reported gains in health may be due to people's tendencies to view things positively or present a positive view to researchers. Even if the health-protecting effects of hardiness are real, they may have various explanations. For example, hardiness may influence health by changing people's views of negative events, enhancing their capacity to use resources to buffer the effects of a stressful event, or influencing the practice of healthy behaviors.[32]

Explanatory Style

Explanatory style refers to the tendency to explain events in certain ways. For example, a person who fails a math test may explain the low grade by saying he or she has low math ability, will always have low math ability, and that this low math ability will affect many other opportunities. Such an explanation would reflect a *pessimistic explanatory style*. Alternatively, someone with an *optimistic explanatory style* may conclude that he or she failed the test because the test was too hard, that she or he didn't try hard enough and can improve in the future, and that today's failure does not necessarily predict future failures on math tests or other activities. There is evidence that young people with a pessimistic explanatory style will have worse physical health thirty-five years later, even though their initial physical and emotional health was the same as that of a comparison group of people without the pessimistic explanatory style.[33]

Pessimistic explanatory styles have been found to be associated with unhealthy habits (such as lack of exercise, smoking, and alcohol consumption), lack of confidence that those habits can be changed, and a greater number of stressful life events.[34] It has also been found that blaming oneself for negative events (as is characteristic of the pessimistic explanatory style) may affect immune functioning. For example, HIV seropositive men who attributed negative events to themselves rather than to others* had a subsequent decline in immune functioning over the following eighteen months.[36]

Dispositional Optimism

Optimistic explanatory style refers to the ways in which one attributes causes to events; *dispositional optimism* refers to an overall optimistic state in which one generally expects that the future will be good. Dispositional optimism has been linked to better reports of physical health and quicker recovery from illness. In a study of coronary artery bypass surgery, for example, it was found that optimism was associated with greater use of problem-solving coping strategies, less use of denial,

---

*It would be a mistake to conclude from these findings that blaming other people for negative events is good for one's health. In fact, a strong tendency to blame other people is a coping style that is also associated with poor outcomes over time.[35] Instead, these findings suggest that the relationship between self- and other-blame is a matter of degree and that blaming oneself for all or most negative events can be detrimental.

fewer complaints about physical symptoms, a faster rate of recovery, and a more complete return to normal recreational, social, and sexual activities six months later.[37]

A number of studies show that optimism is linked to psychological well-being in other stressed populations, including people with HIV, women with early-stage breast cancer, college freshmen, and emigrants from the former East Germany to West Germany.[38] These studies have also provided consistent evidence that the benefits of optimism can be explained by differences in coping strategies. Specifically, optimists are more likely to use active forms of coping, such as problem solving and seeking social support, and less likely to use avoidant forms of coping, such as wishful thinking or substance use. Finally, some new evidence suggests that optimism may assist people in attending to and remembering information about their own health risk behaviors, which may assist them over time in avoiding threats to health.[39]

Psychological Inhibition

The process of concealing problems and negative emotions, known as *psychological inhibition*, can be detrimental to one's psychological and physiological health. Since Roman times, medical practitioners have speculated that the tendency to conceal or suppress negative emotions is implicated in cancer and other diseases. Although cause and effect between psychological and physiological states is difficult to determine, recent studies have found some support for those ancient speculations. Two separate studies on emotion suppression, for example, showed that people who later developed malignant tumors showed stronger tendencies to suppress feelings of anger and to hold back the expression of depressed feelings than people who did not go on to develop cancer.[40]

Psychological inhibition may have such effects because it takes energy to keep secrets and suppress negative emotions—energy that might otherwise be spent doing things that promote health and healing. It could also be that putting unpleasant things into words helps us to understand them better. For example, in one experiment, participants were randomly assigned to write journal entries over a period of four days about traumatic events they had never disclosed to anyone else. Compared to participants who did not write about trauma, the disclosing participants not only subsequently reported fewer major illnesses and fewer visits to the doctor, but also demonstrated better immune functioning.[41] Other studies have shown that there are also indirect health benefits: an improvement in mood, more active coping strategies, and a more positive reframing of the traumatic experiences.[42]

Social Support

There are many forms of social support, including practical support (such as rides to the doctor's office or help with meals), emotional support (such as reassurance), and appraisal support (such as help in figuring out what is happening and how to cope with it).[43] Health psychologists have extensively studied the association between social support and mental and physical health and have found that social support may be particularly beneficial in highly stressful situations.[44] They have also documented the important role of family relationships in patients' adaptation to serious illness. For example, the family seems to be a vital resource in the overall adjustment of women with breast cancer, especially when the family is an expressive one in which there is little conflict.[45] For married women with breast cancer, the husband is often described as the most important and stable source of social support.

Unfortunately, family and friends may not always be psychologically available to the patient. They may feel unpracticed or uncomfortable in their attempts to provide support, so they may avoid the patient, send mixed signals (for example, by smiling while standing ten feet away from the hospital bed), say nothing to avoid saying the wrong thing, or say the wrong thing just to have something to say.[46] If patients find that other people respond negatively, they may conclude that it is better to keep their problems to themselves, a choice that may compound their psychological distress.

For individuals who have difficulty getting support from established social networks like the family, support programs may be beneficial. These programs usually consist of formal and informal gatherings of persons who share a common concern. The best-known support groups are the twelve-step programs, such as Alcoholics Anonymous and Overeaters Anonymous. It is estimated that up to 15 million individuals attend support group meetings each year.[47]

Support groups for individuals with medical conditions come in many formats. They may be led by professional therapists who work with a particular patient population, or by people who have the condition themselves. Group meetings may focus on a variety of activities; education, emotional support, and social activism are all commonly seen in support groups for persons with medical conditions. As such, they can provide important information, as well as a means of taking greater control of one's health. There are also support groups for patients' friends and family members who may also be dealing with stressors associated with the illness.

QUALITY OF LIFE MEASUREMENTS

Think for a moment about the quality of your life. What score would you give yourself on a scale of 1 to 100? What factors did you take into account in determining your score? Would you focus on how happy you are, how healthy you are, how many friends you have, how much you like your job? Do you think that other people would consider the same factors to be the most important ones? Now imagine that you are diagnosed with cancer. Consider how the quality of your life may change.

In addition to posing an interesting philosophical question, serious consideration of what quality of life is and how it is affected by major illnesses or negative life events is an important practical matter. Quality of life measures are used to evaluate the impact of illness and treatments on patients, to compare the effectiveness of different kinds of treatment for the same illness, and to decide among different treatments when funds are limited. Quality of life issues may also be important in understanding patients' adherence to treatment, because some widely prescribed treatments, such as surgery for prostate cancer or drug treatment of hypertension, produce a lower quality of life than no treatment because of side effects such as impotence, incontinence, or pain.[48] Understanding how medical treatment affects patients' quality of life may allow additional interventions to be designed to meet patients' needs, and thereby improve both quality of life and adherence to treatments.

Physicians, researchers, and health policymakers have struggled with what quality of life is and how it should be measured. To date, there is no widely accepted definition. As an example of how much disagreement there is, a search of studies conducted between 1980 and 1984 revealed sixty-nine medical studies of quality of life that used eighty-three different measures of this concept. The most frequently used measures of quality of life are *functional status* measures. These measures rate a person's ability to perform everyday activities, such as eating, bathing, and dressing, or rate a person's health on a continuum ranging from 0 ("dead") to 100 ("normal with no complaints and no evidence of disease").[49]

There are a number of limitations to functional status measures, however. One is that they do not make very fine discriminations. For example, people who do not experience impairments in everyday activities would all receive the same score, even though their quality of life may vary considerably. The measures also do not take pain into account,[50] so cancer patients with the same ability to function but with different amounts of pain would get the same score. Nor do these measures assess psychological or social functioning. For this reason, people who are severely depressed and socially isolated as a result of illness would receive the same score as those who, in spite of the illness, are cheerful much of the time and able to maintain social contacts with friends.

Another limitation of these measures is that they are often administered by physicians whose ratings of quality of life may be substantially different from the patients' own ratings. In one survey of the quality of life among hypertensive patients, physicians' ratings indicated that 100 percent of them had improved, whereas only 49 percent of the patients thought they had improved.[51] Moreover, only 4 percent of the patients' relatives, who saw the patients on a daily basis, thought the patients had improved. It seems that these ratings were so discrepant because physicians are trained to evaluate medical outcomes, not psychological or social ones. Therefore, although the patients' medical problem, hypertension, was responding well to treatment, the patients and their relatives were more concerned about the patients' overall well-being, social relations, and perhaps other factors, such as financial pressures.

More recent measures take a broader view of what might affect the quality of life. Using ratings provided by healthy people, they consider factors such as a person's mobility, physical and social activity, and physical symptoms (such as fatigue, pain, and shortness of breath).[52] However, as we saw earlier in this chapter, healthy people often overestimate the amount of distress patients experience and may rate symptoms and physical limitations as taking a greater toll on quality of life than is actually the case.

Finally, in addition to the problems inherent in quantifying the effects of illness, there remains the concern that current measures of quality of life are not closely tied to psychological aspects of well-being, such as self-acceptance, autonomy, positive relations with others, purpose in life, and personal growth, all of which have been shown to be important to adults at all stages of life.[53] For example, a woman who has had a mastectomy without reconstructive surgery may pass a physical exam and be pronounced cancer free, but she may show less acceptance of herself, feel less in control of her environment, and experience impaired relations with others. These reactions, in turn, may affect her physical health by influencing how she copes with rehabilitation and whether she follows recommended treatments.

CHALLENGES TO ADOPTING AND MAINTAINING SPECIFIC HEALTH BEHAVIORS

Health psychologists James Prochaska and Carlo DiClemente have outlined five distinct stages of change involved in stopping high-risk behaviors or adopting healthy behaviors.[54] In the *precontemplation* stage, people are not intending any behavior change within six months (they haven't even thought about it); in the *contemplation* stage, people intend to change their behavior within six months; in the *preparation* stage, people seriously plan to change within the next thirty days and are making some attempt to do so; in the *action* stage, people have changed their behavior for up to six months; in the *maintenance* stage, people have continued their behavior change for more than six months. As repeated New Year's resolutions would indicate, people can stay in the contemplation stage for many years or try actions for a few months but not maintain them.

The challenge to health psychologists and others is to increase the number of people in the action and maintenance stages of health behavior, and to prevent people who are attempting to enact healthy behavior from backsliding into a previous stage. To illustrate in greater detail the difficulties involved, let's consider research on three kinds of health behavior: safer sexual behavior (an example of a preventive behavior), willingness to undertake breast self-examinations and mammography (an example of illness-detection behavior), and compliance with taking medication for hypertension (an example of adherence to prescribed treatment). Each of these behaviors has the potential to save lives, information is easily obtained about them, and their medical value is clear. Unfortunately, there is great resistance to practicing these behaviors.

Prevention: The Case of Condom Use and Safer Sexual Behavior

Safer sexual behavior is a classic example of preventive behavior that must be practiced regularly to be effective, in this case, in reducing one's risk of HIV infection and other sexually transmitted diseases (STDs).

Approximately 50 to 60 percent of sexually active heterosexual adults *never* use condoms for sexual intercourse, a small percentage (16 to 20 percent in various studies) uses condoms 100 percent of the time for any insertive sexual activity, and many report using condoms only some of the time. For example, college women reported using condoms in 60 percent of their sexual encounters.[55] Condom use also varies considerably depending on the type of relationship. People report using condoms more frequently for sex with secondary sexual partners (those outside of their primary relationship) than with their primary partner.[56]

What makes findings like these vexing (and interesting) to health psychologists is that people's use of condoms some of the time, or with some partners, suggests that they understand that condoms are effective in preventing HIV and STDs, acknowledge some degree of vulnerability to infection, are willing to use condoms, and know how to do so. Why don't people adopt precautions all of the time and with all partners? Why don't they change their behavior? Here are some of the psychological and social factors that are known to interfere with safer sexual behavior.

Fear of AIDS The intense fear of AIDS may actually result in an increase rather than a decrease in risky sexual behavior.[57] Perceiving oneself to be at risk for such a serious illness creates considerable stress and fear. As a consequence, people may feel overwhelmed by their risk and powerless to reduce it, or they may deny the risk. If sexual behavior is a person's preferred way to release tension, then increased stress from increased risk could actually increase risky sexual behavior. Consequently, it may be important to recognize that intervention programs that focus on increasing fear have the potential to backfire. Indeed, stress-reduction programs have been effective for reducing psychological distress and sexually risky behavior among gay men who are HIV seropositive.[58]

Fear and Guilt About Sex Fear of sex or guilt about sex is known to result in less regular use of contraceptives and may also interfere with obtaining information about AIDS or safer sexual practices.[59] A recent experiment provides support for this idea. When students in a college marketing class were shown advertisements for personal care products, such as toothpaste, shampoo, and condoms, women who scored high on a measure of sex guilt recalled less of the information from the condom ads and listed fewer thoughts about the ads than women with medium or low levels of sex guilt.[60]

Impression Management The need to look good, to convey a desired impression of the self, affects a wide range of human behaviors, including sex-related behaviors.[61] For example, many people report that buying condoms is embarrassing. Additionally, people who are trying to be seen as sexually attractive want to avoid seeming "wimpy," "uncool," overly concerned about HIV risk, or as having planned for sex. Consistent with these ideas, research on attitudes toward condoms has revealed that impression management issues— beliefs that condoms stigmatize the user as sexually experienced, promiscuous, or planful, and that purchasing condoms is embarrassing—are important to both men and women.[62]

Goals The goals of sexual activity may interfere with safer sex practices. For example, the establishment of intimacy and trust is a critical goal for many couples. Using a condom for every act of sex between partners in a close relationship is seen by many to convey a lack of trust, to raise unpleasant questions (Does the person have other partners? Has the person lied about his or her sexual history?), and to decrease intimacy.[63] Understanding the goals that people are pursuing in their sexual relationships turns out to be quite useful in understanding their behavior. For example, Catherine Sanderson and Nancy Cantor examined two different kinds of goals that adolescents may be pursuing in their social dating and sexual behavior: intimacy goals and identity goals.[64] Intimacy goals involve open communication, sharing, and trust with one's partner(s), whereas identity goals involve personal development behaviors, such as self-reliance, self-exploration, asserting one's independence, and trying out multiple roles. These two goals were found to influence the effectiveness of differing types of interventions aimed at promoting safer sex. For teens focused on intimacy goals, programs that focus on communicating with one's partner tend to be effective, whereas for those with identity goals, interventions that focus on condom use skills have more impact.

Gender Roles Different gender roles may also affect safer sex practices in heterosexual couples. For men, safer sex involves wearing a condom; for women, it involves persuading a male partner to wear one. These are different behaviors, and different factors, such as power differences and relationship factors, may be involved from the start.[65] Some women, for example, may hesitate to take an active role in negotiating safer sexual behavior because their perceived inferior social status leads them to develop characteristics such as passivity and submissiveness to please men. Additionally, they may fear the conflict or problems in the relationship that may result from negotiating safer sex; women who have experienced abuse may be especially wary of angering their partners. Different factors may influence men. For example, traditionally masculine beliefs about sex and gender, such as feeling less responsible for preventing pregnancy and believing that relations between the sexes are adversarial, are linked to lower levels of condom use and greater numbers of sexual partners among adolescent males.[66]

Situational Factors Even people who enter a sexual situation intending to practice safer sex often fail to do so in the heat of the moment. Researchers interested in understanding people's failure to practice safer sex have looked closely at the circumstances in which sexual decisions are made. One very interesting approach to this difficult problem has been to examine people's *sexual scripts*: their description of the behaviors and situations leading up to sexual activity.[67] Researchers found that a typical script for first-time sex starts when one member of the couple proposes to move to a private location to get more comfortable, followed by gradual increases in physical intimacy, escalating sexual behavior, establishing mutual intent to have sex, and moving to a better location, such as a bed or floor. These scripts were also analyzed for when and how often alcohol and other drugs were used, and when condoms or other forms of contraception were mentioned, if at all. The findings were striking: nearly 70 percent of the scripts included alcohol use, but only 20 percent of college students' scripts (but more than 60 percent of middle-aged adults' scripts) included condom use. If condoms are mentioned, it seems to be during a brief period of time following the moment the couple mutually establishes their intent to have sex. This "discussion" (it is actually rarely verbal) takes place under conditions of intense sexual arousal and often when people are drunk or high on drugs—in other words, when they may not be making their best and most considered decisions and when it is difficult for them to modify their behavior.

Mistrust Finally, mistrust of government health agencies may interfere with preventive health behaviors. For example, some African Americans believe that the spread of HIV is part of a government conspiracy to wipe out minority communities.[68] In one study, 67 percent of African Americans participating in a focus group about AIDS-related attitudes expressed the belief that the U.S. government was not "telling the whole story about AIDS." Only 34 percent of European American respondents expressed this belief. Additionally, 51 percent of African Americans and 41 percent of European Americans believed that AIDS was being used to "promote hatred of minority groups." Similar suspicions and fears may be present in the gay community, where some people believe that AIDS was "invented" to wipe out homosexuals or decrease gay male sexual activity.[69] With such beliefs as a backdrop, resistance to sexual behavior change and to HIV testing takes on different political and cultural meanings. As such, this resistance cannot simply be understood as a question of health beliefs.

In conclusion, unsafe sexual behavior is the product of many psychological, social, and cultural factors. Therefore, the most successful interventions include not just one, but several of the factors from the preceding list.[70]

Illness Detection: The Case of Breast Cancer Screening

Not all illness can be prevented, but early detection can minimize the impact of a disease. Early illness-detection procedures are widely available, yet they are infrequently used. Many of the factors that interfere with preventive behavior also apply to illness-detection behavior. For example, illness-detection behaviors may be time-consuming or awkward. Additionally, many people do not practice behaviors such as breast or testicular self-examination or HIV testing because they fear discovering that they have cancer or HIV infection.

How can such barriers to illness-detection behavior be surmounted? Researchers in the areas of health psychology, attitude change, and decision making have found that emphasizing what people will *lose* rather than gain seems to have huge effects on behavior.

In a test of this idea, researchers interested in promoting mammography randomly assigned women over the age of forty to view one of two videos, *The Benefits of Mammography* or *The Risks of Neglecting Mammography*.[71] The major topics covered in the two videos were identical; the only difference was whether the information was presented in terms of gain or loss. For example, the *Benefits* video noted,

"We will show that detecting breast cancer early can *save* your life," whereas the *Risks* video stated, "We will show that failing to detect breast cancer early can *cost* you your life." The video emphasizing losses was superior in prompting the women to get mammograms (43.3 percent versus 33.8 percent at six months follow-up, 66.2 percent versus 51.5 percent at twelve months follow-up).* The emphasis on losses is particularly effective for women who believe that breast self-exams and mammography are "risky" because they may find a lump or cancer. For those who do not believe that these behaviors are "risky," a message that emphasizes gains (what women might learn about their bodies) may be more effective.

Nonadherence to Treatment: The Case of Hypertension

Treatment adherence has received extensive research attention because of the startlingly high level of nonadherence to medical recommendations. It is estimated in some studies that as many as 93 percent of all patients fail to follow their doctor's recommendation and nearly 70 percent do not take their medicine as prescribed.[72] Are people who fail to take prescribed medication naive, forgetful, foolish, and rebellious? The answer seems to be no; rather, they have their own beliefs about their illness and its prescribed treatment, and those beliefs may not match those of their physicians.[73]

The classic example of treatment nonadherence is resistance to drug treatment for hypertension. The drugs for treating this disorder have many undesirable side effects, and many people question whether the medication is really helping them if it makes them feel worse instead of better. To complicate matters, hypertension is a silent killer, which means that it creates serious health problems without creating detectable symptoms. Although it is impossible to tell when one's blood pressure is elevated without measuring it, people frequently develop their own theories about when their pressure is up, and they use this information to decide whether they need to take medication. As one woman said: "Are you really certain that people can't tell when their blood pressure is up? I mean, maybe you didn't get the right data (reading)? I know I can tell when my blood pressure is up, like if I have a headache. I take it, I have a pressure cuff, and it's high! And I take my medications, whenever I have a headache or if my face feels warm. So, I know I can tell and I don't need meds all the time."[74]

In a study investigating this phenomenon, 80 percent of hypertensive patients believed their doctor's statement that people in general cannot detect elevated blood pressure, but 90 percent believed that they *personally* could do so.[75] That is, they believed the information applied to others but not to them. Unfortunately, patients who reported that they could monitor their own blood pressure were three times more likely to drop out of treatment than those who didn't mention such a belief.†

---

*Similar results have been found for breast self-exams and HIV testing.
†Similar results have been reported with diabetes patients and also with arthritis patients, who often experiment with their anti-inflammatory medication even though they have been told that the medications are effective only when taken regularly.

CONCLUSIONS

Let's review the major lessons learned from the application of theories and research in health psychology and then conclude by identifying some areas in which health psychology can potentially contribute to the understanding and improvement of human health in the future.

Lesson 1: It is important to ask patients about coping, adjustment, and quality of life. Numerous studies of physically disabled people, people with cancer, and people with other serious illnesses, such as rheumatoid arthritis and AIDS, reveal that they can and do cope with extreme challenges to physical and mental health. Often they adjust differently, and better, than most other people think. Putting the research focus on how people respond to such challenges psychologically and socially has the potential to tell us a lot about human adaptability and the impact of illness not only on the disease state, but also on the total person. Efforts to assist people with serious illnesses, whether they are formal interventions or informal attempts by friends and family to help the person, will be more successful if they are informed by a more complete understanding of the challenges posed by illness to patients' views of themselves and their future and to patients' interactions with other people.

Understanding how people cope with such changes is a booming research area in health psychology. Researchers are continuing to examine how certain beliefs and personality factors are related to more or less adaptive ways of coping, how people respond to violations of beliefs, how such responses are influenced by social support, and, in turn, how different ways of responding to serious illness and other stressful events affect one's social resources and health over time.

Lesson 2: It is important to understand that health behaviors are multiply determined. Many illness-prevention and illness-detection measures seem simple but may actually be very difficult to implement and maintain. We reviewed several perceived barriers to change that keep people from enacting life-saving behaviors, even when they have high levels of relevant knowledge and agree that such behaviors would reduce their risk of illness. As is true for research on adjustment to serious illness, major advances in understanding health behavior have been furthered by asking people why they do or do not practice certain behaviors and by examining the psychological and social context in which such behaviors occur. Fortunately, interventions that address the psychological and social factors involved in health behaviors show great promise in increasing healthy behaviors and reducing risky ones.

Lesson 3: It is important to understand the mind-body connection. A major contribution of health psychology has been to expand our knowledge of this connection. Research on the links among psychological distress, social support, and immune function has yielded intriguing evidence that psychological, social, and physical factors jointly influence health. Such research has stimulated the development of support groups and stress management training to bolster immune function among people with serious illnesses such as cancer and AIDS. Additional research on cognitive styles and disclosure of emotions may also further intervention efforts. Ultimately, it may be possible to employ such interventions prospectively, to prevent serious illness from developing.

The Future

The advent of medical procedures that seemed impossible a generation ago—genetic testing, infertility technologies, organ transplantation, and other procedures to extend life—presents new challenges to researchers in health psychology and raises new questions. How do people understand the probabilistic risk information provided by genetic testing? How do people make decisions to be tested or to change their life plans following testing? More generally, how do people think about such topics as future disability and death, advanced medical directives, and physician-assisted suicide?

Although our understanding of illness-prevention and detection behaviors has increased considerably over the past thirty years, there are several crucial preventive health issues where relatively little progress has been made. Specifically, teen smoking is on the rise; unplanned teen pregnancies in the United States remain at high levels relative to other industrialized nations; the incidence of skin cancer, especially deadly melanoma, has increased dramatically; and HIV continues to spread, especially among women, teenagers, and members of ethnic minority groups. All of these remain as pressing public health problems.

The difficulty of getting patients to adhere to treatment regimens—especially those that are complex and time-consuming, have few detectable immediate benefits, and have unpleasant side effects—will become more important with the advent of more sophisticated therapies, such as protease inhibitor drug "cocktails" to treat HIV infection. It will be important to understand how patients perceive such complex illnesses and treatment regimens because compliance with treatment often depends on patients' understanding of their condition. Hence, future studies will continue to provide insight into medically risky behaviors that look foolhardy or ignorant to the detached observer, but may make good sense to the patient. Additionally, as new forms of early intervention become available (e.g., to limit the damage caused by heart attacks or the severity of HIV infection), it will become increasingly important to study how people appraise and respond to the first symptoms of illness in order to understand how to motivate them to seek treatment early enough for the treatment to be most beneficial.

Great progress in the prevention and treatment of illness has been made, but such benefits have not been evenly distributed. At this writing, deaths from HIV infection have declined sharply among white men, but to a lesser extent among members of ethnic minority groups. The difference in mortality has been attributed to differing access to expensive new drug therapies. Therefore, health psychology researchers and public policymakers must work strenuously to involve women and ethnic minorities in clinical trials and other research studies and to ensure fair access to life-saving treatments and psychological interventions.

Finally, the impact of managed care on the delivery of interventions to promote psychological well-being must be carefully monitored. Health psychologists must continue to demonstrate not only that their interventions can improve physical health and quality of life, but also that they are cost-effective. By increasing the practice of preventive and illness-detection behaviors, improving treatment adherence, reducing psychological distress, and reducing unnecessary doctor visits, interventions grounded in psychological theory and research have the potential to save millions of dollars and greatly reduce the personal and societal costs of illness. Paying attention to psychological and social factors in health is not a frill, but a scientific, personal, and societal necessity.

SUGGESTIONS FOR FURTHER READING

American Psychological Association Science Directorate. (1995). *Doing the right thing: A research plan for healthy living. A Human Capital Initiative strategy report.* Washington, DC: American Psychological Association.

Blechman, E., & Brownell, K. (1998). *Behavioral medicine for women: A comprehensive handbook.* New York: Guilford.

Buunk, B. P., & Gibbons, F. X. (1997). *Health and coping: Perspectives from social comparison theory.* Hillsdale, NJ: Erlbaum.

Kato, P. M., & Mann, T. (1996). *Handbook of diversity issues in health psychology.* New York: Plenum Press.

Taylor, S. E. (1998). *Health psychology* (4th ed.). New York: McGraw-Hill.

Journals—for example, *Health Psychology, Annals of Behavioral Medicine, Psychology and Health, Psychosomatic Medicine, Women's Health: Research on Gender, Research and Policy, and Journal of Clinical Psychology in Medical Settings*—are also good starting points for further reading.

PSYCHOLOGY APPLIED TO PSYCHOLOGICAL DISORDERS

Astrid M. Stec

P eople sometimes shy away from psychologists in social settings because they worry that psychologists will search for, and maybe find, something abnormal in their character or behavior. In fact, most psychologists are interested in *normal* behavior and have no expertise, or even interest, in dealing with the abnormal. It is mainly the subset of psychologists, called *clinical psychologists,* who are interested in the abnormal. Actually, the term *abnormal* may be inappropriate because clinical psychologists are curious not only about conditions that seem far removed from the normal (such as schizophrenia), but also about common ones such as stress, anxiety, relationship difficulties, or problems of low self-esteem. Clinical psychologists are interested in studying, assessing, treating, and preventing these conditions. I will describe each of these activities after offering a brief history of clinical psychology and a description of how clinical psychologists are trained.

A BRIEF HISTORY OF CLINICAL PSYCHOLOGY

Today most people associate clinical psychology largely with the treatment of behavioral and emotional difficulties. But that is not how it started. Clinical psychology began in 1896 when a school teacher asked a psychologist named Lightner Witmer to help her with a student who was a "chronic bad speller." Witmer tested the student and found that he had a number of learning disabilities. He then established a "clinic" in which other children with speech disorders, sensory problems, and learning difficulties could be assessed and treated. In his clinic, Witmer and his staff not only tried to help the children, but also gave advice to teachers and parents. Witmer is thus credited with founding clinical psychology, but because he worked exclusively with children in relation to educational settings, he would probably be called a school psychologist today, not a clinical psychologist.

It was other psychologists who expanded clinical work to include the assessment of adults in mental hospitals and prisons. In hospitals, their assessments helped psychiatrists diagnose and plan treatment for patients with brain damage and other problems. In prisons, psychologists helped assess convicts and plan rehabilitation programs for them. They also continued Witmer's work with children by becoming involved in child guidance clinics, but these focused mainly on behavioral and emotional problems, not educational problems.

It was World War I that brought even more psychologists into clinical functions. The war required that recruits be assigned to positions based on their abilities, and psychologists, who by this time had much experience administering and designing various tests, were called on to help select and classify more than 2 million military recruits. As a result of this massive testing effort, the public became more aware of psychological services, especially those of assessment.

After World War I, psychological clinics proliferated, and gradually clinicians began to be involved not just with assessment but also with treatment. A few established private practices. But there was still no formal training for psychologists as therapists because it was psychiatrists who were perceived to be responsible for treatment. Psychologists were still largely restricted to their assessment function.

World War II changed all of that. Although psychologists' work focused on assessments, so many veterans were emotionally scarred at the end of it that psychiatrists could no longer meet the demand for treatment services. This was the chance that psychologists, who had been wanting to expand their therapeutic opportunities, were waiting for. In the United States, the Veterans Administration began to fund the training of clinical psychologists, and it soon became the largest single employer of psychologists in the country.

Since the end of World War II, clinical psychology has gained public and legal recognition, and has become the most popular area of study for students of psychology. Of the three thousand or more doctoral degrees granted in psychology during the 1980s, 40 percent of them were in clinical psychology.[1] Clinical psychology graduates work in a wide variety of educational, business, forensic, and health settings. A large proportion (about 35 percent) are established in private practice.[2]

Although the years after World War II saw a burgeoning of opportunities for clinical psychologists, the past fifteen years or so have been a time during which funding for all health care services, including those of clinical psychologists, has been cut back or restricted by, for example, managed care systems in the United States. Consequently, the most recent challenge for clinical psychologists has been to develop more efficient therapeutic techniques and to focus on prevention so that fewer people will require treatment.

PROFESSIONAL TRAINING AND REGULATION

The most common training programs for clinical psychologists are based on the *scientist-practitioner* model. There are two important aspects to this model. First, it requires that clinical psychologists, like all other psychologists, have expertise as scientists. A knowledge of scientific methods enables psychologists to investigate their hypotheses objectively and encourages a scientific attitude, which ideally engenders, ideally, open communication, constant evaluation, and a willingness to be proved wrong. Second, the scientist-practitioner model requires that clinical psychologists have a clear understanding of normal psychological processes—perception, learning, memory, cognition, biological bases of behavior, and social influences—as well as of the assessment and treatment of psychological disorders.

This model distinguishes the training of clinical psychologists from that of other mental health professionals. Psychiatrists, for example, are educated as medical doctors, which means that the focus of their training is on diagnosing and treating disease, physical or mental. In their undergraduate years, they take many science courses, but there is not an emphasis on normal psychological processes or on scientific research methods.

One of the responsibilities of any profession is to protect the public from incompetent or untrained practitioners. In clinical psychology, legislation in all North American states and provinces ensures that those who offer clinical services to the public cannot use the title "psychologist" unless they have met appropriate professional criteria, such as having a certain level of education, a certain amount of supervised clinical experience, and a general knowledge of their field, including relevant laws and ethical standards. If these criteria are satisfied, then the psychologist becomes—depending on state or provincial law—a certified, registered, or licensed psychologist.

CLINICAL ASSESSMENT

Clinical assessment involves gathering a wide variety of information about people's behavior, thoughts, emotions, and abilities. The information may then be used to help clinicians and others to choose the best treatment strategies or optimal vocational, educational, or rehabilitation programs. It may also be used for screening people to participate in psychological research, or to make decisions about mental competency or other legal issues (see Chapter 8). Clinical psychologists rely on three main forms of assessment: interviews, tests, and observations.

Interviews

Interviews are the most common form of assessment.[3] The purpose of the clinical interview is typically to identify the nature of the client's* problems, decide if the client has come to the right place, clarify the terms for further contact, and, even more important, set the tone of the client-therapist relationship. There are three stages of the interview: the beginning, middle, and end.

A successful *beginning stage* is critical because the first contact with a clinician will often determine whether a client will agree to further assessment or treatment; almost half the clients who attend an initial interview fail to return for scheduled treatment.[4] What makes for success in the interview is similar to what makes for success in any budding relationship or conversation: we are more likely to want to continue the interaction if we feel that the person talking to us appears interested in us and does not do anything verbally or nonverbally to make us feel anxious or

---

*Note that many psychologists use the term *client,* not *patient,* to denote that they do not endorse a strictly medical model of psychological disorders.

unimportant. Thus, a warm smile, some eye contact, a friendly greeting, and a handshake are excellent beginnings. The clinician also helps clients ease into the interview with, for example, some small talk about the weather or difficulty in finding the office. The interview then usually begins with a general, open-ended question such as, "So what brings you here today?" indicating that the clinician is open to hearing whatever the client wishes to reveal.

As the conversation starts and initial rapport has been established, the interview enters its *middle stage.* Sometimes this stage follows a structured format in which particular questions are asked in order to elicit specific information; at other times it proceeds in a more easy-going, nondirective way. The nondirective interviewer encourages an easy flow of communication by asking open-ended questions that allow a diversity of answers, not questions that limit answers. For example, "How do you feel about having dinner with your father?" is preferable to, "Do you feel better after having dinner with your father?"

The degree of structure in an interview depends partly on the theoretical orientation of the psychologist. The clinician who follows the behavioral or cognitive-behavioral model (described later) is more likely than a humanist therapist to impose some structure. The degree of structure is also influenced by the purpose of the interview. If the purpose is to arrive at a diagnosis (for example, to decide whether a client displays a mental disorder and, if so, which disorder it is), a carefully planned question-and-answer format is usually employed.

The last part of the interview, the *termination stage,* requires care and consideration because some clients may now feel vulnerable after having confided highly personal information. Some may feel a sense of loss if they have enjoyed the comfort of a supportive relationship, and some may even be angry because they fear that the therapist is rejecting them by ending the interview. In view of these potential reactions, the clinician usually prepares the client for termination by stating, in advance, that the interview will soon be finished. This closing phase gives the clinician an opportunity to review what has occurred during the interview, plan for further sessions, and address, or at least acknowledge, the emotional issues that have been raised. It also gives the client a chance to ask questions about the interview, the clinician's techniques and goals, and anything else that seems relevant. Ending the interview by responding to clients' questions may be particularly effective because it helps provide clients with a much-needed sense of control and closure as they make the transition from the special atmosphere of the interview to face the demands of their day-to-day world once again.

Tests

Compared to interviews, tests are more formal, structured ways of obtaining information. They involve presenting a person with particular tasks or sets of questions in order to assess some area of functioning. Tests provide a quick, comprehensive, objective, and (ideally) accurate assessment. For this reason, they are popular in school (at least with teachers); indeed, many of us enjoy filling out tests in popular magazines that promise some quick assessment of our personalities, social skills, or intellectual capabilities.

One of psychology's main contributions to testing is the development of measures of reliability and validity, the two main criteria that evaluate the accuracy of tests. A test is *valid* if it measures what it is supposed to measure. For example, a test of mathematical ability should reflect mathematical skills, not reading comprehension. A test *reliable* if its results are stable, as when the same results are obtained on repeated occasions. (By the way, tests published in popular magazines are usually neither valid nor reliable.)

Psychologists have been responsible for designing thousands of tests to measure countless human characteristics.[5] Many of these tests have strict rules governing their use, administration, scoring, and interpretation, and are available only to appropriately trained psychologists. This restriction is similar to that imposed on prescription medications; only a physician is trained to know when and how these medications should be taken and monitored.

Clinical psychologists have been particularly active in the development of tests of intelligence and personality. Let's consider some of the most popular tests in these areas.

Intelligence Tests The first intelligence test—a version of which is still popular today—was designed in 1908 by Alfred Binet, then revised in 1911 by Lewis Terman of Stanford University, and hence is known as the *Stanford-Binet*. The test was originally intended to be administered to school children in order to determine if they could function in the regular school system, but it has subsequently been used to determine intelligence for many purposes other than school placement.

The Stanford-Binet consists of a number of tasks that measure verbal skills (e.g., defining words, answering questions) as well as nonverbal ones (e.g., copying a drawing, solving puzzles). The tasks are age-graded, which means they are designed to tap the capabilities of children of differing ages. For example, three-year-olds are expected to be able to touch their eyes, nose, and mouth; seven-year-olds should be able to copy simple geometric figures; and eleven-year-olds ought to be able to define abstract terms, such as *honesty*.

Early versions of the test contained six tasks at each age level, and a child's mental age was calculated by assigning two months of "credit" for each successfully performed task . The child's mental age was then compared to his or her chronological age. Later, the scoring formula was changed to provide an "intelligence quotient," or IQ, obtained by dividing mental age by chronological age and multiplying by 100. If the mental and chronological ages were the same, the child would have an IQ of 100, about average in the general population. If mental age was higher than the chronological age, the IQ was over 100; if mental age was lower than chronological age, the IQ would fall below 100.

The Stanford-Binet underwent a number of minor revisions in order to modernize its tasks, but only the latest revision, published in 1986, contained major changes in organization and content.[6] The current version's items are no longer organized on the basis of age, but rather reflect four areas of intellectual functioning:

verbal reasoning, abstract/visual reasoning, quantitative reasoning, and short-term memory.

The other major method for measuring intelligence is a series of tests designed by David Wechsler: the *Wechsler Adult Intelligence Scale* (WAIS), the *Wechsler Intelligence Scale for Children* (WISC), and the *Wechsler Preschool and Primary Scale of Intelligence* (WPPSI). These scales were developed in the 1930s, 1940s, and 1950s and were last revised in 1981. The WAIS, developed first, became the first test specifically designed to measure adult intelligence. All three tests include one set of items that taps verbal abilities and another set that measures nonverbal abilities. Overall IQ is determined by comparing an individual's score on the various tests with norms collected from thousands of others who have taken the test.

Both the Stanford-Binet and the Wechsler scales are administered individually and take about an hour for full administration. Clinicians not only score the client's answers for correctness, but also observe how test takers approach the challenge of the tests. For example, they observe how well an individual attends to and persists at each task, what kinds of errors the person makes, and whether and how he or she corrects those errors. No official scores are attached to these observations, but they can be informative supplements to test scores.

Personality Tests   *Personality* refers to our characteristic ways of behaving, thinking, and feeling: the way we see the world, the way we consistently assess and react to situations, the preferences we have, and the like. These characteristics describe what we are like and how we are different from others. Psychologists have constructed many tests for measuring a multitude of personality characteristics. These tests generally fall into two categories: objective and projective.

Objective tests consist of relatively clear, specific tasks, questions, or statements to which the test taker responds with direct answers, choices, or ratings. The scoring of objective tests is so quantitative that computers are often used to do it. Sometimes computers are even used to administer the tests.

The most widely used objective test is the *Minnesota Multiphasic Personality Inventory* (MMPI). Developed during the late 1930s and revised in 1989 (MMPI-2), the test consists of 567 sentences such as: "I usually feel that life is interesting and worthwhile"; "It makes me uncomfortable to have people close to me"; and "I like to arrange flowers." Test takers indicate whether each statement is true or false for them, or if they "cannot say." The answers to most items are scored on ten clinical scales, which are associated with various mental disorders such as depression, paranoia, and schizophrenia. Answers to other items, known as content scales, reflect characteristics such as anger, cynicism, anxiety, and low self-esteem. Finally, answers to still other items, called validity scales, are scored to detect test taker characteristics that may undermine the validity of the test, such as whether the test taker is trying to conceal, or perhaps exaggerate, personality characteristics. Doing either is made more difficult by the fact that the MMPI is constructed so that the person taking the test does not know what a particular answer will reveal. This structure ideally gives a more accurate assessment than might come from an interview, but there is considerable debate among clinicians and researchers about whether this is indeed the case.

Another popular objective test of personality is the *California Personality Inventory* (CPI), designed in 1957 and revised in 1987. In contrast to the MMPI, which was originally intended to aid in psychiatric diagnoses, the CPI is aimed at assessing personality in the "normal" population. It measures more positive characteristics such as sociability, self-acceptance, and responsibility. Like the MMPI, it consists of many true-false statements (462 of them) and contains validity scales.

Both the MMPI and the CPI tap a broad range of personality characteristics. Other personality tests (such as the NEO Personality Inventory) are based on recent research that has aimed to describe personality along only five dimensions: openness, conscientiousness, extroversion, agreeableness, and neuroticism.[7] Still others address one specific characteristic such as a tendency toward depression[8] or bulimia.[9]

Projective tests present a person with stimuli that have no obvious, "correct" interpretation or answer. For example, a client may be asked to finish an incomplete sentence such as, "I wish . . . ," or to draw a picture of a house, a tree, a person, or a family. The assumption is that when there is no one way to perceive or answer something, people will project their own wishes, fantasies, impulses, and other characteristics onto the test stimulus.

The best-known and most frequently used projective test is the *Rorschach Inkblot Test,* a set of colored and black-and-white inkblots created by Swiss psychiatrist Hermann Rorschach between 1911 and 1921. Ten of these inkblots are presented, one at a time, and clients describe what they see in the blots and where they see it. In scoring the test, the psychologist considers not only what clients say but also how they justify their responses. Do they interpret the whole blot? Do they pay attention to special details? Do they focus on the white spaces rather than the solid parts? Do they rely more on color than on shape? The psychologist also looks for themes that may emerge from responses to the ten pictures. For example, the client may repeatedly perceive animal forms, human figures, blood, or sexual objects. In addition, although there are no "right" or "wrong" ways to interpret the blots, the psychologist notes how unusual the client's perceptions are in comparison to those of others. Psychologists' overall assessment of a client's responses is based on either formally designed scoring techniques[10] or, more commonly, subjective judgments based on their clinical experience and intuition.

Another commonly used projective test is the *Thematic Apperception Test* (TAT), developed in 1935 by Christina D. Morgan and Henry Murray. The TAT consists of a set of drawings that clearly represent people or objects but are vague enough to be open to many interpretations. The client's task is to tell a story about each picture: What is happening? What led up to it? What is going to happen next? The psychologist's analysis of the client's stories takes into account their content, logic, organization, language, and emotional reactions that appear in the telling. As with the Rorschach, there is more than one way to score and interpret TAT responses. In fact, by 1965 there were over twenty systems available.[11] Most clinicians tend to combine a formal scoring system with their own clinical judgment.

In summary, tests have been designed to provide a comprehensive assessment of various client characteristics. They have also received much legitimate criticism from within the profession and outside it. Psychologists themselves continue to be concerned about the validity and reliability of tests, and they argue about the potential for misuse and misinterpretation of tests. Along with the public, psychologists have also become aware of biases in psychological tests, especially biases that can place minority group clients at a disadvantage. Accordingly, the use of IQ tests is restricted in some school systems, and the Civil Rights Act of 1991 prohibits their use in hiring decisions. There is also a concern that tests may invade respondents' privacy. Thus, personality tests have been eliminated from routine selection procedures for federal employees. Nevertheless, the judicious use of psychological tests can provide useful information—for example, to help teachers identify the intellectual abilities and areas of difficulties in students or to aid personnel departments in matching workers' personalities with job opportunities.

Observation

We are all aware that watching someone do something is often more informative than listening to a description of it. Similarly, psychologists' observations can often provide more information about the client than tests or interviews can. An intelligence test may show that a child has difficulty solving problems in the allotted time, but it will not show how the child deals with failures, frustrations, and distractions in the classroom. A woman may disclose during an interview that she flies off the handle easily, but watching her at home will demonstrate what sets her off, how other family members react to her temper, and how she copes with their reaction.

At first glance, observation seems like a simple procedure, but making accurate observations is a challenge. Observers must know exactly what to observe, must not be distracted from focused observation, and must avoid being biased by their own expectations. Because the task can be so demanding, psychologists often rely on trained observers, including teachers, nurses, family members (including children), or even the clients themselves. Frequently, several observers work together in order to ensure consistent, unbiased, and reliable observations.

Observers are trained to pay attention to particular behaviors, and they sometimes use special monitoring devices or shorthand symbols to help keep track of the frequency, intensity, and duration of behavior. In order to cope with the staggering amount of data that is potentially observable, they may collect data intermittently by sampling behavior at specific time intervals or focusing on particular activities. For example, an observer may record a child's behavior in the classroom by noting how often the child gets up from the seat, how frequently the child interrupts the teacher, or the number of times the child acts aggressively during recess.

Observers are also trained to act in ways that minimize the effect their presence may have on the observed behavior. There is probably no way of eliminating this *observer effect* altogether, but observers are taught to be as unobtrusive as possible. For example, when they are conducting *naturalistic observation* in a home or a school, they will sit where they can see what is happening but not where they will be an integral part of the activity. When the observation takes place in a more controlled setting, observers may analyze audiotapes or videotapes or watch from behind a two-way mirror.

TREATMENT

Clinical psychologists provide treatment for a wide range of problems, from debilitating disorders such as schizophrenia to less incapacitating ones such as low self-esteem. In treating these problems, psychologists rely on a variety of therapeutic methods. Hundreds have been identified, but most of them stem from one of four basic models of therapy: the psychodynamic, behavioral, cognitive-behavioral, or phenomenological-experiential. Each of these models organizes the therapist's thinking. They are like guides for a trip that tell the basic laws of the land, what to pay particular attention to, how best to negotiate the terrain, what to watch out for, where the main roads are, which roads are connected, and even which language to speak. (In this chapter, the terms that are characteristic of the language of each therapy model are in italics.) Therapy models also help therapists organize their perceptions, so in a sense, each model influences the portrait that will be drawn of each client. Peter Bankart, comparing therapists and artists in his book *Talking Cures: A History of Western and Eastern Psychotherapies* writes, "How your portrait looks when the artist is done has less to do with how skinny or short or bald or old you are than with whether the painter was Picasso in his Blue period, van Gogh at the height of his powers, or a Zen monk painting you with his eyes closed."[12]

Psychodynamic Models

Psychodynamic therapies assume that the expression of our overt acts and feelings provides clues to deep inner processes. What we can observe of ourselves and others is like the visible parts of a tree. Underneath the surface may be a mass of seething emotions and conflicts whose roots extend far into our past. Psychological problems arise from the pressure of these effervescent emotions and conflicts, which can erupt into our conscious experience and cause distress and confusion. The aim of therapy is gradually to uncover the hidden roots, bring them into the light of consciousness, and thus release some of the pressure.

The first, and probably best-known, psychodynamic model is the *psychoanalytic* one. The initial road map for this model was designed by Sigmund Freud in the late nineteenth and early twentieth century.[13] Freud's ideas are fundamental to understanding many of the processes and terms used in various therapeutic methods, so we will begin with a description of the key elements of the Freudian approach and then briefly describe some variations on Freud's original theory.

The basic goal of psychodynamic therapy is self-knowledge, or *insight*. It is assumed that once people understand the reasons for their actions, feelings, and thoughts, they will be able to change them if necessary. According to Freud, these reasons are hidden in the *unconscious,* a part of ourselves that is largely inaccessible to our conscious mind. But although the unconscious is hidden, there are clues to its contents in our everyday behaviors, especially when our memory or attention seems to slip. For example, when we cannot remember someone's name, it may be because we are unconsciously angry at the person; when we misplace our car keys, we may do so because at some deeper level we really do not want to go where we were supposed to go; or when we accidentally say, "I had a grim on my face," instead of, "I had a grin on my face," we are trying to cover some unacceptable, unpleasant feelings. All of these are examples of what are now called "Freudian slips."

Freud said that other clues to the unconscious can be obtained by asking the patient to *free-associate*—that is, to say everything that spontaneously comes to mind without editing or censorship. The rationale for free association is that by removing the constraints of logic, social niceties, and other rules, unconscious material will surface more readily.

Freud saw another route to the unconscious through the analysis of dreams. When we are dreaming, he said, the censorship that is characteristic of the waking state is not as active, so the unconscious mind can reveal itself more readily. One of the main reasons for Freud's famous strategy of asking patients to lie on a couch during treatment was his assumption that the more relaxed we are, the freer we are to let the unconscious surface.

Still another avenue to the unconscious derives from the relationship established between patient and therapist. Freud referred to the patient's feelings toward and relationship with the therapist as *transference* because he assumed that patients transfer onto the therapist the characteristics of earlier significant relationships.* For example, the patient may accuse the therapist of being angry all the time when it is not the therapist but the patient's mother who was consistently angry. Or patients may fear that the therapist will betray them, when it was actually their father who betrayed them. When patients reveal the nature of their past relationships in this way, the therapist can more easily identify their problems from the past and understand how they recur in the present.

The first task for the psychodynamically oriented therapist, then, is to find various paths and clues to the unconscious. The second task is to recognize, and find ways to overcome, the patient's *resistance* to exposing what is in the unconscious. There is resistance because the feelings, thoughts, wishes, and conflicts in the unconscious are often distressing, so even though people seek help, they will—unconsciously, of course—put up some roadblocks. Some typical signs of resistance are arriving late for appointments, or diverting the conversation to less personal topics by, for example, engaging the therapist in intellectual discussions of abstract issues, or by talking about someone else's problems. The therapist's role is to interpret these strategies to the patient by suggesting that they are aimed at warding off painful, distressing, or shameful matters.

Closely related to resistance are the *defense mechanisms* that Freud said people use daily, whether they are in therapy or not. Defense mechanisms are ways of un-

---

Countertransference refers to the *therapist's* feelings toward a patient, reactions to the transference of the patient, or the therapist's own transference to a patient.

consciously armoring ourselves against our internal conflicts. We rely on defense mechanisms when we cannot rationally and consciously cope with our feelings. These mechanisms camouflage discomfort by (1) pushing it into the unconscious (*repression*), (2) not acknowledging that it exists (*denial*), (3) acting as though it is someone else's problem (*projection*), (4) taking it out on someone else (*displacement*), (5) experiencing the opposite feeling (*reaction formation*), (6) explaining it away (*rationalization*), or, if all else fails, (7) *regressing* to a dependent, childlike state, in the hope that someone else will take care of our problems. The therapist's goal is to help patients uncover some of these mechanisms so they can develop less defensive ways of coping with their inner and outer worlds.

Freud also emphasized the impact of childhood experiences on adult personality. Specifically, he said that if we experienced either a lack of gratification or excessive gratification of particular needs at specific stages of development, we may become *fixated* (or stuck) at those stages. For example, signs of fixation at the earliest (*oral*) stage may include excessive dependence and reliance on oral pleasures such as eating, drinking, smoking, and talking too much, all to satisfy a variety of oral needs symbolically. The role of the therapist is to help identify the critical stage at which development became delayed and to try to move the person to a more mature stage.

A further task for the therapist is to help patients understand the impact of unconscious conflicts and defenses on their current relationships. It would do little good, for example, if a woman knows that she maintains unconscious childhood feelings of anger toward her mother, yet fails to see that these feelings continue to create difficulties in sustaining close relationships with other women.

Reaching the ambitious goals set by the traditional psychodynamic approach requires a lot of time (three to five sessions each week for two to fifteen years), a lot of money, and a great deal of therapeutic skill. Consequently, the therapy is most suitable for people who can afford the time and the money, and these people are generally adults who can function reasonably well outside the therapeutic setting.

There are also variations on the psychodynamic model that demand less intense therapeutic work and challenge some of Freud's principles. We cannot do justice to all of the variations here, so we will focus on a few representative ones.[14]

Individual Psychology   The key aspects of therapy based on individual psychology were first outlined by Alfred Adler.[15] Adler began as a follower of Freud but then broke ranks with him. He agreed with Freud that the traces of adult personality can be found in childhood experiences, but he was also interested in how the past affects patients' goals and expectations. Thus, having patients write a "future biography" was as central to understanding their current state as having them recount their past. He also agreed with Freud that excessive pampering or neglect by parents is detrimental, but he emphasized influences of the broader social world context outside the family.

One of Adler's favorite targets in therapy was the *inferiority complex,* which he saw as being created not only by the family but also by larger societal forces. Part of the treatment for this problem consisted of convincing patients that a desire to be superior, to be "Superman" or "Miss Perfection," or to live in general as if one is someone else, would only exaggerate (and conceal) deeper feelings of insecurity and helplessness. Instead, patients were encouraged to rethink and reconstruct their lives and beliefs so that they could achieve a sense of control and responsibility. In order to foster this sense of control and responsibility, Adler, unlike Freud, sat face to face with the patient, thus creating a more equal relationship between the patient and the therapist. Virtually all modern therapists (except those who still practice traditional psychoanalysis) use this arrangement.

Analytical Psychology   Analytical psychology was developed by Carl Gustav Jung. Like Adler, Jung initially had a close connection with Freud but then developed his own theory of human nature and therapy, which expanded the ideas of both Adler and Freud.[16] For example, whereas Freud had focused on the primary family's influence on personality development, and Adler had enlarged the focus beyond the family, Jung believed that the personality structure of each individual contained, in miniature, a reflection of the entire universe.[17] Therefore, Jung was concerned with exploring not only a patient's personal unconscious, but also a *collective unconscious,* which comes from the experience of past generations and cultures and is part of the intrinsic inheritance of each individual. In order to access the contents of the collective unconscious, Jung analyzed patients' dreams, memories, and fantasies, as well as myths and rituals. Religious experiences were important to Jung because they provided information about universal symbols (*archetypes*), such as a concept of God, a wicked witch, a pure virgin, or a hero on a quest. Discovering the connections between individual and universal experiences would, he proposed, provide patients with an enriched sense of the meaning of their existence—"a life of fuller awareness."[18] But before this discovery could be accomplished, Jung believed that people have to achieve a sense of union within themselves—a union that was impeded by two obstacles.

The first obstacle is that we attempt to camouflage what is inside us by wearing *masks,* that is, appearing as we would like others to see us and as we would like to see ourselves. For example, we may wear the mask of a cheerful person, an organized person, or a cynic. These masks often cover the second obstacle, that of seeing what is in our *shadow*—the parts of ourselves that we would prefer to keep in the dark and that are usually the opposite of who we think we are. For example, if we see ourselves as cheerful, then an angry person is in hiding; if we think we are organized, a disorganized part lurks in the shadow; and if we portray ourselves as a cynic, there is a soft, generous part, which is concealed. Thus, for Jung, acknowledging the masks and throwing light on the shadow parts were the first significant steps of a patient's journey toward a more creative, integrated being. Once they took these steps, patients could face larger issues, such as the overall meaning and purpose of life. In essence, then, Jung was "a scholar of the spiritual and transcendent"[19] and perceived patients not only as seeking treatment but as being "pilgrims on a sacred journey."[20]

Object Relations Therapy   Developed by a number of British analysts beginning in the 1950s, object relations therapy is one of the modern variations of the psychodynamic model.[21] These analysts believe that the relationships one forms during adulthood are determined by the earliest relationships one had with "objects" in the world, especially one's primary caregiver (usually the mother). The key task of the *primary object* is to provide a source of information to the infant about himself or herself. The infant, in a sense, learns to see himself or herself through the eyes of the mother. It is as though the mother holds up a mirror to the infant to let the infant know who he or she is. If this *mirroring* is successful, then the mother is in tune with the infant's needs for self-knowledge and will understand, encourage, and fulfill them, as well as nurture and protect the infant. Object relations therapists believe that if a child does not experience that kind of closeness with the mother, problems ranging from relationship difficulties to serious mental disorders will ensue. Therapy in such cases provides a second chance to experience the ideal qualities of a primary relationship. The therapist becomes the empathic, nurturant person who "holds" the client,* that is, accepts and contains whatever feelings are expressed by the client without feeling overpowered by them, as the mother might have done. Thus, the warm, responsive, and accepting relationship between the client and the therapist, rather than hosting any complex analysis of past experiences, becomes the avenue for developing improved relationships outside of therapy.

Feminist Psychotherapy   Psychodyamic therapists who take a feminist perspective have two objections to the traditional psychodynamic therapies. The first is that therapists are often unaware of how their own culture colors their interpretation, understanding, and treatment of individuals. For example, a white, economically privileged, male therapist may not appreciate the experiences of a client whose gender and background are different from his. Furthermore, feminist therapists argue, many therapists essentially help people to adjust to the world as it is rather than helping clients to question the impact of existing political, economic, legal, and social structures. Therefore, many feminist therapists believe it is important to develop the awareness of these influences in their clients.

The second objection is that the patriarchal society in which traditional psychodynamic approaches developed did not do sufficient justice to the understanding of women's positions in society and the difficult demands placed on women by their family and culture. As a result, women and others (especially members of minority groups) have often been judged to be in psychological distress that is assumed to be due to internal deficiencies. In fact, say feminists, their distress is actually *caused,* by attempts to cope with exceedingly difficult external demands such as being the primary caretakers for the family, or facing discrimination and restricted opportunities in the workplace. In order to help clients deal with these societal pressures, feminist therapists focus on *empowerment,* that is, encouraging clients to develop their own strengths. Empowerment is aimed not at developing authority over someone else but at developing faith in one's own judgments, perceptions, feelings, skills, and competencies. For feminist therapists, the therapeutic

---

*Note that recent models of psychodynamic therapy refer to "clients," not "patients."

setting becomes an arena for demonstrating that clients can feel empowered in their own lives. Therefore, feminist therapists often address the power differential between a therapist and client, and aim to empower clients by listening to, understanding, and *validating* (or confirming) the clients' feelings and perceptions.[22]

Behavioral Models

Therapies based on behavioral models of disorder focus on problematic behaviors that are observable in the present rather than searching for unobservable, unconscious causes from the past. Where psychodynamic therapists engage in long-term detective work to find hidden clues to inner motivations, behavioral therapists are more like teachers aiming to identify and correct mistakes and hoping to encourage more appropriate solutions in as short a time as possible. Consistent with the teacher role, behavioral therapists base their techniques on three learning models that have been demonstrated in the psychological research laboratory.

The first set of learning principles used in behavioral therapies are those of *classical conditioning*. The basic principle of classical conditioning is that we automatically make connections between things that happen at the same time; and we then react to both of them in a similar way.

The connections formed by classical conditioning are generally helpful to us. For example, after a dog bite, the learned fear serves to alert us to possible danger from dogs. Although this is an adaptive reaction, it may become problematic if we avoid going anywhere we could possibly see a dog. In other words, these reactions may become so excessive as to qualify as phobias, meaning that they cause so much anxiety that they interfere with our ability to meet the demands of everyday life.

The most common behavioral treatment of such phobias is called *systematic desensitization*. It involves helping clients to associate gradually more intense versions of once-feared stimuli with relaxation. Desensitization can be done in real life or in the imagination. Clients terrified of dogs, for example, may systematically be taught to relax and then remain relaxed while imagining a small dog in the distance that gradually comes closer and closer.[23]

Behavioral therapists also use the principles of *operant conditioning*. The basis of operant conditioning is that we make connections between our behavior and its consequences (reward or punishment), and then repeat what brings positive consequences and avoid doing what brings negative consequences. So, for example, we go back to restaurants that serve good food and avoid those that don't. Again, operant conditioning serves us well. It can be used to encourage or discourage many behaviors, but problems arise when people have been rewarded for maladaptive behavior. For example, although parents can use operant conditioning to teach their children appropriate behavior, they can also inadvertently reward tantrums in their children by giving more attention to the children when they are misbehaving than when they are being quiet.

Behavioral therapists might treat such problems by changing the pattern of consequences. For example, therapists may deliberately set up a way of systematically rewarding desirable behavior in the client, perhaps teaching parents the correct way to reward a child for desirable behavior and to ignore the child for unacceptable behavior. In hospital settings, a popular system of operant conditioning is called a *token economy.* It involves systematically providing poker chips or other tokens after the client performs some desirable behavior, such as being friendlier or engaging in better self-care. These tokens can subsequently be exchanged for snacks, TV time, or some other reward.

In addition to providing positive consequences for desirable actions, behavioral therapists may also directly teach clients behaviors that will result in positive consequences. *Assertiveness training,* for example, involves teaching clients various ways of expressing their needs so that they are more likely to be met. In *social skills training,* clients are taught basic social skills that allow them to have more rewarding interpersonal relationships.

Sometimes operant conditioning techniques are used to teach clients that the negative consequences they have learned to expect in certain situations will not happen. Since we generally avoid situations that we assume will bring pain or other negative consequences, we often do not have the opportunity to learn that our expectations are wrong. For example, avoiding all dogs because of one bad experience would deprive a person of the opportunity to learn to interact positively with friendly dogs. Behavioral therapists use *exposure techniques* to overcome such avoidance. These techniques focus on exposing clients to whatever they fear until they are no longer afraid. So, clients who are terrified of dogs might be placed in a room with a dog until they realize that the dog will not bite; their fear reactions subside through a process called *extinction.*

Classical and operant conditioning involve learning on the basis of our own experiences. But we also learn by watching the behavior of others and what happens to them. Behavioral therapists use the process of *modeling* or *observational learning* in social skills training, assertiveness training, and anxiety-reduction treatments by presenting either a live or videotaped model to demonstrate appropriate behavior.[24]

Cognitive-Behavioral Models

Cognitive-behavioral therapies are based on the recognition that it is not just the objective features of our external reality that influence us, but how we think about that reality: the assumptions we make, the explanations we give, the expectations we have about what happens (or is going to happen), and the beliefs we have about ourselves. These thoughts affect our emotions, our ability to relate to others, and our confidence about ourselves (this is also known as self-efficacy).[25]

An example may help to clarify the cognitive-behavioral view. Imagine having the following thought: "I want to go to the party, but I am shy." Would you go? Now imagine saying to yourself, "I want to go to the party, *and* I am shy." Would you be more likely to go? If so, then you can see how the cognitive substitution of *and* for *but* can make a difference in your behavior and also your feelings about a situation. The "but" statement may lead you to feel apprehensive; the "and" statement might give a little confidence that you could somehow manage the party *and* your shyness. Now compare how you might feel after thinking, "I *want* to visit my parents," as opposed to, "I *should* visit my parents." The former might feel fine; the latter, like any other "should," "ought," or "must" statement, may evoke feelings of guilt or resentment. These simple examples illustrate the power of saying one thing to ourselves rather than another. There is even more power in more general self-statements such as, "I'm no good" or "Nobody will ever care for me," and greater punch yet in even more elaborate stories of positive or negative thinking.

The aim of cognitive-behavioral therapists is to identify the nature of the words, statements, and stories we use in "talking" to ourselves and to focus especially on those that cause us difficulties by distorting or exaggerating reality. Aaron Beck, for example, has identified the kinds of cognitive distortions that accompany depression. Many depressed people seem to filter out the positive and pay special attention to, and even magnify, the negative.[26] This is the "glass is half-empty" syndrome or the "My partner left me so I must be worthless" pattern.

In order to change patterns of thinking—about specific situations or life in general—the therapist will guide clients toward evaluating the evidence for and against these patterns. The goal is to show clients that there are different ways to interpret their reality. For example, if a client says, "Nothing I do ever works out," the therapist would elicit specific information about experiences that have indeed had negative outcomes, but also encourage the client to attend to experiences that have resulted in positive outcomes.

Therapists such as Albert Ellis[27] believe that the best way to convince clients to change patterns of thinking is to confront their irrational and self-defeating thinking directly, sometimes even abrasively. In Ellis's rational-emotive behavior therapy (REBT), having a warm and nurturant relationship with a therapist is thought to be less crucial than receiving a direct message that we cause our own anxiety, grief, and mental distress by repeatedly relying on unrealistic beliefs about the world. Thus, Ellis does not hesitate to tell his clients that they are "big babies" before encouraging them to behave in a more mature way and rewarding them for making more rational choices.

Phenomenological-Experiential Models

The therapy models described so far concentrate on explaining human behavior on the basis of unconscious conflicts or past learning experiences. In contrast, phenomenological-experiential models emphasize the idea that people are striving, creative beings who aim to reach self-fulfillment or *self-actualization*. The focus of these models is on the present, not the past, and the concern is not on how we are alike, but how we are each unique. Further, psychological problems are seen as stemming from factors that inhibit us from reaching our fullest unique potential. The therapist's task, then, is to recognize and encourage the client's potential for growth and to acknowledge that the client has the best understanding of his or her own uniqueness, choices, and destiny. Thus, the role of the therapist is not that of detective or teacher, but that of facilitator—a person who provides a setting and relationship that will encourage the client's growth toward self-knowledge, self-acceptance, and ultimately self-fulfillment or self-actualization. The two most prominent examples of phenomenological-experiential therapies are Carl Rogers's client-centered therapy[28] and Fritz Perls's Gestalt therapy.[29]

Client-Centered Therapy In Rogers's therapy, it is the client, not the therapist, who is perceived to have the responsibility for making changes. Hence, it is the client who takes the lead; the client decides what will be discussed. The therapist encourages the client's self-disclosure, mostly by listening without interrupting, changing the subject, or guiding the interaction in any particular direction. In the process, the therapist shows respect, trust, acceptance, caring, and emotional connectedness with the client. Client-centered therapists believe that given this kind of therapeutic environment, clients will be able to explore and experience themselves freely, and eventually will come to respect, trust, accept, and care for themselves in the same way the therapist does. Providing this sort of atmosphere can be a daunting task, since most of us (psychologists included) find it easier to control and criticize than to nurture and accept. Rogers provided a number of guidelines for meeting this challenge.

First and foremost, the therapist offers *unconditional positive regard*. This means that the therapist refrains from communicating judgments about the client because doing so would create what Rogers called *conditions of worth*—the idea that a person is worthwhile only if he or she thinks or behaves in certain approved ways. Conditions of worth force people to distort their real feelings and prevent them from being who they are, who they want to be, or who they could be. Growth is stymied when one's aim is mainly to please other people by meeting their expectations rather than pursuing one's own agenda. The client-centered therapist tries to communicate an acceptance of the client even when the therapist does not approve of what the client says or does. This acceptance, which demonstrates an inherent faith that the client will eventually choose his or her own best path, is considered more important than defining for the client what constitutes "appropriate" behavior.

It is also crucial for the client-centered therapist to avoid giving advice and thus undermine the client's freedom to make decisions, a freedom that is considered more important than any advice the therapist could give. Giving advice would also imply that the therapist does not trust the client to make choices and that the client ought to be dependent on the therapist.

In order to appreciate the client fully, the therapist must try to see the world as the client sees it, that is, understand what it must be like to be the client. Rogers referred to this as *empathic understanding*. Therapists communicate this understanding by being attentive to the client and *reflecting* what the client has said. For example, if the client tells a story about a scary event, the therapist might say, "I sense that you were feeling afraid." This response places an emphasis on the client's feelings and demonstrates that the therapist acknowledges those feelings. The client, of course, is always free to correct the therapist's interpretation.

Finally, the therapist's own behavior and feelings have to be *genuine* and *congruent* with one another. This means that the therapist has to monitor his or her own feelings constantly, be honest about them with the client, and make sure that the actions and the words spoken reflect those feelings instead of camouflaging or betraying them. For example, if the therapist is feeling some frustration with the client, then it is preferable for the therapist to say, "I'm feeling frustrated by what you have just said," rather than pretending to feel calm.

Gestalt Therapy   Like Carl Rogers, Fritz Perls was concerned with helping clients to differentiate those aspects of themselves that are "real" from those that were adopted as a result of internalizing other people's expectations. For Perls, as for Rogers, personal growth consists of developing awareness of the complete, real self and abandoning the *phony* self. Once clients recognize and resolve the conflicts between the two, they can stop diminishing themselves, their symptoms of disorder will disappear, and they can be free to grow again.

To facilitate recognition of various parts of the self, Gestalt therapists pay special attention to the discrepancies between what clients do and what they say. For example, clients may say that they want to be treated like an adult while, at the same time, acting in a childlike manner. Or, they may claim that they are nervous all the time while sitting in a relaxed position. Gestalt therapists do not ask for explanations of these discrepancies, but instead focus on pointing them out so that the client becomes more aware of them. Sometimes the therapist will ask the client to exaggerate certain nonverbal behaviors so that their significance becomes even clearer. For example, if the client is wiggling his foot, the therapist will draw attention to that and ask the client to wiggle the foot even more so that he can focus on it and perhaps be able to express what it is intended to communicate.

Gestalt therapists see dreams as providing another opportunity to develop awareness of various parts of the self because aspects of the dream are assumed to reflect various aspects of the dreamer. To demonstrate this, clients in Gestalt therapy may be asked to role-play the different parts of the dream. If they have dreamed of throwing a rock, they will be asked to "play" that rock as well as to play the person throwing the rock; if they have dreamed of an angry person chasing them, they will be asked to "play" that angry person as well as the person being chased. The hope is that once clients become aware of all the aspects of their dreams, they will be able to reintegrate the parts of themselves (positive and negative) that have become alienated.

The Gestalt therapist may also deliberately frustrate clients to help push them toward self-awareness. Perls, for example, would put a group therapy client on what he called the "hot seat," where the group would focus its attention on that client, pointing out his or her interpersonal strategies, games, defenses, and manipulations. Like Albert Ellis, Perls would not hesitate to tell his clients when they are "playing stupid" or "playing dependent."

Gestalt therapists also promote clients' self-awareness by forcing them to focus on the present, the *here and now*. Dwelling on the past or dreaming about the future, they say, are simply ways of diverting attention from current feelings and thoughts; the past or the future is relevant only insofar as it is represented in immediate experience. Gestalt therapists often use role playing to keep the focus on the here and now. Thus, a client may be asked to imagine that a significant person from his or her past is sitting in the empty chair nearby and then engage in "conversation" with that person. The imagined presence of the other person helps to bring forth the client's current feelings toward that person. In another version of this technique, the client is asked to write a letter to the absent person. The letter is not mailed, but the process of writing it helps the client to become aware of current feelings.

Finally, Gestalt therapists encourage clients to take responsibility for their own actions and feelings by helping them to express themselves directly. Instead of asking questions, they are encouraged to make statements. Thus, "You don't really want to go away with me for the weekend, do you?" becomes, "I'm feeling scared because it sounds as if you don't want to spend the weekend with me." Clients are also taught to make "I" statements. "*You* make me angry" or "*It* makes me feel really good" becomes "*I* am angry at you" and "*I* feel really good." This kind of rephrasing is believed to lead the client to a stronger, clearer, more assured sense of self.

Combined Approaches and Common Themes

We have described four different approaches to psychological treatment, but most clinical psychologists do not slavishly follow just one, or all aspects of one approach. Each therapist tends to add unique variations based on his or her history, experiences, and personality. Those who adopt an eclectic (or combined) approach use multiple techniques tailored to suit a particular client, problem, or situation.

Regardless of their theoretical underpinnings, all forms of psychotherapy are similar in several ways. They all (1) aim to give clients a sense of hope that they will be able to function better and feel less distress (that sense of hope and faith may be one of the most critical aspects of therapy); (2) promote self-examination, self-knowledge, and self-analysis in order to foster independence and avoid repeating errors from the past; (3) encourage releasing, or at least voicing, emotion; and (4) encourage therapists to be involved with the client's welfare, and yet keep enough distance to be able to remain objective.

COMMUNITY PSYCHOLOGY, PSYCHOSOCIAL REHABILITATION, AND PREVENTION

Clinical psychologists recognize that the political, economic, social, physical, and educational environment of an individual can contribute to psychological difficulties. Therefore, many of them are involved not only in providing the kind of treatment described in the previous sections, but also in facilitating social and societal changes that may either prevent problems from occurring or can facilitate people's adjustment to their environment and the stressors it presents.

Community psychologists focus on trying to understand the connection between the individual's problems and the social structure in which he or she functions. In addition to working with individuals, community psychologists consult with various groups within a community in order to identify the strengths and resources within it. For example, they might train nonprofessional helpers from the community to provide child care and mental health support or do peer counseling or abortion counseling. They may support self-help groups such as Alcoholics Anonymous, GROW (a support group for the mentally ill), or a variety of other organizations that help people deal with psychological disorders or other crises in their lives.

Individuals suffering with schizophrenia or major mood disorders used to be confined in public mental institutions, but over the past several decades, there has been a move toward reintegrating them into the community, where they may live more normal, independent, productive lives. Psychologists active in *psychosocial rehabilitation* are especially interested in helping people with these severe disorders to cope with life while living in their community—either following hospitalization or as an alternative to it. Along with other mental health workers, such as nurses and social workers, psychologists have helped to design rehabilitation programs that teach formerly hospitalized mental patients basic skills such as cooking, grooming, buying groceries, making change, using public transportation, obtaining medical care, applying for jobs, and interacting adaptively with other people.

Some psychologists are working to establish programs designed to prevent disorders. For example, they may help parents strengthen their relationships with their children; they may work to reduce the incidence of physical and sexual abuse or severe neglect; they may be instrumental in teaching children and adolescents the cognitive, emotional, and interpersonal skills that are crucial to their later development and adjustment; and they may help those who have traditionally felt powerless to feel more confident in taking more control over their lives.

RESEARCH

With their scientific background, all psychologists like to make sure that their work is based on empirical evidence rather than unsupported faith and speculation. Hence, many clinical psychologists are involved in scientifically evaluating all facets of their work. They explore the reliability and validity of tests and other forms of assessment, and they evaluate the relative benefits of various treatments. With regard to the latter, they may ask questions such as: Are people better off with therapy, or will they improve as much without it? Can therapy make things worse? Which treatments produce the best results? What is the usual rate of progress? How long do the benefits last?

The answers to these questions are of interest not only to psychologists and their clients, but also to the wider audience made up of those who interact with those clients or pay for the treatment. Effective psychotherapy also benefits society at large because it can help reduce crime, violence, and health care costs.

It is often difficult to employ precise scientific methods to address these questions about therapy because clinical psychologists must deal with variables that may be difficult to quantify (such as "improvement"), and they must study vulnerable individuals whose need for therapy and confidentiality has to be respected. For example, the only way to find out if any therapy is better than no therapy requires depriving some people of treatment by placing them on a waiting list and comparing their progress with that of treated individuals. Or one can alternate periods of therapy with periods of no therapy. In both cases, people may temporarily be left without the help they need, and this may raise some ethical issues. Yet if we can't compare a treatment group (or period) with a no-treatment group (or period), we cannot confidently conclude that it was treatment that caused any observed improvement. If we simply compare a client's functioning before and after therapy, any improvement might have been due to therapy or to any number of external circumstances: the client may have improved simply because some time had passed; the client may have found a new partner, a new job, or a better place to live; or the client may even have read a book or watched a TV program that gave some sudden insight into how to deal with a problem.

One of the ways around the dilemma of depriving individuals of treatment is to treat all who need it on an ongoing basis, but to treat some problems and not others. For example, therapists may address difficulties in verbal communication, but not immediately treat problems in nonverbal behaviors, such as making eye contact. If the treatment is truly effective, only treated behaviors should show significant improvement.

Another somewhat more controversial approach, is to conduct surveys of former clients. A recent example of this method appeared in a *Consumer Reports Survey* of over seven thousand readers who answered a series of questions about their own treatment experiences.[30] This approach is controversial because it is impossible to check the accuracy of the answers and because the results may be representative only of readers of *Consumer Reports.*

In summary, conducting research on psychotherapy always involves making compromises. Psychologists have to balance the demands of good scientific research against the needs and rights of the clients they study.[31] Nevertheless, quantitative analysis of the results of large numbers of research studies suggests the following conclusions about psychotherapy:

1. The average person is far better off at the end of therapy than the majority of those who do not receive therapy.[32]
2. There seems to be very little indication that therapy makes clients worse. Deterioration does happen, but in a very small percentage of clients. We still do not understood why or how the deterioration occurs.[33]
3. In general, all treatments appear about equally successful, and the therapist's theoretical orientation or therapeutic methods do not appear to make much difference. However, some disorders may be more effectively treated by some approaches than others.[34] And it also seems to matter that the client perceives the relationship with the therapist to be a warm, caring one.[35]
4. The benefits for at least half the treated clients are evident after the first six to eight sessions; the majority of those who improve do so by the twenty-sixth session. The rate of progress is quickest at the beginning and then slows, possibly because it takes time to start dealing with the most difficult problems.[36]
5. The benefits of therapy are greatest immediately after therapy, but have been shown to last over periods of six to eighteen months. There is even some evidence that further improvement continues for longer periods of time.[37]

FUTURE DIRECTIONS

You may have gathered by now that clinical psychologists do not rely on magic, but depend on careful, hard work and critical thinking skills. Like them, I do not possess a crystal ball, so the following thoughts about the future are based on trends that are already evident in the discipline.

One current trend is to streamline the therapeutic process as much as possible. Therapists began by adopting Freud's intensive, long-term model, but thanks largely to the development since the 1960s of the behavioral, cognitive-behavioral, and phenomenological models, clinical psychologists have recognized that many clients do not need to take such a long road to improvement. In the 1990s, partly as a result of managed health care programs, psychologists have gravitated toward treatment models that aim to be even more efficient. A quick perusal of psychology sections in bookstores or descriptions of workshops designed for therapists will affirm the popularity of brief or time-limited therapies.[38] Although some psychologists are skeptical of the prevailing optimism of quick cures,[39] time-limited therapies will likely remain popular given the appeal of their promise of more efficient solutions.

Finally, clinical psychologists are becoming increasingly involved in the prevention of psychological problems. The more cognizant we are of the causes of psychological distress, the more insight we can have into how to prevent that distress. Some of this understanding is coming from exploring what works in therapy. For example, if the relationship with the therapist is important, then perhaps there are ways of teaching people to develop the relationship skills that a good therapist has. If prevention programs are successful, the total cost of health services can be expected to decrease. The 1990s have seen a significant decrease in funding for health care, including mental health care, and it is unlikely that this trend will soon reverse itself. For this reason, and because they are genuinely concerned about reducing human suffering, clinical psychologists will probably become even more involved in programs designed to prevent or provide early identification of psychological disorders.

SUGGESTIONS FOR FURTHER READING

Bankart, C. P. (1997). *Talking cures: A history of western and eastern psychotherapies.* New York: Brooks/Cole Publishing Company.

Cohen, R. J., & Swerdlik, M. E. (1999). *Psychological testing and assessment: An introduction to tests and measurement* (4th ed.). Mountain View, CA: Mayfield.

Nietzel, M. T., Bernstein, D. A., & Milich, R. (1998). *Introduction to clinical psychology* (5th ed.). Englewood Cliffs, NJ: Prentice Hall

Stangor, C. (1998). *Research methods for the behavioral sciences.* Boston: Houghton Mifflin.

CHAPTER 4

PSYCHOLOGY APPLIED TO EDUCATION

Anita Woolfolk Hoy

W hat are the best ways of learning? What are the most effective ways to assess learning? Which teaching objectives are most helpful? Should a teacher present the information, or should students discover it on their own? How can students best be motivated? Is it better to provide simple examples or to challenge students with complex problems? What is the best way of grouping students with different abilities? How important is the social environment in learning? Which methods of teaching reading are most beneficial? These are some of the questions that educational psychologists address.

Educational psychologists "study what people think and do as they teach and learn a particular curriculum in a particular environment where education and training are intended to take place."[1] These activities can take place in any setting, including colleges, consulting rooms, corporations, industry, the military, and religious institutions, but educational psychologists tend to concentrate on the more traditional context of classrooms in elementary and secondary schools. In this chapter, I will review the work of today's educational psychologists, but first, a look backward.

EARLY HISTORY OF PSYCHOLOGY AND EDUCATION

Long before there was educational psychology, there was thinking about psychology and education. In the third and fourth centuries B.C., the philosophers Socrates, Plato, and Aristotle discussed topics that are still studied by educational psychologists today: the role of the teacher, the relationship between teacher and student, methods of teaching, the nature and order of learning, and the role of emotion in learning. Similarly, the writings of eighteenth- and nineteenth-century European philosophers and reformers such as Pestalozzi and Herbart have a familiar ring for educational psychologists.[2] For example, Pestalozzi emphasized the value of students' activity and Herbart stressed the importance of their prior experiences and interests. In fact, Herbart's five-step approach to pedagogy sounds quite current: (1) preparation (of the learner's mind), (2) presentation, (3) association and comparison, (4) generalization or abstraction, and (5) practical application.

When the formal study of psychology began in the United States late in the 1800s, it was almost immediately linked to education and teachers (see the story of Lightner Witmer in Chapters 1 and 3). However, not all educators of the day welcomed the intrusion of psychology into their domain. Many argued that education was a moral and religious endeavor that could not be informed by research and experimentation. Teaching decisions, they thought, were best made by educators with religious and philosophical—not scientific or psychological—training.[3] Good teaching was considered simply a matter of exercising the mind, and demanding hard work and obedience.*

Nevertheless, in 1890, William James, one of the founders of psychology in the United States, gave a lecture series for teachers entitled *Talks to Teachers About Psychology.* These lectures were first presented around the country in summer schools for teachers, and then, in 1899, they were published both as a book and in the *Atlantic Monthly* magazine. Among the modern ideas that James supported were the use of discussion, projects and activities, laboratory experiments, writing, and drawing.

It was one of James's students, G. Stanley Hall, who founded the child study movement in the United States. He wrote books about children and adolescents, started the journal *Pedagogical Seminary,* and developed courses in child study for teachers. In his teachings and writings, Hall encouraged teachers to make detailed observations and keep careful records to study their students' development, as his own mother had done when she was a teacher.[5]

John Dewey, a philosopher-psychologist who became known for his philosophy of education, was a student of Hall. Before completing his doctorate in psychology, Dewey had been a high school teacher and had great respect for the practice of education. He founded the Laboratory School at the University of Chicago when he was head of the university's Department of Philosophy, Psychology, and Pedagogy. Indeed, Dewey is considered to be the father of the progressive education movement in North America (although he credited educational reformer Francis W. Parker with this accomplishment).[6] Dewey emphasized the ways that interest and effort affect students' motivation to solve problems of all sorts: social, intellectual, and practical. He encouraged the use of individualized and experience-based curricula to reach each child best. He believed that inquiry, problem solving, and active learning (working with the material rather than just listening to a lecture about it, for example) were superior to passive learning.

The first educational psychology textbook was written in 1903 by E. L. Thorndike, another of William James's students. In founding the *Journal of Educational Psychology* in 1910, Thorndike was also responsible for shifting the study of educational issues from the classroom to the laboratory. In the preface to the first issue of his journal, Thorndike asserted that educational psychology would bring the methods of exact science to bear on the problems of education. In his labora-

---

*Many of these concerns are echoed today in the opposition of some religious groups to approaches such as whole language, cooperative learning, or inquiry methods.[4]

tory, Thorndike developed popular methods for teaching and assessing reading, spelling, arithmetic, handwriting, English composition, and drawing. Thorndike's research approach was popular for about fifty years. Then, in the early 1960s, the Soviet Union successfully launched the first earth-orbiting satellite, *Sputnik*, creating insecurity over the apparent inferiority of education in the United States and spurring congressional funding of both basic and applied research in education.

At about the same time that Thorndike was developing measures of reading and arithmetic abilities in the United States, Alfred Binet was working in France on a measure of general intelligence. In 1904, just after the introduction of compulsory education there, the minister of public instruction in Paris confronted Binet with the following question: How can students who will need special teaching and extra help be identified early in their school careers, before they encounter failure in regular classes? In response to this question, Binet and his collaborator, Théophile Simon, decided to develop a test that would objectively measure learning ability and not discriminate against students who came from an impoverished background.

After trying many different test items and eliminating those that did not discriminate between successful and unsucessful students, Binet and Simon finally identified fifty-nine useful test items, sets of which were appropriate for children in each age group from three to thirteen. Binet's test allowed the examiner to determine a child's *mental age* by noting which age group's items the child could pass. For example, a child who succeeded on test items usually passed by most six year olds was considered to have a mental age of six, whether the child was actually four, six, or eight years old. The concept of the intelligence quotient, or IQ, was added later, after Binet's test was brought to the United States and revised by Lewis Terman at Stanford University, to become the Stanford-Binet test. IQ scores were computed by comparing a child's mental age score with chronological age, using the following formula: IQ = (Mental age/chronological age) × 100.* The success of the Stanford-Binet led to the development of several other modern individual intelligence tests.

Another major change in understanding children's learning abilities came as a result of the work of Jean Piaget. In 1920 Piaget took a job in Binet's laboratory, where he became intrigued with the kinds of errors that children made as they completed mental tasks. He noticed, for example, that if five pennies are widely spread out on a table, preschoolers would think there were more pennies than if the pennies were placed closely together. He noted as well that by the time they were in elementary school, children could count objects accurately. They could also define concrete objects such as "shoe," but were unable to define abstract concepts like "liberty." It was not until adolescence that children could think abstractly and solve problems systematically (this explains the haphazard attempts by younger children to find their shoes or other possessions). Over the next several decades, Piaget devised a model of cognitive development to account for the thinking behind these

---

*More recently, the concept of *deviation IQ* was introduced. The deviation IQ score relies on the comparison of a person's score with that of others in the same age group, rather than a comparison between mental and chronological age.

errors.[7] According to this model, children pass through several stages as they gradually develop the cognitive capabilities to solve increasingly difficult problems and make sense of their world. Although some of the details of Piaget's stage model have turned out to be incorrect (for example, younger children tend to be more capable than he thought), teachers have found Piaget's description of cognitive development useful in understanding their students' ways of thinking, matching instructional strategies to students' abilities, and fostering the development of students' thought processes.

While Piaget was outlining his description of the development of children's thinking, B. F. Skinner, an American psychologist, was proposing a very different view of learning. Where Piaget focused on how children's experiences result in increasingly complex cognitive processes, Skinner concentrated on studying the effects of experience on overt behavior. According to Skinner, the most important influences on people's behavior (what they can be observed to do in a particular situation) are not invisible and mental, but obvious and environmental. Behavior is shaped, he said, as a function of two sets of factors: stimuli that precede it (its *antecedents*) and stimuli that follow it (its *consequences*).[8] A given consequence then becomes the antecedent for the next behavior. Generally a positive consequence (*reinforcer*) makes it more likely that the preceding behavior will occur again, while a negative consequence (*punisher*) makes it less likely to occur again.

Skinner's approach, which emphasizes principles known as *operant conditioning* and the *functional analysis of behavior,* has been applied extensively to education, by both Skinner himself and many of his followers. For example, Skinner encouraged teachers to strengthen appropriate student behavior through the systematic use of attention, recognition, praise, and other rewards (reinforcers). He noted that punishment, such as reprimands and social isolation, can also help change classroom behaviors, but that it must be used with caution, and always combined with reinforcers for more appropriate behavior.

Operant conditioning procedures were very popular during the 1960s in regular classrooms as well as in special education, military training, coaching, and many other educational settings. Indeed, the basic principles of reinforcement that Skinner developed continue to be emphasized and used, but it is also clear to psychologists and educators that people do more than simply respond to reinforcement and punishment. Today, learning is also seen as a reflection of cognitive processes (the ways we think about situations and incorporate knowledge) as well as being influenced by expectations, feelings, and the interactions we have with others.

THE DEVELOPMENT OF MODERN EDUCATIONAL PSYCHOLOGY

In the 1960s, a number of educational psychologists developed approaches to teaching that foreshadowed some of the applications and debates seen in educational psychology today. We will focus on the work of three of these individuals: Jerome Bruner, David Ausubel, and Benjamin Bloom.

Jerome Bruner: Discovery Learning

Jerome Bruner's early research on thinking stirred his interest in educational approaches that encourage the development of thinking.[9] His work emphasized the importance of understanding the structure of a subject being studied, the need for active learning as the basis for true understanding, and the value of inductive reasoning in learning.

Subject *structure* refers to the fundamental ideas, relationships, or patterns of a subject—the essential information in a field. Because structure does not include specific facts or details about the subject, the essential structure of an idea can be represented simply as a diagram, a set of principles, or a formula. According to Bruner, learning will be more meaningful, useful, and memorable for students if they focus on understanding the underlying structure of a subject, and especially how the key concepts fit into a *coding system*. A coding system is a hierarchy of related concepts in which the most general concept is at the top and the more specific ones are below. For example, the most general concept for this chapter is "psychology in education"; the subtopics are more specific, and each of these has subsections that are even more specific.

Bruner believed that students must be *active* in order to grasp the structure of the information: they must identify key principles for themselves. To help them do this, teachers should provide problem situations and examples that stimulate students to question, explore, experiment, and discover the subject's structure. This process has been called *discovery learning,* and it is thought that the younger the student, the less guided and the more like discovery the learning should be.

Working from specific examples in order to formulate a general principle is the basis of *inductive* reasoning. For instance, if students are presented with enough examples of triangles and nontriangles, they will eventually discover what the basic properties of any triangle must be. The inductive approach requires intuitive thinking on the part of the students. Bruner suggested that teachers can nurture this intuitive thinking by motivating students to make guesses based on incomplete evidence and then to confirm or disprove the guesses systematically. For example, after learning about ocean currents and the shipping industry, students might be shown old maps of three harbors and asked to guess which one became a major port. Then students could check their guesses through systematic research.

David Ausubel: Expository Teaching

David Ausubel's approach is frequently contrasted with that of Bruner because, according to Ausubel, knowledge is acquired through *reception* rather than through discovery. This means that concepts, principles, and ideas are presented and understood, not discovered. The more organized and focused the teacher's presentation is, the more thorough the learning will be. Ausubel also stressed what is known as *meaningful verbal learning*: learning that is connected with existing knowledge and not simply memorized. In this approach, when teachers present materials in a carefully organized, sequenced, and somewhat finished form, students receive the most usable material in the most efficient way. Ausubel recommended that content be presented in terms of basic similarities and differences, using specific examples. But unlike Bruner, who stressed inductive thinking, Ausubel emphasized the importance of *deductive* thinking, that is, working from the general to the specific, or from the rule to the example.

According to Ausubel, optimal learning generally occurs when there is a potential fit between the student's current knowledge and the material to be learned. To make this fit better, a lesson taught in accordance with Ausubel's strategy always begins with an *advance organizer*—an introductory statement of a high-level concept broad enough to encompass all the information that will follow. The organizer acts as a kind of conceptual bridge between new material and the students' current knowledge.[10] Advance organizers are appropriate for students above the fifth or sixth grade and are especially helpful when the material to be learned is quite unfamiliar, complex, or difficult.[11] This is why textbook chapters often contain overviews, previews, and other advance organizers. Concrete models, diagrams, or analogies also seem to be especially good organizers.[12] Organizers can serve three purposes: they direct students' attention to what is important in the coming material, they highlight relationships among ideas that will be presented, and they remind students of relevant information that they already know. In an English class, for example, a teacher might begin a unit on rites of passage in literature with a very broad statement such as, "A central character who is coming of age must learn to know himself or herself, must make some kind of journey of self-discovery, and must decide what in society is to be accepted and what rejected." Of course, the effects of advance organizers depend on how good they are and how students actually use them.

Benjamin Bloom: Goals of Learning

Several decades ago, Benjamin Bloom led a group of experts in educational evaluation whose goal was to improve college and university examinations. The impact of their work has touched education at all levels around the world; indeed, it would be difficult to find an educator trained in the past thirty years who has not heard of the work of the Bloom group.

Bloom and his colleagues developed a taxonomy, or classification system, of educational objectives. The objectives in the cognitive domain are:[13]

1. *Knowledge:* Remembering, recognizing, or simply paying attention to something without necessarily understanding, using, or changing it.
2. *Comprehension:* Understanding the material being communicated without necessarily relating it to anything else.
3. *Application:* Using a general concept to solve a particular problem.
4. *Analysis:* Breaking something down into its parts.
5. *Synthesis:* Creating something new by combining different ideas.
6. *Evaluation:* Judging the value of materials or methods as they might be applied in a particular situation.

These objectives are usually viewed as a hierarchy, with "knowledge" at the bottom and "evaluation" at the top. Each skill is assumed to build on those below, although this is not always the case because some subjects do not fit this structure very well.[14] Nevertheless, Bloom's hierarchy of objectives has been used extensively in teacher education and training. Teachers are encouraged to include a range of objectives in their lesson plans, ask questions at all levels of the hierarchy, and match assessment procedures with learning objectives.

CONTEMPORARY CONTRIBUTIONS OF PSYCHOLOGY TO EDUCATION

The contributions of psychology to education today can be organized around three major perspectives on learning: behavioral, cognitive, and constructivist. Let's briefly examine these perspectives and then consider examples of teaching and learning techniques that are based on them.

Psychological Approaches to Learning

The *behavioral* approach to learning developed from work by Skinner and others who emphasized the role of antecedents and consequences (especially reinforcers) in behavior change. Learning was defined as a change in behavior brought about by experience. This approach focuses on overt behavior, so there is little concern for the mental, or internal, aspects of learning.

The *cognitive* approach, in contrast, sees people as active learners who initiate experiences, seek out information to solve problems, and reorganize what they already know to achieve new insights. In fact, from the cognitive perspective, learning is seen as "transforming significant understanding we already have, rather than simple acquisitions written on blank slates."[15] What the individual brings to the learning situation is the most important element. The knowledge base "is a scaffold that supports the construction of all future learning."[16] So instead of being passively influenced by environmental events, people actively choose, practice, pay attention, ignore, reflect, and make many other decisions as they pursue goals. To cognitive theorists, reinforcement is merely a source of information; it is changes in knowledge, not just consequences, that make changes in behavior possible.

Constructivist theories, which are increasingly influential today, are grounded in the work of Piaget, Bruner, and Dewey, as well as others such as Lev Vygotsky and the Gestalt psychologists.* The essence of the constructivist approach is that it puts "the students' own efforts to understand at the center of the educational enterprise."[17] According to the constructivists, students should not be given stripped-

---

*Vygotsky, a Russian psychologist, proposed a sociocultural theory of cognitive development that emphasized the role of cultural practices (especially language) and interactions with other people in the development of thinking. Vygotsky suggested that children learn by appropriating or "taking for themselves," the ways of acting and thinking provided by their culture, family, and other "teachers." Gestalt theorists described several principles explaining how we make sense of information in the environment. For example, rather than perceiving bits and pieces of unrelated information, we tend to organize what we see into patterns or organized, meaningful wholes.

down, simplified problems and basic skills drills, but instead should deal with complex situations and "fuzzy," ill-structured problems. The world beyond school presents few simplified problems or step-by-step directions, so schools should ensure that every student has experience solving the kinds of complex problems that the real world presents.

Another goal of constructivist-oriented teaching is to develop students' abilities to establish and defend their own positions while respecting the positions of others. This also encourages students to be aware of the influences that shape their thinking.

Applications of Behavioral Approaches

Two prominent examples of the contributions of behavioral approaches to education are the development of learning objectives and the use of mastery learning techniques.

Learning Objectives   Although there are many different approaches to developing learning objectives, each assumes that the first step in teaching is to decide what changes should take place in the learner. An *instructional objective* is a clear and unambiguous description of the teacher's educational intentions for students. Today many school districts require teachers to complete lesson plans that include learning objectives.

Robert Mager has developed an influential system for writing behavioral objectives.[18] According to Mager, a good objective has three parts. First, it describes the intended student behavior: What must the student be able to do? Second, it lists the conditions under which the behavior will occur: How will this behavior be recognized or assessed? Third, it gives the criteria for acceptable performance (usually on a test). This system, with its emphasis on final behavior, requires learning objectives to be described in very explicit statements. Mager contends that students often can teach themselves if they are given well-stated objectives.

Research has shown that providing objectives for students does seem to improve their achievement, but only under certain conditions. First, objectives can best promote learning in the context of loosely organized, relatively unstructured activities such as lectures, films, and research projects. With highly structured materials such as programmed instruction, objectives seem less important. Second, learning objectives are especially helpful when the importance of some information is not clear from the learning materials and activities themselves; here, instructional objectives will probably help focus students' attention on relevant information and thus increase achievement. However, when the task is simply to get the gist of a written passage or transfer the information to a new situation, objectives are not as effective. In these situations, it is better to use questions that focus on meaning and to insert questions right before the material to be read.[19]

Mastery Learning   *Mastery learning* is based on the assumption that, given enough time and the proper instruction, most students can master any learning objective.[20] To use the mastery approach, a teacher must break down a course's material into small units of study. Each unit might involve mastering several specific objectives. "Mastery" usually means a score of 80 to 90 percent on a test or other assessment. In mastery learning, the teacher informs the students of the objectives and the criteria for meeting each. Students who do not reach the minimum level of mastery or who reach this minimum but want to improve their performance (and their grade) can repeat the unit. When they are ready, they take another form of the unit test. The challenge for teachers using the mastery learning approach is to provide the extra help needed by students who do not attain mastery. Teachers must also have enough versions of learning materials available to allow students to "recycle" through objectives they failed to meet the first time (just repeating the same materials usually will not help). It is also important to have several forms of tests or other performance assessments for each unit.*

Mastery learning is most useful when the focus of instruction is on key concepts or skills that serve as a foundation for later learning. In mathematics, for example, some students will fall further and further behind if they move from addition of fractions to more advanced topics before they really understand addition of fractions. By the time they reach division of fractions, these students may be at a loss. Mastery learning has been successful when students get the extra time and support they need to learn, especially through corrective instruction outside class or through in-class peer tutoring or cooperative learning groups.[22]

In practice, mastery learning has not helped to erase achievement differences among students, as some proponents had hoped.[23] Left to work at their own pace, some students will learn much more and leave a unit with a much better understanding then others. Some will work hard to take advantage of the learning opportunities that mastery learning provides, while others will be frustrated instead of encouraged by the chance to recycle.

Applications of Cognitive Approaches

Many psychologists have used cognitive theories of learning and memory to help students develop better learning strategies. Underlining, highlighting, taking notes, visual mapping, and mnemonics are examples of such strategies.

Underlining or Highlighting   Underlining or highlighting is one of the most common study techniques college students use, yet few students ever receive any direct instruction in the best way to apply this technique. It is no wonder that many fail to use it effectively. One common problem is that students underline or highlight more material than they should; it is far better to be selective. Thus, when students are limited in how much they are allowed to underline—only one sentence per paragraph, for example—learning improves.

Taking Notes   Taking notes during lectures serves at least two important functions. First, it focuses attention and helps encode information, thus increasing the chances

---

*A form of mastery learning that has been successful in college is the Keller Plan, or the Personalized System of Instruction (PSI).[21]

that it will get into long-term memory. In order to record key ideas in their own words, students have to translate, connect, elaborate, and organize. So even if they do not review their notes before a test, just having taken them appears to aid learning, especially for those who lack prior knowledge in an area. Of course, if note taking distracts students from listening to and making sense of the information, then it may not be effective. Second, notes provide extended external storage that allows for more effective reviewing for exams. Students who use their notes to study tend to perform better on tests, especially if they take high-quality notes—those that are lengthy and capture key ideas, concepts, and relationships.[24]

In one interview study of 252 college students, researchers concluded that understanding is improved for students who use note taking to focus their attention on important ideas and to construct representations that reflect the organization of the lecture.[25] As the course progresses, these expert students match notes to their anticipated use and modify their strategies after tests or assignments. They also use personal codes to flag material that is unfamiliar or difficult, they fill gaps in their understanding by consulting relevant sources (including classmates), and they record information verbatim only when a verbatim response will be required. In other words, they are generally strategic about taking and using notes.

Visual Mapping   Effective use of underlining and note taking depends on an understanding of the organization of the information to be learned. Visual mapping strategies have been developed to help students with this key element of learning. There is evidence that, when learning from textbooks, creating graphic organizers such as maps or charts is more effective than merely outlining the text.[26] "Mapping" these relationships by noting causal connections, comparison and contrast connections, and examples has been shown to improve students' recall of information. It also helps for students to compare one another's maps and discuss the differences between them.

Mnemonics   Systematic procedures for improving memory are called mnemonics (pronounced "knee-monics"). Many mnemonic strategies use imagery. For example, to remember a grocery list, you might visualize each item in an especially memorable place in your house (perhaps a bunch of bananas hanging from the kitchen light fixture or a quart of milk perched on top of the refrigerator). Then when you go shopping, you think of the familiar places in your house that trigger a memory of the grocery items. If information needs to be remembered for a long time, an acronym may be the answer. An acronym is a form of abbreviation—a word formed from the first letter of each word in a phrase, such as NAFTA for the North American Free Trade Agreement, or HOMES for the names of the Great Lakes (Huron, Ontario, Michigan, Erie, and Superior). Another method forms phrases or sentences from the first letter of each word or item in a list, for example Every Good Boy Does Fine, to remember the lines on the G clef—E, G, B, D, F. Another mnemonic is to incorporate all the items to be memorized into a rhyming jingle, such as "*i* before *e* except after *c*."

The mnemonic system that has been most extensively applied in teaching is the keyword method. A person using this method to remember a foreign word, for example, would first choose an English word, preferably a concrete noun that sounds like the foreign word or part of it. The second step is to associate the meaning of the foreign word with the English word through an image or sentence. Thus, the Spanish word *carta,* which means "letter," sounds like the English word *cart.* The words can be linked with the image of a shopping cart filled with big letters or perhaps stamped envelopes, or the sentence: "The cart full of letters tipped over."[27]

Applications of Constructivist Approaches

Constructivist teaching approaches recommend complex, challenging learning environments in which the focus is on student-centered instruction.[28] Inquiry and problem-based learning, and cooperative learning such as jigsaw and scripted cooperation are examples of techniques that illustrate the constructivist approaches.

Inquiry and Problem-Based Learning   John Dewey described the basic inquiry learning format in 1910. There have been many adaptations of this strategy since, but inquiry still usually includes the following elements: The teacher presents a puzzling event, question, or problem. The students then (1) formulate hypotheses to explain the event or solve the problem, (2) collect data to test the hypotheses, (3) draw conclusions, and (4) reflect on the original problem and on the thinking processes needed to resolve it.

At times, teachers present a problem and encourage students to ask yes or no questions to help the students gather data and test hypotheses. This method allows the teacher to monitor students' thinking and to guide the process. Here is an example:

1. After explaining the overall method, the teacher presents a puzzling event by, for example, blowing softly across the top of an 8½- by 11-inch sheet of paper. The paper rises, and the teacher asks the students to figure out why.
2. Students ask questions to gather more information and isolate relevant factors. The teacher answers only by saying yes or no. The students might ask if temperature is important (no), if the paper is a special kind (no), if air pressure has anything to do with the paper rising (yes), and so on.
3. Students test causal relationships. In this case, they ask if the nature of the air on top causes the paper to rise (yes). They ask if the fast movement of the air results in less pressure on the top (yes). Then they test the rule with other materials, for example, thin plastic.
4. Students form a generalization (principle): "If the air on top moves faster than the air on the bottom of a surface, then the air pressure on top is lessened, and the object rises." Later lessons expand students' understanding of the principles and physical laws through further experiments.
5. The teacher leads a discussion of the students' thinking processes. This discussion would include topics such as: What were the important factors? How did the students put the causes and effects together?[29]

Computer and video technologies can support problem-based learning. For example, the Cognition and Technology Group at Vanderbilt University has developed a videodisc-based learning environment that focuses on mathematics instruction for the fifth and sixth grade. The series, called "The Adventures of Jasper Woodbury," presents students with complex situations that require problem-finding; setting subgoals; and the application of mathematics, science, history and literature concepts to solve problems. Even though the situations are complex and lifelike, the problems can be solved using data embedded in the stories presented. In one adventure, Jasper sets out in a small motorboat, headed to Cedar Creek to inspect an old cruiser he is thinking of buying. Along the way Jasper has to consult maps, use his marine radio, deal with fuel and repair problems, buy the cruiser, and finally determine if he has enough fuel and time to sail his purchase home before sundown.

The Vanderbilt group calls its problem-based approach *anchored instruction.* The "anchor" is the interesting situation, which provides a focus, a reason for setting goals, planning, and using mathematical tools to solve problems. Initial research indicates that students as young as fourth graders and as old as high schoolers can work with the adventures. Students are highly motivated as they work in groups to solve the problems; even group members with limited math skills can contribute to the solutions because they might notice key information in the videotape or suggest innovative ways to approach the situation.

Group Work and Cooperation in Learning

Cooperative learning has a long history in American education. In the early 1900s, John Dewey criticized the use of competition in education and encouraged educators to structure schools as collaborative, learning communities. These ideas fell from favor in the 1940s and 1950s, when there was a resurgence of the value of competition. In the 1960s, there was a swing back to individualized and cooperative learning structures, stimulated in part by concern for civil rights and interracial relations. Today, interest in collaboration and cooperative learning is fueled by evolving constructivist perspectives on learning. Many forms of cooperative learning are used in schools today. Two examples are jigsaw and scripted cooperation.

Jigsaw   The jigsaw method is an early form of cooperative learning that emphasizes high interdependence among groups of students. Each group member is given access to only part of the material to be learned by the whole group and becomes an "expert" on that part. Because the students are then asked to teach each other, everyone's contribution is important. (A more recent version of this method, called Jigsaw II, adds "expert" meetings where students from different groups who have access to the same material confer to make sure they understand their assigned part and to plan ways to teach the information to their groups.) In the end, students take an individual test covering all the material to be learned, but they earn points based on the score of their entire group.

Scripted Cooperation   Donald Dansereau and his colleagues have developed a method for learning in pairs called scripted cooperation.[30] Here, students work together in reading a section of text, solving math problems, editing writing assignments, or almost any other learning task. On a reading task, for example, both partners read a passage, then one student gives an oral summary to the other. The partner comments on the summary and notes any omissions or errors. Next, the partners work together to elaborate the information—creating associations, images, mnemonics, ties to previous work, examples, analogies, and the like. The partners switch roles (as summarizer versus listener) for the next section of the reading, and continue to take turns until they finish the assignment.

Motivation in Education

Closely tied to learning is student motivation, the engine that fuels learning and the steering wheel that guides its progress. Just as there are various theories of learning, there are various theories of motivation.

Behaviorists explain motivation with concepts such as reward and incentive. Rewards are desirable consequences for appropriate behavior; incentives provide the prospect for future rewards. Giving grades, stars, and so on for learning—or demerits for misbehavior—is an attempt to motivate students by extrinsic (external) incentives, rewards, and punishments. *Humanistic* views of motivation emphasize intrinsic (internal) forces such as a person's need for "self-actualization,"[31] the inborn "actualizing tendency,"[32] or the need for "self-determination."[33] From the humanistic perspective, to motivate students means to encourage their inner resources: their sense of competence, self-esteem, autonomy, and self-actualization. *Cognitive* theorists believe that behavior is determined by our thinking, not simply by whether we have been rewarded or punished for the behavior in the past. From this perspective, behavior is initiated and regulated by plans,[34] goals,[35] schemas (generalized knowledge),[36] expectations,[37] and attributions (the causes we see for our own and other people's behavior).[38] *Social learning* theories of motivation are integrations of behavioral and cognitive approaches. They take into account both the behaviorists' concern with the effects or outcomes of behavior and the cognitivists' interest in the impact of individual beliefs and expectations. Many influential social learning explanations view motivation as the product of two main forces: (1) the individual's expectation of reaching a goal and (2) the perceived value of that goal.

Teachers are concerned about developing a particular kind of motivation in their students: the motivation to learn, defined as "a student tendency to find academic activities meaningful and worthwhile and to try to derive the intended academic benefits from them."[39] Motivation to learn includes planning, concentration, awareness of the goals and plans for learning, the active search for new information, clear perception of feedback, pride and satisfaction in achievement, and little or no anxiety over failure. Motivation to learn involves more than intending to learn; it includes the quality of the student's mental efforts. For example, reading the text ten times may indicate intention and persistence, but motivation to learn implies more thoughtful, active study strategies, like summarizing, elaborating basic ideas, outlining in your own words, drawing graphs of key relationships, and so on.[40]

CHARACTERISTICS OF EFFECTIVE TEACHERS

Researchers have long thought that the key to success in teaching must lie in the teacher's personal characteristics,[41] so some of the earliest research on effective teaching focused on those qualities. This assumption proved incorrect, or at least incomplete, but research on the topic did provide some important lessons about teacher characteristics.

Teacher Knowledge and Enthusiasm

Teachers who know more facts about their subject do not necessarily have students who learn more. However, teachers who know more may give clearer presentations and explanations, which seem to help students learn more and make them like their teachers better.[42] Teachers who are more knowledgeable may also be more organized and recognize student difficulties more readily. Thus, they are ready for virtually any student question and do not have to be evasive or vague in their answers. So knowledge appears to be a necessary but not sufficient condition for effective teaching.

Some studies have found that ratings of teachers' enthusiasm for their subject are related to student achievement gains. Correlated with enthusiasm are warmth, friendliness, and understanding, and these teacher traits seem to be the ones most strongly associated with student attitudes.[43] In other words, teachers who are warm and friendly tend to have students who like them and the classes they teach. Keep in mind, though, that these conclusions come from studies that found an association, or correlation, between teacher warmth and better student learning, but which cannot tell us whether teacher warmth caused these changes, whether better students generate teacher enthusiasm, or whether some other factor is responsible for the relationship between the two variables. And while teachers trained to demonstrate enthusiasm do tend to have students who are more attentive and involved, those students are not necessarily more successful on tests of content.[44]

Teacher Expectations

The impact of teacher expectations was dramatically illustrated over thirty years ago by Robert Rosenthal and Lenore Jacobson. Their research captured the attention of the national media in a way that few other studies by psychologists ever have.[45] The study also caused great controversy within the professional community and prompted additional research.[46]

What did Rosenthal and Jacobson find that caused such a stir? After choosing several students at random from a number of elementary school classrooms, they told the students' teachers that these children were "bloomers" who would make significant intellectual gains during the year. Indeed, the selected students did show unusually large gains that year. The researchers suggested that these gains were stimulated by a self-fulfilling prophecy, an outcome that occurs simply because it has been expected. In this case, the teachers' expectations about certain students' improvement were said to somehow bring about the very behavior the teachers expected.

Actually, two kinds of expectation effects can occur in classrooms. The first is the self-fulfilling prophecy, which can be based on a groundless prediction. The second kind of expectation effect occurs when teachers are reasonably accurate in their initial expectations about various students' abilities and then give these students extra attention if they need it. Problems arise, however, when "slow" students begin to show improvement but teachers do not alter their expectations accordingly. This pattern is called a *sustaining expectation effect,* because the teacher's unchanging expectation might serve to sustain the student's performance at the initially expected level. When this happens, the opportunity is lost to provide more appropriate teaching, and encourage greater student achievement. In practice, sustaining effects are more common than self-fulfilling prophecy effects and may affect students' achievement, motivation, aspiration level, and self-esteem. Also, some students are more sensitive than others to teachers' opinions. In general, students who are young, dependent, or conforming or who, like their teacher, are most likely to be affected, especially in terms of self-esteem, by teachers' views of them.[47]

Research on Teacher Effectiveness

Much of educational psychologists' research on effective teaching points toward a teaching model called *direct instruction, explicit teaching,* or *active teaching.*[48] Various versions of this model outline six important teaching functions: (1) review and check the previous day's work, (2) present new material, (3) provide guided practice, (4) give feedback and correction, (5) provide independent practice, and (6) review weekly and monthly. In this model, the successful teacher combines learning time with effective classroom management; makes clear and organized presentations; maintains an academic, "learning-is-serious-business" focus; makes good use of review, learning probes, understanding checks, and guided practice; asks higher- and lower-level questions and then gives students sufficient time (called "wait time") to come up with answers; and moves at a steady pace to cover key topics. Study after study has associated these teacher behaviors with better student learning.[49]

Researchers identified these direct instruction elements by comparing teachers whose students learned more than expected (given their prior knowledge) with teachers whose students performed at an expected, or average, level. Teaching effectiveness was usually defined in terms of the average improvement in standardized test scores for a whole class or school. So the results of direct instruction hold for large groups, but not necessarily for every student in the group (in fact, although average achievement improves, the achievement of some individuals may decline).[50] Further, the researchers focused on existing practices in American classrooms, and because the focus was on traditional forms of teaching, the research did not assess successful teaching innovations.

Given these considerations, you can see that direct instruction models apply best to the teaching of basic knowledge and skills, such as science facts, mathematics computation, reading vocabulary, and grammar rules. These skills involve tasks that are relatively unambiguous; they can be taught step by step and tested by standardized tests. Direct instruction approaches are not necessarily appropriate for objectives such as helping students to write creatively, solve complex problems, or become more mature emotionally. Still, there is ample evidence that direct instruction and explanation can help students learn. Without guidance, younger and less prepared learners may construct incomplete or inaccurate knowledge.[51] Deep understanding and fluid performance, whether in dance or mathematical problem solving or reading, require models of expert performance and extensive practice with feedback.[52] These elements are at the heart of the direct instruction model.

THE PRESENT AND THE FUTURE: ISSUES AND CONTROVERSIES

Among the controversies surrounding applications of psychology to education are debates about the nature of intelligence, the prevalence of testing, ways of dealing with students of differing abilities, and the best approach to teaching reading and writing.

The Nature of Intelligence

The idea that people vary in what we call intelligence has been with us for a long time. Plato discussed variations in mental abilities over two thousand years ago. Most early theories about the nature of intelligence included one or more of the following three themes: (1) the capacity to learn, (2) the total knowledge a person has acquired, and (3) the ability to adapt successfully to new situations and to the environment in general.

Today there is considerable controversy over what intelligence is and how it should be measured. At a 1986 symposium, for example, twenty-four psychologists offered twenty-four different views about the nature of intelligence. Over half of the experts mentioned higher-level thinking processes such as abstract reasoning, problem solving, and decision making as important aspects of intelligence, but they disagreed about whether intelligence is a single ability or many separate abilities.[53]

Some theorists believe intelligence is a basic ability that affects performance on all cognitively oriented tasks. Thus, an "intelligent" person will do well in computing mathematical problems, analyzing poetry, taking history essay examinations, and solving riddles. Evidence for this position comes from studies comparing the results of various measures of intellectual abilities. In study after study, moderate to high positive correlations are found among all the tests that are designed to assess separate intellectual abilities.[54]

Other theorists insist that there are several separate "primary mental abilities." Years ago, for example, Louis Thurstone listed the following major mental abilities underlying intellectual tasks: verbal comprehension, memory, reasoning, ability to visualize spatial relationships, numerical ability, word fluency, and perceptual speed. The most prominent modern proponent of the concept of multiple cognitive abilities is Howard Gardner.[55]

According to Gardner, there are at least seven separate kinds of intelligences: linguistic (verbal), musical, spatial, logical-mathematical, bodily-kinesthetic, understanding of others (interpersonal), and understanding of the self (intrapersonal). Gardner based his notion of separate abilities partly on evidence that brain damage (from a stroke, for example) often interferes with functioning in one area, such as language, but does not affect functioning in other areas. Gardner has also noted that individuals often excel in one of these seven areas but have no remarkable abilities in the other six. There are now hundreds of articles, books, newsletters, and organizations that encourage the application of Gardner's theory to teaching.[56]

Recent work in cognitive psychology has emphasized the importance of thinking processes rather than fixed abilities in defining intelligence. Robert Sternberg's *triarchic theory of intelligence* is an example of a cognitive process approach to understanding intelligence.[57] As you might guess from its name, this theory defines intelligence as having three aspects: analytic, creative, and practical. *Analytic intelligence* involves mental processes that lead to more or less intelligent behavior. These processes are defined in terms of components—elementary information-processing abilities that are classified by the functions they serve and by how general they are. Some components are specific, that is, they are necessary for only one kind of task, such as solving analogies (for example, food is to body as _____ is to car. The answer is "gasoline"). Other components are general and may be necessary in almost every cognitive task. *Creative intelligence* involves coping with new experiences. Thus, some intelligent behavior is marked by two characteristics: (1) insight, or the ability to deal effectively with novel situations, and (2) automaticity, the ability to become efficient and automatic in thinking and problem solving. *Practical intelligence* involves choosing environments in which success is likely, adapting to that environment, and reshaping it if necessary. People who are successful often seek situations in which their abilities will be valuable, then work hard to capitalize on those abilities and compensate for any weakness. This third aspect of intelligence is seen in practical matters such as career choice and social skills. No matter what conception of intelligence proves most enduring, the message to educators from current perspectives on intelligence is that students have many potential abilities and these abilities can be developed.

The Use of Standardized Tests

Psychology has had a profound impact on education through its development of tests of mental ability, aptitude, and achievement. On average, more than 1 million standardized tests* are given per school day in classes throughout the United States.[58] But controversy surrounds these tests. Critics of standardized testing argue that these tests measure disjointed facts and skills that have little or no use or meaning in the real world. Often, they say, test questions do not match the content of courses taught in the schools, so tests cannot measure how well students have learned the curriculum. In addition, the results of the tests are all too often used to label students as low achievers, possibly setting up "sustaining expectation effects."[59]

Despite these criticisms, there is great pressure on teachers to produce students who score high on standardized tests. Teachers' jobs, principals' pay raises, and even the value of real estate in the school district may be affected by the test score average at each school. Consequently teachers find themselves "teaching to the test," that is, focusing greater attention on material they know or suspect will be on the test. Because standardized tests are best at measuring lower-level objectives, facts, and skills, these tend to become the content of school curricula.

Defenders of standardized tests note that it is the responsibility of the school to select appropriate tests and recognize that standardized tests are designed to sample what is typically taught. The fit with any school's curriculum will not be perfect. Further, they point out that a standardized test is only one source of information about student learning, and that to redesign a curriculum to match a test's content or to make classroom placement decisions on the basis of test scores alone is to overuse—and misuse—the test. No test is reliable and valid enough to serve as the only basis for making important decisions. Tests do provide useful information, but the test scores do not tell all. A hundred years ago, William James suggested that we must combine test results with observations made "upon the total demeanor of the measured individual, by teachers with eyes in their heads and common sense and some feeling for the concrete facts of human nature in their hearts."[60]

Dealing with Diverse Student Abilities

In the early 1900s, before group intelligence tests were readily available, teachers dealt with students who differed in ability and achievement by promoting those who performed adequately and holding back the others. This worked well for those promoted, but not for those who failed, so the idea of social promotion was introduced to keep age-mates together. Once intelligence tests became widely available, failing students could be promoted but then grouped into classes based on their ability. Ability grouping was popular through the 1930s, but fell from favor until the early 1960s when, as noted earlier, the era of *Sputnik* raised concerns about U.S. children's math and science skills. In the late 1960s and early 1970s, ability grouping was criticized again, partly because of concerns about its creation of expectancy-sustaining effects. Today, teachers are encouraged to use various forms of coopera-

---

*Standardized tests are examinations given, usually nationwide, under uniform conditions and scored according to uniform procedures. The tests may assess subject-matter knowledge such as mathematics or reading, learning aptitude, vocational interest, or other domains.

tive learning and heterogeneous grouping to deal with ability differences among their students.[61]

What do we know today about ability grouping? Research has consistently shown that segregation of whole classes by ability (often called *tracking*) may benefit high-ability students but causes problems for low-ability students.[62] Low-ability classes seem to receive lower-quality instruction in general because teachers of these classes tend to emphasize lower-level objectives and routine procedures, with less academic focus. Furthermore, there are often more management problems and, because of these problems, increased stress and decreased teacher enthusiasm. These effects on instruction and teacher attitudes may mean that low expectations are communicated to the students. Indeed, students' self-esteem suffers almost as soon as they are assigned to "dummy" English or math. This drop in self-esteem may be followed by less frequent class attendance. In addition, because the lower tracks often enroll a disproportionate number of students from ethnic minorities and economically disadvantaged groups, ability grouping, in effect, can lead to re-segregation of schools.

There are two exceptions to the general finding that between-class ability grouping leads to lower achievement. The first is found in honors or gifted classes, where high-ability students tend to perform better than comparable students who remain in regular classes. The second exception is seen in the nongraded elementary school and the related Joplin Plan. In these arrangements, students are grouped by ability in particular subjects, regardless of their age or grade. A reading class might have students from several grades, all working on the same level on reading. This cross-grade grouping seems to be effective for students of all ability levels as long as the grouping allows teachers to give more direct instruction to the groups. But when cross-age grouping is used to implement individualized instruction, the effects are much less positive.[63]

Another approach to dealing with diversity in student ability is to create within-class ability grouping. Here, students are clustered by ability but remain in the same class. Many elementary school classes are grouped for reading, and some are grouped for math, although there is no clear evidence that this approach is superior to others. It appears that within-class ability grouping can be effective if groups are formed on the basis of actual achievement in the subject being taught, not general IQ, and if students are mixed for many other activities and subjects.

Teaching Reading and Writing

For years, educators have debated whether students should be taught to read and write through code-based (phonics skills) approaches that relate letters to sounds, and sounds to words, or through meaning-based (whole language, literature-based, emergent literacy) approaches that do not dissect words and sentences into pieces, but focus instead on the meaning of the text.

Advocates of the whole language approach believe that learning to read is a natural process, much like mastering one's native language. Reading is a kind of guessing game in which students sample words and make predictions and guesses about meaning based on the context provided by other words in the passage and on their prior knowledge. This suggests that words should not be presented out of context, and "sounding out" words, and "breaking whole (natural) language into bite-size abstract little pieces" should be avoided.[64] Rather, children should be immersed in a print-rich environment, surrounded by books worth reading and adults who read—to their children and for themselves. From the whole language perspective, teaching and learning are seen as reciprocal and collaborative. The teacher becomes an astute observer of students, noticing what support or resources they need in order to learn. Together, teacher and students make decisions about curriculum. When students write, they are encouraged to write for an audience. The goal is to help them communicate effectively, making writing a relevant and meaningful activity. As David Pearson put it, "[We] should ask students to read and write for real reasons (the kind real people in the real world have) rather than fake reasons we give them in school. School is too school-like."[65]

Despite the arguments for the whole language perspective, there are now two decades of research demonstrating that skill in recognizing sounds and words does support good reading skills. Advocates of the code-based approach cite research showing that the ability to identify many words in reading does not depend on using context to guess meaning. In fact, it is almost the other way around; knowing words helps to make sense of the context. The more fluent and automatically one can identify words, the more effective one will be in getting meaning from context.[66] It is the poorest readers, as well as beginning readers, who resort to using context to help them understand meaning.

Probably the best way to teach reading and writing is to combine whole language and code-based approaches. Indeed, excellent primary school teachers do use a balance of explicit decoding-skills teaching and whole language instruction.[67] Given that context is important to beginning readers, the whole language approach to reading and writing is most effective in preschool and kindergarten. Whole language seems to give children a good conceptual basis for reading and writing. Also, the social interactions that occur in relation to reading and writing—reading books, writing shared stories, examining pictures, discussing meaning—are all activities that support literacy and mirror the early at-home experiences of children who come to school prepared to learn. In addition, the whole language approach seems to improve students' motivation, interest, and attitude toward reading and to help children understand the nature and purposes of reading and writing.[68] On the other hand, phonemic awareness (the sense that words are composed of separate sounds and that sounds are combined to make words) in kindergarten and first grade predicts literacy in later grades. If children do not have phonemic awareness in the early grades, direct teaching can dramatically improve their chances of long-term achievement in literacy.[69]

CONCLUSION

It is likely that psychology will continue to contribute to education as psychologists understand more about the processes of learning, teaching, and intellect and as they continue to explore variations in human abilities, ways of assessing learning, and the creation of multifaceted learning environments. They will continue to ask questions such as: What is a useful and appropriate balance of discovery and direct instruction? How can teachers, who must work with groups, adapt instruction to individual variations? What should the role of testing and grading be in education? What are the goals of education, and how do we balance cognitive, affective, and psychomotor objectives? How can learning technologies be used to best advantage for students? How can we help students understand, remember, and apply knowledge? And if we think these are new questions, we need only attend to the history of psychology and its applications to education to see that they have existed for a long time. The same questions will probably continue to shape the application of psychology to education.

SUGGESTIONS FOR FURTHER READING

Berliner, D. C. (1993). The 100-year journey of educational psychology: From interest, to disdain, to respect for practice. In T. Fagan & G. VandenBos (Eds.), *Exploring applied psychology: Origins and critical analyses.* Washington, DC: American Psychological Association.

Berliner, D., & Rosenshine, B. (Eds.). (1987). *Talks to teachers.* New York: Random House.

Bloom, B. (1994). Reflections on the development and use of the taxonomy. In L. Anderson & L. Sosniak (Eds.), *Bloom's taxonomy: A forty-year retrospective.* Ninety-third yearbook for the National Society for the Study of Education. Chicago: University of Chicago Press.

Board of Educational Affairs of the American Psychological Association. (1995). *Learner-centered psychological principles: Guidelines for school redesign and reform.* Washington, DC: American Psychological Association.

Collins, A., Brown, J. S., & Holum, A. (1991). Cognitive apprenticeship: Making thinking visible. *American Educator, 15* (3), 3839.

Derry, S. J. (1989). Putting learning strategies to work. *Educational Leadership, 47* (5), 4–10.

CHAPTER 5

PSYCHOLOGY APPLIED TO CONSUMER BEHAVIOR

Frank R. Kardes

I magine that you have a cold and decide to visit the grocery store to buy cold medicine. You walk up to the pharmaceutical section, only to find dozens of different brands, varieties, and sizes of cold medicines. Now you need to ask yourself a series of questions: Do you need the kind that treats stuffy noses, sore throats, or flu and body aches? Do you need overnight, twelve-hour, or twenty-four-hour relief? Do you want pills, tablets, caplets, coated caplets, liquicaps, gel caps, or solid gel caps? Should you buy extra strength or regular, and if you buy regular, should you take twice as many? Despite the staggering array of choices available to consumers, the typical consumer spends only twelve seconds per product category to choose a specific brand, and only twenty-one minutes altogether on a typical shopping trip.[1]

Information overload exists in many other consumer environments as well. The typical North American consumer is exposed to over three hundred television, radio, newspaper, and magazine advertisements per day.[2] And this estimate is rather conservative because it does not include all the direct marketing junk mail that stuffs your mailbox, phone calls from telemarketers, posters, billboards, and internet advertising.

How do consumers deal with all this information? What influences them to make their choices? What kinds of errors do they make in deciding about products or services? What are the best marketing strategies to persuade consumers to buy particular products? These are the basic questions that consumer psychologists address as they scientifically study human responses to products, services, and the marketing of products and services.

HISTORY OF CONSUMER PSYCHOLOGY

John B. Watson was the first prominent psychologist to apply psychology to advertising.[3] His work reflected his belief that psychology could not be recognized as a science until its practical usefulness in many fields was demonstrated. He wrote, "If psychology would follow the plan I suggest, the educator, the physician, the jurist, and the businessman could utilize our data in a practical way."[4] Following the success of World War I propaganda campaigns, the advertising industry was very receptive to Watson's scientific ideas about controlling and predicting behavior (see Chapter 6).

In 1920, when his highly publicized divorce forced Watson to leave academia, he accepted a position at the J. Walter Thompson advertising agency, the largest in the world at the time (and still one of the largest). After an initiation process that included participating in Thompson's training program, selling Yuban coffee to wholesalers and retailers, and serving as a sales clerk at Macy's, Watson quickly became a spokesperson for Thompson, addressing business executives, trade associations, and industry leaders throughout the world. His main message was that psychology is a science and could be used to predict and control consumer behavior. He helped develop new advertising techniques, such as appealing to consumers' fear and other emotions to motivate them to buy and the use of expert testimonials to impress consumers with products. Today these techniques are commonplace. Watson rapidly worked his way up the corporate ladder to become vice president at J. Walter Thompson. His success opened the doors of ad agencies, market research firms, and manufacturing firms to other psychologists and helped open the public's eyes to the relevance and importance of psychology to everyday life.

Early consumer psychologists were heavily influenced by Watson, B. F. Skinner, and other psychologists who emphasized the importance of controlling and predicting behavior. But today, consumer psychologists concentrate on understanding the thinking processes that influence how decisions are made.

THE THINKING BEHIND CONSUMER DECISIONS

When we are faced with too much information, too little time, or other constraints on our reasoning and thinking processes, we often take mental shortcuts, that is, we take the quickest route to arriving at decisions, without considering all possibly relevant information. These shortcuts, which allow us to make decisions more easily and quickly, are called *heuristics*. Heuristics are often useful, but they can also be problematic because they may lead us to neglect or overlook important information. Such oversights, in turn, can result in errors and biases in our thinking.[5] An understanding of heuristic thinking allows us to appreciate how we make decisions, and it also throws light on the marketing techniques that are based on a knowledge of those heuristics. I will describe four common heuristics: prediction, persuasion, compliance, and choice.

Prediction Heuristics

The ability to predict is crucial to a wide variety of judgments and decisions. How long will my new car last before I have to buy another? Will I still like this new product five years from now? Which ad should I pay attention to? Psychologists Amos Tversky and Daniel Kahneman identified four main kinds of prediction heuristics that people tend to use more or less automatically.[6]

Representativeness Heuristic The *representativeness heuristic* involves judging one thing on the basis of how similar it is to another. If an object looks like a fish, people will predict that it is a fish. If a new product reminds people of an old product they liked a lot, people predict that they will like the new product too. But sometimes people focus on irrelevant similarities, especially under conditions of information overload, time pressure, or ambiguity, so their judgments may be led astray. For example, if the new product and the old product share only similar packaging, then the prediction about the new product may be incorrect.

Availability Heuristic   The *availability heuristic* involves making predictions based on the ease with which instances or examples can be retrieved from memory. Events that have occurred frequently in the past are more easily remembered. We also tend to assume that these events are likely to occur frequently in the future. However, memory-based judgment can be highly inaccurate when memory is influenced by factors other than objective frequency. For example, the media highlight sensational events, such as an obscure person's winning a multimillion dollar lottery prize, and rarely cover less sensational topics such as heart attacks, diabetes, and other illnesses. Consequently, people often overestimate the likelihood of winning the lottery (and are therefore more likely to buy a lottery ticket), but underestimate the likelihood of heart attacks, diabetes, and other illnesses (and are therefore less likely to buy disability insurance).

Simulation Heuristic   The *simulation heuristic* involves making predictions based on the ease with which a sequence of events can be simulated or imagined. For example, it is hard to imagine how a new product could flop in its first year yet become a tremendous success in its second year. Consequently, people predict that this is very unlikely. However, it is easy to imagine how this outcome could occur *if* a plausible sequence of events is outlined, such as the company's being bought out by a larger and more powerful organization that improves the product and its marketing in its second year. In fact, however, success in the second year is far more likely to occur through some other sequence of events than the one that is easiest to imagine.

Anchoring and Adjustment Heuristic   The *anchoring and adjustment heuristic* involves forming an initial judgment or first impression (the anchor) and then adjusting this judgment in a positive or negative direction depending on further evidence. Because anchoring is relatively easy and adjustment is relatively effortful, final judgments tend to be too close to initial judgments. In other words, people tend not to change their minds enough to reflect the new information they get. Consequently, it is surprisingly difficult to change first impressions of people, products, or services, even when the new information is dramatically different from the old. Not even experts are immune from this anchoring tendency. In a recent experiment, expert real estate agents were shown either a low, medium, or high list price for a house. Even after spending several hours examining the house thoroughly, these experts' estimates of its value were remarkably close to the anchor established by the stated list price. Those who heard the low list price undervalued the house; those who received the high list price overvalued it.[7]

Persuasion Heuristics

When consumers are motivated, able, and have the time to process advertisements, package labels, brochures, or other types of persuasive messages, they tend to reason carefully and base their judgments on large amounts of highly relevant and complex information.[8] But when the motivation or ability to scrutinize information carefully is low (due to low involvement, disinterest, distraction, ambiguity, intense emotional states, information overload, time pressure, and the like), people tend to form attitudes quickly and easily based on one or more of the following persuasion heuristics.[9]

Length-Implies-Strength Heuristic   People may rely on the *length-implies-strength heuristic*, which assumes that long messages filled with lots of facts and figures indicate that the advertised product is of very high quality.[10] Consequently, when consumers note that an advertisement contains an impressively long list of reasons for buying a particular brand, the length-implies-strength heuristic often leads them to quickly and easily form favorable attitudes toward that brand without bothering to read the contents of the message.

Liking-Agreement Heuristic   The *liking-agreement heuristic* is based on the idea that people generally agree with people they like.[11] As a result, persuasive messages delivered by likable people—or people who are physically attractive or have attractive personalities—are often more influential than the exact same messages presented by neutral or unlikable people. Thus, famous and likable actors, athletes, comedians, supermodels, and other celebrities are frequently used in advertising because the more that consumers like the endorser of an advertised brand, the more they will like the advertised brand itself.

Consensus-Implies-Correctness Heuristic   The *consensus-implies-correctness heuristic* suggests that the majority opinion is usually considered to be valid.[12] Hence, when people hear a large audience applauding or agreeing with a speaker, they tend to view the speaker as highly credible and persuasive. Similarly, information about the results of large-scale polls and surveys, as in "Ernie's Cleaners rated number one in town," tend to be highly persuasive.

Compliance Heuristics

Salespeople, fund raisers, politicians, con artists, spouses, friends, and relatives all try to get us to comply with, or say yes to, their requests. Consumer psychologist Robert Cialdini has identified six key heuristics that dramatically increase people's tendency to comply with such requests.[13]

Commitment-and-Consistency Heuristic   Research on the *commitment-and-consistency heuristic* shows that once people agree (commit) to a request, they tend to stick to the agreement (be consistent) even if the nature of the request changes.[14] Accordingly, salespeople may use the "low-ball" strategy, which involves offering a good deal on a product, such as a car, and getting a commitment from the customer to buy it. After getting the commitment, the salesperson goes away for a few minutes in order to "check with the boss" or " fill out some paperwork." When the salesperson returns, the initial deal is changed either by raising the price (using hidden options) or removing options the customer thought were standard. Even though the deal has changed so that it is no longer a good deal, customers often buy the product anyway.

Furthermore, once people are induced to agree to a small request, they seem to feel committed to agreeing with a subsequent larger request. This is called the "foot-in-the-door" effect.[15] For example, car salespeople often ask customers to buy relatively inexpensive options and accessories first because this increases the likelihood that they will comply with larger requests later. People are more likely to buy expensive options like a compact disc player or an air conditioner after first agreeing to buy inexpensive options, such as white walls or floot mats. In other settings, salespeople find that customers who comply with a small request, such as completing a short survey, are more likely to comply with a larger request later, such as purchasing the product or service described in the survey.

Reciprocity Heuristic   The *reciprocity heuristic* convinces people to return favors automatically, without being asked.[16] So if a salesperson gives you, say, a meal coupon or free sample, you are more likely to return the favor by buying something from that salesperson. This is why many salespeople offer "door openers," which are relatively worthless gifts designed to activate the reciprocity heuristic. They may also try to create the "door-in-the-face effect" by making an initial request (such as to buy a $3,500 set of encyclopedias) that you are likely to refuse.[17] Having done so, however, you are more likely to agree to a more moderate and reasonable request, such as to buy the $50 dictionary, which was, in fact, the original target. This strategy can be particularly effective if the salesperson makes a series of concessions, such as repeatedly lowering the price of a product or service until the customer begins to feel guilty for not reciprocating by buying it.[18] A related strategy is to create the "that's-not-all effect," which involves gradually sweetening a deal by throwing in "free" bonuses, such as air conditioning, a juicer attachment, or other items that would have been included anyway. Appearing to compromise in this way, too, is often more successful than offering the best deal right from the start.[19]

Scarcity Heuristic   The *scarcity heuristic* exploits the consumer's desire to want possessions that most other people cannot have. Valuable objects are scarce, and most people assume that the reverse is true as well—that scarce objects are valuable. Prime real estate, diamonds, popular new toys, and other scarce objects are highly prized by consumers. Moreover, consumers often experience an intense desire for things they are not supposed to have. To cigar smokers in the United States, Cuban cigars are a coveted prize, much as alcohol is to many underage youngsters. Accordingly, suggestions that items for sale are scarce or illicit tend to increase their appeal. These suggestions are usually conveyed through statements about "limited time offers" or "limited availability." For example, on home shopping channels, a running count of the dwindling number of sale items remaining is always on the screen. Establishing a limited distribution area can have the same effect. Before Coors beer was distributed outside Colorado, consumers routinely drove hundreds of miles to buy it, even though these same people may now ignore it in their local liquor store. Some salespeople make ordinary products seem less ordinary, and thus more desirable, by selling them from a shabby storefront or the trunk of a car, implying that the products are stolen and setting a "bargain" price that is actually no lower, and may be higher, than would be found anywhere else.

Social Validation Heuristic The *social validation heuristic,* or *proof in numbers principle,* reflects a way of thinking that can be surprisingly powerful in promoting compliance. Building on the consensus-implies-correctness heuristic mentioned earlier, advertisers create the impression that lots of other people have already purchased a product or service, thereby exerting implied peer pressure for us to comply as well. Thus, billboard, television, and radio advertisers tell us that their products are "world famous," the "fastest growing," or the "largest selling." Hundreds of satisfied customers, we assume, cannot be wrong! Every day, we are reminded that McDonald's has sold over 1 billion hamburgers. Telethon organizers and fund raisers also know that people are more likely to donate to a charity when they are exposed to a long list of people who have already contributed (and to a constantly updated display showing the total collected so far).[20]

Liking Heuristic The *liking heuristic* has been well demonstrated by Joe Girard, the man described in the *Guinness Book of World Records* as the world's greatest car salesman. Girard regularly sends thousands of customers greeting cards with the simple message, "I like you." As suggested by the reciprocity heuristic, people are then inclined to like him too. When we think about someone in positive terms, we find it easier to comply with his or her requests. One of the ways to be liked is to associate oneself with people, objects, and issues that are positively evaluated and to avoid being associated with those that are negatively evaluated. Advertisers do this by spending millions to hire revered figures like Michael Jordan and by firing anyone, such as O. J. Simpson, who does anything to create a negative public image.[21]

Authority Heuristic The *authority heuristic* causes us to take especially seriously requests coming from authority figures. Accordingly, people who want us to comply often create "authority cues," such as impressive surroundings, lofty titles, elegant clothes, or expensive possessions to suggest that they are legitimate authorities to whom we should pay heed. Doctors, lawyers, teachers, executives, politicians, religious leaders, and other experts and authority figures can often get other people to do things they would not normally do, such as remove clothing on command, spend hours studying obscure topics, or work overtime for no extra pay. It is no wonder that TV ads for pain relievers or investment firms feature people who look like doctors or successful stockbrokers, not homeless street people. Merely wearing a white coat and carrying a clipboard may create authority cues powerful enough to persuade people to inflict serious harm to others.* It seems that people question authority only when they are sufficiently motivated to do so and when they are able to avoid the trap of heuristic thinking.

Choice Heuristics

When we make judgments, we are essentially rating someone or something on a continuous scale, such as from 1 to 10. When consumers make choices, however, their task involves a noncontinuous scale: they choose either to purchase a particular brand or they choose not to. Sometimes their choice reflects objective judgments based on an analysis of the pluses and minuses of each specific attribute or feature of each product or service being considered. But when consumers' motivation or ability to process information carefully is low—as when grocery shopping under time pressure with small, noisy children—their choices tend to be based on the following heuristics.

Lexicographic Heuristic   The *lexicographic heuristic* leads us to choose a brand based on the single attribute—such as price, safety, efficiency, power, or the like—that is most important to us at the time.[22] Focusing on a single attribute, while ignoring all others, greatly simplifies consumer decision making, but it may have a hidden cost: it may cause us to overlook other important and less desirable attributes.

Elimination-by-Aspects Heuristic   What happens when the attribute we consider most important appears in more than one of the alternatives we are considering? The *elimination-by-aspects heuristic* helps us to make a choice efficiently by first eliminating all options that do not have the desired attribute and then examining all the remaining options for the second-most-important feature.[23] Those that lack this feature are then eliminated. If this process still leaves more than one option, those that do not offer the third-most-important attribute are dropped, until only one brand remains. For example, when buying a new car, a particular consumer may prefer a car with a sporty appearance. Any models that do not look sporty are quickly rejected, and the number of choices decreases. Next, the consumer may decide on front-wheel drive, thereby eliminating more models. Then the consumer may want room for passengers in the back seat. Once again, the choices are reduced. Eventually the number of choices will be small enough to allow for a careful comparison of the remaining alternatives.

Additive-Difference Heuristic   The *additive-difference heuristic* is often used when consumers have only two brands to compare. Here, sometimes without realizing it, we compare the difference between the values of each attribute for the brands, weigh the difference by importance, and then add the weighted differences.[24] Essentially what this means is that we not only pay attention to attributes, such as price

---

*This was demonstrated in a classic experiment by Stanley Milgram, in which participants were persuaded by a laboratory researcher to deliver what appeared to be dangerously high levels of electric shock to a helpless victim.

and reliability, but also how important each of these is for us. If one brand is expensive but reliable, and price is less important to us than reliability, we will choose that brand over a cheaper and less reliable one.

Conjunctive and Disjunctive Heuristics   Sometimes consumers examine only one brand, as when they are in a hurry and the first satisfactory brand they encounter will be good enough. Accomplishing this task requires relatively little mental effort, and that effort is further reduced by using either the conjunctive heuristic or the disjunctive heuristic. Using the *conjunctive heuristic* means that we set a minimum acceptable cutoff point for each attribute of the product we are looking for (e.g., the blank videotape has at least four hours of recording time and costs less than five dollars), then select the first brand that is acceptable on *all* counts. Using the *disjunctive heuristic* means setting an acceptable, usually somewhat higher-than-minimum, cutoff point for each attribute and then selecting the first brand that is acceptable on any *one* of them.

THE EFFECTS OF CONTEXT ON CONSUMER CHOICES

So far we have described the kinds of shortcuts that consumers use in thinking about the complex choices they have to make as they decide to purchase a product or service. In this section, we focus on the second major influence on consumer decisions: the context, or background, against which consumers view the products and services they buy.

In any situation, we tend to notice what is novel or different, we pay attention to anything that moves against a background of stillness, we are intrigued by complexity, and our interest is aroused by anything that is intense. Consequently we are more likely to pay attention to a roaring tiger in the middle of a suburban street than to a lamppost. Similarly, Rolls Royce automobiles, cylindrical Pringles packages, pink Energizer bunny commercials, and bright neon lights stand out and are more likely to attract our attention than ordinary automobiles, bagged potato chips, run-of-the-mill commercials, and dull signs. However, "noticeable" stimuli are noticeable only if they are surrounded by the ordinary. Thus, the same Rolls that might snap your head around as it drives by your house might not even be noticed in a parking lot filled with Rolls Royces just like it. We *can* pay attention to one particular Rolls in that situation, but it takes motivation, effort, and the ability to process information carefully.[25]

The context provided by information that is already in our memory also affects how we respond to new information. Whenever we learn something new, we not only store what we have learned but also some of the background, or context, in which it appeared. This is why it is easier to recall what we learned if some of the background information, or cues, are available to jog our memory. Advertisers are happy to provide these cues in the hope that they will help us recall their products. Accordingly, television commercials include memorable background information in the form of music, scenery, or characters that are presented again at the point of purchase. In stores, consumers find themselves surrounded by hundreds of context cues—from the Keebler elves to Elvira, Mistress of the Dark—on product packages, banners, cardboard cutouts, and other attention-getting displays. The greater the overlap between the cues present in advertisements and at the point of purchase, the better the consumer's memory of the product will be.[26]

We are also more likely to remember what we think about most often, or what we have learned most recently. For example, when rumors circulated several years ago about McDonald's using worms in their hamburgers, "McDonald's" and "worms" were strongly associated in the memories of many consumers.[27] Merely seeing McDonald's ads or signs made worms come to mind spontaneously for these consumers and had a depressing effect on sales of McDonald's hamburgers, even though most consumers did not actually believe the rumors. One way to eliminate this unfortunate association is to enter new information into consumers' memories, thus encouraging them to associate new things with McDonald's. Having customers answer a survey that prompted them to think about other qualities of McDonald's restaurants—such as cleanliness, convenience, service, the taste of the shakes and the fries—helped counteract the effects of the worm rumor.[28]

Context can also affect our judgments about the world, including about consumer products. A given object can seem large or small, heavy or light, good or bad, depending on what it is compared to. For example, a Ford Taurus seems large when compared to a Geo, but small when compared to a Cadillac sedan. Similarly, the quality of a Taurus is likely to be judged as higher when compared to a Yugo than to a BMW. Further, the more a particular object stands out from another, the greater the judged difference is likely to be. Thus, the BMW will get a better quality rating when it is compared to the Geo than when judged in isolation. Conversely, if two objects are very similar, the two will be judged to be more similar if compared to each other than they would had they been judged independently, that is, without reference to the other. This effect occurs even if a consumer is simply asked to think about the comparison. One researcher asked participants to complete a word puzzle that led some of them to think about automobiles that were either inexpensive (e.g., Citation, Escort), moderately priced (e.g., Grand Prix, Cutlass), or extremely expensive (e.g., Mercedes, Porsche). Then, in an apparently unrelated second experiment, the same participants were asked to judge another automobile that was described only in terms of a few attributes that did not include its brand name or price. The participants' judgments about this target automobile's price were made in relation to the kind of cars they had thought about in the puzzle task. Thus, those who had thought about extremely expensive automobiles in the puzzle rated the target automobile as inexpensive; the ones who had thought about inexpensive cars rated the target as expensive.[29]

Contextual factors can also influence how sensitive we are to evidence about products. People rarely receive complete and accurate information about anything, including consumer products, but they often form strong opinions anyway.[30] In forming these opinions, they tend to give too much weight to whatever information they have, and too little weight to the possible impact of information they don't have. For example, "I don't know how much it would cost to fix this washer if it breaks, but it's on sale and repairs couldn't be *too* much." However, when the context provides cues implying that relevant information is missing, people often adjust their judgments toward a more moderate and defensible position.[31] They are particularly likely to adjust their judgment in the light of missing evidence if they are presented with a similar, comparable object, such as two different brands of washers. Just making people aware of the idea of comparison seems to produce more moderate judgments and highlights the importance of getting more evidence.

Several studies have demonstrated the effect of context on consumer choices when three, rather than only two, brands are presented for consideration. It might seem obvious that adding a third brand should result in fewer people choosing either of the original two brands because some of them will choose the new third brand. Surprisingly, this is not always the case. Suppose that Brand A is excellent on attribute X (say, reliability) but poor on attribute Y (say, appearance). Suppose also that Brand B is just the opposite: poor on attribute X but excellent on attribute Y. As expected, if these two attributes are equally important to consumers, half of them will choose Brand A and half will choose Brand B. Now suppose the salesperson changes the context of the information by mentioning the availability of a Brand C, which is inferior (in all ways) to Brand A but better than Brand B. Doing this will increase the proportion of people choosing Brand A because they will think about brand A mainly in terms of its superiority to Brand C.[32]

Another way to increase the sales of Brand A is to introduce a Brand C that is superior to Brand A, but only on attribute X; it is far inferior to both Brands A and B on attribute Y. Thus, Brand C would be more reliable than Brand A but clearly the least attractive model of the three. In this case, Brand A becomes a compromise alternative: it now appears to be good (though not the best) on one important attribute and also excellent on the other.[33] This compromise alternative seems safer than either of the other choices, which now seem less desirable because they are excellent on one dimension but very poor on the other. Other research suggests that the same results occur when the context involves more than three brands.[34]

Expectations, especially expectations about gaining or losing, are another important aspect of the context in which people think about information, including product information. For example, we tend to think that winning one hundred dollars is good, especially if we did not expect to win anything. But that same hundred dollar prize might seem less valuable if we had expected to win two hundred dollars. We also tend to see the loss of one hundred dollars as more significant than the gain of that same amount. Accordingly, people are usually more willing to take a risk to avoid a loss than to obtain a gain of the same size. (This is one reason that most people are willing to spend five hundred dollars on an insurance policy but not on a casino bet.)

In a classic experiment to demonstrate this loss aversion phenomenon, participants were told about a hypothetical situation in which a disease was expected to kill six hundred people. They were then asked to choose between a treatment program that would guarantee saving two hundred out of six hundred lives (the "sure thing" option), and a "risky" treatment option that had a 33 percent chance of saving all six hundred lives (but, obviously, a 67 percent chance of saving no one). In this study, 72 percent of the participants chose the sure thing. Then another group of participants was asked to choose between a treatment program in which four hundred out of six hundred people would die for sure (the "sure thing" option) and a "risky" treatment option that carried a 33 percent chance that no one would die and a 67 percent chance that all six hundred people would die. Notice that the outcomes for the two options were the same as in the earlier study, but here they were phrased in terms of losses (deaths) instead of gains (lives saved). Changing the context to emphasize losses instead of gains had a dramatic effect: 78 percent of the participants now chose the risky option! In other words, people tend to prefer a sure thing when outcomes are stated in terms of achieving gain and a risky option when outcomes are framed in terms of avoiding loss. The same loss aversion principle applies to consumers, who, for example, are more likely to buy a particular package of ground beef if it is described as "75 percent lean" (gain) than if it is labeled as "25 percent fat" (loss).[35]

PSYCHOLOGICAL MODELS OF CONSUMER BEHAVIOR

The research described so far is based on principles emerging from cognitive and social psychology. Let's now consider three theoretical models that are more specific to consumer psychology.

The Availability-Valence Model

This model suggests that consumers evaluate products on the basis of two key factors: availability (the ease with which information about the product can be brought to mind) and valence (how favorable or unfavorable that information is).[36] If the total valence of the information retrieved from memory is more favorable than unfavorable (that is, if the pluses outweigh the minuses), the consumer's overall evaluation of the product should be favorable. If the information that can be retrieved is more unfavorable than favorable (the minuses outweigh the pluses), the overall evaluation should be unfavorable.

What determines the availability of information? Many factors are involved, but most of the research on the availability-valence model suggests that the more the consumer thinks about, or "elaborates," product information as it comes in, the more available it will be later.[37]

The availability-valence model can explain many important consumer phenomena. For example, information that is vivid or attention getting is more likely to be available to memory later, and also more likely to be given heavy weight in making judgments about a product. This *vividness effect* is seen in studies showing that interesting speakers are more influential on an audience than boring speakers, even when both speakers present the same information. Interesting information tends to be processed more elaborately and is therefore more memorable and influential than less elaborately processed, boring information.[38]

The *sleeper effect* refers to the tendency for the impact of a persuasive message to increase over time when a believable message comes from a suspect source, such as an untrustworthy advertiser.[39] At first, the message is discounted because the consumer does not trust the advertiser. However, the consumer's memory about the source tends to fade faster than memory of the message itself, presumably because information contained in the message was subjected to more elaborative processing than information about the source. As a result, the negative effect of the source decreases over time, while the effect of the message increases over time, giving it greater persuasive power later on than it did at first.

The *overjustification effect* involves a tendency to discount one reason for buying a product once we are given additional reasons to do so.[40] So, although we may be impressed when advertisers tell us that a product is good (delicious, reliable, or whatever), the impact of the product's good quality on how much we like it can actually be reduced if the advertiser mentions a discount coupon or some other reason to buy. Indeed, research has demonstrated that a coupon can either increase or decrease liking for a product depending on how much elaborative processing about its quality (as opposed to its price) took place when we formed our initial attitudes about it.[41] If we have already used a product, we are more likely to have engaged in a lot of elaborative processing, and that processing results in strong and memorable attitudes. If we have only read about a new product, we will have engaged in less elaborative processing and thus have less memorable attitudes. So a discount coupon will likely increase sales mainly among consumers whose initial attitude toward a product is easily available in memory. The same coupon can activate the overjustification effect, leading to a reduced impact of initial quality information, if one's initial attitude is not easy to retrieve from memory. In that case, the discount may actually result in the consumer's being less favorable toward the product.

The availability-valence model also applies to the foot-in-the-door and the door-in-the-face effects mentioned earlier.[42] Recall that these effects occur when there is a sequence of two requests: an initial request and a target request. The foot-in-the-door effect occurs when a small request is followed by a larger one; the door-in-the-face effect occurs when a large request is followed by a smaller one. It is the relative availability and valence of each of the two requests that underlie the value of sales techniques based on these effects.

Consider the foot-in-the-door effect. While the first request should be relatively small compared to their ultimate goal, salespeople are more likely to get consumers to comply with very high-cost requests if the first one is significant as opposed to trivial. Why? Because if the first request was significant (to buy a car, for example), the consumer is more likely to engage in a lot of elaborative processing about it, and the act of complying with it will be easily available for recall. This highly available memory is more likely to create compliance with later, even more costly requests than if the first request had been merely to read a brochure about the car. Similarly, the door-in-the-face effect is more likely to occur if the second, "compromise," request is made immediately after the initial "excessive" one. This is because the second request will seem far less demanding and far more conciliatory, while the excessive request is still fresh in the consumer's mind, and thus available for comparison.

In short, the availability-valence model of consumer behavior suggests that marketers should attempt to alter consumers' memories so that favorable information about a product is more available than unfavorable information. Taking this approach is more subtle—and often more effective—than attempting to change what consumers initially think about product information.

The Accessibility-Diagnosticity Model

The accessibility-diagnosticity model builds on the availability-valence model by adding a third factor known as *diagnosticity,* or perceived relevance.[43] This model says that consumers' judgment depends not only on the degree to which product information is accessible to memory and has a favorable or unfavorable valence, but also how relevant it is perceived to be in making a buying decision. Accordingly, the accessibility-diagnosticity model has been used to account for all the phenomena explained by the availability-valence model.[44] It has also been used, though, to (1) predict when consumers will base their buying decisions on an overall evaluation of a product versus a comparison of the specific attributes of various options,[45] and (2) explain why consumers' judgments are sometimes altered simply by having them measured.[46] This latter question is of special interest to market researchers who want to get an accurate, unbiased assessment of consumer sentiment about existing or proposed products.

For example, it appears that whether consumers make overall evaluations or compare specific attributes depends on the relative accessibility (memorableness) and the relative diagnosticity (relevance) of product information. As you might expect, the most accessible information is considered first. If that information is also perceived to be highly relevant, the consumer is likely to make an overall evaluative judgment, and a buying decision, based on this information alone. If that information is not perceived to be sufficiently relevant, additional information about specific attributes of various product choices is more likely to be considered and used as the basis for an ultimate judgment and decision.

When consumers are asked to complete a marketing survey, they respond to some of the questions, such as how long they have lived in a particular town, using information that they retrieve directly from memory. These answers and judgments are relatively unlikely to be biased much by simply having them measured. Other questions, however, may ask consumers to think about a topic for the first time, so the answers come not from memory but through thinking about these questions.[47] The judgments that result from this process are said to have self-generated validity, because they are formed for the first time in response to the questions or rating scales presented by the market researcher.[48] Even though they are new, these measurement-induced judgments can exert a powerful influence on a person's other judgments. As a result, the person may then give answers that suggest more consistency than actually exists among their beliefs, attitudes, intentions, and behavior.[49] For example, when asked a question about the importance of weed killer, the consumer may not have thought about the issue before. Nevertheless, he or she will come up with an answer and may also say, in response to related questions, that it is important to have a weed-free lawn, that weed killers are good products, and that he or she not only intends to use weed killer this spring, but has done so in the past. In fact, however, the person may not be this consistent; he or she may *like the idea* of a weed-free lawn but usually does not bother to do anything about it. Researchers have developed a variety of survey methods to discriminate between retrieved versus newly generated judgments and to control for possible measurement effects on judgment.[50] It has been suggested, for example, that the longer consumers take to respond to a survey question, the more likely it is that the answer reflects a newly generated judgment rather than retrieval of a memory.

The Accessibility-Applicability-Adjustment Model

The accessibility-applicability-adjustment model builds on the availability-valence and accessibility-diagnosticity models by (1) defining accessibility more precisely, (2) replacing perceived diagnosticity with the more precise term *applicability,* and (3) emphasizing the role of adjustment and correction processes in judgment and choice. In this model, *available* information is information that is stored in long-term memory.[51] *Accessible* information is both available (present in memory) *and* capable of being activated or brought to mind.[52] Thus, information accessibility can vary along a continuum ranging from very low activation potential to very high activation potential.[53] The term *potential* emphasizes that product information can continue to exist whether or not the consumer happens to be thinking about it at the time, and that the likelihood of bringing the knowledge to mind depends on how much mental energy the consumer exerts to retrieve it. Knowledge accessibility is also determined by how recently, and how often, the information has been activated (more recently and frequently activated information is more easily accessible), and how much effort the consumer has exerted in activating it. According to this model, effortful mental processing leads to the development of elaborate associative networks containing many cues that make information retrieval easier, even by thinking of things that are merely related to that information.[54]

Knowledge activation also depends on applicability, or the goodness of fit between information already stored in memory and information presented now, as in a store display.[55] The greater the overlap, the greater the applicability of stored knowledge for interpreting and judging the stimulus presented in the store. When there is a good match between the stored and the newly presented features of information, the consumer's judgment about a product will likely be based on the stored information.[56] This means that the consumer's prior knowledge, along with any heuristics, stereotypes, and preconceptions stored in memory, are likely to determine the ultimate judgment. When the match between stored and newly presented information is low, then the judgment is more likely to be based mainly on the attributes of the product on display.[57]

Sometimes consumers suspect that their initial judgments have been influenced by an irrelevant or an inappropriate contextual factor. Under these circumstances, they may attempt to adjust or correct their initial judgments in light of the potentially biasing factor. Recent research has shown that adjustment can result in reduced acceptance of false product claims.[58] For example, after judging the desirability of Hawaii as a vacation spot, Kansas City may seem very undesirable to a consumer. This contrast effect is reduced, however, if consumers suspect that judging Hawaii first may have influenced their judgments of Kansas City. Consumers are most likely to make such judgment adjustments if (1) the influence of potentially biasing factors is clear, (2) knowledge about the effects of these factors on judgment is stored in memory, and (3) people are motivated and able to engage in the relatively effortful process of adjusting and correcting judgments.[59] These factors also influence the amount of adjustment that takes place; the stronger they are, the more likely it is that judgments will be affected by them.

Finally, it should be emphasized that each stage of the accessibility-applicability-adjustment model is likely to be influenced by the consumer's need or motive for *cognitive closure*: the "desire for a firm answer to a question and an aversion toward ambiguity."[60] Consumers with little need for closure tend to be more concerned about making a correct decision than about making it quickly, so they are willing to suspend final judgment until they have carefully considered, weighed, and integrated all of the relevant information. Those with a strong need for closure tend to jump to conclusions on the basis of whatever apparently relevant information happens to be readily available (a phenomenon known as *seizing*), and they tend to avoid, ignore, or discount information that may threaten these conclusions. This rush to judgment is called *freezing* because the person not only seizes on a choice but then seems frozen to it. Consumers who have a strong need for closure, then, are the ones most likely to make judgments based on whatever information happens to be accessible and apparently applicable (even if it is not), and to fail to adjust initial judgments in the light of additional information.[61]

CONCLUSION

Theories of consumer psychology are continually evolving. As the field of consumer psychology grows, new insights about how and why consumers behave as they do will undoubtedly emerge. These insights can be used to improve judgment and decision making on the part of consumers and on the part of those interested in influencing consumers.

How can we use current knowledge about consumer psychology to become better consumers ourselves? First, we need to be aware that heuristic thinking can lead us to overlook important information, which can lead to poor decisions. The best way to avoid the trap of heuristic thinking is to constantly ask ourselves if we have enough information to make an informed decision about a product. If our decision is based on only one or two pieces of information, it may not be an ideal one. Second, we should try to consider many different brands and use the information about various brands systematically and consistently, that is, using the same criteria and the same processes to weigh and evaluate the information for each brand. This helps to reduce the magnitude of context effects because contextual changes often lead us to be unsystematic and inconsistent in our thinking.

Suggestions for Further Reading

Cialdini, R. B. (1993). *Influence: Science and practice.* New York: HarperCollins.

Eagly, A. H., & Chaiken, S. (1993). *The psychology of attitudes.* Fort Worth, TX: Harcourt Brace Jovanovich.

Kardes, F. R. (1993). Consumer inference: Determinants, consequences, and implications for advertising. In A. A. Mitchell (Ed.), *Advertising exposure, memory and choice* (pp. 163–191). Hillsdale, NJ: Erlbaum.

Kardes, F. R. (1994). Consumer judgment and decision processes. In R. S. Wyer & T. K. Srull (Eds.), *Handbook of social cognition* (Vol. 2, pp. 399–466). Hillsdale, NJ: Erlbaum.

Kardes, F. R. (1999). *Consumer behavior and managerial decision making.* Reading, MA: Addison Wesley.

CHAPTER 6

PSYCHOLOGY APPLIED TO BUSINESS

Winfred Arthur, Jr., and Ludy T. Benjamin, Jr.

In the early evening of October 20, 1909, agents of the U.S. government stopped a truck outside Chattanooga, Tennessee, and, under federal authority over interstate commerce, seized its freight. The "contraband" consisted of forty barrels and twenty kegs of Coca-Cola syrup on its way from the headquarters plant in Atlanta, Georgia, to the bottling plant in Chattanooga. The seizure was ordered from Washington, D.C., under the authority of the recently passed Pure Food and Drug Act. In the lawsuit that was to follow, the Coca-Cola Company would be charged with marketing and selling a beverage that was injurious to health because it contained a harmful ingredient, caffeine.

As the Coca-Cola Company prepared for trial in the spring of 1911, its scientists realized that their research evidence on caffeine consisted primarily of studies on physiology, with almost nothing on behavior other than a few experiments on animals. Human behavioral studies were needed, and soon. The company approached Harry Hollingworth, a psychologist at Barnard College in New York City, who had earned his doctorate only two years earlier. Hollingworth was cautious about accepting the research assignment. He was aware that others, more senior than he, had already turned down Coca-Cola's offer. He was concerned as well about questions of scientific integrity that would be raised by a large company's spending a lot of money for research it hoped would be favorable to its legal and commercial needs. Hollingworth sought to minimize that concern in his contractual arrangement with the Coca-Cola Company. The contract specified that he would be allowed to publish the results of the studies regardless of their outcome, and that the results of the research would not be used in any Coca-Cola advertising.

Hollingworth designed a series of studies that he carried out with his wife, Leta Hollingworth (who would herself become an eminent psychologist). These studies involved a scope of testing and a sophistication of methodology that had not been seen before in applied psychology. The research was designed to test the effects of caffeine on sensory, cognitive, and motor functioning in humans. A battery of thirty different tests was given to participants under differing drug dosages and at different intervals. Some of the control procedures used in this carefully conducted research included presenting tasks in all possible orders, giving some participants inactive substances to assess placebo effects, and keeping participants (as well as experimenters) "blind" to which participants received what substances (double-blind testing).[1]

The results indicated that even high doses of caffeine (much higher than would ever be consumed by heavy drinkers of Coca-Cola) had no ill effects on behavioral or cognitive performance. The data were some of the most impressive scientific evidence presented at the trial in Chattanooga, but although the court found in favor of Coca-Cola, the company eventually lost the case in the Supreme Court. It was required to pay court costs, and, on its own, it reduced the caffeine content of its soft drink.

Hollingworth's research for Coca-Cola was important on several levels. It marked perhaps the earliest example of funding by a large corporation of psychological research. The success of the research advanced Hollingworth's reputation in the business community and resulted in many other business research opportunities that led to a very successful career for him in applied psychology. Of greatest significance, though, was that the work helped bridge the gap between academic psychology and the business world, opening doors for psychologists seeking to consult with businesses and showing psychologists how they could use their science in the service of business.[2]

THE BEGINNINGS OF A PSYCHOLOGY OF BUSINESS

When psychology emerged in Germany at the end of the nineteenth century, the new psychological scientists quickly recognized the applicability of a science of mind. Initial forays were made in the fields of education and business, and were soon followed by a host of other applications. Nowhere was applied psychology more at home than in the United States, which in the late nineteenth century was undergoing a social metamorphosis brought on by increased industrialization, new waves of immigration, growth of the cities, and calls for educational reform. There were numerous problems inherent in such social upheaval. What was needed was an applied science to help solve those problems. The business world beckoned in particular. With "the formation of large industrial empires . . . came new management problems and a growing preoccupation with efficiency. Applied psychologists, with their widening variety of psychological tests, provided a timely management tool that attracted attention among the leaders of some of America's largest corporations."[3] Business was changing and growing, and the new science of psychology was invited to be a part of that growth. Traditionally business had concerned itself with such issues as product development, acquisition of cheap materials, more efficient ways of processing, and so forth. Psychology's entry into the business world shifted the focus to the worker, for greater productivity and efficiency lay in having workers who were better selected, better trained, and more satisfied.

Business is king in the United States. Of that there can be no doubt. Despite having less than 7 percent of the world's population, the United States generates almost 40 percent of the world's income.[4] Today psychologists are an integral part of the business world, serving in a wide variety of roles in small companies and global corporations alike. The psychological specialty most closely allied to business is *industrial/organizational psychology,* known as I/O psychology, for short.

Some historians date the beginnings of I/O psychology to the work of Hugo Münsterberg, a professor of psychology at Harvard University from 1892 until his death in 1916. Münsterberg's 1913 book, *Psychology and Industrial Efficiency,* was a watershed publication for the psychology of business. It stimulated interest in business among psychologists, thus fostering rapid growth in industrial psychology, yet it also was quite popular with business executives and the general public. For a while the book even appeared on best-seller lists for nonfiction.[5] Münsterberg recognized the business community's growing concern with efficiency, and in his book he touted the promise of psychology in that regard. Efficiency meant more effective advertising, better training of workers, more science-minded management, improved employee selection procedures, better accounting methods, and better ways to control the performance of workers and the quality of their output. Münsterberg argued that psychology was the science that could best ensure such efficiency.

Although Münsterberg is an important figure in the history of I/O psychology, the field did not begin with him. Applications of psychology to business in America predate his book by more than fifteen years. For example, University of Minnesota psychologist Harlow Gale began studies on the psychology of advertising as early as 1896,[6] and Northwestern University's Walter Dill Scott followed in 1903 with the first of his two books on the psychology of advertising.[7] Hollingworth, too, was involved in advertising and selling even before his work for Coca-Cola. He began his advertising work in 1910 and published his first book on the subject in 1913. These early applied psychologists who worked with the business community were often called business psychologists or economic psychologists, and, most commonly, consulting psychologists. By the 1920s they were called industrial psychologists, and only much later (in the 1970s), industrial-organizational psychologists.

Most of the early twentieth-century work by business psychologists was centered on mental testing: tests that typically measured sensory and motor abilities as well as cognitive performance. Psychologist James McKeen Cattell coined the term *mental test* in 1890 and pioneered the development of many of the early mental tests. Hollingworth was his student at Columbia University, and virtually all of the tests he used in his work for Coca-Cola had been developed by Cattell. Mental tests were used to measure advertising appeals, sales strategies, management styles, consumer behavior, and were also valuable in personnel matters such as worker selection, job analysis, production, and efficiency. For example, potential perfume advertisements were tested by asking people to indicate which slogans induced sensory impressions of aroma. Worker efficiency was assessed by a variety of mental tests such as calculation tasks (mental arithmetic), eye-hand coordination, and visual and auditory reaction time measures. Other business psychologists focused their work on testing and counseling individuals with regard to career selection, a field usually known as *vocational guidance* or *vocational counseling.*

INDUSTRIAL PSYCHOLOGY IN THE 1920S AND 1930S

Personnel issues were a product of the rise of big business in America in the early twentieth century. As companies became larger and jobs grew more specialized, businesses found that new practices were needed to ensure workers' efficiency. To meet these needs, companies established personnel departments that served as centralized offices for hiring and job placement. By the 1920s, these departments typically included psychologists, either as consultants or full-time employees, and emphasized (1) job analyses to identify the individual components of all jobs, and (2) testing of current and potential employees to make appropriate matches between work skills and job requirements. Making successful matches was no doubt important for employee satisfaction; however, for management the impetus for a good match between worker and job was improved production, which ultimately meant more profit for the company. Some personnel departments were seen as psychological laboratories wherein all kinds of company-relevant psychological questions could be answered, such as which employees would remain loyal to a company (rather than leaving for greener pastures after expensive training), or what kind of employees have the personality traits to handle jobs in complaint departments.

Advertising was another important component of big companies. There too psychologists had an impact. One of the first psychologists involved in advertising was John Watson, the founder of behaviorism. He was employed full time in two of New York City's largest advertising agencies, first at J. Walter Thompson and then at William Esty, where he conducted research on the effectiveness of various advertising strategies. Perhaps his greatest contributions were made in the development of testimonial advertising, particularly indirect testimonials, a subtle kind of advertising that focuses not on the product but on the psychological reaction of the consumer. Watson believed that indirect testimonials were particularly effective because they appealed to the basic human emotions of fear, rage, and love.[8] For example, in a magazine advertisement for toothpaste, Watson showed a seductively dressed young woman smoking. The appeal was not to brushing teeth for hygienic reasons but for enhancing sexual attraction via the independence implied by women smoking in the 1920s and the need for the toothpaste to ensure fresh breath.

Companies were also affected by the work of many female psychologists who joined the world of business in the 1920s because university faculty positions were often unavailable to them. Marion Bills, for example, earned her doctorate in psychology in 1917 and spent her career of more than thirty years at Aetna Life Insurance Company, where she was involved with personnel selection and sales research. Another pioneer among female business psychologists was Elsie Bregman, a student of Cattell who received her Ph.D. in 1922. She worked for Macy's department store in New York City, where she established a psychological laboratory for personnel testing and selection. In her first two years there, she tested more than twenty thousand individuals in an impressive program of research designed to identify persons who would be successful in sales and clerical positions. The battery of tests she developed for selecting people for these positions was used not only at Macy's but in other businesses as well.[9] Bregman found three kinds of tests that were useful in

Macy's personnel decisions. One measured the ability to follow written instructions. Another test, which Bregman called a judgment test, would likely be called a reasoning test today. The third test measured the person's ability to see similarities and dissimilarities in the meanings of pairs of words.

Applied psychologists were much in demand during the 1920s, partly because of their successes of testing and selection during World War I, but also because newspaper columnists argued that individuals could not secure happiness and success without the advice of psychologists.[10] They suggested that psychologists were needed to help people select mates, raise their children, and choose a career. Among the new popular magazines appearing in the United States during this decade was *Industrial Psychology Monthly,* a publication written by psychologists and business executives for the use of business leaders.[11] The practical nature of this magazine is illustrated by the titles of some of its articles: "Tests for Chauffeurs," "Personality: A Secret of Success in Retail Selling," and "Handling Men Through Their Self Interests."

Another force behind the popularity of industrial psychology in the 1920s was the rise of Frederick Winslow Taylor's concept of *scientific management.*[12] Scientific management, also known as *Taylorism,* recognized the basis of conflict inherent in the employer-employee relationship: workers wanted higher wages, and management wanted cheap labor. Taylor, a mechanical engineer, argued that efficiency resulted only when both sides understood that mutual cooperation was mutually beneficial. He called for scientific job analyses, better employee selection and training, and better cooperation between labor and management, including some degree of shared decision making. Other engineers also sought to improve industrial efficiency. Frank Gilbreth, for example, used the new technology of motion pictures to do time-motion studies of jobs such as bricklaying, thus allowing better inspection of worker behaviors and determination of how they might be made more efficient. He was aided in his work by his wife, Lillian Gilbreth, a psychologist, who greatly expanded the scope of his work after he died. She also made a number of important contributions on her own, including product design (especially of office machines), vocational rehabilitation programs for disabled individuals, and programs for improving employee satisfaction. It has been said that she was the popularizer, if not the inventor, of the suggestion box.[13]

The work of Taylor and the Gilbreths was not without criticism, especially from worker groups and some members of Congress.[14] One of the outcomes of their work was management's greatly increased expectations for improved production. Many workers felt that such heightened productivity contributed to the wealth of the owners and management but added little to their own wages. The psychologists' work was nevertheless exceptionally popular with American business executives, and psychologists were able to capitalize on that popularity, expanding their presence in business through the 1920s and 1930s. Even in the midst of the Great Depression, businesses continued to rely on psychologists, whose focus on increasing efficiency seemed even more important in a faltering national economy. Morris Viteles, a leading industrial psychologist based in Philadelphia, reminded the business community that "the stability of the business enterprise depends no less upon the soundness of its psychological foundation than upon the solidity of its economic and technical supports. . . . The failure to study . . . the effectiveness of human behavior in industry can only result in serious waste in the form of individual maladjustment and of industrial inefficiency."[15] Businesses heeded these words by acknowledging the value of psychology and seeking the services of psychologists.

In fact, the demand for psychologists' services by business and the general public was so great in the 1920s that there were not enough trained psychologists to meet the need. In this climate of intense demand and limited supply, individuals who were self-taught psychologists or even charlatans offered their services as "psychologists." For example, although phrenology (identifying personal traits by examining bumps and indentations of a person's skull) had largely been discredited in the nineteenth century, other pseudosciences retained some credibility, including physiognomy (identifying personal abilities from facial characteristics), graphology (handwriting analysis), and character analysis based on physical characteristics. The last of these proved particularly popular with American businesses during the 1920s and 1930s.

There were several prominent character analysis systems, the most popular of which was described by Katherine Blackford, a physician. In her books, she urged companies to hire blond men because they were more likely to have the convex facial profiles that allegedly indicated positive, dynamic, driving, aggressive, domineering, impatient, active, quick, hopeful, speculative, changeable, and variety-loving characteristics. Blonds, in short, were assumed to be people of action.[16] Blackford also argued that character traits such as honesty, courtesy, cheerfulness, and a good work ethic could be measured only through her observational system, not by standard psychological tests. According to Blackford, businesses failed because they ignored the science of human nature and thus hired individuals for jobs for which they were wholly unsuited. Her books offered advice on how to use the job interview to observe physical and behavioral traits that would match with various job demands.

It was no wonder that scientifically oriented psychologists sought ways to distinguish themselves from nonpsychologists and from nonscientific "psychologists" as well. James McKeen Cattell and others founded the Psychological Corporation in 1921 as a way to identify legitimately trained psychological consultants to industry. That same year, the American Psychological Association began a credentialing program to certify consulting psychologists. Many psychologists wrote books and magazine articles warning businesses and the general public about "pseudo-psychologies." Unfortunately, many business executives could not tell the real psychologists from the rest, and as a result, psychology declined in popularity in the business community in the latter half of the 1930s. The downturn would be only temporary though; psychology's considerable successes on behalf of the military in World War II would restore the faith of American business leaders. The renewed popularity of industrial psychology did not, of course, eliminate pseudopsychologies. Techniques like graphology continue to be used to a minor extent in the United States even today (it is a very popular personnel selection tool in France), and some character analysis techniques are also still used, often in the context of job interviews. However, these methods are not among the research or practice tools of the modern I/O psychologist in America.

INDUSTRIAL PSYCHOLOGY IN AMERICA AFTER WORLD WAR II

Much of the activity in applied psychology during World War I had involved selection research and drew on the work of business psychologists like Scott. Applied psychology during and after World War II was much more diverse. It involved not only selection, but also job analysis, military training, marketing research, propaganda, and human factors research, that is, on the ways in which, for example, equipment design affects the performance of the people who use that equipment. This latter field was subsequently called engineering psychology (see Chapters 10 and 11).

By the 1970s, the growth of theory in social psychology, which studies how individual behavior is affected by other people, and the growth of corporate America created new interests among psychologists in organizational issues. There was a growing realization that to effect change in business, one had to do more than change a few workers or a single department. To make a difference, one had to change the entire organizational climate. So industrial psychologists became industrial/organizational psychologists, interested both in studying organizational behavior and development and using that information to bring about significant changes in business and industry.[17] Accordingly, in 1973, the American Psychological Association's Division of Industrial Psychology (Division 14) changed its name to the Division of Industrial and Organizational Psychology.

Today industrial/organizational psychology is one of the major applied specialties in psychology, with researchers and practitioners working in a wide variety of settings.

SOME APPLICATIONS OF PSYCHOLOGY TO BUSINESS

For most of the twentieth century, I/O psychologists have led the way in devising better ways to select, place, promote, train, develop, organize, evaluate, lead, motivate, and compensate people in the workplace. Given this range of activities, most I/O psychologists tend to describe themselves as either personnel (I) or organizational (O) "types." Those in personnel tend to focus on analyzing particular jobs and finding the best methods for selecting suitable employees for those jobs, while organizational psychologists concentrate on overall working conditions and look at issues such as leadership, job satisfaction, and employee motivation. Both personnel and organizational psychologists work in a wide variety of settings. During the summer and fall of 1994, members of the Society for Industrial-Organizational Psychology responded to a survey regarding their primary employment positions. Over a third of the membership identified academia as their primary place of employment, with the remainder primarily consultants or in-house practitioners (corporate consultants).[18]

Personnel Psychology

One of the most successful applications of personnel psychology to business was in the development of *assessment centers* at AT&T in 1956 under the leadership of Douglas Bray, Donald Grant, Richard Campbell, and Ann Howard.[19] In assessment centers, many techniques (such as situational exercises and job simulations, leaderless discussions, business games, and presentations) are used to assess participants on behavioral dimensions or competencies such as team building, decision making, organizing and planning. Assessors observe and document participants' performance in the exercises and simulations and then write reports on what they observed. Afterward, the assessors get together and reach consensus on ratings for each participant's skill level on each of the competencies or areas being measured. Finally, assessors meet with each participant individually to review and discuss the participant's performance on the assessed behavioral dimensions and to suggest strategies and activities that might lead to improvement on those dimensions.

The George Bush School of Government and Public Service at Texas A&M University is the site of a unique and innovative application of assessment centers. All students entering the school begin the Master of Public Service and Administration degree program with the Leadership Assessment and Development Center, which is designed to evaluate their relative strengths on such leadership skills or competencies as team building, oral and written communication, innovation, and dispute mediation. Based on the confidential results of this assessment, each student works with an adviser to select activities to strengthen his or her skills on specified competencies. In addition, students are expected to attend various professional developmental seminars scheduled throughout the year.

Prior to the start of the second (and final) year, students' performance on the leadership competencies is reassessed by ratings obtained from the students' professors, internship employers, and fellow students, as well as by self-ratings from the student. This information, coupled with that obtained from the assessment center in the first year, is used to evaluate the progress students have made during their first year, and also to generate another developmental feedback report.

Assessment centers have proved to be useful for a wide range of human resource management purposes, including selection, promotion, placement, career planning, training and development, and improvement of managerial and leadership skills.[20] They have been used most frequently in the context of managerial and administrative jobs in a wide variety of organizational sectors, such as manufacturing, government, public utilities, oil companies, and academia.[21]

Studies of the usefulness of assessment centers typically compare judgments of performance made in the center with job-related criteria, such as job performance, promotion rate and career advancement, and salary. The results have generally shown short-term as well as long-term benefits.[22]

Assessment centers offer many other advantages.[23] For example, it has been demonstrated that assessment center evaluations appear to be less biased by participants' ethnicity or gender than are some other measures used in personnel selection.[24] Indeed, although the assessment center cost per candidate is about ten times more than that for an aptitude test (usually a paper-and-pencil test that measures basic job skills), the results are so much less affected by ethnicity or gender that they can be much more useful to organizations in the long run.[25]

Overall, then, the empirical evidence on the effectiveness of assessment centers is quite positive. They are widely recognized as good tools for identifying individuals with potential for success in management and developing leadership and managerial skills. The success of assessment centers is reflected in the fact that they are used all over the world as both selection and development tools.

Organizational Psychology

A good example of the successful application of organizational psychology to business is the reorganization of the Ashanti Goldfields Corporation Limited mining operations in the West African country of Ghana, a corporation that had been described as a "permanently failing organization."[26] The strategies that reversed the decline of this corporation are described in a study by Winfred Arthur, Jr., and his colleagues.[27] Major emphasis was placed on the development and establishment within the management group of new ways of thinking about performance, the introduction of managerial goal setting, the development of managerial teams, and an improvement in the basic standard of living for employees. Although the specific methods were diverse, a number of points were emphasized. First, any changes were to be sensitive to the cultural context within which the company was operating. In particular, there was a need to transfer decision-making power to the local level, so that decisions were made by managers who were both physically close to and aware of the cultural values of the employees most affected by those decisions. Second, there was a need to create a shared vision of performance based on more clearly measurable goals for both production and costs. Third, participation in decision making would be encouraged among employees throughout the organization in a fashion that reflected their abilities, needs, and motivations.

The results of this intervention remain impressive. Costs went up only 5 percent at a time when the country's currency devaluation rate went up 500 percent. This limited increase in cost was remarkable because, as a country's currency is devalued, the cost of importing goods increases, and Ghana imports almost all of the supplies needed for production. During the same time period, gold production increased by over 25 percent. In the years since the intervention, annual net profits have been well over $45 million. The company is currently the largest foreign exchange earner in Ghana, generating approximately 90 percent of the country's total earnings. Finally, the company has expanded its operations internationally, acquiring mines and subsidiary operations in other countries, and in February 1996, it became the first African company listed on the New York Stock Exchange.

Unfortunately, not all applications of I/O psychology are equally successful. One prominent example of an unsuccessful case from organizational psychology was the use of *T-groups* (the "T" stands for "training") or *sensitivity training* as a means of helping managerial personnel to relate better to each other and to their employees. T-groups began in the late 1940s and were popular through the 1960s and early 1970s. A T-group typically consisted of ten to twelve trainees who met for several hours each day for anywhere from two days to several weeks. Although there was no agenda or format for the group discussions, the members ideally would begin to talk about themselves and each other and, in the process, point out each others' weaknesses and strengths. Although T-groups increased interpersonal sensitivity or empathy, it was never clearly demonstrated that they changed the behavior of individuals in organizations. Furthermore, because sensitivity training sessions are often emotionally charged and very intrusive, some participants experience emotional and psychological harm. Studies of the aftereffects of participation in T-groups show psychological "casualty rates" of up to 50 percent.[28] It is not surprising that T-groups are rarely, if ever, used in business organizations today.

THE EFFECTS OF I/O PSYCHOLOGY ON PEOPLE IN THE WORKPLACE

Employment testing is one application of I/O psychology that has a major impact on the lives of many people. Personnel psychologists assist organizations in the development and implementation of employment practices that are nondiscriminatory, that is, they do not violate rules and guidelines set by the Equal Employment Opportunity Commission (EEOC) and other employment-related legislation. As part of this work, personnel psychologists devote a substantial amount of their time to the development and validation of employment tests, which constitute a major component of personnel selection in many organizations. I/O psychologists are particularly involved in efforts to ensure that tests or other tools used to make employment decisions are clearly job related, nondiscriminatory, and unbiased. The tools they evaluate include employment interviews, references and biographical information, work sampling procedures, assessment centers, drug testing, and tests of cognitive and personality dimensions such as conscientiousness and integrity, job knowledge, and job experience.

Demonstrating the fairness and job relatedness (relevance to job performance) of a selection system or other employment practice is not only important from a scientific and professional standpoint, but is also mandated by Title VII of the Civil Rights Act of 1964 and the Civil Rights Act of 1991. These statutes make it unlawful to discriminate on the basis of race, color, religion, sex, or national origin in employment settings. The Americans with Disabilities Act of 1990 and the Age Discrimination in Employment Act of 1967 make it illegal to discriminate on the basis of physical and mental disability and age (over age forty), respectively.

When a personnel tool results in a rate of selection in hiring, firing, promotion, or other employment decisions that is substantially different for, and work to the disadvantage of, members of a protected group, that tool is said to have an adverse impact. So, when an employment test displays adverse impact (say, by favoring men over women), the employer is required to demonstrate the job relatedness or business necessity of the test or else refrain from using it. Suppose that a fire department requires fifty push-ups and fifty pull-ups in its physical ability test for entry-level firefighters. To demonstrate the job relatedness of this test, I/O psychologists might be asked to design and implement studies that evaluate whether performance on the test is related to performance on the job, such that high performers on the test will also be high performers on the job and low performers on the test will do poorly on the job.

As part of their efforts to improve the usefulness of personnel tests, I/O psychologists have also evaluated the validity of employment interviews. Many employers believe that they can distinguish good employees from poor ones just by talking to them. However, the research on employment interviews demonstrates without a doubt that the typical unstructured employment interview conducted by supervisors is a poor predictor of job performance. Indeed, good interviews—those whose results *are* predictive of future job performance—call for a lot of work in their design and development. Most important, they must be structured and standardized.[29] This means that in a given application, all interviewees be asked the same questions in the same order and in the same way, and the resulting responses must be scored according to a common system.

Prominent Theories and Methods in I/O Psychology

Job performance is perhaps the most important construct in I/O psychology and human resource management. However, despite its importance, relatively little is known in theoretical terms about the structure of job performance.[30] Some recent research focusing on this issue has led to the development of some interesting theories of job performance.[31] These theories consider job performance to consist of task-specific elements (e.g., how good an auto mechanic is at fixing cars) and contextual elements, such as whether the employee volunteers for additional shifts or hours when a coworker calls in sick, socializes, helps and cooperates with other employees, and in general displays organizational "good citizenship."[32] The task-specific elements may best be predicted by looking at individuals' ability levels or what they are capable of; the contextual elements might be more evident in the answers to personality tests.[33] For example, a computer programming aptitude test may predict how good a programmer an individual will be, but a personality test that measures agreeableness and sociability may be a better predictor of how well the person will get along with other employees.

Another prominent I/O theory involves *goal setting*.[34] Goals have two major functions: they serve as the basis for motivation, that is, for deciding how much effort to put into a task, and they also direct behavior. Thus, goals are intended behaviors that influence actual behavior. There are two conditions that must be met before goals can positively influence behavior: (1) the individual must be aware of the goal and know what must be accomplished (so the goals must be clear and specific), and (2) the individual must see the goal as something that she or he is willing to work for (in other words, accept the goal and be committed to it). Given these conditions, the basic assumptions of goal-setting theory, which have been supported for more than twenty years through hundreds of empirical studies, are that specific, short-term, difficult goals lead to higher performance than either no goals, easy or moderate goals, or "do your best" goals.[35] Thus, the major factors that influence goal attainment are goal difficulty and how immediate the goal is. Feedback about how one is progressing toward a goal is important as well. Other factors that may be important, but have received less empirical support, include whether the goal is chosen by the individual or is imposed by someone else, how much monetary reward is associated with achieving the goal, the effect of type and complexity of the goal, and the influence of personality characteristics on various goal-related behaviors.

In business settings, the concept of goal setting underlies management by objectives (MBO), a management technique meant to increase employee performance. The MBO process has three steps. First, employees meet with their supervisor to set goals to achieve during a specified period of time. Consistent with goal-setting theory, the goals are specific, short term, and difficult but attainable. As part of this process, employees and supervisors may also discuss and establish how performance will be assessed or evaluated at the next review session. Second, throughout the performance period, progress toward the goal is monitored, although the employee is generally free to determine how to go about meeting the goals. Third, at the end of the performance period, the employee and supervisor meet to review the employee's performance, evaluate whether the set goals were achieved (feedback and knowledge of results), and decide on a new set of goals.

Management by objectives was a popular method of evaluating the performance of managers in the 1970s and 1980s. For instance, in surveys of performance appraisal techniques, more than half of the organizations responding reported using some kind of MBO procedure to evaluate managers' performance.[36] However, MBO is not as popular as it used to be.

Meta-analysis (also called validity generalization) is a relatively recent methodological development that has had a major impact on I/O psychology. Meta-analysis refers to a set of statistical procedures that combine the results of many studies and estimate the average outcomes or validity of the entire body of research.[37] Studies evaluating the ability of personnel assessment methods to predict future job performance have been conducted since the early twentieth century, but a review of these studies revealed that the results of different studies, using similar methods to predict performance on the same or similar jobs, failed to agree with one another. For example, three organizations might use the same test to select clerical staff, but each organization found different results. In one organization, the test scores might be very good at predicting job performance; in the second, the test scores might be less accurate in predicting job performance; and in the third, the test scores might have little relation at all to job performance. Findings such as these initially led to a belief that the relationship between tests and job performance is specific to each situation and does not generalize from one organization or setting to another (the *situational specificity hypothesis*). However, it turned out that some of the evidence for situational specificity was actually due to quirks in statistics and measurement methods, not to real differences in the jobs.[38] Thus, the results of meta-analyses have generally refuted the situational specificity hypothesis and demonstrated that the same test can indeed be useful across different settings. In fact, the conclusion that cognitive ability is the best predictor of performance across all jobs is based primarily on the results of meta-analyses.[39]

I/O PSYCHOLOGY AROUND THE WORLD

With the globalization of economies and marketplace, there is an increasing need to investigate the efficacy and generalization of I/O interventions to cultures and economic systems beyond those of North America.[40] Consequently, a number of studies of the effectiveness of I/O interventions, and their potential gain to organizations, are being pursued in various parts of the world.[41] For example, I/O psychologists found that Japanese organizations' job performance appraisal systems are quite different from those found in U.S. organizations.[42] Japanese organizations assume that employees will be with the company for a long time, so they focus on long-term rather than short-term results. Consequently, promotions and raises are based on seniority, there is an absence of demotions, and managers rely on appraisals from many sources instead of any particular one. In addition, the appraisal information is mainly used for promotional and bonus-related evaluations and less so placement, training and development, career guidance, or other purposes.

Approaches to management have also been found to be substantially different across various cultures.[43] For example, in response to a test of management styles and behavior (the Laurent Management Questionnaire), 63 percent of Chinese managers, but only 18 percent of U.S. managers, agreed that "the main reason for having a hierarchical structure is so that everyone knows who has authority over whom." Similarly, 34 percent of Chinese managers agreed that "most organizations would be better off if conflict could be eliminated," while only 6 percent of U.S. managers agreed with that statement. The overall pattern of responses to the test usually successfully described management styles and behavior in Europe and North America, but it failed to produce an accurate description of Chinese managerial behavior. The pattern of responses to the questionnaire items by Chinese managers was so different from that obtained for Western managers that it led the researchers to conclude that traditional Western conceptions of managerial behavior may not be transferable to Chinese organizations.[44]

In two West African countries (Ghana and Nigeria), on the other hand, researchers found that I/O practices were very similar to those reported for U.S. organizations.[45] Organizations in the West African countries generally used the same procedures for recruitment, selection, and performance appraisal, but there were some notable exceptions. For instance, it appears that organizations in Ghana and Nigeria do not routinely use standard U.S. recruitment techniques such as the use of employment agencies, college recruiting, and advertisements in professional and trade publications. This is not surprising, however, given that developing nations tend to have fewer colleges, agencies, or professional publications than are to be found in the United States.

In Europe, researchers have observed that available personnel selection procedures are comparable in different countries, although there is great country-to-country variation in the extent to which certain procedures are actually used.[46] For instance, in contrast to the United States, France still relies heavily on the use of handwriting analysis, and there tends to be a greater reliance on personality assessments and less use of biographical information.

In summary, there is increasing recognition that in spite of some similarities, cultural and national differences influence work values, organizational behaviors, and I/O and human resource management practices.[47]

ISSUES, CONTROVERSIES, AND INNOVATIONS IN I/O PSYCHOLOGY

As I/O psychology continues to expand, its practitioners find themselves facing a number of issues, controversies, and innovations in their work. Let's consider just a few of them.

Banding

Banding refers to a set of personnel evaluation procedures in which scores falling within a range, or band, are considered to be the same. Thus, for example, in college grades, test scores falling between 90 percent and 100 percent might all be considered A, scores between 80 percent and 89 percent B, and so on. When banding has been recommended or used in personnel selection, it has been based on the premise that since tests and other personnel assessment methods are never perfectly reliable, small differences in test scores do not necessarily represent real differences in the attribute being measured. Consequently, advocates of banding recommend that if several employees' test scores fall within the same range, then other factors, such as experience, should be used to rank-order these individuals for hiring or promotion. On the other hand, opponents of banding have been quick to point out what they see as its basic conceptual flaw. Specifically, scores differing by a relatively large magnitude (e.g., 90 percent versus 100 percent) might be considered to be "the same," while scores differing by only 1 percentage point (e.g., 89 percent versus 90 percent) might be "different." The scientific merit of banding, or lack thereof, is yet to be resolved.

There have also been some questions raised about the legal status of banding. Section 106 of the U.S. Civil Rights Act of 1991 states that it is unlawful for an employer "in connection with the selection or referral of applicants or candidates for employment or promotion to adjust the scores of, use different cutoffs for, or otherwise alter the results of employment related tests on the basis of race, color, religion, sex, or national origin." Because banding can be seen as a form of score adjustment, there has been some concern that its use is a violation of the Civil Rights Act of 1991. The current prevailing view is that banding per se does not violate the act, although the rank ordering or selection of individuals within a band on the basis of race, color, religion, sex, or national origin would be a clear violation.[48]

Predicting Job Performance from Personality

The importance of considering personality characteristics is attracting renewed attention in personnel selection and other employment contexts.[49] A search of PsycINFO, a computerized database, using "job performance and personality" as key words resulted in 205 citations from 1990 to 1997 compared to only 52 during 1960 to 1969. The renewed interest is attributable partly to the development of a new model of personality and partly to the results of recent meta-analytic studies and findings.

Meta-analytic statistical procedures make it possible to combine the results of many different studies. These procedures have made it possible to demonstrate more effectively the relationships between various personality differences and job-related issues.[50]

The new model of personality, called the "Big Five," or Five-Factor Model (FFM) of personality, describes people's personality in terms of openness, conscientiousness, extroversion, agreeableness, and neuroticism.[51] Because there are only five dimensions, it has become easier to get a clearer picture of personality differences and how they relate to some important behaviors.[52] For example, when researchers examined the relationship between conscientiousness and the likelihood of having an accident while driving, they found that individuals who rate themselves as more conscientious (more self-disciplined, responsible, reliable, and dependable) are less likely to have accidents than those who rate themselves lower on these qualities.[53] Consequently, companies hiring employees for positions that require a lot of driving may want to assess candidates not only for their driving ability but also for their conscientiousness.

The search for ideal personality traits is also supported by the opinions of workers. When they are asked in job analysis interviews to describe what is required for effective performance in the positions they already hold, "they typically describe characteristics such as 'being a team player,' 'remaining calm under pressure,' 'being responsive to the client's needs,' 'being persistent,' and 'taking initiative' as crucial for their jobs. These characteristics are precisely what well-constructed measures of normal personality assess."[54] Indeed, it seems that assessing qualities of personality as well as the skills required for the job will improve employers' ability to predict job performance and select the best employees.

Teams

The concept of teams is very popular in organizational development and management today. Teams are defined as a "distinguishable set of two or more individuals who interact interdependently and adaptively to achieve specified, shared, and valued objectives."[55] In other words, when people work as a team, they work together to figure out how best to accomplish a particular goal. Teams have received a great deal of research attention recently and have become a critical element in many organizations.[56] Today, organizational environments and the problems they generate are increasingly complex, unpredictable, and interrelated. Consequently, teamwork can be more effective than individual effort in addressing these problems. Furthermore, companies undergoing downsizing (layoffs) have had to change their organizational structure in order to operate with a smaller workforce. Accordingly, the work team is one of the most common organizational structures associated with downsizing.[57]

In a recent survey, three thousand managers and executives from twelve countries rated the development of good teamwork as one of the top business priorities for the year 2000.[58] Research shows that teams can work more effectively, innovatively, and productively because team members bring diverse resources and expertise to bear on a task. Many corporate leaders expect teams to improve production, increase profit margins, and bolster poor organizational morale.

With the surge in the use of teams in organizations, there has been a concurrent interest among I/O psychologists in how to select[59] and effectively train teams to work together.[60] Several studies[61] have furnished information on the differences between effective and ineffective teams, and others[62] have begun to develop guidelines for team training—for example, that every team member should be able to state the title and purpose of the team mission and there should be no more than six members in a group when performing problem-solving or decision-making tasks.

360-Degree Feedback

Traditionally, efforts to measure and understand job performance have been accomplished by using supervisors' ratings of employees' performance or, in some instances, objective indicators of performance, such as sales volume. More recently, I/O psychologists have begun to evaluate performance through multirater systems known as the *360-degree approach* (sometimes referred to as multi-rater feedback, multisource assessment, or upward feedback), which involves obtaining performance ratings from the employee, as well as the employee's supervisors, peers, and subordinates. A 1996 study by the American Management Association revealed that 13 percent of the companies surveyed used a 360-degree system, and the number is growing.[63]

There is some debate about whether multi-rater feedback is more appropriate to guide promotion, salary increase, and other administrative decisions or to provide feedback for training and self-improvement purposes. In any case, there is little doubt that 360-degree evaluation systems are innovative and allow employees to receive performance-related information from multiple perspectives. Ideally, this feedback provides a fuller, and thus more useful, description of work behaviors and performance. It also provides an excellent way for members of the growing number of organizational teams to provide constructive feedback to one another. These 360-degree systems can even be structured to incorporate performance data from sources outside the organization, such as customers and clients. Unfortunately, what little empirical research exists on the approach suggests that agreement among raters is generally lower than one might wish,[64] a finding that has led some researchers to question the value of 360-degree performance evaluation systems.[65]

New Modes of Assessment

In an attempt to identify employee performance predictors that are as free as possible from some of the problems typically associated with traditional paper-and-pencil tests, I/O psychologists have recently begun to focus their attention on developing tests based on simulated situations.[66] There are five major categories of simulation-based assessment techniques: (1) video-based job-related tests, (2) computerized simulation-based assessment of typical managerial decision making, (3) computerized case management simulations, (4) computerized dynamic case simulations, and (5) computerized microworld simulations.[67]

By far the most popular of these simulation-based assessments are video-based tests in which job applicants respond, orally or in writing, to videotaped items or stimuli, usually situational exercises or scenarios. In one such exercise, a job candidate is presented with the following scenario: A manager is upset about the condition of the department and takes it out on one of the department's employees. The manager says to the employee, "Well, I'm glad you're here." The employee answers, "Oh? Why's that?" The manager replies, "Look at this place! That's why! I take a day off and come back to find the department in a mess. You should know better." The employee's rebuttal is, "But, I didn't work last night," to which the manager responds, "Maybe not. But there have been plenty of times before when you've left this department in a mess." The job applicant is then asked to choose whether he or she would:

a. Let the other associates responsible for the mess know that he or she had to take the heat.
b. Straighten up the department, and try to reason with the manager later.
c. Suggest to the manager that he talk to the other associates who made the mess.
d. Take it up with the manager's boss.

The simulated situation is presented on a video screen preceded by an introductory narrative and is portrayed by professional actors. The assessment question and response options are then read by the narrator as they appear on the screen.[68]

Proponents of video-based testing claim that it has several advantages.[69] First, these tests have the ability to depict events and incidents that are richer and more detailed than the material contained in written stimuli. Second, for jobs that do not require reading skills, the use of video-based tests minimizes or eliminates the influence of a person's reading ability on test performance. Third, watching video-based stimuli provides job applicants with a realistic preview of the types of activities they are likely to encounter if they are hired. Fourth, applicants for a job are less likely to object to a test that appears to be measuring abilities that are important for doing the job than to one that appears to assess unrelated qualities.

The primary disadvantage of video-based tests is their cost—as much as $1,500 per finished minute of tape.[70] Another disadvantage is that the size of group test administrations is limited by the amount of equipment, especially video monitors, available. So although they are an innovative and potentially valuable tool for personnel assessment, simulation-based assessment methodologies do have their limitations,[71] and the jury is still out as to whether these new testing methodologies actually have less adverse impact than more traditional methods.[72] Just how serious the limitations of simulation-based assessment are is yet to be determined because research on it is still rather sparse.

CONCLUSION

I/O psychology has an impact in one way or another on every person in the workforce. Assessment centers are commonly used as a way to more accurately predict the performance of individuals in particular job settings. Employment tests are better and fairer than in the past, largely due to EEOC guidelines, which were shaped substantially by the research of I/O psychologists. Due to the efforts of I/O psychologists, many companies are more productive, workers have higher morale, and job safety has been improved. This is not to say that all of the problems of the business world have been solved, but as the field of I/O psychology improves its methods, its ability to solve the problems of businesses improves as well. Work is an important part of most people's lives, so by enhancing people's jobs, I/O psychologists are improving people's lives. Indeed, this is the ultimate source of satisfaction for psychologists who work with business and industry.

SUGGESTIONS FOR FURTHER READING

Aamodt, M. G. (1996). *Applied industrial/organizational psychology* (2nd ed.). Pacific Grove, CA: Brooks/Cole.

Dipboye, R. L., Smith, C. S., & Howell, W. C. (1994). *Understanding industrial/organizational psychology: An integrated approach.* New York: Harcourt Brace.

Miner, J. B. (1992). *Industrial-organizational psychology.* New York: McGraw-Hill.

Muchinsky, P. M. (1997). *Psychology applied to work: An introduction to industrial and organizational psychology* (5th. ed.). Pacific Grove, CA: Brooks/Cole.

Schultz, D. P., & Schultz, S. E. (1998). *Psychology and work today: An introduction to industrial and organizational psychology* (7th ed.). Saddle River, NJ: Prentice Hall.

Smither, R. D. (1998). *The psychology of work and human performance* (3rd ed.). New York: Longman.

CHAPTER 7

PSYCHOLOGY APPLIED TO SPORTS

Glyn C. Roberts and Darren C. Treasure

Mark was able to perform his gymnastics floor routine more or less flaw-lessly in practice—but not in competition. When a sport psychologist was asked to consult with the gymnastics team, his coaches were exasper-ated, and Mark was thinking of quitting. Mark's ability should have made him the top gymnast on the team in the floor exercise. But he always "choked" (his term) during competition, and his performance was hurting the team. When the psychologist began to work with the team, Mark was one of the "problems" he was asked to deal with.

When sport psychologists work with a team or an individual athlete in any sport, they begin by taking stock of the situation. In Mark's case, the psychologist began by chatting with him about his "choking," asked him to talk about how he felt when competing, and asked how it was different when he was in the practice gym. After these conversations, it became clear that Mark was probably experiencing acute competitive anxiety that was severe enough to affect his concentration and performance. In fact, he stated that he knew he was going to "blow it" before he competed. Observations of Mark in practice and in competition made it clear that he functioned differently in the two situations. In practice, he was relaxed and chat-ted with his teammates; in competition, he was agitated and did not speak very much with the rest of the team. The psychologist asked Mark if he was willing to try some things that might help his performance, and he agreed. Mark first learned some relaxation skills along with visualization so that he could begin to control his anxiety in competition. This training used simulated competition situations in which he could try using his anxiety management skills. Mark practiced his relax-ation techniques diligently, used thought blocking to erase visual images of failing, and learned to replace them with more positive images, such as performing the rou-tine correctly, just as he did in practice. With the psychologist's help, he developed a precompetition routine that included using relaxation techniques to keep his anxi-ety under control and to keep him loose while waiting to perform. Indeed, his per-formance began to improve. But the psychological work did not end there. Mark asked the psychologist if he would speak to his coach about the coach's behavior during gymnastic meets. He said that the coach typically came up to him just before he competed and "got in his face" about how important it was for him to do well on his routine. Mark knew the coach was trying to motivate him, but this approach was only making Mark more nervous. Accordingly, during a meeting with the coach and the psychologist, Mark told the coach how he wanted to be dealt with just before a competition. The coach agreed to change his behavior, and did so. Mark began to feel more comfortable, and by the end of the season he was beginning to hit his routine most of the time. Although he still got somewhat apprehensive, the techniques he learned helped him to cope with the anxiety associated with athletic competition.

The case of Mark is typical of what applied sport psychologists do: they consult with individuals or teams to help athletes develop and use psychological skills that optimize those athletes' performance in competition. Sport psychologists are employed on a full-time or part-time basis by the U.S. Olympic Committee (USOC), many professional teams, and some major universities. Many individual athletes, including professional golfers and tennis players, track and field competitors, and equestrians, also engage sport psychologists as consultants. And almost all sports medicine clinics today employ a sport psychologist as part of their efforts to deliver sports science services to athletes. One of the newest trends is for sport psychologists to be employed as consultants to the fitness industry. Still, helping athletes perform better is only one aspect of sport psychology. In this chapter, we will review its other aspects, beginning with the story of how sport psychology developed as an academic and applied field. We will also discuss some of the critical issues facing this rapidly emerging arena of applied psychology.

A BRIEF HISTORY OF SPORT PSYCHOLOGY

It can be argued that the first social psychology experiment, published in 1897 by Norman Triplett in the *American Journal of Psychology,* was also the first study in sport psychology. Triplett was fascinated by the fact that bicycle riders always seemed to perform better when riding or competing with others than when performing alone. In his now-classic study, he proposed a "dynamogenic" explanation for the phenomenon, suggesting that the presence of others arouses riders' competitive drive. To demonstrate this effect, he asked children to perform a fishing-reel-winding task, either alone or with another child. Most of the time, he found, the children performed the task faster when they were in the presence of a peer who was doing the same task at the same time.

It was not until 1920 that the world's first sport psychology laboratory was founded by Carl Diem at the Deutsche Sporthochschule in Berlin, Germany. Five years later, in 1925, A. Z. Puni opened a sport psychology laboratory at the Institute of Physical Culture in Leningrad. That same year, Coleman Griffith of the University of Illinois at Urbana–Champaign established the first sport psychology laboratory in North America. Griffith had begun his research into psychological factors that affect sport performance in 1918, and in 1923 he offered the first course in sport psychology.[1]

Griffith was interested in the effects on athletic performance of factors such as reaction time, mental awareness, muscular tension and relaxation, and personality. He worked with the University of Illinois football teams (including legendary coach Robert Zupke and famous players such as Red Grange), consulted with the Chicago Cubs baseball team in 1938,[2] and corresponded with Notre Dame coach Knute Rockne about psychological and motivational aspects of coaching and athletics.[3] Between 1919 and 1931, Griffith published two books, *The Psychology of Coaching* (1926)—the first book in sport psychology—and *Psychology of Athletics* (1928), and twenty-five articles on sport psychology. Because of the financial constraints imposed by the Great Depression, Griffith's laboratory was closed in 1932, and although he continued his academic career (he was university provost from 1944 until his retirement in 1953), he was a "prophet without disciples."[4]

In North America, little or no research in sport psychology took place between the closing of Griffith's laboratory and the 1960s. True, a few books were published,[5] and people such as Franklin Henry at the University of California at Berkeley taught and conducted some research on motor learning, but it was not until the late 1960s and early 1970s that sport psychology again emerged with any real momentum on North American campuses. Then, rather quickly, physical education departments in many institutions began to offer courses in sport psychology, and graduate programs in sport psychology started to appear. The upsurge in interest resulted from coaches' growing recognition that although they had a lot of knowledge about the physiology and mechanics of performance, the influence of psychological factors was not well understood. Many of the new courses were initially aimed mainly at helping students apply psychological principles in their future roles as coaches and physical education teachers.[6] However, as physical education departments began to shift their focus away from preparing teachers and toward research on athletic performance, the role of sport psychology within these departments also changed. These changes were reflected in the fact that during the 1970s and 1980s many departments of physical education changed their names to "kinesiology" or "sport science."

Important as these developments were, the most significant stimulus to the growth of sport psychology was the formation of academic societies and scholarly journals devoted to professionals in this emerging field. In 1965, the International Society of Sport Psychology (ISSP) was formed by scientists from across Europe, and its first international congress was held that same year in Rome. Several scientists from North America who attended this first ISSP meeting were asked to consider hosting the next international congress. In 1966, a group of sport psychologists met in Chicago to discuss the formation of a society for sport psychology. They became the steering committee that founded the North American Society of Sport Psychology and Physical Activity (NASPSPA) and held its first official meeting in Las Vegas in 1967. Arthur Slatter-Hammell of Indiana University was the first president of NASPSPA, whose membership jumped from around 60 to 214 in just the first three years. As of 1997, that figure had increased to 550 members whose interests focus on three main areas: sport psychology, motor learning, and motor control.

The first scholarly journal devoted to sport psychology, the *International Journal of Sport Psychology,* was established in 1970, followed in 1979 by the *Journal of Sport Psychology*. Its name was changed in 1988 to *Journal of Sport and Exercise Psychology* in order to reflect the expanding research base dealing with exercise and health psychology issues.

Increasing interest in conducting sport psychology research in settings outside the laboratory was stimulated in 1979 by an article written by Rainer Martens, "About Smocks and Jocks." Martens criticized the laboratory-based research findings that dominated the field at the time because they often did not generalize to the situations in which athletes actually found themselves.[7] He said it was time for researchers to get out of their labs and into actual athletic competition settings. This article stimulated research in applied settings and led to a transformation of academic sport psychology that included application as a major focus of the field.[8] So although NASPSPA continued to focus primarily on theoretical research and academic issues, a new society, the Association for the Advancement of Applied Sport Psychology (AAASP), was formed in 1985 to focus more directly on applied psychology in both the health field and the sport context—that is, on the delivery of psychological services to athletes and coaches of collegiate and professional teams, and to discuss and compare experiences related to these services.

With nearly a thousand members, AAASP is now the largest international sport psychology society in the world. Its purpose is to provide a forum to address applied aspects of sport psychology such as the promotion of applied research in the areas of social, health, and performance enhancement psychology; the promotion of the appropriate application of these research findings; and the examination of professional issues (such as ethical standards) qualifications for becoming a sport psychologist, and certification of sport psychologists.[9] Among AAASP's other objectives, it seeks to promote the field of sport psychology within psychology itself and to encourage membership from interested individuals trained in other areas of psychology and related disciplines, as well as from sport scientists trained in departments of physical education, sport and exercise, and kinesiology. These latter objectives appear to have been met: 40 percent of AAASP's members hold degrees in some area of psychology.[10] Further, mainstream psychology's recognition of the growth and impact of professional sport psychology was formalized by the establishment in 1987 of Division 47 (Exercise and Sport Psychology) within the American Psychological Association (APA). The growth in applied sport psychology research during the 1980s was reflected in the development of two journals devoted exclusively to publishing that research. *The Sport Psychologist,* an official ISSP journal, which first appeared in 1987, focuses mainly on research and articles dealing with performance enhancement. In 1989, the *Journal of Applied Sport Psychology* was established as the official journal of AAASP. Its content is somewhat broader, including the areas of social psychology, health psychology, and performance enhancement.

The growth and recognition of applied sport psychology has been supported by publicity stemming from sport psychologists' work with elite athletes, particularly those who compete in the Olympics or in professional sports. The nature of this consultation activity has shifted dramatically since it first became common-place in the 1960s. In those years, as sport scientists' research helped illuminate the physiological demands of competition, applied sport science focused on helping athletes employ new and improved ways of becoming physically fit. Consultation included advising athletes on dietary practices that would better meet the nutritional demands of their sport and on refining athletic techniques on the basis of research in biomechanics. It was not until the late 1970s that consultants in applied sport psychology began to center on the psychological aspects of athletic performance. During the 1980s and 1990s, there was an explosive growth in athletes' use of sport psychology consultants to help them prepare mentally to do their best. Many athletes balked initially at the idea of hiring a sport psychologist, because—as tends to be true for people in general—they perceived that they would be confessing a weakness or revealing a psychological disorder. Today, however, most athletes recognize that sport psychologists can help them to take a better mental approach to their sport. Indeed, many athletes don't bat an eye as they talk about their use of a sport psychologist. And in professional sports, where athletes, coaches, and team owners can earn astronomical sums of money, anything that can give an athlete or team a competitive edge is important, including the mental and emotional strength they can get with the help of sport psychologists.

The first indication of interest by the USOC in using sport psychologists to help Olympic athletes improve their performance came in 1978, when the committee recruited expert advisers in four branches of sport science: biomechanics, exercise physiology, nutrition, and sport psychology. This step came only two years after a psychologist, for the first time, had been assigned to be with the U.S. athletes during the 1976 Olympic Games. By 1983, the USOC had established a Sport Psychology Committee and a registry of qualified sport psychologists identified as specializing in research, educational, or clinical sport psychology. As a result, sport psychologists have played an increasingly prominent role in the preparation of U.S. Olympic athletes. In 1984 psychological services were routinely provided to U.S. team members at both the Summer and Winter Olympics,[11] and in 1989, an entire issue of *The Sport Psychologist* was devoted to reporting on the delivery of sport psychology services to U.S. and Canadian athletes during the 1988 Olympics.[12] (The following year, an issue of the same journal was devoted to sport psychologists' work with professional teams.)[13] Since then, the involvement of sport psychologists in Olympic competition has continued to increase.

The recent publication of books by prominent sport psychologists—such as *Golf Is Not a Game of Perfect*,[14] *The New Mental Toughness Guide to Sport*,[15] and *The Achievement Zone*[16]—has also helped to propel sport psychology into public awareness and to interest many individuals trained in various subfields of psychology and related fields to consider the research and consultation opportunities that may exist for them in sport psychology. Although the early history of sport psychology was dominated by physical education, sport psychology has now evolved into an interdisciplinary field, involving sport scientists from disciplines such as physiology, nutrition, biomechanics, and psychology. Similarly, although initial interest focused on sport performance, particularly the performance of elite athletes, sport psychol ogists have broadened their interests considerably. Performance enhancement remains a significant area of research and applied work, but understanding and improving the quality of physical activity for all segments of the population has emerged as an emphasis of many sport psychology researchers and practitioners.[17] As the backgrounds of the researchers and practitioners in the field have become more diverse, debate has inevitably arisen over issues such as the training needed to become a sport psychologist, the competencies required to be publicly labeled as a sport psychologist, and the ethical standards of professional conduct to be expected of those in the field.[18] We will discuss these issues later.

Today, the academic discipline of sport psychology in the United States is almost exclusively housed in university departments of kinesiology, sport science, or physical education. Indeed, no more than 20 percent of the 1989–1994 doctoral graduates in sport psychology received their degrees from psychology or counseling departments, and of those who did complete psychology degrees, some focused on nonclinical areas.[19] In other words, there does not appear to be any trend for psychology or counseling departments to replace kinesiology or sport science departments as the dominant home for graduate programs in sport psychology.

It should come as no surprise that courses in sport psychology, and most faculty who consider themselves sport psychologists in U.S. universities, are still found in departments of kinesiology or sport science. These academic sport psychologists conduct research on the impact of psychological variables on sport and exercise performance and participation, and vice versa. The picture in applied sport psychology is more complicated. Although many psychology professionals working in nonuniversity settings in North America call themselves sport psychologists, few have received any formal education in sport psychology. Few psychology training programs offer course work in the sport area, and the study of athletes is almost nonexistent in graduate psychology and counseling programs.

Individuals who have a doctorate in clinical or counseling psychology and work in the area of sport psychology are trained to assume a variety of traditional clinical roles, both in and out of sport, but their graduate programs do not prepare them for the unique situations created by the competitive sport experience or to deal with the performance enhancement goals that many of their athlete-clients seek. In one survey involving more than a thousand athletes seen over a six-year period at the Olympic Training Center in Colorado Springs, typical complaints included anxiety at competitions, concentration during performance, lack of motivation in the face of grueling training schedules, worry over whether they would be successful and their efforts rewarded, and problems communicating with a coach or fellow athlete.[20] So although athletes can, and do, develop psychological disorders (e.g., eating disorders and substance abuse) that require the specialized skills of a clinician, many teams and athletes prefer to consult with individuals who have a more extensive sport science background. As a consequence, opportunities have emerged for practitioners of a new field known as *educational applied sport psychology*. Psychologists working in this field are trained with less focus on the assessment and treatment of mental disorders than on sport and exercise science. Thus, many students pursuing sport psychology degrees in programs housed in departments of kinesiology or sport and exercise science take advanced training in counseling and psychology as part of their graduate degree requirements. Through individual and group sessions, these professionals then educate athletes (and coaches) on the use of anxiety management, confidence building, time management, and other psychological skills that may help athletes cope with intense pressure. Though their approach is educational rather than clinical, it may be wrong to assume that all their athletic clients are emotionally or mentally stable and interested only in performance enhancement goals.[21] Doing so can lead the unwary practitioner to ignore an athlete's serious psychological problems.

As one might expect from this history, considerable confusion exists in the field of sport psychology concerning its nature, goals, and priorities, primarily because three groups of professionals regard themselves as sport psychologists: the academic and research oriented, the clinically trained, and the educational sport psychologist. And because of their different educational experiences and training, these three groups see the issues in their field from different perspectives. For example, in applied sport psychology, educational psychologists are concerned that the field is, or will soon be, dominated by clinicians who have little, if any, knowledge of sport and who are perpetuating the idea that sport psychologists are "shrinks" who deal with "crazy" athletes. Clinical psychologists argue that people who take mainly an educational approach, primarily by teaching athletes psychological skills, will not be sensitive enough to any underlying psychopathology. And the academic and research-oriented psychologist may be concerned that those who focus too much on application will rely on their own experiences rather than information obtained from more objective and controlled experimental studies. Let's now turn to some of the most significant issues facing the field of sport psychology today.

CURRENT ISSUES IN APPLIED SPORT PSYCHOLOGY

Current issues in applied sport psychology focus on questions such as: What credentials should a sport psychologist have and how and where should sport psychologists be trained? What are the unique ethical issues facing sport psychology? What opportunities exist for sport psychologists?[22]

Credentials and Training

Since sport psychology is a relatively new field and draws practitioners from many different backgrounds, there has been some controversy over who can call themselves a "sport psychologist." Could it be someone who is a psychologist as well as an experienced athlete or coach? Is it enough to be a psychologist who is familiar with the literature in sport psychology? In general, the answers are "no" because the guidelines of the APA stipulate that psychologists working within a specialized area are competent to practice only within their boundaries of competence.[23]

In order to help define the areas of competence, the APA and the Association for the Advancement of Applied Sport Psychology (AAASP) have recently developed criteria that are now used in two national certification programs.[24] The criteria include, first, a doctoral degree from an accredited institution of higher education. Second, they require knowledge in various areas: scientific and professional ethics and standards; sports-related intervention and performance enhancement procedures, as well as the historical, philosophical, social, or motor behavioral bases of sport; health and exercise psychology; social psychology; psychopathology and its assessment; and the biomechanical and physiological, cognitive, affective, and social bases of behavior. Third, it is essential to be familiar with skills in research design and statistics, basic skills in counseling, and particular skills and techniques related to sport or exercise. In addition to meeting these criteria, supervised experience with a qualified person (one who has an appropriate background in applied sport psychology) is required. During supervision, the individual receives training in using sport psychology principles and techniques with an appropriate sport or exercise population. In 1994, AAASP also approved requirements for the recertification of certified consultants and requirements for an increase to four hundred hours for the certification supervised internship. Meeting the AAASP criteria means that the title "Certified Consultant AAASP" may be used. It does not, however, allow use of the title "psychologist" because such use is restricted by laws in each state and province of North America. Individuals who satisfy both AAASP and APA standards can become members of the USOC's Registry of Sport Psychologists.

AAASP certification is recommended by the Executive Committee of Division 47 (Exercise and Sport Psychology) of the APA if a psychologist wants to practice sport psychology or use the title "sport psychologist," but considerable debate about the validity and fairness of the AAASP criteria continues within the psychology and sport science communities. Some, for example, argue that the criteria are not defined precisely enough, and others fear that the criteria may exclude many qualified individuals, especially those whose main training is in kinesiology. Still others are concerned that the criteria, which bridge the fields of psychology and kinesiology, are so extensive that few existing university programs can satisfy all the necessary courses and experiences for students to achieve AAASP certification. Consequently, graduate students currently in training have to take courses in at least two, and perhaps more, different university departments.[25] However, a recent tracking survey of the 1989–1994 graduates of sport psychology programs has found that most graduate students were able to take course work that satisfied most of the AAASP criteria.[26] Finally, there is some debate about the different needs of students who wish to pursue a career in applied sport psychology (that is, those planning to work directly with athletes) versus those who want to focus on research. For the latter, some of the AAASP criteria, such as those involving counseling skills, may not be necessary. The British Association of Sport and Exercise Sciences has recognized this issue and accredits individuals as either research scientists in sport and exercise science, or as consulting sport psychologists.

Although there is no consensus about the competency and knowledge base of applied sport psychology, most individuals in the field agree that those wishing to enter the profession of applied sport psychology must participate in a recognized training experience that adequately prepares them for practice. However, it remains to be seen whether the AAASP certification criteria will be widely accepted by the sport psychology community, colleges, universities, and, perhaps most important, the institutions of sport and the elite athletes who pay for the services of applied sport psychologists and who may be more impressed by someone who has "smelled the sweat" in a top-level dressing room as a player than by someone with a long list of academic credentials.

Ethics

Sport psychologists, like all other professionals serving the public, sometimes encounter situations in which it is not easy to determine the right course of action. For example, although coaches usually recruit sport psychologists, athletes become the clients. This situation can create ethical problems if the coach asks the psychologist for information about an athlete that may violate the athlete's right to confidentiality. Another situation requiring ethical considerations arises when a professional or Olympic athlete informs the sport psychologist that he or she is going to credit the psychologist publicly for improved performance, a situation that occurs frequently in the world of sports but rarely in other consulting and clinical settings.[27] The problem here is that psychologists' ethical guidelines, which currently are the same for sport psychologists as for clinical psychologists, do not allow them to solicit testimonials from clients.[28] Therefore, although the endorsement is tempting because it may provide the psychologist with future clients, the sport psychologist has to ensure that the testimonial was in no way requested from the client. Because situations such as this one present different ethical challenges from those encountered in other clinical or therapeutic situations, many in the field of sport psychology propose that sport psychology develop its own specific ethical guidelines.[29] These guidelines are needed, they say, because much of the work done by sport psychologists is not necessarily clinical or therapeutic in nature, as when the focus is on performance enhancement or training in psychological skills such as relaxation techniques and positive imaging.[30] Indeed, it has been suggested that a code of ethics designed specifically for sport psychology is a vital aspect of the professionalization of the field.[31]

Opportunities

The primary employment opportunity for individuals trained in sport psychology at the Ph.D. level is an academic position at a university. A recent study tracking the careers of graduates in sport psychology found that 59 percent of them hold positions in kinesiology departments, 13 percent in psychology or counseling departments, 9 percent in private practice, 7 percent in university or private research, 3 percent in business, 3 percent in student services for athletes, 2 percent in physical education or coaching, 1 percent in sports medicine, and 3 percent in other areas.[32] Of those in kinesiology departments, the majority taught sport psychology or conducted research in the area (88 percent and 75 percent, respectively). Fifty-one percent consulted with athletes, although only 2 percent spent more than half their time consulting. The graduates who were employed in psychology departments spent much less time teaching, doing research, or consulting about sport psychology. Therefore, if an individual wishes primarily to consult with athletes, a university position in kinesiology or psychology does not currently offer that opportunity.[33]

CONCLUSION

There are still many unanswered questions about the future of sport psychology in North America.[34] For example, will sport psychologists take a more active role in educating coaches and athletes regarding psychological training and techniques for improving performance and personal growth? What will be the impact of AAASP's certification standards on graduate curricula? Will the training of sport psychologists take place in kinesiology, sport science, and/or psychology departments? Will the acceptance of sport psychology by mainstream psychology continue to grow? How will the emergence of exercise psychology affect sport psychology at the graduate level and in the university job market? How can the various organizations in sport psychology— AAASP, NASPSPA, and APA Division 47—complement each other? Will the demand for applied sport psychology increase as, for example, professional and collegiate teams hire more sport psychologists? If so, what services will future sport psychologists be expected, and qualified, to deliver?

It is probably safe to say that sport psychology programs will continue to be housed in departments of kinesiology and/or sport science, not in psychology departments. A recent survey of clinical psychology chairpersons indicated that they do not consider sport psychology to be a major component of psychology departments.[35] This situation is not unusual[36] and reflects developments in some other areas of psychology. For example, school psychologists are often trained in departments of education, not psychology departments, and some clinical psychologists are trained in independent professional schools specifically geared to provide clinical training. However, with regard to sport psychology, more collaboration in the future between departments of psychology and home departments of current programs of sport psychology may eventually place sport sciences as a specialty area within psychology departments.

If present trends continue, and they show no signs of abatement, demand for sport psychologists will continue to grow. Thus, opportunities to consult will likely grow. But, when one considers that most sport psychologists today consult only part time and that most sport psychologists are currently employed full time in university departments, there may be restrictions on the growth of sport psychology due to reduced funding at universities and the downsizing of many programs, including sport psychology. Already there is some overproduction of graduate students in sport psychology, and the competition to be employed is keen. Thus, the future is not as rosy as one would wish. Still, other employment opportunities may develop. One area growing rapidly is health and exercise psychology. As many people become aware that healthy lifestyles can significantly improve their quality of life, demand for exercise psychology consultants may increase. Also, more university athletic departments are employing full-time sport psychology consultants to work with teams (for example, Pennsylvania State and Ohio State University Athletic Departments now employ full-time sport psychology consultants*).

The greatest growth in sport psychology may result from increasingly sharing information gained from sport psychology research and practice with those who would benefit from that information: physical education teachers, coaches at all levels, fitness instructors, physical therapy professionals, parents whose children are involved in sports, sports medicine consultants, and the like. Thus, sport psychology in the future may expand beyond the traditional university appointments and services to elite athletes, to provide consultation and information to a much broader audience.

Suggestions for Further Reading

Hardy, L., Jones, G., & Gould, D. (1996). *Understanding psychological preparation for sport: Theory and practice of elite performers.* New York: Wiley.

Roberts, G. C. (in press). *Advances in motivation in sport and exercise.* Champaign, IL: Human Kinetics.

Weinberg, R., & Gould, D. (1999). *Introduction to sport psychology* (2nd ed.). Champaign, IL: Human Kinetics.

Williams, J. M. (1998). *Applied sport psychology* (3rd ed.). London: Mayfield Publishing.

---

*This title was chosen by AAASP, although many who work with athletes believe that "Performance Enhancement Consultant" would be a more descriptive title.

PSYCHOLOGY APPLIED TO THE LEGAL SYSTEM

Michael T. Nietzel

P sychology's application to legal issues has become one of the fastest-growing and most controversial areas of research and practice in contemporary applied psychology.

The history of psychology's relevance to the legal system dates at least to the turn of the twentieth century. In 1901, William Stern studied the accuracy of memory by presenting pictures to students for forty-five seconds and then asking them to recall the content of the pictures at various intervals.[1] These experiments preceded today's research on the reliability of eyewitness testimony and led Stern to conclude that inaccurate memories were very common, particularly in answer to leading questions.

Hugo Münsterberg is often credited as being the first forensic (law-related) psychologist; however, his book, *On the Witness Stand,* was not published until 1908, several years after Stern's work and after Alfred Binet and Sigmund Freud had already proposed that psychological tests could have implications for judicial proceedings. Both Binet and Freud suggested that unusual delays or responses in either word association or reaction time tests might reveal the guilt or innocence of defendants. These ideas anticipated modern techniques of lie detector tests.[2]

Applications of psychology to law enforcement began in 1916, when Lewis Terman, the Stanford University psychologist who revised Alfred Binet's intelligence scales to produce the Stanford-Binet intelligence test, assessed the intelligence of thirty applicants for police and firefighting jobs in San Jose, California. A few years later, another testing pioneer, L. L. Thurstone, tested the intelligence of police candidates in Detroit. Assessments of this type gradually became an accepted practice, and psychological screening of police candidates for intelligence and personality characteristics is now routine in most departments.

The use of psychological research and theory to critique legal practices, guide attorneys in trial preparation, and formulate theories of criminal behavior appeared periodically throughout the 1920s and 1930s. In addition, special interest developed in extending psychological practice to police work.

Currently, the demand for psychologists to contribute in various ways to the legal system has grown to the point where almost two thousand psychologists belong to the American Psychology-Law Society, a division of the American Psychological Association.[3]

THE SCOPE OF LEGAL PSYCHOLOGY

The roles that applied psychologists play in the legal system are concentrated in four general areas: law enforcement psychology, the psychology of litigation, correctional psychology, and forensic psychology.

Law enforcement psychology is devoted to research on the activities of law enforcement agencies and direct clinical services to these agencies. A psychologist might test candidates for police work to screen out those who are not psychologically fit, offer crisis intervention to police officers who have been involved in violent encounters, consult with detectives about what kind of individual might have committed a certain type of crime, or hypnotize witnesses for the purpose of enhancing their recollection of crime events.[4]

The *psychology of litigation* is concerned with the effects of various legal procedures used in civil or criminal proceedings. Litigation consultants offer advice to attorneys about jury selection, study the factors that influence jury deliberations and verdicts, and analyze the effects of different portions of the typical trial (such as opening statements, cross-examination of witnesses, or closing arguments).

Correctional psychology is concerned primarily with the delivery of psychological services to individuals who are confined in prison after having been convicted of a crime. Most correctional psychologists are employed in prisons, penitentiaries, or special juvenile facilities, but they may also work out of a probation office or be part of a special community-based correctional program.

Forensic psychology (and forensic psychiatry) involves applying mental health knowledge and expertise to questions about individuals who are involved in a legal proceeding. Such questions cover an enormous range of issues. For example: Is an individual so mentally ill and potentially dangerous as to justify involuntary hospitalization? Is a person charged with a crime mentally competent to stand trial? Has a person suffered psychological harm as a result of an injury or trauma, and if so, how serious are the consequences? Did a person possess an adequate understanding at the time he or she drafted a will? These are just a few of the questions answered by forensic psychologists, who apply the skills and techniques of their profession to individual cases and then offer testimony at civil and criminal trials or other legal proceedings.

From the public's point of view, a psychologist's role as *expert witness** is one of the most controversial of all legally related activities. Psychologists and psychiatrists have testified in some of the most notorious trials in recent U.S. history, including those of the Menendez brothers, O. J. Simpson, Jeffrey Dahmer, Susan Smith, and John Hinckley. In his 1994 book, *The Abuse Excuse,* attorney Alan Dershowitz denounced much of this type of testimony as simply providing obviously guilty defen-

---

*In this role, not only forensic but also clinical, social, and school psychologists may offer their expertise.

dants with a way to avoid being held responsible for their crimes. One commentator summed up such skepticism when he referred to trial testimony by mental health experts as the time to "send in the clowns."

Psychologists and psychiatrists testify in approximately 8 percent of all trials held in federal civil courts, and mental health professionals participate in as many as 1 million cases each year.[5] Three factors are responsible for the widespread use of mental health experts. Expert testimony is frequent, first, because there are a lot of topics to testify about. For example, experts may testify about the characteristics of a defendant, such as his or her mental condition, ability to understand the legal proceedings, prospects for benefiting from rehabilitation, or potential for being a danger to society. Or they may address procedural issues, such as the accuracy of eyewitness identifications and the effects of various pretrial or trial processes. They may also offer their expertise in relation to the psychological damage an individual may have suffered as a result of an assault or other wrongful conduct. In child custody or adoption cases, they may prescribe which psychological factors ought to be considered in deciding on the placement of the child. In addition, psychologists have been called on to contribute their knowledge to larger social issues, such as the effects of pornography, violence, and spouse abuse. As scientists learn more about human behavior, attorneys are likely to find psychological information even more helpful in court cases.

Second, expert testimony flourishes because the law encourages it. Since the mid-1970s, U.S. courts have relaxed their standards for admitting the testimony of experts. In general, a qualified expert can testify on a topic if "scientific, technical, or other specialized knowledge will assist the trier of fact to understand the evidence or to determine a fact in issue" (Federal Rule of Evidence 702). In 1993, the U.S. Supreme Court ruled in *Daubert* v. *Merrell Dow* that judges can decide when expert testimony is based on sufficiently relevant and reliable scientific evidence to be admitted. This decision encourages consideration of innovative testimony, such as references to new psychological syndromes that victims are alleged to suffer and psychological profiling of certain types of victims or assailants. Many critics, including experts themselves, fear that this kind of testimony will lead judges—especially those who cannot distinguish valid from invalid research—to expose jurors occasionally to testimony based on "junk science" rather than standard empirical methods and sound scientific principles.

Finally, expert testimony thrives because it can be lucrative. At hourly rates ranging from $100 to $400, forensic experts can earn thousands of dollars per case. Moreover, if one party in a trial hires an expert, the other side usually feels compelled to do so as well. Consequently, the use of psychological expertise feeds on itself and has become a significant source of income for many professionals.

This chapter concentrates on the practice of forensic psychology. The following five areas of practice illustrate the range of cases in which forensic psychologists become involved: (1) competence to stand trial and criminal responsibility, (2) psychological damages in civil trials, (3) civil competencies, (4) psychological autopsies and criminal profiling, and (5) child custody and parental fitness. These five areas only scratch the surface of forensic topics. New research issues are constantly being addressed, and professional psychological services are continuing to expand in law enforcement agencies, courtrooms, and prisons.[6]

CRIMINAL COMPETENCE AND RESPONSIBILITY

No other area of law illustrates the controversies surrounding expert testimony as dramatically as testimony about whether a defendant was insane while committing an illegal act. Proving insanity can result in a defendant's being acquitted or, if convicted, protected from the punishment that would otherwise ensue.

Courts allow defendants' mental condition to be considered at trial because most societies believe it is immoral to punish people who, as a result of a mental disorder, either do not know that their actions are wrong or cannot control their conduct. These societies see punishment as fully deserved only by those who can understand the nature and wrongfulness of their criminal behavior.

Criminal Competence

In the United States and Canada, it is not permissible to continue criminal proceedings against a defendant who is unable to understand the nature and purpose of those proceedings. Thus, before a court ever considers whether a defendant is guilty or not guilty, sane or insane, it must first decide about the defendant's competence to stand trial. Defendants are considered incompetent if, as a result of a mental disorder, they cannot (1) understand the nature of their trial, (2) participate meaningfully in their own defense, or (3) benefit from consultation with their attorney. Note that competence refers to the defendant's mental condition *at the time of the trial,* whereas insanity, described next, refers to the defendant's mental condition *at the time of an alleged offense.*

The law requires defendants to be competent for several reasons.[7] First, legal proceedings are more likely to arrive at accurate results with the participation of competent defendants. Second, punishment of convicted defendants is morally acceptable in our society only if they understand why they are being punished. Finally, the perceived fairness of our adversary system of justice (prosecution versus defense) requires participation by defendants who have the capacity to defend themselves against the charges of the state.

Since competence refers to an understanding of legal proceedings, the criteria for competence depend partially on whether the defendant understands those proceedings. Psychologists are sometimes asked to evaluate a defendant's competence to confess to criminal charges, waive the right to an attorney, refuse use of the insanity defense, or be executed after conviction of a capital crime. Different questions are involved in each of these evaluations because different tasks require different capabilities. (Questions about other competencies also arise in civil law, which are discussed later in this chapter.)

Here is an example of a case in which the question of competence to stand trial was raised:

Jamie Sullivan was a twenty-four-year-old grocery store clerk charged with arson, burglary, and murder in connection with a fire he had set at a small grocery store in Kentucky. The evidence in the case was that after closing hours, Sullivan had returned to the store where he worked and forced the night manager, Ricky Ford, to open the safe and hand over $800 in cash. Sullivan then locked Ford in a small back-room office, doused the room in gasoline, and set the store on fire. Ford was killed in the blaze. Police arrested Sullivan within hours at his grandmother's apartment on the basis of a lead from a motorist who saw Sullivan running away from the scene. If convicted on all charges, Sullivan faced the possibility of a death sentence.

Jamie Sullivan was mentally retarded. He had dropped out of school in the eighth grade, and a psychologist's evaluation of him at that time reported his IQ to be 68. He could read and write his name and a few simple phrases, but nothing more. He had a history of drug abuse and, after vandalizing five homes in his neighborhood, had spent several months in a juvenile correctional camp at the age of fifteen. The army refused his attempt to volunteer for service because of his limited intelligence and drug habit. His attorney believed that Sullivan's mental problems might render him incompetent to stand trial and therefore asked a psychologist to evaluate him.

After interviewing and testing Sullivan, and reviewing the evidence the police had collected, the psychologist found the following: Sullivan's current IQ was 65, which fell in the mentally retarded range; he did not suffer any hallucinations or delusions, but he expressed strong religious beliefs that "God watches over his children and won't let nothing happen to them." The psychologist asked Sullivan a series of questions about his upcoming trial, to which he gave the following answers:

Q: What are you charged with?
A: Burning down that store and stealing from Ricky.
Q: Anything else?
A: They say I killed Ricky too.
Q: What could happen to you if a jury found you guilty?
A: Electric chair, but God will watch over me.
Q: What does the judge do at a trial?
A: He tells everybody what to do.
Q: If somebody told a lie about you in court, what would you do?
A: Get mad at him.
Q: Anything else?
A: Tell my lawyer the truth.
Q: What does your lawyer do if you have a trial?
A: Show the jury I'm innocent.
Q: How could he do that best?
A: Ask questions and have me tell them I wouldn't hurt Ricky. I liked Ricky.
Q: What does the prosecutor do in your trial?
A: Try to get me found guilty.
Q: Who decides if you are guilty or not?
A: That jury.

At a hearing to determine whether Jamie Sullivan was competent to stand trial, the psychologist testified that Sullivan was mentally retarded, and consequently his understanding of the proceedings was not as accurate or thorough as it might otherwise be. However, the psychologist also testified that Sullivan did understand the charges against him, as well as the general purpose and nature of his trial. The judge ruled that Sullivan was competent to stand trial. A jury convicted him on all the charges and sentenced him to life in prison rather than to death by execution.

It is estimated that, like Jamie Sullivan, thirty thousand or more defendants are evaluated annually to determine their competence to stand trial or plead guilty.[8] The question of criminal competence can be raised at any point in the criminal process, and it is usually raised by defense attorneys who believe that a client may be suffering from a mental disorder. Defense attorneys question the competence of clients in up to 15 percent of all felony cases and about half that often in misdemeanor cases.[9]

If a question of competence is raised, the judge will order an evaluation. Typically, the defendant is taken to a special hospital for observation and examination. In fact, most mentally disordered offenders who have been committed to hospitals are there either because they are waiting for a competency evaluation or they have been found incompetent and are receiving treatment to restore their competence. In most states, psychiatrists, psychologists, and social workers are authorized to perform competency evaluations, and they often use special structured interviews. For example, the Competency Assessment Instrument addresses questions such as: Is the defendant aware of his or her possible legal defenses and protections? Is the defendant able to trust and effectively communicate with the average attorney? How well can the accused understand, participate, and cooperate with counsel in planning a strategy for the defense that is consistent with the reality of the circumstances? Is the accused able to understand the roles of defense counsel, prosecuting attorney, judge, jury, defendant, and witnesses? How well can the defendant understand the basic sequence and impact of events in a trial? Does the accused understand the nature and seriousness of the charges, as well as the conditions and restrictions that may be imposed as a result of a guilty verdict? Is the accused able to give a basically consistent, rational, and relevant account of his or her motivation and actions at the time of the offense? Is the accused able to recognize and communicate distortions in prosecution testimony? Would the defendant's inappropriate behavior disrupt a trial?

Over 70 percent of defendants referred for such evaluations are ultimately found competent to stand trial,[10] and judges seldom disagree with the consensus of the clinicians who have examined a given defendant.

One study revealed that of more than five hundred defendants found incompetent, many were "marginal" men who were undereducated and deficient in job skills, with long histories of being involved in both the legal and mental health systems.[11] Substance abuse was common. Minorities were overrepresented, compared to their presence in the general population. Other studies have found relatively high percentages of psychosis and lower intelligence among incompetent defendants.[12]

One other consistent finding is that incompetent defendants are charged with more serious crimes than defendants in general.

If a defendant is found competent, the legal process resumes, and the defendant again faces trial. If the defendant is found incompetent, the picture becomes more complicated. For minor crimes, the charges might be dropped, sometimes in exchange for requiring the defendant to receive treatment. If the charges are serious, the defendant usually will be returned to an institution for treatment, which, if successful, will result in the defendant's ultimately standing trial. In most states, this mandatory treatment can last up to six months; if the person is still judged incompetent, a different form of hospitalization will be arranged, or the person might be released. Outpatient treatment of incompetent defendants is seldom used, even though it could often be justified.

How successful are efforts to restore defendants' competence? One study evaluated an experimental treatment for a sample of incompetent defendants sent to one of three Philadelphia facilities.[13] In addition to receiving the usual psychiatric care, defendants assigned to these special treatment groups watched videotapes and received special instructions on courtroom procedures. They also discussed different ways of resolving problems that they might face during a trial. A matched control group received treatment for their general psychiatric needs, but no specific training to improve competence. Following treatment, defendants in the special competence-restoration group showed significant increases in their knowledge of competence-relevant information compared to the controls. Hospital staff judged 43 percent of the experimental subjects to be competent to stand trial after treatment, compared to 15 percent of the control subjects.

Criminal Responsibility: The Insanity Defense

Insanity is not a psychological concept; it is a legal term based on the legal requirement that defendants are presumed to be mentally capable and can be held responsible for the crimes with which they are charged. Therefore, if defendants plead not guilty by reason of insanity (NGRI), they must present evidence that they lacked the state of mind necessary to be held responsible for a crime. How that state of mental responsibility is determined has evolved over time.

Rules Defining Insanity   The original standard for judging insanity was introduced in 1843 and is known as the *McNaughton rule*. It states: "To establish a defense on the grounds of insanity it must be clearly proved that, at the time of committing the act, the accused was laboring under such a defect of reason, from disease of the mind, as not to know the nature and quality of the act he was doing or, if he did know it, that he did not know what he was doing [was] wrong."[14]

McNaughton remains the standard for insanity in about twenty U.S. states. It "excuses" criminal conduct by defendants whose mental illness either (1) causes them not to know what they are doing (e.g., believing they are stabbing a space alien rather than killing a person) or (2) leaves them incapable of knowing that what they are doing is wrong (e.g., having the delusion that the victim is about to abduct them). The McNaughton rule has been criticized over the years because it focuses only on cognition—knowing right from wrong—and ignores how mental illness might affect motivation or emotions. Thus, in 1954, a new standard for judging insanity was proposed as an alternative to the McNaughton rule. The new standard, known as the *Durham rule,* or the product test, states that "an accused is not responsible if the unlawful act was the product of a mental disease or mental defect."

At first, the Durham rule was popular with mental health professionals, but it soon ran into trouble with attorneys and judges, who believed that it gave too much weight to expert testimony about any mental illness that could cause criminal behavior. As a result, the Durham rule was never accepted by more than a few states; in 1972, it was replaced with the Brawner rule, also known as the ALI rule.

The *ALI rule* (named for the American Law Institute, which formulated it) holds that a defendant is not responsible for criminal conduct if, "at the time of such conduct as a result of mental disease or defect [the defendant] [lacks] substantial capacity either to appreciate the criminality [wrongfulness] of his conduct or to conform his conduct to the requirements of the law." The ALI rule, or something close to it, is used by about half the states, and one part of it is used in all federal courts as the test of insanity. The ALI rule differs from McNaughton in three main ways:

1. By using the term *appreciate* instead of *know,* the ALI rule acknowledges that emotional factors as well as cognitive ones influence criminal conduct.
2. The ALI rule does not require that offenders have a total lack of appreciation for the wrongfulness of their behavior, only that they lack "substantial capacity."
3. The ALI rule defines insanity in both cognitive and volitional terms. Defendants can be considered insane even if they appreciated that certain conduct was wrong, as long as a mental illness rendered them unable to control their conduct.

Consequences of Using the Insanity Defense An ABC News poll conducted in 1982 showed that 67 percent of Americans believed justice had not been served after some highly publicized defendants were found not guilty by reason of insanity. However, despite widespread public dissatisfaction with the insanity defense, it is used much less frequently than most people assume, and with very infrequent success. Across the United States, experts estimate that fewer than 1 percent of all criminal cases result in a finding of NGRI.[15]

One of the public's concerns is that defendants found not guilty by reason of insanity go "scot free," but this is seldom the case. For example, one New York study found that NGRI defendants were hospitalized for an average of three and a half years and that defendants who had committed more serious offenses were confined longer.[16] In many states, most NGRI defendants are kept in a mental institution until a judge is convinced that it is safe to release them. A survey of more than 1 million indictments across seven states showed that defendants found guilty were more likely to be released from confinement than those acquitted on the basis of insanity, and compared to convicted defendants, insanity acquittees in four states spent less time in confinement, but in three states they spent more time in confinement.[17]

Does hospital confinement and treatment produce any benefits for defendants found NGRI? Some studies show that individuals who complete their hospital treatment do better than those who run away from the institution,[18] but another found no difference in the posttreatment behavior of NGRI defendants who were officially discharged and those who escaped.[19] Robert Nicholson and his colleagues collected data on all NGRI defendants in Oklahoma who had been treated in the state forensic hospital over a five-year period. Within two and a half years of their release, half of these patients had been rearrested or rehospitalized, a rate that is about the same as for criminals in general.[20]

Judges once used criteria for releasing NGRI defendants that were more stringent than those set for other kinds of involuntary commitments. In the 1992 case of *Foucha* v. *Louisiana,* the U.S. Supreme Court eliminated this discrepancy, ruling that it is unconstitutional to keep a defendant in an institution if the person no longer meets the standard for involuntary civil commitment—that is, if the person is no longer mentally ill *and* dangerous. This ruling seems fair, but cases like that of E. E. Kemper III raise certain doubts about it. Kemper was released from a California hospital for the insane after spending five years there for murdering his grandparents. He petitioned a court to seal his psychiatric records, which it did after psychiatrists pronounced him sane. Neither the court nor the examining psychiatrists knew that, since his release, Kemper had killed his mother and seven other women. The last murder occurred three days before the court hearing that sealed his records.

Cases like Kemper's are rare, but they add fuel to the argument that the insanity defense puts the public at risk. The dangerousness of NGRI defendants is difficult to determine, partly because it is hard to know how dangerous *anyone* might be. Assessing the dangerousness of NGRI defendants is complicated by the fact that most of them are immediately removed from the community and confined in a hospital, where they receive drugs and other treatment. Although people with serious mental disorders (including NGRI defendants) are a bit more likely to be violent than people without such disorders, this relationship is typically found only for people who are currently experiencing psychotic symptoms.[21] If drugs or other treatments reduce these symptoms, the potential for violence is reduced as well.

The Role of Expert Witnesses in the Insanity Defense   There is great concern that testifying about insanity allows mental health experts to give opinions for which they lack proper competence or certainty. Three issues are pertinent to this problem. First, can experts reliably and validly diagnose mental illness and therefore identify this component of legal insanity? Second, can experts accurately assess a defendant's criminal responsibility for acts committed in the distant past? Third, even if the answers to the first two questions are "yes," are clinicians any more capable than nonprofessionals of making these judgments?

Many psychologists doubt that their field has any special expertise in determining a defendant's sanity at the time of an alleged offense.[22] They also believe that experts have too much influence on the outcomes of insanity trials, contending that decisions about criminal responsibility are legal questions best left in the hands of juries or judges. Finally, they worry that the public loses confidence in psychology and other behavioral sciences when juries see, and the media report, a parade of mental health experts who contradict one another about a defendant's sanity.

Revisions and Reforms in the Insanity Defense   For many decades, juries deliberating cases involving the insanity defense could only reach verdicts of guilty, not guilty, or not guilty by reason of insanity. Since 1976, however, about a quarter of the states have passed laws giving juries a fourth possible verdict: *guilty but mentally ill* (GBMI). A defendant found GBMI is usually sentenced to the same period of confinement as any other defendant convicted of the same crime. Ideally, however, the GBMI prisoner's confinement begins in a treatment facility, and transfer to a prison occurs only after treatment is complete. The real intent of GBMI laws is to offer a compromise verdict that will decrease the number of defendants found NGRI. It is unclear how successful these laws have been in this respect; NGRI verdicts have declined in some GBMI states but not others.

Several other problems with the GBMI verdict have caused authorities to take a second look at this reform. First, it complicates an already confusing situation for juries. GBMI laws require jurors to distinguish between mental illness that results in insanity and mental illness that does not. Second, the claim that the GBMI verdict would result in more treatment for mentally ill prisoners has proved unfounded. Overcrowding at most facilities prevents adequate treatment from taking place. In one Michigan study, 75 percent of GBMI offenders went directly to prison without any treatment.[23] Finally, the GBMI verdict, and any opportunity for treatment it might bring, is available only to the small proportion of defendants who raise an insanity defense. A severely disturbed defendant who does not claim insanity cannot be found GBMI.

Another major change occurred in 1984, when, in the wake of the John Hinckley* trial, Congress passed the Insanity Defense Reform Act (IDRA). Its purpose was to limit the number of defendants in federal courts who could successfully use the insanity defense. The IDRA changed the insanity defense in the federal courts in three important ways:

1. It placed the burden on the defendant to prove insanity, rather than on the prosecution to prove sanity, which had previously been the case.
2. It eliminated the volitional prong of the ALI rule. Lack of behavioral control because of mental illness is no longer a basis for insanity in federal courts. Insanity is restricted to the cognitive part of the rule: that as a result of mental illness, the defendant could not appreciate the nature or wrongfulness of his

---

*Hinckley was found not guilty by reason of insanity for the attempted murder of President Ronald Reagan.

acts. This reform was introduced because of the view that the ability to control one's acts cannot be assessed reliably and that the issue of volition was a loophole through which too many criminal offenders were walking to freedom. Substantial empirical research contradicts both these claims, however.

3. The IDRA allows experts to describe a defendant's mental condition and the effects it might have on behavior, but they may not give "ultimate opinion" testimony. That is, they may not state any conclusions about a defendant's insanity. The reformers hoped that this change would prohibit experts from having too much control over verdicts, but empirical studies suggest that the prohibition might not have much effect on juries. In one study, for example, participants read one of several versions of a trial where a defendant pleaded NGRI in the killing of his boss.[24] One group of participants read a transcript in which mental health experts for both sides offered only diagnostic testimony, that is, that the defendant was mentally ill at the time of the offense. A second group read a version in which the experts testified about their diagnosis and also gave a "penultimate opinion," that is, stated how the disorder might have affected the defendant's understanding of the wrongfulness of his or her act. A third group read a transcript in which the experts discussed the diagnosis, gave penultimate opinions, and then offered an ultimate opinion as to whether the defendant was sane or insane at the time he killed his boss. In this study, participants' verdicts were not affected by the type of testimony they read. These results could mean that a ban on ultimate opinion testimony does not accomplish much, but it could also mean that the ban can shorten expert testimony without sacrificing essential information.

Psychologists have questioned whether the typical juror comprehends legal definitions and then applies them as intended by the courts. One study found that jurors could correctly answer only 51 percent of a series of questions testing their comprehension of the McNaughton rule.[25] Other investigators[26] have obtained similar results: regardless of what insanity rule was used, college students showed low rates of accurate recall and comprehension of the crucial components in various insanity definitions.

Most mock jury studies of the IDRA have found that verdicts are little affected by whether jurors hear the ALI definition, the IDRA definition, or no definition of insanity at all.[27] Jurors appear to depend on their own views about what constitutes insanity and interpret the evidence according to those views, regardless of the formal instructions that judges give them.[28]

In response to the difficulties with the insanity defense, a few U.S. states, such as Idaho and Montana, have abolished it. However, issues associated with insanity remain because to be convicted of a crime in any state, one must have intended the illegal act. Defendants can be found guilty of theft, for example, only if it can be proved that they intended to steal. Accordingly, even states with no official insanity defense allow evidence to be introduced about a defendant's *mens rea* ("guilty mind") during alleged crimes. If, because of a mental disorder, defendants lack the *mens rea* for a crime, they should be found not guilty. And so, to help juries decide, experts including psychologists, continue to offer testimony about the effects of mental illness on defendants' *mens rea,* even in states that have no insanity defense.

In short, a defendant's mental state can never be entirely eliminated from jurors' consideration, simply because it makes no sense to talk about guilt without knowing something about a defendant's state of mind. In one form or another, the issue of insanity remains a part of court decisions about criminal responsibility.

PSYCHOLOGICAL DAMAGES IN CIVIL TRIALS

When one person is injured by the actions of another party, the injured individual can sue the second party to recover money damages as compensation. Such lawsuits are covered by an area of civil law known as *torts.* A tort is a wrongful act that causes harm to an individual. When the criminal law exacts compensation for wrongful acts, it does so on behalf of society as a whole. Tort law, on the other hand, provides a mechanism for *individuals* to redress the harm they have suffered at the hands of someone else.

Many kinds of behavior can constitute a tort. Slander and libel are torts; so are cases of medical malpractice, the manufacture of defective products resulting in a personal injury, and intentional or negligent behavior producing harm to another person.

A person can suffer various kinds of damage from a tort, including destruction of personal property, physical injuries, and emotional distress (sometimes called "pain and suffering"). The law has always compensated victims who are physically hurt or sustain property losses, but it has been reluctant historically to compensate emotional distress largely out of concern that such damages are too easy to fake and too hard to measure. When recovery for emotional damages was allowed, the courts often required that a physical injury had to accompany the psychological harm or that a plaintiff who was not physically injured at least had to be in a "zone of danger" in order to get compensation (e.g., even though the plaintiff was not injured by the attack of an escaped wild animal, she was standing next to her children when they were attacked).[29]

In recent years, however, the courts have taken the view that psychological distress can be compensated regardless of whether any physical damages are inflicted on the plaintiff. Two types of mental injuries are now common in civil lawsuits: those arising from "extreme and outrageous" conduct intended to cause distress, and those arising from "negligent" behavior. In the latter type of cases, plaintiffs are allowed to sue for psychological damages if they are bystanders to an incident in which a loved one is injured (e.g., a parent sees her child crushed to death when a defective roller coaster derails).

In the case of an intentional tort causing psychological distress, a plaintiff has to prove that a defendant intentionally or recklessly acted in an extreme and outrageous fashion (sometimes defined as "beyond all bounds of decency") in order to cause emotional distress. In addition, the plaintiff must prove that the distress is severe—in other words, something more than merely annoying or temporarily upsetting.

In recent years, an increasing number of tort cases have dealt with sexual harassment in the workplace. A plaintiff who claims to have been sexually harassed at work can sue the worker(s) responsible for the harassment, and the company itself, if the plaintiff can show that the company knew (or should have known) about the harassment and took inadequate measures to stop it. Plaintiffs can seek both compensatory damages for emotional harm as well as punitive damages, which penalize the company for its failure to respond properly to the misconduct.

Although a mental health expert might be called to testify about the emotional consequences of harassment, such testimony is not necessary to establish that the harassment created an abusive work environment for which the plaintiff can recover monetary damages.

When psychologists assess civil plaintiffs, they typically conduct an evaluation that, like most other evaluations, includes a social history, a clinical interview, psychological testing, and perhaps interviews with others and reviews of available records. Based on these data, the clinician reaches a decision about what, if any, psychological problems the person might be suffering. Thus, much of the evaluation is not too different from what a clinician might do with any client, regardless of whether the person was pursuing a lawsuit.

The more difficult question the clinician must answer is whether the psychological problems were caused by the tort, aggravated by the tort, or existed before the tort. There is no established procedure for answering this question, although most clinicians try to locate as many records and other sources of data as possible that will help date the first appearance of any disorder. In some situations, a plaintiff might allege that he or she was selected for harassment precisely because the defendants knew of some prior difficulty that made the plaintiff vulnerable to a particular kind of harassment. In such cases, the clinician must consider this additional factor before reaching a conclusion about the significance of some prior psychological problem.

When a worker is injured on the job, the law provides for the worker to be compensated, and it does so by using a streamlined system that avoids the necessity of proving a tort. This system is known as *workers' compensation law;* in the United States, all fifty states and the federal government have a workers' compensation system. Prior to the development of workers' compensation, a person who was injured at work had to prove that the employer was responsible for a tort in order to receive compensation. This requirement proved difficult because employers used any of several defenses to defeat the worker's claim. They often blamed the employee's negligence or the negligence of another worker for the injury. In other cases, employers said that a worker's injuries were simply the unavoidable risks of the job and that the worker was well aware of these risks. As a result, up to the beginning of the twentieth century, many seriously injured workers and their families were denied compensation for work-related injuries.

In workers' compensation systems, workers can seek compensation for physical and psychological injuries sustained at work, the cost of the treatment they receive, lost wages, and the loss of future earning capacity. Because psychological injuries or mental disorders arising from employment can be compensated, psychologists are often asked to evaluate workers and render an opinion about the existence, cause, and implications of any mental disorders in a given case. Claims for mental disability usually arise in one of two ways.

First, a physical injury or threat can cause a mental disorder and psychological disability. A common pattern in these *physical-mental cases* is for a worker to sustain a serious physical injury—say, a broken back or severe burns—that leaves him or her with chronic pain. As the pain continues, the worker begins to experience psychological problems, usually depression and anxiety. These problems sometimes worsen until they become full-fledged mental disorders, resulting in further impairments in overall functioning.

The second work-related pathway to mental disability is for an individual to suffer a traumatic incident at work or to undergo a long period of continuing stress that leads to psychological difficulties. A night clerk at a convenience store who is the victim of an armed robbery and subsequently develops posttraumatic stress disorder is an example of such *mental-mental* cases, as is the clerical worker who, following years of overwork and pressure from a boss, experiences an anxiety disorder.

In a third kind of case, known as *mental-physical,* work-related stress is blamed for the onset of a physical disorder such as high blood pressure. Many states have placed special restrictions on these types of claims, and psychologists are seldom asked to evaluate them.

In recent years, the number of psychological claims arising in workers' compensation litigation has increased dramatically; much of the increase has been attributed to a surge in mental-mental cases. In the 1980s, stress-related mental disorders became the fastest-growing occupational disease category in the United States.[30] It is not clear what accounts for this surge in psychological claims, but three explanations have been proposed. First, because more women have entered the workforce and because women are more often diagnosed with anxiety and depression disorders than men, the increase in psychological claims might be due to the growing percentage of female workers.[31] A second possibility is that shifts in the job market from manufacturing and industrial jobs to service-oriented jobs have produced corresponding increases in interpersonal stressors and decreases in physical injuries. A third speculation is that claims of psychological impairments are motivated primarily by financial incentives, producing a range of cases in which genuine impairments are mixed in with exaggerated or malingered claims.

CIVIL COMPETENCY

When we discussed competence to stand trial earlier, we focused on the competency of criminal defendants to engage in certain behaviors and make certain decisions during the course of a trial. However, the question of mental competence is raised in several noncriminal contexts as well; these other situations involve issues of *civil competency.*

Questions of civil competency focus on whether an individual has the capacity to understand information that is relevant to making a specific decision and then making an informed choice about what to do. Questions about civil competency include the following: Is a person competent to manage his or her financial affairs? Can an individual make competent decisions about his or her medical or psychiatric treatment? Is a person competent to execute a will?

The legal standards used to define competence have evolved over many years, but scholars who have studied this issue agree that four abilities are essential to competent decision making.[32] A competent individual is expected to be able to (1) understand basic information that is relevant to making a decision, (2) apply that information to a specific situation in order to anticipate the consequences of various choices that might be made, (3) use logical or rational thinking to evaluate the pros and cons of various strategies and decisions, and (4) communicate a personal decision or choice about the matter under consideration.

The specific abilities associated with each of these general criteria vary with the decision that a person must make. Deciding whether to have risky surgery demands different kinds of information and thinking processes than does deciding whether to leave one's estate to one's children or to a charitable organization.

One area where researchers have focused their attention is on the competence of individuals with severe mental disorders to make decisions and give informed consent about their own psychiatric treatment. Can persons with serious mental disorders make competent treatment decisions? Do their decision-making abilities differ from persons who do not suffer mental disorders? These are some of the questions that have been investigated in the MacArthur Treatment Competence Study. This large-scale study has resulted in the development of several structured interview measures that can be used to assess the four basic abilities involved in legal competence: understanding information, applying information, rational thinking, and expressing a choice.

In one phase of this study, standardized interviews were conducted with patients suffering from schizophrenia, major depression, or heart disease, and with healthy persons from the community who were demographically matched to the patient groups.[33] Only a minority of the people in any of the groups showed significant impairments in competent decision making about various treatment options they were asked to consider. However, the patients with schizophrenia and major depression had a poorer understanding of treatment information and used less adequate reasoning in thinking about the personal consequences of treatment than did the heart patients or community sample. These impairments were more severe and consistent across different competence abilities for the patients with schizophrenia than for the patients with depression, and the more serious the symptoms of mental disorder were (especially those involving disturbed thinking), the poorer was the understanding.

These results have implications for social policies involving people with mental disorders. First, contrary to popular impressions, the majority of patients suffering from severe disorders such as schizophrenia and major depression appear to be capable of competent decision making about their treatment. Second, a significant number of patients, particularly those with schizophrenia, do show some impairments in their decision-making abilities.

The question of competence to consent to treatment usually arises when a patient refuses treatment that seems to be medically and psychologically justified. Under these circumstances, the first step might be to break down the explanation of the treatment decisions facing the patient into smaller bits of information. This kind of presentation may help the patient understand how a recommended treatment would be in his or her best interests. Should the patient and treating professionals remain at an impasse after such a presentation, it would be important to have a clinical assessment instrument that could be administered in a brief period of time to determine whether the patient lacks the necessary abilities to reach a competent decision. The development of just such an instrument, based on the initial results of the MacArthur Treatment Competence Study, is underway.

The questions involved in civil competencies illustrate that mental health laws and policies are not just abstract principles. They can have significant positive or negative effects on patients, leading many mental health professionals and attorneys to consider the therapeutic implications of legal rulings in this area, not just the effects of such rulings on case law or on broad issues such as individual versus social rights. This perspective, known as *therapeutic jurisprudence*,[34] views the law as having the potential for being helpful to patients and argues that all mental health laws should be evaluated to determine their therapeutic impact. In other words, therapeutic jurisprudence would frame the issues discussed in this section partly on the basis of the impact that different solutions would have for individual patients.

PSYCHOLOGICAL AUTOPSIES

The typical forensic assessment involves a clinician's (for example, a psychologist, psychiatrist, or social worker) interviewing, observing, and testing a client in order to arrive at an understanding of the case. However, in a few unusual circumstances, clinicians may be called on to give opinions about a deceased person's state of mind prior to death. Obviously, in these cases, the clinician must conduct an evaluation without the person's participation. These postmortem evaluations are termed *psychological autopsies* or *equivocal death analyses*.[35]

The first psychological autopsies are believed to have been performed in the 1950s when a group of social scientists in Los Angeles began assisting the Coroner's Office in determining whether suicide, murder, or accident was the most likely cause of death in certain cases. The use of psychological autopsies has become more commonplace over the years, especially in the following kinds of cases:

- Determining whether someone's death was due to suicide or accident (this question is raised by an insurance company that could deny death benefits if it is shown that the policy holder committed suicide)
- Assessing claims in workers' compensation cases that stressful working conditions or work trauma contributed to a worker's accidental death or suicide
- Evaluating whether a deceased individual had the necessary mental capacity to execute or modify a will
- Supporting the argument made by some criminal defendants that a victim's cause of death was suicide rather than homicide

Although there is no standard format for conducting psychological autopsies, most of them rely on information from two general sources: archival records and interviews with third parties who knew the decedent. In a sense they resemble a technique known as *criminal profiling* in which psychologists try to piece together the characteristics of an as-yet unidentified serial killer, for example. Both approaches attempt to infer an individual's motives and state of mind by assessing archival information a person has left behind. In the case of the psychological autopsy, the identity of the person in question is known, but the nature of his or her behavior remains in question; in the case of the criminal profile, the behavior is known, but the identity of the culprit is not.

Some general guidelines about what psychological autopsies should include have been published.[36] Some investigators concentrate on data from the time just before the person's death. What was the person's mood? How was the person doing at work? Were there any pronounced changes in the person's behavior? Others—especially those who take a Freudian, or psychodynamic, perspective on behavior (see Chapter 3)—look for clues about family dynamics and the person's early life. As a child, how did the person interact with his or her parents? What was the individual's approach to school? To competition with peers?

How has testimony about psychological autopsies fared in court? In workers' compensation cases and trials about whether insurance benefits should be paid, the courts have usually admitted psychological autopsy testimony; in criminal cases and those involving the question of whether a person had the mental capacity to draft a will, the courts have been reluctant to permit the testimony. Judges are more skeptical in general about allowing expert testimony in criminal cases than in civil ones, perhaps because the risks of prejudicial testimony are greater when one's liberties can be taken away. One reason for the courts' hesitancy in permitting psychological autopsy testimony in cases involving the validity of wills might be that the state of mind of the deceased is the critical legal question the jury must answer. Allowing expert testimony on this matter might therefore be viewed as invading the province of the jury.

CHILD CUSTODY AND PARENTAL FITNESS

One of the fastest-growing areas of forensic psychology is the evaluation of families in order to recommend the custodial arrangement that is in the best interests of children whose parents are divorcing or separating. The increase in these cases is attributable to two facts. First, half of all marriages in the United States now end in divorce. Consequently, more than a third of children in the United States will spend some time living in a stepfamily, and over half will spend time in a single-parent household.[37] Therefore, the issue of custody is a practical concern for millions of families. Second, from the end of the nineteenth century to the middle of the twentieth century, the prevailing assumption was that awarding custody of young children (sometimes called children of "tender years") to their mothers was usually in their best interests. The preference for maternal custody has weakened over the years, so that now many courts prefer knowing about the parenting abilities of each parent before making a decision about custody.

Child custody evaluations usually arise in situations in which divorcing parents disagree about which of them can better meet the needs of their children and should therefore retain custody of them. Most states permit two kinds of custodial arrangements. The more common is *sole custody*, in which one parent is awarded legal custody of the child and the other parent is granted rights of visitation and other types of contact with the child. In *joint custody* arrangements, both parents retain parental rights concerning decisions about the child's general welfare, education, health care, and other matters. Joint custody does not mean that the child spends an equal amount of time with each parent. Usually one parent is given physical custody of the child, and the child spends more time living with that parent.

Evaluations of parental fitness involve a question that differs from that of a custody dispute. The issue is not which of two parents would be the better custodial parent, but whether children should be removed from the custody of a parent who is not fit to *be* a parent. The legal definition of parental unfitness varies from state to state, but the law generally prefers to have biological parents retain custody of their children. In some states, the type of evidence necessary to prove unfitness is that the parent (1) inflicted, or allowed someone else to inflict, physical injury, emotional harm, or sexual abuse on the child, (2) is morally delinquent, (3) abandoned the child, (4) is mentally ill, or (5) fails to provide essential care for the child for some reason other than poverty. In most states, it must be shown in a "clear and convincing" manner that one or more of these conditions is substantially threatening a child's welfare.

Child custody cases are among the most ethically challenging and clinically difficult forensic evaluations that psychologists perform. First, the emotional stakes are extremely high, and both parents are often willing to spare no expense or tactic in the battle over who will win custody. Associated with this conflict is the fact that the children are usually forced to live—for months, if not years—in emotional limbo; they do not know in whose home they will be residing, where they will be going to school, or how often they will see each parent. Second, a thorough competency evaluation requires that the clinician evaluate assessment data from the children, both parents, and, when possible, other people who have been in positions to have observed the family. Often, not all the parties agree to being evaluated or do so only under coercion, resulting in a lengthy and unfriendly process. Third, to render an expert opinion, a clinician must possess a great deal of knowledge—not just about the individual children and parents under evaluation, but about child development, bonding and attachment, family systems, the effects of divorce on children, adult and childhood mental disorders, and various kinds of testing. Added to these factors are changes in what we have traditionally defined as a family. With increasing acceptance of different lifestyles, clinicians must often confront questions about whether parents' sexual orientation or ethnicity should influence custody decisions. Finally, child custody evaluations are highly adversarial processes, in which one side will challenge any procedures or opinions by an expert with which it disagrees. Clinicians who conduct custody evaluations must brace themselves for all sorts of attacks directed at their clinical methods, scholarly competence, personal character, and professional ethics.

Clinicians conduct custody evaluations under any of three scenarios: (1) a judge can appoint one clinician to conduct a custody evaluation that will be available to all the parties, (2) each side can retain its own expert to conduct independent evaluations, or (3) the sides can agree to hire the same expert to conduct one evaluation. Most informed observers prefer either the first or third option because they minimize the adversarial pressures that arise when separate experts are hired by each side. Guidelines for conducting custody evaluations have been developed by the American Psychological Association and the Association of Family and Conciliation Courts. Although the methods used in custody evaluations vary with the specific issues in each case, most evaluations include the following components:

1. Clinical, social-history, and mental status interviews of the parents and the children
2. Standardized testing of the parents and the children
3. Observation of interactions between each parent and the children, especially when the children are minors
4. Interviews with other people who have had opportunities to observe the family (e.g., adult children of the parents, grandparents, neighbors, the family physician, school teachers)
5. Documents that might be relevant to the case (medical records of children and parents, report cards, arrest records)

A 1980s U.S. national survey of mental health professionals who conduct child custody evaluations found that they devoted an average of nineteen hours to each custody evaluation.[38] By the 1990s, this figure had increased to twenty-six hours, largely because of more time being taken to review records and write longer reports.[39] A substantial amount of this time was devoted to interviewing and observing the parties. More than two-thirds of the respondents indicated that they conducted individual interviews with each parent and each child, observed each parent interacting (separately) with each child, and conducted formal psychological testing of the parents and the children.

These experts also reported how often they recommended various custodial arrangements. Limited joint custody (parents share the decision making, but one parent maintains primary physical custody) was the most common recommendation, and single-parent custody without visitation was the least recommended alternative.

Because divorce is such a potent stressor for children and because protracted custody battles tend to leave a trail of emotionally battered family members in their wake, increasing attention is being given to helping parents and children cope with these transitions or to finding alternatives to custody fights. *Custody mediation* services by psychologists are now being used more often in lieu of adversarial court procedures. The supposed benefits of custody mediation are that resolutions are reached more quickly and with better compliance among the participants than with adversarial procedures.

It is not clear, however, that mediation always leads to better adjustment by divorcing parents or by their children. To assess the impact of mediated versus adversarial child custody procedures, Robert Emery and his colleagues at the University of Virginia randomly assigned divorcing couples to settle their custody disputes through either mediation or litigation. They found that mediation greatly reduced the number of hearings necessary and the total amount of time to reach a resolution. Parents who mediated did not differ in terms of psychological adjustment from those who litigated, but a consistent gender difference in satisfaction with the two methods did emerge. Fathers who went through mediation were much more likely to report feeling satisfied with the process than did fathers who litigated; mothers who went through mediation, on the other hand, were less likely to express satisfaction with its effects, and some measures actually favored mothers who litigated their disputes.[40]

Concern over Expert Testimony by Psychologists

Judges, lawyers, and psychologists themselves have expressed a great deal of concern about the reliability, validity, propriety, and usefulness of expert forensic testimony. Sharply worded critiques of psychologists' expert testimony can be found in several sources,[41] and one well-known guidebook has been devoted entirely to the subject of how to cross-examine expert testimony by psychologists.[42]

What are the main problems with testimony by psychological experts? The following eight concerns are among the most important:[43]

1. The scientific foundation for much of the testimony offered in court is often less than adequate, leading to invalid information and potentially incorrect verdicts.
2. Much of the testimony is of limited relevance, therefore wasting court time and burdening an already crowded docket.
3. Experts are too often permitted to testify about ultimate issues (Is the defendant insane? Was the plaintiff emotionally damaged?) which are more appropriate for juries to decide.
4. Expert testimony is frequently used to introduce information that would otherwise be prohibited because it is hearsay. (Experts are permitted to share this information with juries if it is the kind of information they routinely rely on in reaching their opinions.)
5. The adversary system compromises experts' objectivity. Experts readily testify to opinions that favor the side that pays them, becoming little more than "hired guns" whose testimony can be bought.
6. Expert testimony is expensive, so reliance on experts gives an advantage to the side with more money.
7. Testing the reliability and validity of expert opinions through cross-examination is inadequate because attorneys are usually not well equipped to conduct such

cross-examination, and juries often fail to understand the significance of the information uncovered during the cross-examination.

8. The spectacle of experts' disagreeing with one another in trial after trial ultimately reduces the public's esteem for mental health professionals.

In response to these concerns, several reforms of expert testimony have been proposed. Most are aimed at reducing the undue influence or excessive partisanship that is thought to plague expert testimony. Several commentators have recommended that experts not be allowed to testify about the ultimate issue in forensic cases. As noted earlier, this reform was part of the overhaul of the federal law concerning insanity that occurred in the 1980s. There is little evidence that limiting expert testimony in this way has had much impact on the use or success of the insanity defense, and it is no more certain that it would have any larger impact in other kinds of cases.

Another suggestion has been to reduce the adversarial nature of expert testimony by limiting the number of experts each side could introduce to testify about a given topic, requiring that the experts be chosen from an approved panel of individuals reputed to be objective and highly competent, or allowing testimony only by experts who have been appointed by a judge rather than hired by opposing attorneys. Although these changes would appear to reduce the "hired gun" problem, it is not clear that consensus could be reached on which experts belong on an "approved" list or that being appointed by a judge guarantees an expert's objectivity.

Several scholars have suggested that courts not permit expert opinion testimony unless it can be shown that it passes the scientific reliability standard established by the *Daubert* decision.[44] Such a requirement might lead to a dramatic decline in testimony by forensic psychologists and psychiatrists, but unless attorneys and lawyers are educated more thoroughly about scientific methodology, it is not clear that they can make informed distinctions between "good" and "bad" science.[45]

A final, modest reform is to ban any reference to witnesses as providing *expert* testimony, a term that seems to suggest that jurors should pay extra attention to it. Instead, judges would always refer—in the presence of juries—to *opinion* testimony or witnesses.[46]

SUGGESTIONS FOR FURTHER READINGS

Melton, G., Petrila, J., Poythress, N., & Slobogin, C. (1997). *Psychological evaluations for the courts* (2nd ed.). New York: Guilford Press.

Sales, B., & Shuman, D. (Eds.). (1996). *Law, mental health, and mental disorder.* Pacific Grove, CA: Brooks Cole.

Wrightsman, L., Nietzel, M., & Fortune, W. (1998). *Psychology and the legal system* (4th edition). Pacific Grove, CA: Brooks Cole.

Recent issues of two journals: *Behavioral Sciences and the Law* (Wiley) and *Law and Human Behavior* (Plenum).

CHAPTER 9

PSYCHOLOGY APPLIED TO THE ENVIRONMENT

Robert Sommer

C rime has been a serious problem in American public housing for many years. Although politicians often blame the tenants, a team of research architects and psychologists has suggested that faulty architecture and living environments have been the major culprits. They checked police records and found that smaller projects with three-story walk-up buildings had less crime and vandalism than large high-rise projects with anonymous towers surrounded by open space not associated with particular buildings. People in three-story walk-ups can more easily become acquainted with other residents, receive support from them, see what is happening at ground level, keep track of potential troublemakers, and watch their children at play.[1] In effect, the residents are able to defend their space and feel that they have some control over their territory.

A notorious example of poorly designed public housing was the Pruitt-Igoe project in St. Louis, Missouri, completed in 1956. Completely foreign to the lifestyles of the tenants, the structure of the eleven-story towers destroyed the mutual support systems that had existed in their previous neighborhoods. One of the consequences was a very high crime rate in the public areas. In 1976, all the occupants were relocated and the buildings were dynamited.

Interviews with burglars have revealed that visibility and territorial control by residents make a building appear less desirable as a potential target.[2] These factors were addressed by city planner Oscar Newman at the Clason Point Housing Project in New York City, where crime was rampant. Improvements included new fencing to enclose the areas behind the buildings, paths and hedges to mark front yards, painting the facades different colors to give the buildings individual identities, and adding new street lights and benches to increase usage of the outdoor areas. These measures reduced maintenance costs, and decreased the overall crime rate more than 50 percent and the burglary rate by more than 25 percent.[3]

Newman subsequently used similar strategies to reduce crime in the Five Oaks neighborhood in Dayton, Ohio. There, the solutions included street closures that reduced through-traffic and created mini-neighborhoods that were easier for the residents to control. The effects were dramatic. Within a year of implementing the changes, nonviolent crime fell by 24 percent and violent crime by 50 percent, and the average price of a single-family home in the area rose by 15 percent.[4]

These examples are good illustrations of the ways in which environmental psychologists can work with architects and city planners to improve the quality of urban life.

DEFINITION OF THE FIELD

The field of *environmental psychology* is concerned with the relationships between people and their physical surroundings, including the effects of environments on people and peoples' effects on their environment. From its beginnings less than half a century ago, environmental psychology has been interdisciplinary, field oriented, and dedicated to problem solving. Interdisciplinary teams are required because environmental changes can produce complex physical and social consequences. Hence, the composition of a team varies from project to project, as does the role of the environmental psychologist. For example, an urban project on which I worked was headed by an architect and included an urban planner, a transportation engineer, an architectural historian, an economist, and a behavioral scientist (me). My assignment was as liaison with the social agencies serving the street people who would be displaced by the project. I had a different role on a bikeway project. This team was headed by a civil engineer and included a transportation planner, physical education specialist, mechanical engineer, and two psychologists who studied cyclists' attitudes and behavior.

Environmental psychology research is often done in the field, that is, in real-world settings, rather than in the laboratory, because it is difficult and expensive to simulate real-world problems in the laboratory. The research does not end with identifying problems but continues to search for solutions. This requires ongoing collaboration with engineers, designers, planners, and others who direct change in the physical environment.

ORIGINS OF THE FIELD

Research in environmental psychology began in the 1950s as part of a national campaign to improve mental hospitals. Among the problems identified were dirty, drab, and dysfunctional buildings. Architects, who were knowledgeable about formal characteristics of buildings but less so about human needs, turned to psychologists and other behavioral scientists for assistance. They approached psychologists because their theories of perception, cognition, and social behavior are relevant to an understanding of human needs; their research methods offer the possibility of obtaining systematic information about human behavior; and they possess skills in human relations useful in planning and advocacy. For example, psychologists can facilitate communication among the architect, the architect's client, and building occupants, and thereby ensure a good fit between the occupants and the building. Because of its origins in collaboration between architects and psychologists, the field was originally known as architectural psychology, and its researchers worked in a variety of university departments (e.g., environmental behavior studies at the University of Wisconsin at Milwaukee, social ecology at the University of California at

Irvine, and architecture at the University of California at Berkeley). Over the next few decades, as the field expanded into new problem areas outside architecture, such as parks and natural landscapes, it became known as environmental psychology.

From the beginning, there was resistance from some architects who were enamored with pure form and wanted to sculpt buildings without regard to their practical or social functions. This purist position was succinctly stated by noted architect Philip Johnson in his comment, "The job of the architect is to create beautiful buildings. That's all."[5] Some corporate clients, too, did not want their building plans complicated by the need to take into account the diversity of occupant needs, preferring instead the simpler one-style-fits-all approach.

Collaborative research by architects and psychologists to create more suitable hospital conditions increased awareness of the effect of the physical environment on social behavior. The first task for environmental psychologists was to identify mismatches between people and their physical settings. In order to do this, they developed new techniques for studying human response to the environment, such as postoccupancy evaluation and behavioral mapping. *Postoccupancy evaluation* is the systematic examination of how a building or other facility works in practice from the standpoint of occupants and other users. A researcher may interview occupants or distribute questionnaires asking about various aspects of the building, such as lighting, heating, color scheme, use of decorations, noise level, and so on. *Behavioral mapping* tracks the behavior of people in an area. For example, it is used in studies of shopping malls to see where and how people spend their time. Building owners may then use this information to shift traffic patterns into less visited areas.

Once environmental psychologists identified the mismatches between people and their environment, they tried to ease these problems through improved design. Although this work was initially aimed at understanding the relations between people and institutional environments, later research included indoor settings other than institutions, and then moved outdoors to study larger urban spaces and natural settings. A field that had begun with investigations of color and chair arrangements in mental hospitals was soon tracking visitors in national parks and studying the stresses associated with urban commuting.

Today there are active environmental psychology research programs throughout the world. The type of research and training occurring in each area reflects local cultural and environmental contexts. For example, the dense population in Japan has stimulated research on human crowding, and Scandinavian researchers have examined responses to natural environments such as forests and oceans. In Brazil, environmental psychologists have studied squatter settlements around major cities, the social life of street children, and the quality of life in Brasilia, a planned city that is the nation's capital.

RANGE OF APPLICATIONS

The range of environmental psychology applications has been wide, from airports to zoos, although the coverage in all but a few areas is still thin. The most studied settings have been large institutional and corporate buildings, such as hospitals, schools, libraries, dormitories, and offices where a captive population is easy to observe and is willing to fill out questionnaires. Studies of prisons, however, have been hindered by difficulties in gaining access to and collecting honest responses from inmates. Indeed, most research in correctional facilities has been done at a distance using archival measures to, for example, relate the frequency of assaults and illness to crowding and other environmental conditions.

Currently, office design is a hot area for environmental psychologists because it is attracting financial support from corporate clients and furniture manufacturers who wish to develop and test new office systems. Dealing directly with corporate clients allows researchers in environmental psychology to test new systems under realistic conditions. Among the latest innovations is the "office neighborhood," a concept aimed at increasing workplace collaboration and spontaneous interaction. Other environmental psychologists are exploring new developments in high-tech offices.

Settings studied least by environmental psychologists include single-family homes (where the researcher's presence might distort behavior) and mundane settings, such as street corners, convenience stores, gas stations, churches, and parking garages, all of which tend to be overlooked as research opportunities.

Typically, the success of an environmental psychology project is measured in relation to a single application. As in the examples described in this chapter, a researcher demonstrates the beneficial effects of an environmental change and publishes the findings, but it is by no means certain that these findings will be applied elsewhere. For example, it was ten years after my first article on airport design appeared before I received a letter from an architect telling me he had used my recommendations on an actual project. Some researchers have reduced the applications gap—the time between publication of research and its application—by becoming team members on design projects or working with government agencies to develop standards. For instance, following my research on bikeways, I served on a task force developing national standards for bicycle paths. Similarly, psychologist Gary Winkel studied space use at Bellevue Hospital in New York City, and hospital officials were so impressed with his report that they brought him into the selection process for the architect who would make the changes.

An important role for the environmental psychologist on a design team is to raise awareness of the needs of future occupants before the building is constructed. This may require opening the eyes of planners and clients to aspects of the environment that are typically overlooked, such as the yard of a school building or the pedestrian areas of a housing development. Are these areas attractive and safe? Do they encourage or discourage interaction? The environmental psychologist may use experiential exercises to raise such issues, asking people to view an area from different perspectives or to play different roles. For example, teachers might be required to view a school building through the eyes of students, or planners might be asked to look at a housing project from the standpoint of teenagers, the police, or criminals looking for easy targets.[6]

Some environmental psychologists address public policy issues by attempting to understand and predict behavior in relation to large national and international trends. Here, the emphasis is on the big picture, considering the planet as one integrated system, and looking at changes associated with global warming, urbanization, deforestation, and overpopulation. This work is also interdisciplinary, but instead of working on design teams with architects, planners, and engineers, the psychologists work with political scientists, demographers, statisticians, politicians, lawyers, and government regulators. The psychologist's role on the team is to answer a number of questions about human behavior that have policy relevance.[7] Can the source of environmental degradation be traced to a value system that gives the environment second-class status compared to human desires? What changes in human behavior are likely to have the most significant effects in reversing pollution and exploitation of the environment? Are global and regional ecosystems too complex for government policymakers and the public to understand? How can policymakers and the public learn to anticipate and prepare for future environmental crises?

Researchers investigating large-scale environmental issues draw heavily on ecological models and concepts. The fundamental principle of ecology is connectedness. In the biological sciences, this refers to the reciprocal relationships between plant and animal communities. In environmental psychology, it describes the two-way relationships between people and their physical surroundings, both natural and human-made. Thus, environmental psychologists are critical both of other psychologists who ignore the effects of the physical environment on behavior, and of architects and planners who emphasize physical features over occupant needs.

Whether solutions to large-scale environmental questions can be developed solely at the level of individual action is an important question. As an example, some environmental organizations see a connection between fast food restaurants in the United States and deforestation in Central America. By purchasing beef from Costa Rica, American fast-food chains encourage small farmers there to convert forest into range land for cattle. Since the soil is not suitable for long-term cattle ranching, there is a continuing cycle of slash-and-burn ranching and abandonment of exhausted fields. Whether a reduction in hamburger consumption at a particular fast-food chain in the United States can reverse deforestation in Central America is debatable, but knowledge of ecological relationships can create an awareness that leads to environmentally sound government policies and regulations, such as eliminating international loans that encourage nonsustainable agriculture.

At the heart of many human-produced environmental problems is what biologist Garrett Hardin has called "the tragedy of the commons."[8] The "commons" is a community pasture open to all. Acting on the basis of self-interest, each herder attempts to keep as many cattle as possible on the pasture. Soon the pasture becomes overgrazed, the grasses die, and the community resource is destroyed. The "commons dilemma," in which the self-interested behavior of individuals ruins a shared resource, has been applied to fishing, forestry, recreation, and many other activities. Although each individual's impact on the resource is slight, the cumulative effects of many individuals rapidly lead to depletion of the resource, and the effects become magnified as population increases. Population growth can also be seen as a commons dilemma, in the sense that each couple's reproduction decision has a slight impact, but when the effects are multiplied across the planet, an unsustainable situation can be created.

Four types of solutions to the commons dilemma have been identified: laws and regulations, education, voluntary organizations, and ethical appeals.[9] With regard to wildlife habitats, for example, laws can limit hunting, and zoning regulations can restrict development. At the same time, local people can be taught the value of species diversity for tourism (ecotourism is a growing international industry), while voluntary organizations can promote ecotourism, advocate for wildlife at the political level, and make appeals on ethical grounds for the preservation of species.

Even when a problem is global, solutions can be implemented and tested in a single community. As an example, deforestation is a worldwide problem with significant implications for climate, air quality, water quality, and wildlife habitat. There is little that an individual in North America can do about the loss of rain forest in Brazil, for example, but action is possible through voluntary organizations such as Global ReLeaf, which is dedicated to planting trees in many nations. These organizations are part of a new movement in urban forestry, and psychologists are working with them to encourage local residents to plant and maintain trees. In this way, the actions of individuals in their own communities are linked through organizational networks to programs that can reduce environmental pollution.

THEORIES IN ENVIRONMENTAL PSYCHOLOGY

Theories in environmental psychology consider the person and environment as a unit rather than separately. Most of these theories have been adapted from other areas of psychology. For example, theories of environmental perception, which deal with issues such as how people view natural and built landscapes, are taken from the psychology of perception. Theories of social behavior (e.g., crowding, personal space preferences, territoriality) in various environments draw heavily on social psychology. Theories of how people organize environmental experience to plan routes from one place to another (wayfinding) employ concepts and methods from research in cognitive psychology.

In accordance with their ecological (interactional) approach, theories of environmental psychology reject the notion of *environmental determinism*, which assumes that environmental conditions directly cause people to act in a certain way. So, although painting a classroom bright colors is likely to provoke comments, it probably won't have a measurable effect on student grades. Similarly, an attractive work environment may be appreciated by employees, but is not likely by itself to raise output. A famous set of experiments in the 1930s at the Western Electric Company (known as the "Hawthorne experiments") revealed the complexity of the relationships between the physical surroundings and productivity. These experiments found that when management, in consultation with employees, improved working conditions, productivity rose. However, when economic conditions later forced management to cut back on the improvements, productivity rose still higher! It appeared that the interest of management in consulting with employees, not just improved working conditions, was responsible for the observed improvements. Yet David Canter, an environmental psychologist in the United Kingdom, describes receiving telephone calls from managers who believe that a fresh coat of paint will solve all their problems, and tells of a housing official who hoped that a different color in his office would reduce the intensity of tenant complaints.[10]

What is interesting is that color *does* affect mood and attitude, but in complex ways. Laboratory experiments and questionnaire studies have shown that red and yellow are associated with increased energy and activity, and blue is associated with lower energy.[11] Indeed, years ago, some mental hospitals used blue rooms to calm excited patients and red rooms to stimulate depressed patients. Yet under most circumstances, color operates indirectly on mood and behavior as one of many background elements. An incompetent computer programmer is not going to become competent suddenly because of new office furniture, pleasant background music, or a coat of red paint on the walls. Most probably, he or she will become a more satisfied, but still incompetent, programmer. In other words, the environment's influence on mood and attitude may or may not translate into effects on performance and productivity. Because attractive surroundings can make people feel better without having a measurable effect on their output, environmental psychologists face a dilemma: they cannot promise too much, but at the same time do not want to ignore people's feelings of comfort and well-being. To find the right balance between promise and delivery, David Canter suggests that the key to applying environmental psychology in the workplace is to understand what the environment means to people and how they view their surroundings, not to impose simplistic formulas—that red walls will raise energy levels; round tables will produce sociability.

Because it is interdisciplinary and problem centered, most research in environmental psychology has employed a variety of theories and methods to deal with a particular problem. However, some investigators have approached the field from a single theoretical perspective. Two noteworthy examples are ecological psychology and behavioristic psychology.

Ecological psychology relies on observation of people in their ordinary surroundings. It began with Kurt Lewin, a social psychologist, who declared that the first step in understanding peoples' behavior is to study the opportunities and constraints in the environment.[12] These environmental features are not accidental, of course, since people select certain settings because of what they offer and are then, in turn, affected by these settings. Lewin's associate, Roger Barker, subsequently compiled maps showing people's interaction with their physical surroundings, much like the maps biologists create to describe animal and plant communities.[13] Studying natural behavior in this way avoids the artificiality and constraints of the laboratory where people (typically college students) spend time answering questions or filling out forms under the watchful eyes of an experimenter, in return for extra credit in their psychology classes.

Examples of ecologically oriented observational approaches in environmental psychology are seen in the city planning studies of William Whyte and the behavioral recordings of the Envirosell firm in New York City. Whyte charted the occupancy of city parks and plazas and found that some were more heavily used than others.[14] Through detailed recording, he was able to relate occupancy levels to physical features of the setting. In 1975, his research was used in the New York City General Plan, which allowed developers to add additional floors to a building, or receive other benefits, in return for pedestrian amenities at ground level. The Envirosell firm still conducts observational studies for commercial clients, charting the behavior of customers in supermarkets, restaurants, and retail stores.[15] They are currently conducting observations designed to improve the efficiency of post offices. Using videotapes and human observers, the Envirosell team records the time people spend in various activities, such as waiting in line, reading instructions, interacting with a clerk, filling out forms, and so on. On the basis of their research, several models for new post office designs have been developed and implemented on a trial basis.

A very different observational approach is seen in *applied behavior analysis* methods, which have their roots in behaviorism, in particular in B. F. Skinner's book, *Functional Analysis of Behavior*. Because this approach relies on experiments to find cause-and-effect relationships, it focuses on behavior that can be observed and tends to avoid measuring people's opinions and attitudes. For example, Scott Geller has used applied behavioral analysis to increase environmentally supportive behaviors such as recycling, composting, energy conservation, use of public transportation, and carpooling.[16] He found that small monetary rewards or "contests with prizes" could encourage people to collect more discarded cans or use more public transportation. These small-scale experiments do not lend themselves to directly confronting large-scale sources of environmental degradation such as industrial pollution, deforestation, global warming, and excessive population growth. However, the approach provides a practical strategy for behavior change that complements larger legislative and regulatory measures.

SKILLS NEEDED BY ENVIRONMENTAL PSYCHOLOGISTS

A wide range of skills is required for applied work in environmental psychology. Some skills can be learned in an academic program, especially if there are class projects, such as evaluating classrooms or behavioral mapping of outside areas (where people sit and stand, and the routes they take from one place to another). However, good intentions and traditional courses are not sufficient. Other aspects of applied work, involving contact with clients, design professionals, and building occupants, are probably learned best through internships or part-time work on design projects. My own campus has two centers that offer consultation and design assistance to communities, and students receive training on projects that improve the quality of life in various types of settings. A recent example concerned the design of a hospital garden intended to provide a restorative environment for patients, visitors, and staff. Another project laid the basis for a skateboard park for teenagers.

Let's consider some of the special skills needed in applied work in environmental psychology.

Ability to Work on Interdisciplinary Teams

Almost all projects involving the environment are multidisciplinary. A city planning team can include urban and regional planners, transportation planners, engineers, economists, architects, landscape architects, and behavioral scientists. To participate on such a team, one must be able to communicate with people from various backgrounds who speak different technical languages. Often the environmental psychologist will have only a small role. On one urban design project, my role was to conduct a needs analysis among street people. This required contact with these people and the social agencies serving them, and bringing this information back to other team members, who had obtained information about traffic circulation, housing, retail sales, employment, bond financing, schools, crime, and other relevant issues. All the information then had to be integrated within a comprehensive plan for developing a part of the city that contained many street people and agencies that had been left out of earlier plans.

A Knowledge of Methods Useful in Natural Conditions

For most applied projects, there is not time or money for laboratory experimentation. All or most of the research is done in the field. This requires flexibility, ingenuity, a knowledge of a variety of methods and when to use them, plus knowledge of the limitations of each method. Survey methods, for example, are used often in environmental psychology, particularly in needs analysis and postoccupancy evaluation. If one wants to know occupants' opinions of apartments and houses in a neighborhood, it will probably be necessary to interview them, conduct a mail survey, or both. Other behavioral research methods that are especially useful in design and planning projects are behavioral mapping, cognitive mapping, the semantic differential technique, and trace measures.

Behavioral mapping is a way of systematically recording people's locations: finding out where they sit, stand, and otherwise spend time. There are two main types of behavioral mapping. In place-centered mapping, observers remain in a fixed location and record the activities of all people within view. Video cameras can be used to record these activities, and human observers later review the videotapes and construct behavioral maps. The second approach, particularly suited to large spaces such as shopping centers, is individual-centered mapping, in which the researcher follows selected individuals throughout their entire stay in an area, recording where they go and what they do. Maps of separate individuals can also be combined into composite maps, with thick lines showing areas of heavy usage. Retailers can use the information to locate displays and redirect traffic into areas not being visited.

Cognitive mapping is used in city planning to learn peoples' mental representations: how they think about places, landmarks, buildings, and other natural features that stand out in their minds. This information can be used to develop user-friendly maps that show buildings and destinations important to residents, to identify dangerous parts of the city that could benefit from improved lighting or more frequent police patrols, or to find tourist destinations that can be featured in advertisements and tourist brochures.

The *semantic differential technique* measures the meanings that people associate with places. Is a neighborhood viewed as safe or dangerous, attractive or ugly, well-kept or rundown, pleasant or unpleasant? This information can guide planning and development decisions. For example, there would be reason to challenge a redevelopment plan for a neighborhood that was highly valued by its residents, when an adjacent area of the city was considered to be an undesirable place to live.

Trace measures are the by-products of interactions. In assessing neighborhood quality, for example, environmental psychologists might look at graffiti and litter, as well as security measures taken by storekeepers and home owners (e.g., bars on windows or Neighborhood Watch signs). Further information about these methods can be found in research methods textbooks.[17]

Flexibility in Time Management

Architects and designers typically keep unusual schedules. When a large project comes along, they work through the night and on weekends to meet critical deadlines. Architecture students learn how to operate in this way during their training. Studios and classrooms remain open throughout the night to allow sleep-deprived students to complete their assignments. Psychology students are usually not accustomed to doing research on this kind of schedule. They expect time to review the literature and conduct studies, plus additional time for data entry and analysis. These expectations are not realistic on most design projects, where deadlines are set in weeks rather than semesters. Information must be gathered and compiled quickly, or it will not be useful in team discussions.

Ability to Conduct Archival Research

It is important to know how to find books and periodicals in landscape planning and urban design, as well as in psychology and other applied fields. Many of the most relevant sources are likely to be unpublished reports from government agencies and private firms. The Internet may also be helpful in locating sources, especially at the beginning of the search, although the amount of information can be excessive, and much of it irrelevant.

Graphic Literacy

Traditional psychology programs emphasize verbal and conceptual skills, but many of the environmental fields rely heavily on visual representation. Large-scale landscape projects require the use of maps, satellite photographs, and geographic information systems. Many projects require video or slide documentation designed to capture on film specific interactions between people and features of the environment. In conducting research on bicycle paths, for example, I took hundreds of photographs of bicyclists riding in traffic. The pictures were useful in identifying problems, such as cyclists' attempting to turn left from a bike line along the right side of the road, and suggesting possible solutions, such as special light signals and turn lanes for cyclists. It is also important to understand the limitations of graphic techniques. For example, architects' drawings tend to show buildings from odd angles and highlight features that occupants would not notice. Architectural scale models usually look appealing even when the actual building may be unattractive and dysfunctional.

Advocacy

Sometimes an environmental problem may call for advocacy in attempting to persuade others to accept a new point of view. This is especially true when groups that will be affected by the project are not represented in the planning. For example, in designing facilities for Alzheimer's patients, an environmental psychologist may advocate for the privacy needs of the patients over the nursing staff's desire for easy observation of patients. Although the eventual solution is likely to be a compromise between these two legitimate needs, it is the task of the environmental psychologist to represent the patients' needs. Thus, the ability to present recommendations persuasively and tactfully is an important aspect of design consultation. There are also occasions when people's preferences must be put aside for valid reasons. For example, corporate employees may want air-conditioning because they have been accustomed to having it. If environmental psychologists assign air-conditioning as a lower priority than energy conservation, they may collaborate with the architect to gain employee acceptance of a climatically responsive building that will require them to adapt their clothing to different seasons. As an advocate, an environmental psychologist does not blindly represent consumer opinion but works to educate consumers about the trade-offs connected with various options.

RANGE OF PROFESSIONAL ACTIVITIES

Environmental psychology is a young field, and the psychologists working within it have been resourceful in creating new niches and roles for themselves as they work for corporations, government agencies, educational institutions, or in private practice. Wherever they work, their activities typically include consultation, research and evaluation, environmental simulation, teaching, and public service.

Consultation

Environmental psychologists consult on a wide variety of projects. Sometimes the participation is invited in a specialty area and broadens during the course of the project as different needs emerge. Consultation is a means by which a psychologist has direct input into the planning of buildings and communities, compared to the slower route of publishing a research paper and hoping that the results will be read and used by practitioners. Typically a consultant is hired and paid for a specified number of workdays.

A consultant's first task is to identify the client. Sometimes this is difficult because the client may have delegated responsibility to someone else, and the consultant has contact only with the delegate and not the original client. The client may be the owner of a building, the manager, an architect, or perhaps a government agency. Rarely will it be the actual occupants of a building or neighborhood.

All applications must be adapted to local conditions. The park or building that is suited to one community may not be appropriate for another. Even methods of consultation will differ across settings. Geographic, cultural, architectural, and economic factors affect the suitability of a design. This increases the value of doing a user needs analysis prior to the actual design and a postoccupancy evaluation afterward to gauge the effectiveness of the design. On large-scale projects, where the occupants will be not available until construction is complete, the environmental psychologist can serve as surrogate and advocate for the users, representing their needs and interests throughout the planning process. Information used in such roles can come from the evaluation of similar projects in other locations and from simulation exercises that can reveal how the building or other project will be perceived when it is occupied.

Some of my experiences as a consultant in environmental psychology provide examples of this activity:

Windowless Offices   A major bank chain planned to build an underground data processing center and wanted to know how the lack of windows would affect employee morale and performance. I reviewed the literature on underground buildings and windowless offices and presented a report to the company architect. I suggested ways of reducing the negative effects of underground work through light wells from above ground, greenery, and artwork with nature themes.

Urban Design Assistance Team   I was part of an interdisciplinary team of architects, planners, economists, and developers that planned the revitalization of downtown areas in Portland, Oregon, and Baton Rouge, Louisiana. My role in Portland was to identify service needs of street people; in Baton Rouge, it was to increase public confidence in the planning process, since voters had become disillusioned by the failure of previous plans.

Ecological Design   I was part of the team that was designing guidelines for the future development of Wakaya Island, an island in the Fiji group that had been uninhabited. Our aim was to ensure that new zoning regulations and design standards would respect the local ecology and culture. I spent a week visiting hotels and resorts on other islands and reading material about Fiji prior to meeting with the design team. I also examined aspects of native culture on other islands that might be introduced into the island, and observed and tracked the activities of the tourist population (who came mostly from Australia and New Zealand).

Bay Area Rapid Transit (BART) Because I had done research on seating arrangements in various public spaces (including airport lounges, library reading areas, hospital waiting rooms, and schools), I was hired by an architecture firm to consult on seating for BART subway cars in the San Francisco area. The goal was to provide a seating arrangement that would comfortably accommodate suburban commuters on longer trips as well as larger groups of tightly packed standing riders during rush hours. We produced a design that combined fixed seats for most riders—two people per double seat—along with separate open areas (away from the seats) for standees or people with bicycles, which are allowed on trains during non-peak-hours.

Research and Evaluation

Environmental psychologists conduct studies for government agencies, design professionals, and client organizations. Many of these fall into the categories of user needs analysis and postoccupancy evaluation. The former takes place before a design is made, the latter after the building is occupied. As an example of a needs analysis, the planning of a convalescent hospital would require knowledge of the special needs of the elderly in terms of illumination, physical support (railings), orientation (signs and color codes), social support, access to medical services, and the like.

A postoccupancy evaluation investigates how the building functions after it is opened for use. In the hospital example, patients and staff of the completed facility would be surveyed regarding specific design features, including those addressed in the needs analysis (e.g., whether the occupants were satisfied with the lighting, the railings, and other features). A postoccupancy evaluation can be converted into a quasi-experiment by constructing a building in stages and using postoccupancy evaluations of the early units to improve later phases of construction. In a similar manner, the management of existing facilities (how space is allocated and used) can be varied systematically according to an experimental plan and the results at each stage evaluated and compared.[18]

Simulation

Another way in which researchers in environmental psychology have influenced design and planning is through environmental simulation, which involves the creation of images or models that show what a project will look like after it is completed. For example, in preparation for manned space flights, the National Aeronautic and Space Administration (NASA) sponsored studies of the effects of short- and long-term confinement on morale, mood, and mental alertness. Some of the studies took place in full-scale models, and others were done in submarines, polar weather stations, and oil drilling platforms, where groups spent long periods in isolation under harsh environmental conditions.

Architects and landscape architects have traditionally used drawings and scale models as simulation tools. A landscape architect will provide drawings of a proposed park containing distinctive geographic features, vegetation, structures, paths, elevations, and equipment. An architect shows a client plans and a scale model of a proposed building. Based on discussions with the client, the architect then redraws the plans and reshapes the model to the client's specifications. As projects became larger and more complex, with multiple clients and user groups, new technologies were needed that could include more people in the design process and present them with alternatives. Both video and virtual reality techniques* permit public assessment and comparison of different design solutions. They are useful techniques because, in general, the responses of people viewing video images or photographs are similar to those of people viewing an actual scene.[19]

The Environmental Simulation Laboratory at the University of California, Berkeley, uses video to explore the public response to design alternatives. A video camera with a tiny lens is moved through a scale model at the speeds associated with either walking or driving, and it provides a videotape that can be viewed and rated by other audiences. By changing the scale model, different design options can be explored (e.g., buildings shown at various heights, or housing of various densities). This procedure was used to create zoning regulations for high-rise buildings in San Francisco where local residents and public officials were shown images of how the city would look as a result of different development strategies.[20]

Computer-generated virtual reality is being used in architecture to give future occupants an idea of what a building will be like, both inside and outside. These methods are also used to check buildings for handicap accessibility. The users wear earphones and special goggles containing a color TV screen, and a computer regulates the users' sensory inputs, coordinating them with body movements tracked by sensors as they "travel" through the building.[21] As the person "walks" through corridors and rooms, the acoustical and visual environments change. Colored images show light and shadow, which change as the individual "enters" virtual corridors and virtual rooms. This procedure has been used to test the acoustical properties of a concert hall. It was also used to create fully detailed models of an office building, complete with furniture, carpets, walls, lighting, doors, indoor plants, and signs. This technology allows viewers to move through the building at their own pace or remain in an area to learn how it might feel to work or live there. It can also reveal design flaws not apparent in two-dimensional blueprints.

Teaching

Environmental psychologists teach students and professionals in many environmental fields. For example, Frank Becker directs the Facilities Management Program at Cornell University. His courses emphasize the design and management of buildings. Rachel Kaplan teaches in the Department of Natural Resources at the University of Michigan, where her students learn how to manage outdoor areas and deal with conflicts between different user groups. Joe Fridgen heads the Department

---

*There are several user groups on the Internet concerned with applications of virtual reality (for example, virtpsy@sjuvm.stjohns.edu).

of Leisure Studies at Michigan State University. His classes on outdoor recreation and tourism attract students and professionals from a wide variety of fields.

Public Service

Environmental psychologists serve on various boards and committees, testify at legislative hearings, and advise planning groups and organizations on environmental issues. For instance, Rich Wener, who teaches at the Polytechnic Institute of New York, serves as adviser to the Bruner Foundation of Cambridge, Massachusetts, which offers a biannual award of $50,000 to recognize urban places that are socially supportive, physically pleasing, and economically viable. Wener is responsible for inspecting the finalist locations in a national competition to ensure that the places operate as described.

On task forces concerned with urban revitalization, environmental psychologists have attempted to ensure that the needs of local residents are not overlooked in the rush to tear down older buildings. Psychologists have also served on panels to select architects for major projects, again ensuring that the architect selected is sensitive to occupant concerns, not just formal design features.

Sometimes there are intangible, unexpected roles for psychologists on design teams. It may, for example, become necessary to be a translator when people on a design project do not understand what others are saying. Occasionally I have been a counterweight to another consultant. This occurred, for example, in a hospital renovation project for a state health agency. The engineers were very impressed with the concrete warehouse-like buildings because they were structurally sound and earthquake-proof, but very negative about several wood-frame structures used for patients in special programs. These views were opposite to those of nurses and patients, who disliked the concrete "barns" as much as they appreciated the small cottages whose windows could be opened. My role was to present data on the views of nurses and patients that could balance the engineers' arguments about earthquake safety. The final recommendations on the project represented a compromise between structural integrity and occupant satisfaction.

SPECIALIZED TRAINING IN ENVIRONMENTAL PSYCHOLOGY

Other than in academic settings, most job opportunities in environmental psychology are at the borders of applied fields. Some of the most exciting work in creating more humane environments is being done by individuals trained in more than one discipline. These people might be architects with a background in psychology or psychologists who have taken courses and conducted research in landscape perception. The membership of the Environmental Design Research Association (EDRA) includes behavior-oriented design professionals and policymakers, as well as design-oriented behavioral scientists. The cross-disciplinary nature of environmental psychology has opened up multiple training models for advanced work in the field. For example, there are programs explicitly in environmental psychology (e.g., City University of New York or Arizona State University) and programs in applied fields, such as facilities management (Cornell University) or housing (University of Illinois); or one can obtain a degree in a traditional design field with a specialty in behavioral aspects of design. I am advising a student who has been accepted by a program in environmental psychology and by programs in urban planning. He has a background in psychology and wants to work on urban issues. His options are to pursue graduate work in environmental psychology while focusing on urban problems in his research, or he could become an urban planner while retaining his interests in behavioral issues.

THE FUTURE OF ENVIRONMENTAL PSYCHOLOGY

Financial support for applied environmental psychology is unpredictable. Government agencies sponsor studies and consultation on an *ad hoc* basis, often reflecting shifts in public policy. The 1960s brought interest in mental hospitals. In the 1970s, it was prisons, energy conservation, and recycling. By the 1980s, there was concern with outdoor settings, and in the 1990s interest has focused on office buildings. Flexibility in one's choice of problems and methods is required for work in this relatively new field. No one can predict with certainty what the next priorities for public support will be.

At the same time, some researchers have managed to devote their careers to a single type of building. For example, Terry Maple concentrates on zoo design, addressing issues such as the environmental needs of various animal species, animal-human interactions, visitor behavior, and the educational value of zoos. Frank Becker specializes in office design, including new high-tech facilities and the home offices used by telecommuters. Jay Farbstein has consulted on numerous jail projects, and Yvonne Clearwater works for NASA on person-environment issues in long-term space flight.

The direction of the field is determined by the activities of its practitioners. The future will depend on the success of their efforts and the ability of researchers to open up new applications. If environmental psychologists are to be hired as full-time employees in design offices rather than as occasional consultants, they will have to keep demonstrating that they can significantly improve people's satisfaction with their environment.

SUGGESTIONS FOR FURTHER READING

Bell, P. A., Greene, T. C., Fisher, J. D., and Baum, A. (1996). *Environmental psychology* (4th ed.). Fort Worth, TX: Harcourt Brace.

Cherulnik, P. D. (1993). *Applicants of environment-behavior research.* New York: Cambridge University Press.

Gifford, R. (1997). *Environmental psychology* (2nd ed.). Boston: Allyn and Bacon.

Stokols, D., & Altman, I. (Eds.). (1987). *Handbook of environmental psychology.* New York: Wiley.

Recent issues of two journals: *Environment and Behavior* and *Journal of Environment Psychology.*

Much of the applied literature in the field is necessarily topical and found in subject area periodicals. For example, in zoo design, more material can be found in the zoo literature than in journals of environmental psychology. There are several organizations where further information about the field can be obtained. The oldest and largest of these organizations is the Environmental Design Research Association (P.O. Box 7146, Edmund, OK 73083-7146). There are also networks of researchers and practitioners concerned with specific types of environments (e.g., health, work, housing, children's environments, gerontological environments) that can be accessed through EDRA (edra@telepath.com).

PSYCHOLOGY APPLIED TO PRODUCT DESIGN

Leon Segal and Jane Fulton Suri

Think about a product you own and like. Why do you like it? What are the qualities you enjoy? Where is it now? Why is it there? Did you buy it, or was it a gift? Did you know you wanted it? Were there alternatives in the same class of product? What particular features make yours special? Do other people consider this object special? Did it change your habits in any way? Did you have to learn anything about it to make it valuable to you?

Whatever product you have in mind—a pen, a book, a CD player—most of the qualities you enjoy about these items, and many you may be unaware of, are the result of decisions made by product designers. The aim of designers is to consider the purpose, form, layout, materials, buttons, screens, functions, and look and feel of products in order to create the experience consumers will have interacting with the product in whatever context they encounter it.

Now take a quick break from reading and look around you. Very likely much of what you see is an *artifact*: a product of human design and manufacturing. This book, the chair you are sitting on, the clothes you wear, the pen or pencil you use, the light fixture illuminating these words: all were designed and manufactured by humans.

Most artifacts we encounter are probably a combination of several types of design and production processes. For example, creation of the pen you use involved several different efforts: designing and manufacturing the hard (probably plastic or steel) outer body as well as the inner plumbing, the mechanisms for exposing and protecting the writing tip, and the production and packaging of the ink. Moreover, the design effort directed at this pen was not limited to these obvious aspects. Notice that in the process of getting the pen into your possession, it was packaged in a box that was also designed by someone. The box probably had some graphics on it that were designed by yet another person, as were the store shelf that displayed the pen, the price labels, and the cash register. In addition, on its way to the store, the pen was transported by train, truck, or plane, themselves products of a design process. Clearly, following the path of any single product results in a complex array of supporting products and artifacts.

It's not surprising, then, that experts from many fields contribute their knowledge to the creation of any one product. Engineers (both mechanical and electrical) select the right materials and processes so that mechanisms and electronic components perform appropriately; industrial designers and interaction designers give objects their overall form and appearance, creating details that have beauty, utility, and meaning. The main role of psychologists in product design is to apply their knowledge of how people think, feel, and act in order to understand the experience of using a product, and, in turn, affect its design appropriately.

This chapter does not cover the contribution of psychology to all artifacts designed and produced; such an undertaking would go far beyond the scope of this book—and probably beyond the practical scope of any book. Instead, we will confine our discussion to the type of artifacts we encounter in our work at a design and product development company. This company develops products that we consider to be of human scale in physical size and complexity—products that are generally used by one or a few people at a time, such as a car or telephone, rather than an oil rig or nuclear power plant.

A BRIEF HISTORY OF PSYCHOLOGY IN DESIGN

The introduction of psychology into the design process is a recent development, but long before product design and psychology were named or recognized as formal disciplines, people were making things with an understanding of the behavior and abilities of the individuals who would use them. Our earliest ancestors made simple tools, adapting stone, wood, and bone to create forms that others would recognize and use as a handle, hammer, or blade. Considering the form and decorations on some of these instruments, the toolmakers at the time were well aware of the aesthetic and symbolic value of their artifacts as well as their function. We can also see how the tools gradually became refined and adapted to users' needs through the sensitivity, care, and skill of the makers.

For thousands of years, the human toolmaker was also the tool designer, but after the Industrial Revolution in the nineteenth century, machines took over the production of most products, and industrialized labor practices separated the activity of design from manufacture. Gradually, specialized engineering functions emerged to design and mass-produce ever more elaborate products. Certainly there were attempts to accommodate users' needs and capabilities, but such goals were often superseded by functional or mechanical considerations as technology became increasingly complex.

The Entrance of Psychology

Psychology began to mature as a science in the first half of the twentieth century, a time that included two world wars. Few machines have been more complex than those produced for war. In World War II, especially, highly complex military equipment was put into action. War is a situation with high penalties for system failure, in terms of both human and equipment losses. And failures there were—some due to mechanical factors, but many more attributable to human factors, including the factors contributing to human error.

Psychologists became involved in redesigning equipment so that failures due to human factors or error could be minimized. Psychological principles of perception and cognition were applied to the design of communications systems, instrument dials, and the layout of controls in aircraft and tanks so that operators could understand them more accurately and react to them more appropriately. For example, as part of the Army and Air Force Aviation Psychology Program, work by M. J. Warrick uncovered operators' intuitive responses about which way to turn a rotary control in order to move a pointer up or down, or to the right or left.[1] He found that people generally expect to turn a rotary control clockwise in order to move a horizontal pointer from left to right; you may have experienced this if you have ever used a rotary control to tune a radio that has a linear dial. Designs that conform to expectations are much easier to use and result in fewer errors than those that contradict them.

The application of psychology to product design at this time was variously known as human factors, engineering psychology, or human factors engineering. In Europe, ergonomics emerged as an applied science linking psychology with physical human sciences, such as physiology and biomechanics.

Following the war, psychologists began to design products geared toward more peaceful and humanitarian ends. For example, one of the psychologists at Dunlap & Associates, the first U.S. engineering psychology firm, improved pill-counting accuracy in a bottling plant.[2] The workers had used boards, with a fixed number of pill-sized indentations in them, which they dipped into a bin of pills. When the workers slid out the boards, most indentations would contain a pill. The worker would then have to find the empty indentations and add the missing pills. Psychologists improved the workers' ability and accuracy in finding empty spots simply by adding a dab of bright orange paint to the bottom of each indentation.

The Birth of Industrial Design

In the period before and immediately after World War II, the profession of industrial design was developing largely in reaction to a perceived lack of aesthetic appeal in the design of most mass-produced products. Industrial designers were concerned with the aesthetic of form and function and also showed concern with designing for people. Firsthand accounts of these early days are given by the leading designers of the time, Raymond Loewy and Henry Dreyfuss.[3]

Henry Dreyfuss pioneered efforts within the design profession to respect human capabilities and limitations, physical as well as psychological. Dreyfuss, and the other designers who worked with him, also embraced the work of human factors professionals, particularly where there were established guidelines or rules of thumb that designers could apply. For example, Humanscale, a system of scales still in use today, was developed at Dreyfuss Associates by Niels Diffrient and his colleagues to allow designers easy access to data on humans' physical characteristics and perceptual abilities.[4] Using Humanscale, designers can select a characteristic or ability by rotating a dial, and then read design values that appear in a cut-out window. For example, one can choose a particular population group, such as ten year olds or adult women, and Humanscale reveals information about that group's maximum reach capacities; or one can select a viewing distance and be shown the size of printed type that would be legible at that distance.

Growth of Consumerism

Technological progress following the war led to the development of many products aimed at labor-saving and entertainment for home, leisure, and work. Vacuum cleaners, refrigerators, lawnmowers, televisions, and telephones were being produced in many versions and styles. Consumers were faced with many choices, and manufacturers learned that in order to convince the consumer to want their particular product, they had to pay attention to what people liked and disliked about the look and operation of that product. As a result, industrial designers were hired by many companies to help them be more sensitive to consumer needs and to design products that were attractive, functional, and pleasurable to use.

Product Design Standards

As products became more powerful and complex, consumers faced greater losses, or even injury, if something went wrong while using them. An electric sewing machine, for example, cost more and was potentially more hazardous than its hand- or foot-driven predecessor. In order to protect consumers, consumer advocates and organizations that set manufacturing standards began to put pressure on companies to take responsibility for damage or injury resulting from the use of their products. The concern was not only with dangers encountered during normal use but also in case of foreseeable misuse (see Figure 1). Consequently, product designers had to start thinking about the behavioral consequences of design decisions, such as making a "stop" button a different color and texture from its surroundings so that it can

Figure 1

Do you see what's wrong here? The person is holding the chainsaw's safety guard instead of its handle because the position and form of the safety guard make it easier (but more dangerous) to hold.

more easily be found during an emergency. As a result of these concerns, some human factors psychologists became specialists in equipment safety and human error and helped frame standards and legislation.*

The Computer Age and "Smart" Products

Developments in computer technology in the 1970s and 1980s brought new opportunities for both designers and psychologists. Since computer programs are based on logical procedures requiring users to be logical as well, psychologists began to apply their understanding of human intelligence and cognitive processes to explore the ways in which people interact with computers. They researched the cognitive demands placed on people by computers and helped design new systems and software to enable efficient and productive use of computer technology.

Computer technology and microprocessors were soon incorporated into everyday products—creating what are today called "smart products." Computers became pocket-sized notebooks and wrist-worn devices. Microprocessors were installed in dishwashers, cars, and cameras. These developments increased the functionality and complexity of most products dramatically. At the same time, an increasingly sophisticated population of consumers sought products that looked good, worked well, and were simple and pleasant to use. In order to meet the demands of consumers, designers turned to human factors psychologists, who became key players in the production of new, complex equipment and intelligent systems.

CURRENT TRENDS IN PRODUCT DESIGN

What are the latest trends in product design and in psychologists' role in it? There are several, and we consider the most important of them in the following sections.

Increased Pace and Competition

Today, product design takes place in an ever more highly competitive business climate. Companies face constant pressure to invent new and better products, and to develop them faster and more efficiently. At the same time, consumers are becoming more demanding about product quality and performance. New media, principally the Internet, offer expanding opportunities for selling products and providing information to consumers about the relative value of the choices available. All of these challenges stimulate product designers and developers to make wise choices about the products they introduce into the marketplace.

---

*Particularly in the United States, this area of safety research has developed into an almost entirely litigious activity, with psychologists acting as expert witnesses in lawsuits involving product manufacturers.

Design as a Strategic Business Advantage

Advertising, quality of service, price, and packaging are all important aspects of a product. But think how your experience of using your toothbrush, washing machine, or automobile contributes to your sense of the company or brand associated with it. Is it just the cost, service, and function, or is it the overall appeal of the design as well? Companies such as Apple, Allessi, Braun, and Philips have long valued design as a central function in their business—a function that is not subservient to marketing, manufacturing, or engineering. And in recent years, because most companies can manufacture products with similar prices, functions, and quality, product design has been recognized as an important way that businesses can differentiate themselves favorably from their competitors.

Psychologists have been able to apply their knowledge of human behavior and motivation to help companies anticipate and provide products that are both useful and appealing to consumers. Psychologists have not only contributed to the design of office furniture, computer products, and photocopiers, for example, but have also helped improve consumers' interactions with products, including game controllers offered by Logitech and Sega, and cameras made by Eastman Kodak.

Availability of Specialized Technology

Technology and equipment originally developed in defense industries have now become available to the civilian population. Many products currently available to the mass market—for example, cellular phones, personal computers, and espresso coffee makers—started out as work-related equipment for people in specialized jobs. Ready access to these items by the general population means that the products have to be instantly understood and usable. In the medical field particularly, this trend has had a significant impact. Equipment once used only by medically trained personnel, such as drug infusion pumps and glucose monitors, are now in the hands of largely untrained people who are taking care of themselves or family members. Human factors psychologists have worked with designers to ensure that people with varying abilities and experiences can use these products easily. For example, the Heartstream ForeRunner defibrillator was designed not just for highly trained paramedics, but for a wide range of people, including cabin crews in commercial aircraft. In order to help inexperienced users, the defibrillator incorporates familiar images, clear indication of buttons and sequence of action, and simple step-by-step on-screen and voice prompts.

Importance of Service

Products are rarely experienced independently of some kind of service offering. Your choice of car, stereo, or computer probably involved some consideration of how easily it could be serviced, upgraded, or repaired. Using a public telephone, for example, has as much to do with the quality of service to which you connect as with the design of the handset and keypad. The recognition that people's perception of products goes beyond the design of the product itself has expanded the scope of product design. Once more, psychologists are in a position to contribute an understanding of how the total experience of use might be improved by the service-related aspects of products.

Complexity of Products

Successful use of even a simple product, such as a door handle or pen, requires more than physical strength and agility. Users of these products must also consider: Does this need a pull, a push, or a twist to open it? Does the pull, push, or twist need to be strong or gentle? Will this brand work like the other, more familiar ones? In order to help users answer these questions, even simple products usually provide cues that guide behavior. For example, as you remove the cap from a pen, you are aware of different materials, textures, and split-lines between the cap and barrel; similarly, some door handles are shaped in a way that induces you to grab and pull them. But we barely notice ourselves reacting to these cues until we pull on the handle of a door that needs a push or shove to open it! Clearly, even with simple operations on everyday items, we are processing a variety of sensory information and drawing on our understanding and memory of similar experiences in order to make proper user decisions.

More complex products that employ electronic technology tend to incorporate possibilities and opportunities that are invisible and unpredictable to users. For example, a product might be wireless and invisibly networked to communicate with others or receive broadcast media, and the software button that operates the communication function has no mechanical connection with the elements it controls. For this reason, cues to indicate the significance of a particular feature have to be designed into the product. Working with designers, psychologists help provide cues that will promote a consistent mental model of the product's operation and guide users to act almost intuitively in achieving their goals.

The Symbolic Value of Products

A key goal of product designers is to ensure that the overall form of the design, selection of materials, layout of control features, and design detailing lead people to use the product effectively. But people's choices are not based on these qualities alone. Swatch's analog watches, for example, have been very successful products despite the fact that their design often makes it quite difficult to tell the time. Their success demonstrates that material possessions can have a profound symbolic significance for their owners, as well as for other people; that is, they influence the ways in which we think about ourselves and others.[5] Thus, our possessions can be a powerful form of nonverbal communication.[6] For example, a BMW car or Rolex watch are widely understood to send messages about wealth and status. Even when you select a briefcase or bag, you probably consider practical issues such as its capacity and features, but you may also think about its look and its image. Does the bag say practical, rugged, serious, professional, or arty? Is its image consistent with your other accessories? Does it have some social significance for you? Is it like the one you used in high school or is it of material similar to the bag your grandfather used to have? Is it a brand your peers carry, or would like to carry?

Impact of Global Markets

There was a time when it was amazing just to have a Walkman that allowed you to carry around your own personal sound system. Now, many versions exist, produced by Sony and its competitors, aimed at different groups of users throughout the world. This market differentiation is a boon for designers, who are now able to create a range of products with different prices, features, functions, and styles to appeal to people with different needs, abilities, tastes, lifestyles, customs, and languages. Here, the contribution of psychology to product design overlaps with psychologists' efforts in market research in order to discover, classify, and interpret the unique design requirements of all the individuals who might be the product's buyers and users.

Environmental Concerns

As more people use more products, as more raw material and energy are consumed in production, and as technology changes more rapidly, there is growing awareness by many people, including designers, of products' possible negative environmental consequences. Legislation in some countries, such as Germany and the Netherlands, requires that manufacturers take responsibility for their product throughout its life cycle, including the cost of its eventual disposal. Designers have responded to environmental concerns by specifying reusable, recycled, or recyclable materials; designing products that can be reused or disassembled for refurbishment or recycling; and considering less energy-intensive and wasteful production methods.

Environmental consequences are beginning to play a role in product choices too. In his book on human and ecological values in design, Nigel Whiteley describes the rapid growth of the "Green Consumer," who registers his or her ecological commitment through buying products that are supposed to be "planet friendly."[7] As professionals concerned with human values, health, and well-being, psychologists, too, are mindful of the environmental impact of design decisions (see Figure 2).

THE WORK OF HUMAN FACTORS PSYCHOLOGISTS

There are four main areas of activity for human factors psychologists as contributors to a design team: research, design, the evaluation and refinement of the product development process, and communication with team members from other disciplines. We will describe each of these in turn, but it is important to note that the activities are not strictly sequential. For example, communication with team members

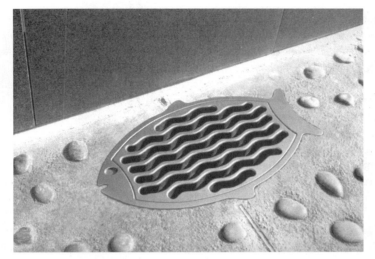

Figure 2

How might the form of a drain cover influence people's behavior? Here, the designers have provided a visual reminder that the drain connects to a life-sustaining habitat. Would you pour hazardous chemicals into it? (Photo courtesy of Mauk Design)

is necessary throughout the process, and each of the development phases may be repeated several times before the end of the entire process. Evaluating a proposed design solution—often by observing users as they interact with a prototype or mock-up of the product—usually leads to new understanding, which subsequently results in ideas for better solutions. These new solutions are implemented in the form of more prototypes and mock-ups, which are then evaluated, and so on.

Research

In this phase, we try to obtain as much information as possible regarding the design problem at hand. We ask a variety of questions: What technology is involved? Is this a revolutionary product that creates a new niche, or an evolutionary product that improves on what already exists? What segments of the population are most likely to interact with the product? What are the expected capabilities or limitations of the users? What is the environment of use likely to be: a home, an office, a construction site, a car, or somewhere else? Would it be best if the product were portable?

At this starting point, we gather information in many ways: reading magazine, journal, or Internet articles connected with the topic; conducting informal interviews and conversations with relevant professionals; buying a range of competitive products; playing with similar products in stores; and sometimes even surrounding ourselves with objects and images that relate to the product. The broader the search, the more likely we are to form a comprehensive understanding of the potential product. Even though this process may initially seem chaotic, coherent patterns begin to emerge. From these patterns we can begin to understand the scope of the project from the perspective of a user of the product.

User Profiles In order to design a product that will meet users' needs, we have to know who our users will be, and especially how a particular user will interact with the product (see Figure 3). For example, if an emergency calling device is intended mainly for the elderly, we have to take into account that the person may have limited dexterity or perhaps hearing difficulties. These restrictions will affect the appropriateness of controls and displays used in the product.[8]

There are usually several user populations of interest, since most consumer products are used by more than one person. For example, a remote control device may be used by both adults and children, and medical products may be used by physicians, nurses, patients, and maintenance people. However, there are also specialty products intended for much smaller audiences, such as a helmet or water bottle for bicycle racers, or a blood gas analyzer for anesthesiologists.

Other aspects of the user profile address perceptions and attitudes toward technology and use of devices. We ask: Is the potential user population familiar with computers or intimidated by them? Are users surrounded by high-tech gadgets in

Figure 3

A product is often contacted by unanticipated users. Who are they? Should they be able to use the product? Should they be protected from the product, or should the product be protected from them?

their daily routine? Do users like—and trust—automated devices, or would they prefer to perform the tasks manually?

Once user profiles are developed, we often create characters who might personify the user. For example, Agnes might be a sixty-year-old retiree, Larry a young architect who bicycles to work, and Pete a computer network administrator on the night shift. These characterizations may be supplemented with photographs to add realism and detail to the description. Making prototypical users seem real helps the design team to stay focused on the users' needs, desires, and limitations.

Field Observations and Interviews   There is no better way for psychologists to develop a sensitivity and appreciation for the richness of the user's environment and to learn about environmental influences on product design than to observe and interview people in their own homes, workplaces, schools or any other setting in which the product may be used.

Human factors psychologists are trained to observe key elements in the environment, such as lighting and noise levels, distractions that interfere with attention to tasks, safety factors, the presence of improvised, home-made versions of what the designers are planning to produce, and variations in the use of existing products. They also pay attention to psychological and social factors, such as what people seem to enjoy about particular products, what frustrates them in their use of products, and how tools and objects seem to affect relationships with other people. In addition, they try to ascertain the cultural significance or symbolic value of any tools, objects, or behaviors.

For example, after being asked to explore new opportunities in the design and use of laptops, we spent many hours observing how people used these devices in places such as airports and libraries. We learned, for example, that starting up and putting away the computer took a long time compared to the time spent doing productive work. We also noticed that users carried a lot of equipment, such as cables, transformer, spare battery, mouse, and additional disk drives. We observed that some laptops, especially those with minimal keyboards and fixed-height screens, seemed to put users in awkward postures. These observations suggested design alterations that would make laptops more self-contained and more easily adaptable to individuals' preferences.

Sometimes we not only observe but also talk to the users in order to find out if they have any complaints about products, and to elicit any suggestions they may have for new or better products. People are usually happy to be asked for their opinions, enthusiastic about contributing their own solutions, and satisfied that they have had an opportunity to make a difference. Not surprisingly, users often provide us with wonderful insights. For example, in looking for ways to improve the design of eyedropper bottles, we asked people how they used their medicine. By doing so, we discovered how the visual and tactile qualities of the bottles might be improved. One elderly lady with failing vision showed us how she wraps a rubber band around some of her eye medicine bottles to remind her which she must use in the morning. A man told us that he keeps the tiny bottle inside a transparent plastic cup on his desk so that he can find it more easily in the midst of the clutter. Similarly, when we asked people about their use of a laptop computer on business trips, we learned that the most frequent use was to retrieve their electronic mail. There was obviously a role for a much smaller, pocket-sized device designed specifically for e-mail connectivity.

Interviewing people requires special skills. Experienced interviewers avoid asking leading questions and instead rely on open-ended ones. For example, it is better to ask, "What do you like best about your camera?" than "Which feature of your camera do you like better: feature X or feature Y?" Similarly, asking, "What's the story behind this handle you improvised?" is preferable to, "Is this handle here because you thought that . . . ?" Posing open-ended questions allows respondents to describe their own experience and to make their own associations, and provides the interviewer with a fuller understanding of needs, preferences, and thought. However, it is also important to guide the interview in a direction that is useful to the design team. Consequently, skilled interviewing is a delicate balancing act between encouraging freedom of expression and directing the interview toward specific goals.

Keeping Records   Since human factors psychologists share their information with other members of the design team at various points in the design process, it is important to keep detailed records of observations and interviews, either at the time or immediately after the interview or observation has concluded.

In addition to taking notes, photos are valuable for capturing information relevant to the design process. Photos often provide a fuller representation of what was observed since they include potentially meaningful details the observer may not have noticed and avoid bias that can exist in the observer's notes. However, just as the presence of someone taking notes can make people feel uneasy, we have to be careful that people are not intimidated by the presence of a camera and that they do not alter their behavior while being photographed. We have found that most people feel less threatened by small, casual-looking cameras than by large, professional-looking equipment. Digital cameras equipped with a display that allows shooting without actually raising the camera to eye level are especially useful.

Videotape records are also valuable, especially for capturing actions and processes that take place over time. Since videos capture sound as well as pictures, they have the benefit of freeing the observer from taking notes. The drawbacks are that keeping track of a moving subject may engage too much of the observer's attention, and reviewing video material can be time-consuming.

Questionnaires   Questionnaires are useful when the product design team wants to quantify, and then compare, people's preferences and habits. For example, one might ask people to rate how easy it is to operate their answering machine by giving them choices from 1 (very easy to use) to 5 (a real nuisance).

Another benefit of questionnaires is that they allow the psychologist to gather information from users who would not be easily accessible otherwise; for example, we can administer the questionnaire by telephone or mail.

However, a questionnaire is only as good as the questions asked. The usefulness of the answers to a questionnaire is completely dependent on how well we were able to formulate our questions. Furthermore, once formulated, the questions cannot be adjusted in tone or content, as can be done during an interview. Consequently, even though questionnaire results may look clear, as when 80 percent of respondents say that they like product A better than product B, we have to remember that this outcome may have been due to the wording of the question. In order to minimize biases and ambiguities of such questions, we often test questionnaires on a small sample of our intended user population before actually administering them on a larger scale. Another drawback of questionnaires is that they do not usually allow psychologists to discover the unexpected, as they often do through photos, videotapes, or observations and interviews. Therefore, we may lose some of the richness of information that helps us understand the reasons for product preferences.

Focus Groups Focus groups are a relatively inexpensive way to get feedback from a group of potential users. Marketing professionals have used focus groups for a long time, but only recently have they been used widely by human factors psychologists. Focus groups involve recruiting eight to twelve potential users, providing them with a comfortable setting, complete with refreshments, and then asking them to participate in a discussion for about two hours. Depending on the goals of the focus group and its timing in the design process, we ask questions about existing products and users' needs, as well as preferences among design alternatives and feedback on a particular design.

In order for a focus group to yield a maximum amount of useful information, the human factors team develops a detailed script and chooses an experienced moderator to guide the discussion. Sketches or models of the product may be presented in order to stimulate ideas and make the design issues more concrete. The aim is to encourage not only discussion, but also interaction with prototypes, models, or products. Because people tend to want to agree with each other and say what others in the room want to hear, group moderators usually structure the session so that all group members have a chance to express themselves candidly, and are not overshadowed by the most outspoken person.

Task Analysis Task analysis captures and describes the tasks people perform when doing a certain job or using a particular product. The human factors psychologist analyzes tasks by identifying all its aspects and then breaking it down into subtasks. In this process they may record task elements and task times. Often they also record users' mistakes and categorize them into standard models of human error—for example, errors of omission and commission, extraneous acts, sequential errors or simply erroneous use of the product (see Figure 4).

A task analysis can be performed in a controlled setting such as a usability lab or in a field setting where a product is actually used. Although it is easier to perform these analyses in a controlled setting, they lack the validity that a field study would have. Further, controlled settings do not provide all the many details that exist in the context of use, nor do they allow us to observe unexpected strategies users have for coping with errors.[9]

The results of task analysis can be used in a variety of ways: to determine what functions a product should have; to allocate functions among the hardware, software, and user; to ascertain the frequency of individual tasks so that important tasks

Figure 4   *These task analysis pictures illustrate the difference between what should be done and what is done in practice. The photo on the left shows how a scanner should be used, but, as shown at right, the stock checker never uses it, finding it easier to key in the codes manually while the scanner hangs uselessly over his shoulder.*

can be made more accessible or easier to perform; to assess what tasks are typically performed in order to uncover dependencies among tasks, common patterns, and complex interactions; and to understand what tasks should be included in usability testing later in the product development process, such as the evaluation phase.

Analysis of Human Characteristics   In the design of any product that will be held, manipulated, touched, or viewed by people, questions about human characteristics arise. Will the tallest person have to bend over to see the display? Will the shortest person be able to see it at all? Will an individual in a wheelchair be able to reach the controls? Will a child be able to open the drawer? Could any of the features hurt an infant? These questions require normative data on human physical characteristics and consideration of people's physical capabilities and limitations. (See Figure 5.)

Over the years, measurements have been taken of various physical characteristics of people in different cultures and populations. Statistical summaries of these data are readily available in various human factors sources and textbooks.[10] We consult these data to ensure that a product will be usable by a large percentage of the population. One way of making the information particularly helpful to the design team is to produce scale drawings that illustrate how people of different sizes will look when using the product. Model makers can also provide three-dimensional

Figure 5

What are the critical characteristics to consider in designing an emergency calling device for the elderly? The device must be designed for limited dexterity, failing eyesight, and hearing difficulties, but the designer, with the help of psychologists, must also think about the users' self-image, independence, comfort with technology, and style preferences.

models of relevant body parts, such as a head or a hand, that serve as reference for understanding the physical issues involved in product design.

Whenever possible, the entire design team tries to experience the product from the user's perspective. To this end, we may use products or product models ourselves. Sometimes we even enlarge product models in order to experience using it from the point of view of, say, a child, or a person with small hands.

In addition to considering users' physical characteristics, human factors psychologists also try to assess emotional reactions. They pay particular attention to any frustrations people may have while trying to use a product. And here too, it is easier for designers to empathize with potential users if they use the products themselves for a while.

Design

What psychologists learn from their product design research serves as a point of departure for the project's designers and engineers. Producing the design is a dynamic process. It involves much sketching; building of cardboard, foam, clay, or wood models; and many discussions of concepts and ideas. The aim is to develop a product concept that meets the user's goals, communicates the desired message, and addresses the key issues identified during the research stages of the process.

During this creative phase, human factors psychologists provide ideas for design concepts and give research-based feedback about concepts that are proposed. Usually the interface between the product and the user is the guiding force for the design. So, although industrial designers frequently have their own ideas about the appropriate look and function of a particular product, they regularly come to psychologists to ensure that their design is in line with what the intended user would expect.

During this part of the design process, as in the earlier research phase, we sometimes create scenarios that will stimulate us to carefully think through the user's interactions with proposed products. Again, we identify a range of potential users and imagine how they might react to a proposed design. For example, in designing a new home security alarm, we might develop several user characters: eighty-year-old Alice with failing vision and mild arthritis living alone in Florida; Jon and Meg, a working couple in Chicago living with adolescent boys who have their own keys, and have friends staying overnight; and visiting students Koechi and Kumiko, whose knowledge of English is limited.

Evaluation and Refinement

Human factors psychologists most often play the role of user advocates on the design team. In order to represent the voices, concerns, and preferences of the expected users, we continually ask ourselves, "If I were a user of this type using this thing, what would my experience be like?" But despite our best efforts, we cannot possibly imagine or predict the perspectives of all potential users. Nor can we rely on the notion of an "average user," as statistics and marketing tools tend to do. On the contrary, design issues and opportunities are best uncovered and identified by looking not at the average, but at the outer limits of the range of users. Thus, if we are helping to design a utility bicycle, we are as likely to focus on the twenty-two-year-old cyclist who uses his bike full time as a delivery messenger, as on the sixty-five-year-old grandparent who occasionally uses the bike for short excursions in the neighborhood.

We also find that designs are more successful if we focus on in-depth, qualitative analyses rather than large sample sizes and statistical analyses, although here, as in the research process, flexibility and creativity are important. In addition, the complexity of the product somewhat dictates the process of evaluation. For example, medical products with complex interaction procedures require extensive, well-structured testing. Software applications need similar testing because they provide users with so many opportunities for misunderstanding and frustration (see Figure 6.) On the other hand, simple products such as toothbrushes can be evaluated adequately with less rigorous procedures.

Testing design prototypes with potential users, whether in a laboratory setting or in the context of use, enables us to discover design problems that need to be resolved for the next round of more highly refined prototypes. For example, a latch might need to be larger, or a key shaped more distinctively. Sometimes the focus of testing is less to discover design issues than to examine a specific aspect of human performance that will bear on the effectiveness of the product. For example, we might need to discover how quickly people can respond to a particular kind of alarm, how much force they exert on a surface when using a mouse, or what barrel shape enables people to place a pointer most accurately. This information will be used to refine details of a design, and the evaluation and refinement continue until the product reaches its final form.

Figure 6

You don't have to be an expert to see that something is troubling this user. By observing nonverbal behavior, psychologists often discover subtle, unexpected details that require adjustments in design.

Communication with Other Disciplines

Human factors psychologists work as part of a team that may include representatives from marketing, mechanical engineering, industrial design, software engineering, interaction design, and manufacturers, each of whom have different responsibilities and preoccupations. Thus, the psychologist's effectiveness depends not only on the technical competence and accuracy of his or her human factors contributions, but also on the ability to communicate relevant information so that members of other disciplines can grasp its significance and respond appropriately. We have found the following techniques to be particularly useful in effective communication.

Making Information Visible Most human factors psychologists are educated within a tradition that emphasizes skills in literacy and mathematics but provides little background in visual media. In contrast, representatives of other disciplines on the design team have more extensive training with visual materials. Each discipline also tends to develop its own favorite terms and definitions. In order to bridge the gap between disciplines, it often becomes necessary for psychologists to rephrase their usual terms and concepts and to illustrate their most important points using nonverbal material, such as photographs, video clips, or even quick sketches of situations and ideas. Making things visible—especially observations of people, contexts, and procedures—is particularly effective because team members are then better able to identify with the situation, to put themselves into other people's shoes.

Creating Shared Experiences Another way to encourage empathy is to devise ways in which team members can personally experience or witness the user-product interface. One strategy is to encourage team members who are not human factors professionals to participate in field observations and interviews. (There are some risks to this approach, because these team members may not be skilled in remaining unobtrusive during observation or in conducting interviews so that the respondent does not feel overwhelmed or coerced to give particular answers.)

Another form of direct experience for team members is to have them witness user-participation sessions. Still another is to use role playing in which team members are asked to take on the characteristics of a specific user performing a particular task. Sometimes we increase the authenticity and drama of role play by providing props and costumes.

CONCLUSION

Psychologists' contributions have gradually become an integral part of the design process. Initially the contributions were exclusively related to complex systems such as airplanes, air traffic control, nuclear power plants, and computer software. Now, psychologists are involved in designs as diverse as computer and consumer communications, medical and industrial products, transportation, furniture, games, and toys. Even the design of apparently simple artifacts—a pen, a toothbrush, an eyedropper—have benefited from the insights of human factors psychologists. As a result, psychologists have progressed from being external consultants to the design process, to becoming fully integrated members of design teams in which they not only help to evaluate and refine established designs, but take on more creative tasks as designers and innovators.

SUGGESTIONS FOR FURTHER READING

Crozier, R. (1994). *Manufactured pleasures: Psychological responses to design.* Manchester, U.K.: Manchester University Press.

Csikszentmihalyi, M., & Rochberg-Halton, E. (1981). *The meaning of things: Domestic symbols and the self.* Cambridge: Cambridge University Press.

Laurel, B. (Ed.). (1990). *The art of human-computer interface design.* Reading, MA: Addison-Wesley.

Norman, D. A. (1990). *The design of everyday things.* New York: Doubleday Currency.

Pheasant, S. T. (1996). *Bodyspace: Anthropometry, ergonomics, and design.* London, U. K.: Taylor and Francis.

Wickens, C. D., Gordon, S. E., & Liu, Y. (1998). *An introduction to human factors engineering.* Reading, MA: Addison Wesley Longman.

PSYCHOLOGY APPLIED TO AVIATION

Christopher D. Wickens and Anthony D. Andre

Aviation psychology is the study of the psychological aspects of flying an aircraft. In order to demonstrate some of these aspects, we will first take a look at the pilot's tasks. Then we will trace the important historical developments in aviation psychology, and follow with a description of current themes in aviation psychologists' research. We will also discuss where aviation psychologists work and what they do, and list some challenges in the future of aviation psychology.

THE PILOT'S TASKS

A pilot's tasks consist of meeting a prioritized set of goals in order to accomplish some flight mission safely.[1] First and foremost, the pilot must aviate, that is, keep the aircraft flying. This involves carefully regulating the aircraft's speed and attitude (roll or pitch) using the flight controls (stick, rudder, and throttle) in order to maintain the flow of air over the wings and thus generate adequate lift. Otherwise the plane will stall. Second, the pilot must navigate, that is, direct the plane to fly to various locations in space, or along various paths, in order to accomplish the mission (e.g., deliver passengers, observe things on the ground, or rescue someone) and avoid hazards (e.g., bad weather, terrain, or other airplanes). In order to aviate and navigate, the pilot depends heavily on a number of cockpit instruments (see Figure 1). These instruments help to create a mental picture of the aircraft's stall potential and flight path. Aviation psychologists study the pilot's perceptions (e.g., of the instruments or of hazards outside the aircraft), attention (e.g., what instruments or tasks are being attended to or ignored), decision-making skills (e.g., deciding to avoid a weather hazard), and the memory processes (e.g., whether the pilot remembers the right sequences of instrument reading and control operation).

Besides aviating and navigating, the pilot must also follow a myriad of procedures to configure the aircraft (e.g., lowering the landing gear, switching fuel tanks, or setting navigational instruments) and to comply with Federal Air Regulations and air traffic controllers' instructions regarding required direction, altitude, and airspeed. Aviation psychologists are interested in exploring questions such as these: Does the pilot remember to carry out the right procedure at the right time? Does

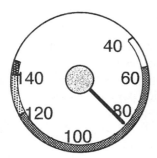
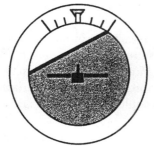

Air speed   Attitude indicator   Altimeter

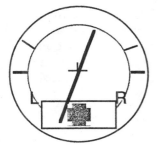
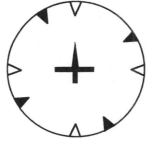

Turn slip indicator   Directional indicator   Vertical velocity

Figure 1 *Layout of traditional flight instruments. The aircraft shown below each instrument portrays the variable described by that instrument.*

the pilot understand and remember the instructions delivered by the air traffic controller?

The pilot must also carefully monitor the many on-board systems (such as fuel supply indicators or automated navigation displays) in order to ensure that these are working properly. Most of the time little action is required, but if there is a problem, the pilot must act promptly and appropriately. Aviation psychologists are interested in exploring how quickly the pilot can detect and respond to any malfunction in these systems.

Finally, the pilot is required to participate as a member of at least three teams: the team composed of the flight deck crew (usually a copilot and sometimes a flight engineer), the team composed of the aircraft's mission crew (for example, the cabin attendants on a commercial aircraft flight), and the team that includes air traffic controllers. Successful coordination with each of these teams requires clear and unambiguous voice communications, and many important social skills, such as encouraging communications along the chain of command so that, for example, the copilot is not afraid to speak up if the pilot makes an incorrect decision.

Although all these tasks are listed in order of decreasing priority, there are often times when it is critical for the pilot to attend to a task or goal that is usually lower on the hierarchy, while performance of a normally higher-priority task is postponed. For example, the pilot may need to check the status of fuel tanks even if it means temporarily ignoring the aircraft's heading. Thus, the pilot must continuously engage in the "supertask" of task management, allocating attention to all flying tasks as necessary in order to maintain the safety of the flight and still accomplish its mission. Aviation psychologists study how pilots perform this "supertask," integrating their various responsibilities and making complex decisions.

A BRIEF HISTORY OF AVIATION PSYCHOLOGY

Aviation psychology has been a pioneer in the broader field of human factors, which studies interactions between humans and machines (see Chapter 10).[2] Thus, historically, aviation psychologists have examined issues and learned lessons that subsequently have been applied to humans working with other real-world systems in the more general domain of human factors.[3]

For example, during World War II, psychologist Norman Mackworth studied the performance of radar operators as they watched their scopes for the appearance of German aircraft crossing the English Channel on bombing missions, and observed the difficulty these operators had in sustaining attention for more than a few minutes at a time.[4] Out of these aviation-related research findings grew the field of *vigilance research*, which addresses how people detect low-frequency events—such as a faulty product on an assembly line, or a subtle indication of a system failure—and studies how these problems can be corrected. For example, after the war, psychologist Paul Fitts and his colleagues investigated how pilots' eyes scanned an aircraft's instrument panel (see Figure 1).[5] This was one of the first of an important series of studies of visual scanning, which have helped to identify the fundamental properties of human selective attention,[6] and raised questions such as the following: How does the brain know what is important in the environment and direct the eye to look at it? How much information can the eye take in before moving to another fixation point? Fitts's work also spawned research on the direction of movement of instrument displays, the direction of movement of the required response, and how aircraft flight instruments might be redesigned in order to improve that compatibility.[7]

Also growing out of World War II was an examination of the kinds and sources of errors that pilots make in interpreting instruments and in responding to their controls.[8] For example, pilots may confuse the flaps control for the landing gear control or misread the altimeter. This research paved the way for many more recent examinations and classifications of the kinds of errors people make in their everyday lives.[9]

Aviation psychology research in the decade after World War II began to examine the issue of pilot training, in particular, how flight simulators could be designed to increase the transfer of skills learned in a safe environment on the ground to the risky environment of an aircraft in flight.[10] Such research has helped to identify the ways in which training simulators have to imitate a real-world (flying or driving) task so that learning on the simulator can successfully transfer to performance in the real task. This research suggested that making the simulator look and feel just like a real aircraft is impressive but, as noted later, is not necessarily helpful for training and is often not cost-effective.

In the 1950s, aviation psychology researchers began to deal with a new generation of jet aircraft that could fly faster and with less stability. They applied the theory of feedback control[11] to the pilot and aircraft[12] and they began to understand how humans control complex dynamic systems, ranging from supertankers to virtual reality devices. Their findings helped show how features such as highly sensitive systems can make human control of such systems nearly impossible.

By the 1970s, aviation psychologists began to study the pilots' mental workload and the limits of human attention in performing several tasks simultaneously and looking at several places at once.[13] These studies provided new insights into how to predict when pilots might become overloaded and fail to carry out critical tasks, how to measure the overload point by looking at heart and brain activity (or subjective ratings), and how to understand the consequences of overload, particularly in regard to distinguishing between pilots' successful and unsuccessful strategies for managing multiple tasks.

CURRENT THEMES OF RESEARCH IN AVIATION PSYCHOLOGY

The characteristics of aircraft flight deck design, the layout of instrument displays and controls, and the basic tasks of flying remained relatively unchanged during the first three decades after World War II. In the 1980s, however, increases in on-board computer power introduced fundamental changes in many aspects of the pilot's tasks. These changes, coupled with the increasing involvement of aviation psychologists, contributed to the emergence of a number of research themes in aviation psychology.

Human-Computer Interaction

Computers have had at least five important impacts on the typical modern flight deck. First, computer-generated displays have the capability of radically altering the depiction of dynamic flight information, from the standard form shown in Figure 1 to a form similar to that shown in Figure 2. Here, the artificial horizon display at the top center of Figure 1 has been changed to appear more like a true horizon, running all the way across the screen. The round dial air speed (top left) and altitude (top right) displays of Figure 1 have been changed to appear as sliding tapes. Most critically, the display has now been equipped with a three-dimensional "tunnel" in the sky to show the pilot's future commanded flight path, and a small predictor symbol to show the future position. This three-dimensional tunnel is extremely valuable for pilots.[14] It exemplifies how the flexibility of computer-based displays has allowed aircraft instrument designers to be more creative in configuring the representation of flight information in a way that best suits pilots' needs for aviating and navigating.

Second, computer technology has affected the very nature of the pilot's interaction with cockpit displays and controls. For example, cathode ray tube (CRT) displays are being replaced by thinner and lighter liquid crystal displays. Head-up displays (HUDs), in which displayed information is superimposed over the pilot's view through the cockpit window, are being installed in more and more aircraft (see Figure 3). In addition, PC-like cursor controls (e.g., touch pads) are being used as a more effective method for interacting with screen menus and other display elements.

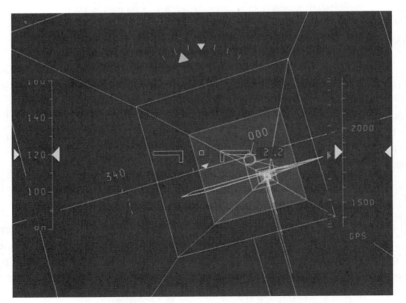

Figure 2

A more advanced concept for representing much of the same flight information shown in Figure 1. (Courtesy Delft University of Technology)

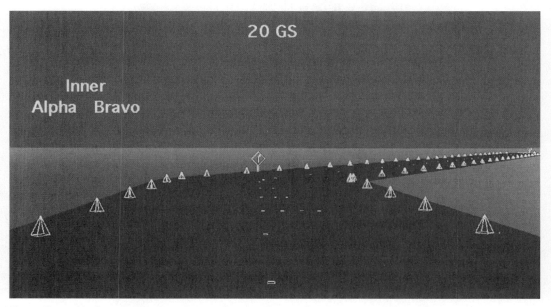

Figure 3 *A head-up display (HUD) image for aircraft ground taxi.*

Third, computers allow new sensory technologies, like infrared radar and satellite navigational signals to bring information to the pilot that was previously inaccessible. The availability of these systems challenges the aviation psychologist to display, prioritize, and organize an ever greater flow of information coming to the pilot.

Fourth, computerized information retrieval systems now allow pilots to access, through keyboards and computer screens, the vast amount of procedural information that was once relegated to paper manuals and checklists. These electronic databases may be physically more manageable, but they raise many of the usability issues studied in the field of human computer interaction, such as confusing menu designs, getting lost while moving through the information (e.g., "How do I get back to the top of the menu?"), or making errors on cumbersome keyboards.[15]

Finally, computers on aircraft have enabled an enormous amount of flight deck automation. In many respects, they have relegated the pilot to the role of a passive monitor who merely observes the autopilot flight management system flying and configuring the aircraft in a way that he or she does not always clearly understand.[16]

The Psychological Impact of Automation Research on and analysis of some high-profile aircraft accidents have revealed a number of psychological factors that influence how effectively people use automation. Particularly relevant in aviation are factors related to understanding and trust of automation. Studies have shown that pilots do not always understand the complicated logic underlying the auto-pilots within the flight management system.[17] They may not understand how, for example, the autopilot system changes altitude on command given that there are five qualitatively different ways of doing so. This lack of understanding is partly the result of the highly complex autopilot system, but also partly a result of the poor feedback provided to the pilot about what the automated system is doing, and why. As a result, some of the system's actions in controlling the aircraft will surprise the pilots, leading them to mistrust it. When this happens, the pilot might intervene, responding in a way that is inappropriate, if not dangerous.[18] However, pilots *must* intervene when, because of computer hardware or software problems, the automated system fails to carry out its task as intended, or gives off false warning signals.[19] Thus, it is important for the pilot to have the right relationship with automation, trusting the system when it is working, but not becoming so complacent about its operation as to fail to notice and correct a malfunction.[20]

Understanding the cognitive factors responsible for pilots' and air traffic controllers' trust, overtrust, and mistrust of automation[21] is a critically important research area for aviation psychology. It is crucial for the broader domain of human factors research, as well. Equally important is an understanding of the features of automation design that can create "human-centered" automation,[22] and that can counteract the problems of understanding, mistrust, and complacency we have described. This means it is best to design automated systems to do tasks in a way that approximates how humans would do them, and to design displays that can make the workings of the automation clearly visible to the pilot or air traffic controller who monitors its operation.[23]

Computer-Based Training

Rapid developments in computer technology have provided a number of alternative possibilities for training pilots' flight skills in an environment that is cheaper, safer, more convenient, and less stressful than that of the aircraft cockpit in flight. Multimedia techniques, including those capitalizing on virtual reality technology, can realistically simulate a cockpit and many of the characteristics of flight. However, more realism is not always a desirable feature in flight training simulators because such simulators must be able to emphasize the particular information and tasks to be learned at any given phase of flight, without overwhelming the student with all complexities of an operating aircraft. The question of how much realism in simulators is necessary, or to what degree it should be scaled back, is a critical issue that will likely continue to engage aviation psychologists.

Situation Awareness

During the late 1980s, the proliferation of new information available in the cockpit regarding factors such as weather, air traffic, and aircraft systems, along with the pilot's new role as a monitor of aircraft automation, led to a growing interest in the commercial and military aviation communities in understanding how pilots maintain awareness of relevant events and use this information to guide their actions or predict future events. The term *situation(al) awareness* (SA) describes the processes of attention, perception, and decision making that together form a pilot's mental model of the current situation.[24]

There has been much debate concerning how best to assess pilot SA, for example, by using measures of eye movements, pilot self-ratings, or answers to SA questions. Some aviation psychologists have questioned the practical value of the SA construct, suggesting that it may be just another term for the already well-defined psychological concepts of attention and memory.[25] Nevertheless, there is general agreement about the need to study how pilots form awareness of the many complex and dynamic events that occur simultaneously in flight, and to develop design and training strategies for optimizing pilot SA. Display interfaces must present pilots with a range of information broad enough to not only allow performance of expected and routine tasks, but also to guide the performance of unexpected tasks if circumstances require it.[26] For example, a pilot needs information about weather conditions on the flight path ahead, and also about bad weather or traffic behind the aircraft in case it becomes necessary to reverse course.

Despite the vast amount of research on the topic of SA, many important issues remain to be studied by the aviation psychology community. One concerns the nature of expertise and the question of why some pilots are successful while others are not. Current knowledge cannot define the extent to which SA may be attributable to some innate trait that the best pilots have, or whether it is based on certain definable critical skills, such as the dynamic and flexible allocation of attention[27] or the skilled use of memory for recent events,[28] that any pilot can learn through appropriate training.

A second issue concerns the development of design principles that facilitate pilot SA, especially as automated systems continue to replace manual control operations, thereby placing a heavier burden on the pilot's visual-perceptual and cognitive systems to monitor and understand the automation.

Third, aviation psychologists need a more sophisticated approach to defining the desired level of SA that can be supported through design or training. To this end, aviation psychologists must define the set of external goals and criteria for achieving these goals before they can begin to evaluate (or affect) a pilot's SA.[29]

Finally, aviation psychologists must identify not only the critical and relevant information required for successful SA, but also the information sources or events that should be ignored or deemphasized in the process.

Crew Resource Management

During the 1970s it became apparent that the traditional strategy of training pilots for specific flight tasks and procedures did not sufficiently address the social, motivational, communication, and cooperative decision-making aspects of flight. After all, pilots work as members of teams,[30] and a large percentage of accidents have been attributed to the crew's failure to manage the flight deck properly. For example, in 1975, a commercial airplane ran out of fuel and crashed over Portland, Oregon. Although the flight crew had warned the captain of the dangerously low fuel status, he had ignored the warning and had generally created an intimidating climate within which the crew members were reluctant to speak up more assertively.

The objective of modern cockpit (crew) resource management (CRM), a concept which arose as a result of a workshop conducted at the Ames Research Center, National Aeronautic and Space Administration (NASA),[31] is to train pilots in the task of managing all resources available to them. Specifically, the goal is to develop effective interpersonal communication, stress management, and task allocation skills so that decision making during abnormal or emergency situations is optimized.

The major sources of CRM training include line-oriented flight training, in which flight crews are videotaped as they confront major problems in simulated flight, and then are debriefed on their effectiveness in handling the problems. They also include crew coordination training in which specific techniques of communication are presented and practiced.[32]

Although nearly all airlines now engage in formal CRM training, it can always be improved, and aviation psychologists help with this task. They seek to develop more effective training scenarios and platform methods; help update CRM requirements in light of newly introduced technology and procedures such as those involved with flying highly computerized aircraft; and they measure and evaluate the effectiveness of CRM programs.

Decision Making

The success of any aviation system rests on the decision-making abilities of the flight crew. Efficient decision-making skills are particularly important in the aviation environment because decisions often have to be made very quickly, and the consequences of a mistake can be disastrous.

Two tragic accidents have had a profound effect on the psychological study of decision making. They involved the *U.S.S. Vincennes* and the space shuttle *Challenger*.[33] In the first case, the U.S. Navy ship *Vincennes* erroneously identified an Iranian commercial aircraft as a hostile warplane and shot it down. This accident demonstrated that decision-relevant information can sometimes be distorted as it is passed from one observer to another (or up the chain of command). The *Challenger* accident resulted from the mission crew's decision to launch the space shuttle despite dangerously low temperatures on the ground. The ensuing explosion destroyed the spacecraft, killing all aboard. This accident highlighted the sometimes catastrophic impact of organizational structure and pressures on the decision-making process.

These accidents prompted aviation psychologists to study new aspects of decision making. Their early studies focused mainly on how pilots make decisions given various amounts of relevant information, time pressure, importance of consequences, and so on.[34] Much attention was also devoted to understanding the range of biases that can affect pilots' ability to make objective decisions and implement appropriate responses.[35] Today, aviation psychologists are more interested in how decision-making performance changes with practice, and in the particular ways experts use their experience to guide their decisions by recognizing problems rapidly and directly recalling (and employing) previously successful solutions.[36]

They also study crew communication, crew coordination, and situation assessment skills that lead to effective team decision making,[37] thus linking this field closely with that of CRM. Ultimately, aviation psychologists are interested in developing decision-making aids, whether they involve new training methods or computer-based decision support systems.

Pilot Selection

Training a pilot is very expensive; in the case of a military pilot, it can sometimes cost millions of dollars. Yet, many pilots who go through the rigors of such training do not ultimately succeed, thus wasting a great deal of time and money. Researchers in aviation psychology have been trying to identify the relevant skills for professional piloting in the civilian or military field and to develop tests that will accurately predict the outcome of an aspiring pilot's training in the complex tasks of advanced aviation. Tests of spatial ability and general intelligence can predict who will make good pilots,[38] and tests of attentional flexibility may also be useful in this regard.[39] Unfortunately, however, tests have not yet been developed that can accurately predict who will have, or can develop, the many skills related to judgment, situation awareness, and crew resource management, that are so critical to good pilot performance.

Air Traffic Control and Maintenance

Since World War II, aviation psychology has focused most of its attention on flight crews and the flight deck, but in the past decade, its attention has broadened to include two of the most critical resources on which the pilot depends: air traffic controllers and maintenance workers.

Psychological studies of air traffic control address attention, memory, work load, and many of the other issues that are so important on the flight deck, but they take a distinctly different perspective.[40] As the manager of a large fleet of aircraft, not a single vehicle, the air traffic controller deals with a more complex system—one that appears on the radar display to change at a rate that is slower than the changes a pilot sees. The controller must rely even more heavily than the pilot on clear, unambiguous communications with other controllers and flight crews.

Psychological research on maintenance workers[41] focuses on issues such as inspections and troubleshooting, and studies the critical role of memory in carrying out procedures (i.e., remembering to perform each critical step).[42] These issues have as much relevance to air safety as do the psychological studies of air traffic control.

AVIATION PSYCHOLOGISTS' ACTIVITIES

Aviation psychologists engage in a wide variety of activities. Let's consider some of them.

Basic Research

In basic research, fundamental principles and concepts of psychology (e.g., attention, parallel processing, color perception) are studied in a context that allows the results to be generalized to the aviation domain. Thus, the goal of basic research is twofold: to validate or refine psychological concepts and theories, and to evaluate empirically the implications of these concepts and theories for the design of pilot-aircraft systems. For example, basic research by David Foyle and Rob McCann on attentional issues associated with head-up displays has contributed to a better understanding of display formats that facilitate parallel processing (that is, paying attention to several things at the same time)[43] and has led to the development of scene-linked symbols for guiding pilots as they taxi around an airport.[44] Here, route signs and guidance cues are presented in a head-up display (see Figure 3) on the window through which the pilot looks to see the runway, but the cues are positioned and moved in such a way that they appear to be attached to the ground beyond.

Basic research studies are typically performed using personal- or low-end graphic computers and often involve the precise measurement of the speed and accuracy of a response to a displayed stimulus. Most often, the research participants are nonpilots, and the tasks are seemingly non-aviation related. Yet these characteristics do not diminish the applicability of basic research to aviation. Indeed, since the focus of basic aviation psychology research is on determining the information processing capacities of the human brain, and since the tasks are carefully chosen to represent the information processing demands of the cockpit, it is reasonable to assume (and it has been shown) that many of the issues addressed by basic aviation psychology research apply directly to pilots and the environment in which they work.

Applied Research

In spite of its inherent value, basic research on aviation psychology issues has declined during the 1990s in favor of more applied research. Budget tightening, shorter development cycles, and political pressures have all created a push for research that has an immediate impact on the aviation community. In contrast to basic research, where psychological concepts are the initial focus, applied research is driven by aviation incidents, accidents, and new system developments. Applied aviation psychology researchers may be assigned the tasks of developing new or improved cockpit interfaces and procedures, or evaluating proposed concepts, such as *free flight*—the possible shift in authority from air traffic control to pilots.[45]

Applied research studies are typically performed on high-end computer workstations and part-task simulators. They often involve some replication of the aircraft display and control environment (as well as the outside world), and usually employ qualified pilots to perform realistic flight tasks. The goal is not to prove the validity of a psychological concept or theory, but rather to compare various human-machine interfaces in order to determine which of them best meets the objectives of the program. The interfaces developed for comparison, however, may well have psychological theory as their basis or justification for design. For example, the design of a digital computer interface between the air traffic controller and the pilot (replacing voice communications) is based heavily on knowledge and theories about short-term memory which indicate that voice communications are often susceptible to error.

Simulation

Simulation studies are in a category of their own, primarily because of the cost and complexity of the equipment and facilities required and also because conducting full-mission simulations is a rare (and expensive) specialty. Simulators are used when a researcher wants to mimic the aviation environment but finds it too costly, dangerous, or time-consuming to conduct the study in operational aircraft. Simulators can be employed, for example, to collect data that forecast the future economic or performance impact of a new cockpit interface. More commonly, simulators have been used by both the military and commercial airlines to teach crews how to perform in both normal and unexpected conditions of flight. For example, the line-oriented flight training mentioned earlier focuses on coordinated crew training rather than on the training of specific, discrete flight and systems tasks.[46]

Finally, it is important to note that much attention has been devoted to the methods and effects of simulation itself. Important issues, such as how to design simulators so that they can produce the greatest transfer of training from simulator to aircraft at the lowest cost, and without creating motion sickness, are still being addressed by aviation psychologists.

Field Observation and Validation

Perhaps the most exciting and important settings in which aviation psychologists work are "in the field," that is, in the airports, cockpits, and taxiways where aviators actually perform their jobs. As aviation psychologists are increasingly asked to evaluate and design applied systems, the need to base their work on field observation and evaluation grows.[47] By observing the relevant issues, users, dynamics, constraints, and environmental factors in real time, aviation psychologists can better apply human factors data and methods to their evaluation, design, and validation tasks.[48]

Through field observation (*ethnography*), aviation psychologists learn how pilots perform their jobs and the critical design or procedural issues that affect them. Field evaluation (*validation*) involves testing the utility of a new or revised cockpit interface design as pilots use these devices and procedures while actually flying an aircraft.

Incident and Accident Analysis

Often, aviation psychologists can draw inferences about the psychological processes of pilots and controllers by analyzing the errors that they have made. The Aviation

Safety Reporting System is a large database of *incidents,* defined as mistakes that did not result in an accident. Maintained by the NASA Ames Research Center, the record of these incidents (around thirty thousand per year) consist of pilots' written or oral statements about the incidents in which they have been involved.

Occurring with much less frequency than incidents are actual *accidents* attributable to pilot or air traffic controller error. Detailed reports of accidents, are kept by the National Transportation Safety Board, and provide a useful source of data for aviation psychologists. Indeed, much of the wisdom underlying crew resource management has been gained from analysis of a few critical accidents such as the Portland crash described earlier. A great deal of what we know about problems with automated systems is also derived from accident analyses.

System Development

Not all aviation psychologists focus primarily on research. Some work directly on the development of new or revised cockpit interfaces. Most of these psychologists do conduct some research in the course of the development process, but they often have to make design decisions on the spot.

Job Opportunities for Aviation Psychologists

Aviation psychologists are employed by various government, academic, and private institutions throughout the world.

Government agencies employing aviation psychologists include NASA, the Federal Aviation Administration, the National Transportation Safety Board, the Department of Transportation, the U.S. Air Force, the U.S. Army, the U.S. Navy, the U.K. Defense Evaluation and Research Agency, and the National Aerospace Laboratory (NLR-Netherlands). Universities that offer aviation psychology programs, and therefore employ aviation psychologists as professors, include the University of Illinois at Urbana–Champaign, Ohio State University, the University of Central Florida, Georgia Tech University, Embry-Riddle Aeronautical University, and the University of Dayton. These universities offer degrees that allow graduates to make direct contributions to aviation psychology with less need for on-the-job training. Most aerospace companies, such as Honeywell, Lockheed Martin, Boeing, and Rockwell Collins, also employ aviation psychologists.

Some aviation psychologists work as individual consultants to, or as members of, consulting firms such as Bolt Beranek and Newman Corporation, Monterey Technologies, Interface Analysis Associates, Klein Associates, and Flight Safety Foundation. These firms advise manufacturers or the government on the human factors of development of aviation products (e.g., new displays) or provide advice on developing testing, training, or flight performance measurement tools. As consultants, aviation psychologists may be involved in litigation procedures by assessing psychological factors that may have contributed to aircraft accidents.

Aviation psychologists interact with one another in many professional groups, societies, and conferences. The most notable of these are the Association of Aviation

Psychologists and the Aerospace Systems Technical Group of the Human Factors and Ergonomics Society.* Conferences that center around, or include sessions on, aviation psychology research include the International Symposium on Aviation Psychology, the Applied Behavioral Sciences Symposium (held at the U.S. Air Force Academy), the Automation Technology and Human Performance Conference, and the Human Factors and Ergonomics Society Annual Meeting.

THE FUTURE

What's in store for future aviation psychologists? In terms of employment, the overall picture is good, as the aging fleet of conventional (nonautomated) aircraft, and the proliferation of advanced sensors and semiautonomous systems bring new challenges to the aviation psychology community. Most likely, the following issues will be at the forefront of future aviation psychology research and development:

- As the cockpit becomes more and more automated, aviation psychologists must determine the consequences of monitoring and interacting with these systems.
- Free flight is a popular new concept that proposes an airspace system whereby pilots have the authority to determine their own air routes, without air traffic controller intervention.[49] Although it is doubtful that free flight will be implemented in its full form in the near future, it is almost certain that significant changes in the relationship between pilots and controllers will take place as pilots begin to assume some of the tasks that controllers previously performed.
- Perhaps the most antiquated aspect of the U.S. airspace system is in the area of air traffic control. New control systems have recently been developed; these systems aim at providing intelligent decision support for controllers and advising them about the most appropriate way to maneuver certain aircraft so that a conflict in the sky or on the airport surface can be avoided.[50] The human factors implications of these systems and their optimal interface design characteristics will need to be addressed by aviation psychologists.
- As sensor technology continues to develop, we will see more and more information displayed to pilots. This capability challenges the aviation psychologist to help manage the presentation of information so that the pilot is not overloaded, and so that the most important information is always more salient and accessible than less important or nonessential information. This goal may be achieved by careful use of highlighting or by computer-driven displays of information that take into account what the computer infers to be the pilot's most pressing information needs from moment to moment.

All of these issues and challenges assure that aviation psychology will continue to be a fascinating field that integrates many subfields of traditional psychology.

---

*The web site address is http://www.hfes.org/About/TG/AerospaceSystems.html.

SUGGESTIONS FOR FURTHER READING

Hawkins, F., & Orlady, H. (1993). *Human factors in flight.* Hampshire, England: Avebury Aviation.

Jensen, R. (Ed.). (1989). *Aviation psychology.* Brookfield, VT: Gower Technical.

O'Hare, D., & Roscoe, S. (1990). *Flight deck performance: The human factor.* Ames IA: Iowa State University Press.

Trollip, S., & Jensen, R. (1991). *Human factors for general aviation.* Englewood CO: Jeppeson Sanders.

Wickens, C., Mavor, A., & McGee, J. (Eds.). (1997). *Flight to the future: Human factors of air traffic control.* Washington, DC: National Academy of Sciences.

Wiener, E., & Nagel, D. (Eds.). (1988). *Human factors in aviation.* Orlando, FL: Academic Press.

PSYCHOLOGY APPLIED TO ANIMAL TRAINING

Stanley Coren

Eleanor Wilson answered the door when the bell rang. Although this everyday act may not seem unusual, it was, because Eleanor has been deaf since the age of five when a viral infection took her hearing. Her husband, Arthur, is also deaf, and although their child, Lori, is not deaf, she is only two years old and not yet able to alert her parents to important sounds. Eleanor knew that someone was at her door because of a springer spaniel named Pete, her hearing assistance dog. When most people think of animals that have been trained to help humans, they tend to think of horses pulling carts or carrying riders, of dogs tracking or retrieving game or guiding the blind, or even of elephants, tigers, bears, and seals entertaining us in the circus. However, animals often are trained for many other complex tasks that improve the lives of humans.

Like other hearing assistance dogs, Pete has been trained to respond to doorbells or knocks by running back and forth between his owner and whichever door the sound is coming from. He jumps onto the bed to wake his family by digging at the blankets when the alarm clock rings. He tells them that the tea kettle is boiling or that Lori is crying by repeatedly running between the source of the sound and his owners. Outdoors, these dogs learn to alert their owners to the sounds of automobile horns, sirens, shouts, and other noises. They do this by jumping up on their masters or stepping in front of them. Pete sits next to Eleanor or Arthur when they are driving, and he has been taught to put his paw on the driver's shoulder when he hears a siren or another car's horn. By looking directly at the sound source, he alerts the driver to a potential problem. For Eleanor and Arthur, Pete provides a measure of safety and independence that they could not otherwise have, unless they lived with someone who had normal hearing.

A BRIEF HISTORY OF ANIMAL TRAINING

Some areas of applied psychology can trace their roots to the early research of medieval scholars, and others can find their origin in the writings of Aristotle or other philosophers who lived some two thousand years ago. The use of psychological principles to train animals, however, goes back much earlier. The beginning of efforts to train animals to perform useful tasks for humans springs from a time well before written language was available to record it.

The domestication of animals probably began with the dog. Recent DNA research suggests that dogs might have been domesticated 100,000 years ago,[1] but the fossil record provides hard evidence that humans were sharing their living spaces with dogs at least as far back as 15,000 years ago, at around the close of the Paleolithic era,[2] and that dogs were already serving a useful function for humans at this time.[3] Cave paintings in Spain dated from this era picture dogs being used to assist in hunting by driving and pulling down prey the size of cows and deer. Dogs were also serving as guards at this time. Excavation of a Cro-Magnon site in southern Europe yielded the skeleton of a Stone Age girl who had been lovingly folded into the fetal-like burial position common at the time. Around her, facing in four different directions, were the skeletons of four dogs. It appears that the dogs were placed there to protect the child during her trip to the nether regions.

The domestication of cats came much later. The earliest evidence of a clearly domesticated cat was unearthed by archaeologist Alaine le Brun, who found its remains in Khirokitia, Cyprus, and dated them to about seven thousand years ago. Indeed, cats were not of any value to humans until the agricultural revolution was well under way, and we had progressed to the point of farming grains efficiently enough to have excess to store for the winter. Especially in towns and villages, these grain stores became an important part of the life cycle of teeming populations of rats and mice, which became a major threat to human subsistence since they contaminated and consumed important stockpiles of nourishment. Although we don't know exactly how it happened, probably somebody noticed that a few wild cats had been lurking around the grain storage areas and that they had been killing and eating the mice. It must have then occurred to this observer that if the cats could be encouraged to do even more of this hunting, it could minimize the proportion of each year's harvest that was lost to rodents. Providing warmth, shelter, and a small amount of food was probably all that was necessary to keep the cats in the vicinity of human habitations.

Notice that the cats could serve functions that were important to humans without any training. The same may have been true when dogs first served as watchdogs for humans.[4] Tossing refuse around the perimeter of a camp or village kept the dogs near, and they would spontaneously sound a barking alarm at the approach of people or predators.

Once humans and dogs began to hunt together, the situation changed. Now human survival depended on animal training. Dogs had to learn, at minimum, not to begin their pursuit of prey until commanded to do so. They also had to learn to return on command when the prey was cornered, killed, or netted. As time went on, dogs were trained to retrieve downed game, track over long distances, and so forth. Similarly, dogs became an essential part of agriculture by making it possible for one person to control and move large numbers of sheep and cattle. Like hunting dogs, herding dogs learned to follow commands, in this case, to gather a flock or herd and drive it in a specified direction. With a well-trained dog, a single human shepherd could care for a flock of more than a hundred animals. Without the dog, it might take a dozen or more humans to do the same job. The ability of humans to train dogs to perform these tasks often determined the well-being of a family or village. Training also came into play as humans successfully taught horses, donkeys, mules, elephants, and many other beasts of burden to transport goods and people and to move heavy objects.

Animals have also been trained for a variety of more specific and esoteric functions. In ancient Egypt, for example, baboons were trained to pick fruit from trees and throw it down to farmers below. War dogs were trained to attack infantry and cavalry, using different tactics for each. Trained circus animals have served as a major source of entertainment for thousands of years. And twenty-five hundred years ago, during the golden age of Greece, there is mention of dogs being used to guide and assist the blind.

All of this animal training occurred well before 1879, when psychology emerged as a formal scientific discipline that eventually began to study animal learning and conditioning. So although they did not know they were doing so, it was the animal trainers of antiquity who began to address the psychology of animal learning.

THE DEVELOPMENT OF PSYCHOLOGICAL RESEARCH ON ANIMAL LEARNING

In recent years, scientific methodology and data from psychology research laboratories have been of great value to those who train animals, but psychologists were slow to focus on the study and modification of animal behavior for its own sake. This delay probably came about because psychologists tended to view animal training not as an area of scientific interest, but as an everyday activity that was understood well enough for practical purposes and therefore merited no systematic investigation. Furthermore, early psychologists viewed their science as the study of consciousness, and since animals were considered to be "furry machines" without consciousness, they were uninteresting and irrelevant subjects for psychological study.

Yet centuries earlier, Aristotle was willing to grant that animals had complex mental capacities, including the ability to perceive the world through sense organs, the capacity for motivation and emotion, and enough intellectual capacity to learn, reason, and analyze.[5] Aristotle appeared to anticipate Darwin's view of animal intelligence, arguing that animals and humans differ only in the degree to which certain mental abilities are found. Aristotle's reasoning was quite influential, and many other great thinkers, including Saint Thomas Aquinas, accepted his views. In the thirteenth century, Aquinas established as formal church doctrine the idea that humans and animals differ only in the degree to which their mental abilities express themselves, rather than in the nature of those mental abilities.[6] Unfortunately, this view led to some complications because philosophers of this era tended to believe that intelligence and consciousness were components of the soul. So, to some scholars, particularly those in the Christian church, accepting the proposition that animals have intelligence would be tantamount to conceding that they also have souls, a conclusion that was unacceptable to many theologians and intellectuals at the time.

The French philosopher René Descartes, always sensitive to the requirements and beliefs of the church, disputed the idea of animal intelligence in his *Discourse on Method*.[7] Descartes argued that animals are only biological machines, similar in some respects to the statues he saw in the royal gardens of Saint-Germain-en-Lay. Each figure was a clever piece of machinery powered by hydraulics and carefully geared to perform a complex sequence of actions when stimulated by the pressure of a visitor's weight on hidden levers beneath paving tiles. Descartes suggested that although there appear to be complex activities going on in animals, these take place without any consciousness or thought. After all, he noted, we don't need consciousness to control our heartbeat, yet the heart seems to respond in an intelligent and adaptive manner. Humans are distinguished from the animals, said Descartes, by the presence of spirit, soul, and consciousness.[8]

Charles Darwin challenged Descartes's view in his *Origin of Species*.[9] Darwin argued that no sharp break exists between the mind of humans and that of animals, and he postulated a continuity of mental and physical characteristics among all species. He sought to demonstrate this point in his book *Expression of the Emotions in Man and Animals*.[10] A friend of Darwin, George John Romanes, attempted a more systematic treatment of mental evolution in 1883.[11] It was his anecdotal and observational data on the learning and thinking capabilities of animals in naturalistic settings that provided the rationale for studying animal behavior in the laboratory.

Still, psychologists originally became interested in animal learning not as an end in itself, but as a means of studying basic processes of learning so that they could better understand human behavior. For instance, early research on reflexology, best known through the research of Russian scientists Ivan Petrovich Pavlov, Ivan Michailovich Sechenov, and Vladimir Michailovich Bekterev, employed dogs, sheep, and other animals to explore the principles of classical conditioning. The potential value of these studies in animal training went unrecognized by those who conducted them.

It was the work of an American psychologist, Edward Lee Thorndike, that started psychology on the path to understanding animal learning in its own right.[12] Thorndike began studying animal learning by observing cats, dogs, and chickens in an apparatus called a puzzle box. He traced the progress of these animals as they learned the sequence of actions, such as pressing a lever or moving a latch, that freed them from the box and allowed them to obtain a food reward. Thorndike believed that learning involved simply establishing connections or associations between the stimuli in a situation and a set of responses to those stimuli. He thought that these connections initially came about through trial and error, in which random responses led accidentally to success. Thorndike formulated two laws to explain the learning process. The first, called the *law of exercise,* stated that associations are strengthened by repetition and weakened by disuse. The second, the *law of effect,* said that "any act which in a given situation produces satisfaction becomes associated with that situation, so that when the situation recurs the act is more likely than before to recur also. Conversely, any act which in a given situation produces discomfort becomes disassociated from the situation, so that when the situation recurs the act is less likely than before to recur."[13]

Thorndike's research established many of the issues, such as the effects of reward and punishment, over which scientific battles about the most effective ways of training animals would rage for almost a century. For example, John B. Watson, the founder of behaviorism, strongly downplayed the role of either reward or punishment in learning. He thought that the simple repetition of certain responses in the presence of certain stimuli would strengthen the association between them.[14] Watson likened this process to classical conditioning, in which an animal comes to salivate in response to a tone that has been associated with food even though the tone itself is not a reward. He also added the notion of *recency,* by which he meant that the response occurring just before a reward is given is most likely to be strengthened. Edwin R. Guthrie took this view a step further, arguing that all that was necessary for learning to take place was that a stimulus and a response occur closely together in time, and that a learned response could develop at full strength after it had occurred just once.[15] Neither Watson nor Guthrie viewed consciousness as a necessary condition for learning; they saw reward and punishment as serving only to preserve any positive or negative associations that stimulus-response pairings had already established.

The value of reward for the training of animals was most clearly established in B. F. Skinner's research on operant conditioning.[16] Much as Thorndike had done, Skinner set up laboratory situations in which an animal must voluntarily emit a behavior, such as pressing or pecking at a lever or key, which is then rewarded, or reinforced, by the presentation of a reward. However, because the animals got their reward while still in this "Skinner box" apparatus and could immediately repeat the behavior that earned that reward, Skinner could observe more precisely the development of learning and the conditions that affect it. He found that animals could learn complex behaviors through *shaping* of successive approximations of the final response pattern. This shaping process has clear practical applications to animal training. For example, if you want a dog to press a doorbell on a wall, you might reward him for first looking at the bell, then for turning his body toward the bell, then for taking an initial step toward the bell, then for moving closer to the bell, and so forth until the desired response pattern appears and can be reinforced.

GENETICS AND ANIMAL TRAINING

Many complex behaviors in animals appear more or less automatically as the result of genetic factors.[17] Early in the history of the domestic dog, for example, it was recognized that by interbreeding animals with specific desirable behavioral traits, one could develop a line of dogs that carried those behaviors in their genes.[18] For example, the Chesapeake Bay retriever breed began with two puppies, a red male and a black female, that were rescued from the wreck of an English ship off the coast of Maryland in 1807. They were found to be good retrievers and were bred together.

The best retrievers from the resulting litters were then also bred together, with an occasional cross-breeding to particularly good retrievers in the immediate area. After several generations, the Chesapeake Bay retriever was uniform and recognizable in its look. More important, members of this breed showed the behavioral characteristics that hunters had been trying to capture. Chesapeakes retrieve virtually automatically, making them incredibly easy to train as gun dogs.

In other words, if an animal has a genetic predisposition toward certain types of useful behaviors, it becomes much easier to train that animal to display desirable variations on those behaviors. In such cases, the trainer does not need to teach a complex response pattern from scratch, but can simply take a pattern of behavior that is already likely to occur, and by using operant conditioning procedures, shape it by successive approximations into the more specific and complex behaviors that are desired.

The herding predisposition of some dogs is inherited from the wolves and other wild canids that hunt in packs.[19] The coordinated activity of the pack involves keeping a group of prey animals together, driving them to a specific location, then cutting out the one animal that is to be killed and eaten. These hunting behaviors are themselves based on five genetically programmed instructions. The first two of these have to do with positioning around the designated prey. Instruction one says that once the quarry is sighted, each wolf should take a position at approximately the same distance from the prey. Instruction two says that each wolf should remain equidistant from its hunting mates on the right and left. Implementation of these instructions results in the pack's forming an almost perfect circle around the prey— a circle that closes steadily during the hunt. Even when working alone, a herding dog tries to fulfill these genetic instructions by performing the role of all members of a hunting pack. First, it chooses its proper or "key distance" from the flock of sheep, for example, then dashes around to occupy the stations that normally would be taken up by other pack members, thus encircling the flock in a wide casting motion. This curving outrun, with pauses at each "outpost" (where a fellow pack member should be), drives sheep on the outer fringes of the flock toward the center of the circle, keeping the flock together.

The third genetically programmed set of hunting instructions relates to ambushing prey. When a wolf pack hunts, a single wolf may separate from the rest of the pack, crouch out of sight, and wait while the rest of the pack drives the herd of prey animals slowly toward it. This genetic tendency accounts for the sheepdog's tendency to run and then drop to the ground while staring at a flock of sheep. It is, in effect, playing the part of a wolf waiting in ambush. The sheep appear to be quite aware of the dog's presence. This "eye," or staring, of the dog seems to mesmerize those sheep that may have started to move away from the flock and tends to hold them in position. As soon as the flock as a whole starts to move again, the dog immediately returns to the actions that mimic the encircling wolf pack.

The fourth genetic program has to do with driving a herd. Wolves have been known to drive a herd of buffalo, antelope, or deer into areas where the herd's movement is restricted by cliffs, shorelines, or other terrain features. Once the avenues of escape have been restricted, it becomes easier to isolate individual members. These herd-driving instructions cause wolves (and herding dogs) to make short, direct runs at the animals, which causes them to run in the opposite direction. The path of driven animals is also altered by nipping at their heels or flanks. Herding animals use this same procedure to control individual members of the flock or herd.

The final genetically based instruction that guides herding dogs is based on the social organization that wolves naturally adopt. Every wolf pack has a leader, usually referred to as the *alpha*. This leader initiates and controls the various moves of the pack, and the other wolves watch him carefully and follow his lead. This arrangement maintains the coordination of the pack's activities and makes it an efficient hunting organization.

The human shepherd serves the function of the pack leader for the sheepdog. The shepherd, in turn, relies on the obedience and intelligence of herding dogs to control their instinctive behavior patterns. To achieve full control, a shepherd need only teach the dog about a dozen commands. These commands include:

> *Come:* Come to the shepherd.
> *Stop:* Stop what you are doing now.
> *Go left or Go right:* These movements are relative to the position of the flock.
> *Circle left or Circle right:* This triggers the encirclement maneuver and indicates the direction in which to start.
> *Lie:* This triggers the ambush position, in which the dog lies down and stares at the flock.
> *Close:* Draw nearer to the flock.
> *Away:* Move away from the flock.
> *Slowly* or *Faster:* These are used to control the speed or vigor of whatever activities the dog is performing at the time.
> *Enough:* This is the dog's cue to leave the herd and return to the shepherd.

These commands can be given orally, with hand signals, with whistle blasts, or by any combination of these. Without these dogs' abilities to refine their genetically programmed heritage on the basis of training, livestock management might never have been possible, and the development of agriculture as the economic base of much of human society might have been delayed or even stopped.

If animals have no genetic predisposition toward the behaviors humans wish to teach, or if genetically programmed behaviors conflict with those desired behaviors, it may be difficult, or even impossible, to train the animal properly.[20] Keller and Marion Breland were attempting to train several species of animals using food rewards. Their goal was to teach these animals to perform amusing sequences of behaviors so that they could perform at amusement parks, fairs and zoos. Unfortunately, the use of food rewards triggered certain inherited behaviors that interfered with the task to be learned.

For example, they describe working with a raccoon that was reinforced with food for taking a coin from a pile and depositing it in a "bank." Although the raccoon would pick up the coin, he seemed reluctant to let it go by putting it into a metal container:

> He would rub it up against the inside of the container, pull it back out, and clutch it firmly for several seconds. However, he would finally turn it loose and receive his food reinforcement. Then the final contingency: we [required] that he pick up [two] coins and put them in the container.
>
> Now the raccoon really had problems (and so did we). Not only could he not let go of the coins, but he spent seconds, even minutes, rubbing them together (in a most miserly fashion), and dipping them into the container. He carried on this behavior to such an extent that the practical application we had in mind—a display featuring a raccoon putting money in a piggy bank—simply was not feasible. The rubbing behavior became worse and worse as time went on in spite of non-reinforcement. (p. 682)

Other species of animals gave the Brelands training trouble too. Pigs, for example, could not learn to put coins in a piggy bank because they began rooting the coins around on the ground. The source of these training difficulties with both species is due to genetically determined behaviors that conflicted with the behaviors that the Brelands were trying to teach. Pigs root along the ground as part of their feeding behaviors, and raccoons rub and dunk food-related items. Using food rewards in the training situation triggered these innate responses, and the genetic programming was sufficiently strong that it took over and effectively competed with the responses the trainers desired. Similarly, it would be difficult or impossible to train a terrier to herd sheep or fowl because their inherited tendencies would cause them to chase and kill these animals.

The Economic and Social Impact of Trained Dogs

It is difficult to assess accurately how much trained animals have contributed to human welfare and security. Obviously, during eras when human transportation depended mainly on horses and other draft animals, the impact was greater than it is today, but even after they have ceased to be our primary conveyance, trained animals remain an economically and socially important resource. For the purposes of illustration, we focus on the domestic dog and its important activities other than shepherding, hunting, and recreational functions.

Dogs on Guard

In North America, one out of every four people lives with a dog. Leaving aside the ownership of dogs as companion animals, the most common urban use of dogs is as watchdogs or guard dogs, the function that probably attracted primitive humans to this species in the first place. Indeed, the domestication of dogs probably began when people started taking in wolf or jackal cubs. Those that proved to be good watchdogs, by barking at any disturbance, were more likely to be kept and bred with others like them. Today police statistics show that a home with a barking watchdog is thirty-one times less likely to be burglarized than a home without such protection.[21] And there are so many stories of dogs' alerting their owners to the presence of wild animals, prowlers, burglars, fires, gas leaks, floods, and other dangers that such tales have lost their novelty value.

Because of its genetic heritage, a dog may require little or no training to sound an alarm, but training usually is required to transform a watchdog into a guard dog, whose function is to intervene if an intruder disturbs property, enters premises, or threatens a person.* A good guard dog is naturally aggressive toward strangers who are entering its territory and generally suspicious of strangers anywhere and anytime. Such dogs may attack if threatened or provoked, or they may simply hold intruders at bay by barking, growling, and adopting a threatening bodily stance. Further training can turn guard dogs into attack dogs, which will pursue and attack any indicated person, either on their handler's command or when the handler is being threatened. Such attack training is often conducted by police canine units and home protection service companies. The process is facilitated if, along with a territorial defense response, a dog has inherited from wolves and other wild canids it has the tendency to rally to the defense of the pack by attacking intruders identified by the pack leader. Indeed, natural guard dogs need very little training to trigger aggressive responses; it takes more training to ensure that these animals will direct their aggression toward indicated targets and that they can be reliably called off or otherwise controlled in an attack situation.

Proper attack training costs from eight thousand to twenty-five thousand dollars initially, and attack dogs must continue to practice their learned skills and take occasional refresher courses or their effectiveness will diminish. The expense is worthwhile, though, because unless guard or attack dogs are well trained, they can cause great difficulties for their owners. The greatest challenge is to teach the dogs to differentiate between harmless strangers and hostile intruders. Each year, many innocent people, including children, are bitten by guard or attack dogs that misinterpreted their approach as a threat. In one case, the damage was not physical, but political.[22]

The event took place around 1530, when King Henry VIII sent the Earl of Wiltshire to the Vatican to petition the pope for annulment of Henry's marriage to Catherine of Aragon (so that he could marry Anne Boleyn). The Earl took his guard dog with him, and when the pope extended his foot so that the Earl could kiss it, the dog, mistaking this movement as a kick directed at her master, launched an attack on the pope's toes. Observers of this incident described it as "riotous"; the pope was not amused. Indeed, his reaction apparently bordered on wrath. We cannot be sure what effect the dog's error had on the pope's decision, since political considerations were also important, but we do know that Lord Wiltshire returned home without the annulment and that Henry broke away from the Catholic church and formed

---

*In ancient Rome, aggressive dogs were kept chained just inside entrances to many homes, and their presence was announced by mosaics showing a chained snarling dog, along with the words *cave canem* ("beware of the dog").

the Anglican church, with himself as its head, to guarantee that his wishes would be granted. One cannot help but wonder if this all would have come about if the Earl had left his dog at home.

Dogs of War

The ultimate use of training to shape dogs' aggressive qualities is seen in war.[23] The ancient Egyptians, Romans, Gauls, and Celts trained war dogs—usually mastiffs—for military attack purposes. Today's mastiffs are quite large enough, weighing in at about 220 pounds (110 kilos), but their ancestors, known as the Molossian dog, tipped the scales at around 280 pounds (140 kilos). These great beasts, fitted out in spiked armor, were trained to tear at horses or infantry who came too near. Some even had lances attached to their backs and were trained to run with them at men or horses. Others, carrying pots of burning resin on their backs, were trained to run under horses. Their function as assault weapons made these dogs the ancient equivalent of a surface-to-surface missile.

Before the era of firearms, war dogs were a major factor in battle. They terrorized infantry and could be extremely effective against cavalry. The Celts trained their dogs to bite the noses of cavalry horses, causing them to throw their riders. This tactic was vital in neutralizing the effectiveness of Roman cavalry during their invasion of Britain. Germanic tribes, too, made effective use of war dogs. Attila the Hun, for example, had in his arsenal giant Molossians and also Talbots, the precursor to the modern bloodhound. In later eras, the war dogs of the Spanish conquistadors played a vital role in crushing the resistance of the native Indians of South and Central America.

In World War I, over seventy-five thousand dogs were pressed into service by both sides. The Germans used dogs very effectively in guard and sentry service, and the French were particularly creative in this regard. They would place sentry dogs at various points along the front, usually in pairs, separated by a hundred feet or so. When one dog sounded an alert to indicate human activity beyond the trench line, the dog's handler would carefully note the direction of the dog's line of sight. The same was done for the second dog, who would also be staring at the same spot, and the spot at which the two sight lines crossed marked the location of the intruder. This triangulation process helped the French to locate and attack snipers, new artillery emplacements, and machine-gun posts.

In World War II, an estimated 200,000 war dogs performed sentry and guard duty, messenger services, and search and rescue work. And prior to the introduction of radar, dogs' sensitive hearing was invaluable in warning warship crews of approaching enemy aircraft. Both sides also used canine kamikaze, or suicide, troops. Twice during the Germans' invasion of Russia, Nazi armored columns were stopped by dogs. These animals had been trained to enter tanks and other armored vehicles to be fed, but before a battle the Russians strapped explosives to the hungry dogs' backs and released them when enemy tanks were sighted. When the animals approached the vehicles for food, a metal-sensitive trigger exploded the bombs they bore, thus disabling the tanks. In the Pacific, the Japanese trained dogs to walk into Allied camps pulling carts containing fifty-pound bombs.

The use of war dogs continued in Korea, Vietnam, and the Gulf War. In Vietnam, for example, dogs helped to stop sabotage and theft at U.S. military installations. Within six months of their introduction, incidents of damage or property loss dropped by 50 percent.

Canine Search and Rescue

Everyone knows that dogs' sense of smell is better than that of humans, but you may not be aware of just how good a dog's scent-detecting ability is. On average, humans have about 5 million scent receptors in their nose; the average dog has around 220 million of them. To put it in another way, if we could flatten out the nasal membranes of a typical dog, it would cover about eight square yards (more than the surface area of the dog); a person's nasal membranes would cover little more than about half a square yard. Dogs' sense of smell is so keen that they can often identify odors so faint that even the most sensitive scientific instruments cannot detect them. It is no wonder that dogs have been trained to find people. In some cases, this means looking for them under rubble following earthquakes, hurricanes, or explosions or in the deep snow of an avalanche. They help police pursue fleeing suspects and locate escaped criminals, and they can track and find missing children or others who become lost in wilderness areas. Depending on the purpose of the search, when the dogs find their quarry, they may be trained to alert their handlers by barking, go back for help, or hold the found person at bay.

Some search and rescue dogs are trained as *trackers,* smelling and following the exact path taken by the person they are pursuing. Others are *trailers,* trained to find a human scent and trace it to its origin without concern for the precise path taken by the person. Trackers are trained to follow a single trail, without deviation, or to pursue a particular category of smells, a particularly important skill when seeking a criminal or a lost child. Trailing skills are needed, too, if the task is to locate multiple accident victims, such as those buried in the rubble of a collapsed building. Here, any scent of human life must be traced to its source. Bloodhounds and other hound breeds are preferred for tracking because their sense of smell is acute and their natural determination and patience make it easy to train them to focus on a particular scent track, even if it is old or weakened by wind and water. When agility and speed at trailing are important, such as at disaster scenes, German shepherds and labrador retrievers are the preferred breeds. Teams of these fast-working dogs were responsible for finding and rescuing over three hundred people buried in the debris of an earthquake that devastated Mexico City in 1985.

One of the most difficult aspects of working with search and rescue dogs is the need to train their handlers to let the animals do the job they have been trained for, without human interference. I once witnessed the impact of this problem during the search for a missing child near Mount Seymour, just outside Vancouver, Canada. The boy had wandered off from a group of classmates, teachers, and parents who were on a nature outing. When the child's absence was noticed at the end of the day, a teacher called for help. A search party was hastily organized, but with darkness falling, attempts at locating the boy failed. Nights on the mountain can be quite cold, and by morning the searchers were in a state of near-panic. It was just after dawn that Max, a labrador retriever trained in search and rescue, reached the site. Max had been working for about three years and was already credited with finding over three dozen people lost in the wilderness. He was given an article of the boy's clothing to sniff, and the people who had been on the outing told his handler in which direction they thought the boy had gone. Max immediately started off in exactly the opposite direction. He had gone only about fifty yards when one of the teachers and the boy's mother ran up to the dog handler.

"He went the other way," the teacher shouted.

"They saw him go back that way," the boy's mother cried, pointing in the reverse direction.

Max's handler replied, "I have to follow the dog wherever he goes. He's the one trained to do the tracking."

The missing child's mother became almost hysterical. Sobbing and pounding on the ranger's chest, she insisted, "The other way! Not this way! My boy is out there in the cold. For God's sake, listen to what these people say. They saw him go, not you or your dog."

As gently as possible, the dog handler repeated that he had to follow the dog. The last words he heard as he moved into the woods were the cries of the boy's mother: "My son is lost. He is going to die because you won't listen to us! Please come back and go the other way. Please!"

Looking sadly over his shoulder, the disconcerted ranger muttered to the small knot of people accompanying him, "God, I hope Max is right this time."

In less than an hour, Max began to pick up speed, and ultimately pulled so hard on his leash that the handler let him run free. Five minutes later, excited barking brought us to a shallow indentation in the mountainside where a small, hypothermic boy sat shivering with his arms around Max and tears on his face. The night before, on the basis of the best evidence they had, the human search party had gone in the wrong direction. It was only by relying on Max's sensory abilities, judgment, and training, even when it appeared to some to be completely wrong, that a child was rescued.

Chemical Detection

With appropriate training, dogs can be used as chemical detectors in a variety of situations. For example, they have been used to detect natural gas leaks and even to find truffles (they are preferable to pigs for this task because, unlike pigs, they don't eat these delicacies when they find them). During World War II, a secret U.S. Army project was aimed at creating a corps of "M-dogs" whose task it would be to sniff out a new kind of land mine the Germans had introduced in North Africa. Because they were made of plastic, these mines were virtually invisible to standard electromagnetic mine detectors and were effectively slowing the Allied advance. The project was showing enough success when the war ended that the idea was revived some thirty years later. Indeed, a 1985 U.S. Army report concluded that no mechanical or electronic device was as good as a dog's nose in detecting mines, booby traps, and explosives. The same report noted that dogs' detection abilities are also superior to a number of other animals the army auditioned, including badgers, coyotes, deer, ferrets, foxes, domestic pigs, wild peccaries, opossums, raccoons (and their South American relative, the coati), and a variety of skunks. The dogs were also described as much easier to train.

Experience with the M-dog project led to a number of spin-off dog training specialties, including those that trained dogs to locate a wider variety of explosives and detect illegal drugs in luggage and other hiding places. In the late 1960s, drug detection training of dogs focused on locating marijuana and hashish; in the 1970s, heroin, cocaine, and several other hard drugs were added to the list. Today, most large police forces have drug-sniffing dogs, and they are also often found at international borders and international airports. Some police forces have also trained dogs to detect firearms.

In recent years, some marijuana and hashish growers have tried to avoid detection by planting their crops in national parks and on other public land where, hidden among the mass of surrounding foliage, the plants are virtually undetectable by the human eye. There are not enough park wardens and drug officers to comb the millions of acres of rugged and isolated terrain, but "dope dogs" have proved valuable in counteracting the growers' tactic. They have been trained to ride in patrolling helicopters and sniff the stream of air from the ground below. Even from a height of several hundred feet, these dogs can easily detect the presence of illegal crops.

The impact of detection dogs on the illegal drug trade has been enormous. At a meeting of the California Narcotic Canine Association, one official reported that each detection dog, in its typical seven-year career with the U.S. Customs Service, can be expected to trigger the discovery and seizure of more than $110 million worth of drugs.[24] With an estimated six hundred to twelve hundred such animals currently in service with customs officials and with local and state police departments, the volume and value of the narcotics that these animals keep off the street is staggering.

A few narcotics search dogs are so good at what they do that they have become famous. For example, a team of Belgian malinois dogs named Rocky and Barco became honorary sergeant majors in the Narcotics Division of the State of Texas. In 1987 alone, they provided evidence that resulted in over 250 arrests and the seizure of narcotics with a street value of over $300 million. The Mexican drug smugglers whose business was most affected by Rocky and Barco's skills put out assassination contracts on the animals, offering $70,000 for the death of each dog. And that was peanuts compared to the $1 million bounty offered by Colombian heroin dealers to anyone who would kill Winston, a labrador retriever working for the British government. Winston had cost them nearly $1 billion in lost drug shipments.

Dogs as Assistance Animals

Guide dogs for the blind, sometimes referred to as "seeing eye dogs," have been around for centuries. For example, around 1574, the French essayist Michel de Montaigne described barbets, the curly-coated dog that served as part of the source stock for today's poodles, guiding their blind and poverty-stricken masters through and around swarms of people, horses, carts, and various other obstacles and pitfalls in the streets of Paris. These animals also seemed to know which residents would give their masters money or food; they made the rounds of the neighborhood, stopping regularly at the appropriate addresses.

The first formal school for training guide dogs was established in 1916 in Germany. Its purpose was to assist veterans who had been blinded during World War I. The first such school in the United States was founded in 1929 by Dorothy Harrison Eustis, near Morristown, New Jersey. There are now many similar training centers around the world.

German shepherds were the first dogs to be given formal guide training, but labrador retrievers and golden retrievers are now often preferred because they are less vigorous dogs, a fact that is appreciated by individuals who may not be strong enough to manage a shepherd. Boxers, poodles, and doberman pinschers are also sometimes used as guide dogs. Interestingly, only about 10 percent of blind people can effectively use guide dogs, and they are *not* the people with residual vision. The reason is that, as in the case of search dogs, partially-sighted people may be unwilling to relinquish control and trust their dog's ability to guide them safely. No matter how poor their residual vision, these people tend to second-guess the dog, or challenge its decisions. Eventually this tendency undermines their confidence in the dog and destroys the dog's carefully developed skills.[25]

The current success of training programs for guide dogs for the blind is due in large measure to the work of two psychologists, J. Paul Scott and John Fuller,[26] who worked at the Jackson Memorial Laboratory at Bar Harbor, Maine, and to a trainer named Clarence Pfaffenberger.[27] Pfaffenberger had trained dogs when he was in the military during World War II and, after the war, trained search and rescue dogs before being hired as the head of the training program at Guide Dogs for the Blind, a charitable organization. In the late 1940s, guide dogs were extremely expensive and difficult to obtain, because the success rate of training them was so poor; only about 11 percent of the dogs entering guide dog programs successfully completed them. It was in 1946 that Pfaffenberger had the first of many long visits with Scott and Fuller, who at that time were studying behavioral development and the interaction between genetics and animal learning.

Pfaffenberger learned during these visits that there are four critical periods in the developing puppy's life and that events taking place in some of them will affect the dog's usefulness and trainability by humans. The first of these critical periods is the twenty-one days after birth, during which the dog is still maturing neurologically; its eyes do not open until around the end of this period. During the second critical period, from four to seven weeks after birth, dogs begin to socialize with their littermates and their mother, and they learn the basics of social behavior that they will need to interact with other dogs appropriately. Dogs separated from their mother and littermates during this period often show an inability to get along with other dogs later. The third critical period, between seven and twelve weeks of age, is the time during which dogs can best learn to accept humans as "pack members" and to bond with them. Dogs lacking in adequate human contact during this period may never respond well to training in complex tasks. The period from thirteen to sixteen weeks is the fourth critical period, during which dogs find their place in the dominance hierarchy of other dogs and in relation to humans. It is during this final period that, through training experiences, dogs learn to see humans as dominant members of their "pack." Any dog that has not been adequately socialized to humans by the age of sixteen weeks has little chance of becoming the kind of animal that one would want as a companion or workmate.

Pfaffenberger learned as well that genetics plays an important role in determining a dog's usefulness as guide animals. The offspring of a good guide dog are much more likely than other dogs to complete a guide training program successfully and became good guide dogs.

Returning to his training school, Pfaffenberger began to apply the principles that he learned from Scott and Fuller. He made sure that in the sixth week of life, his dogs begin to socialize with people and, by the eleventh or twelfth week, received training in responding to basic commands such as "come," "sit," and "down." He established a system of record keeping to track down individual dogs' progress and, using these records, began systematically interbreeding the best of his guide dogs. Over a period of about ten years, this breeding program resulted in a dramatic increase in the success rate of guide dog training, from its original 11 percent to greater than 90 percent. Most other guide dog training programs have now achieved similar success by adopting his programs of early socialization and training, and by starting their own breeding programs designed to produce dogs with characteristics that facilitate the learning of guide dog tasks.

Perhaps the most difficult thing that guide dogs must learn is to ignore commands that, if obeyed, would endanger "their" human. In other words, the dogs must learn to think about what to do, not just to respond in a robot-like way. In essence, the dog must learn to be a companion and coworker, not a slave.

Other Kinds of Assistance Dogs

The number and variety of assistance dogs have been increasing steadily as the public has become more aware of the problems of the disabled.[28] The use of dogs to help hearing-impaired people, for example, is a relatively new idea, developed in Minnesota in 1973, when a professional dog trainer named Agnes Mcgrath trained several dogs in a pilot project with the Society for the Prevention of Cruelty to Animals. A few years later, she established the first formal hearing assistance dog training program at the American Humane Association in Denver. There are now about a dozen training programs for hearing assistance dogs, but the demand far exceeds the supply. The demand is driven partly by the fact that while not all visually impaired people can successfully use guide dogs, almost all deaf people can benefit from hearing assistance animals.

Organizations such as Canine Companions for Independence train dogs to help people who have various physical disabilities. These dogs perform tasks such as opening doors, turning lights on and off, retrieving fallen objects, getting items off shelves, or even taking items out of, or placing items into, the refrigerator. Some assistance dogs provide transportation by pulling people in specially harnessed wheelchairs. When Christopher Reeve, the actor best known for his role as Superman, became paralyzed after a riding accident, he obtained a golden retriever as an assistance dog that fulfills some of these functions.

Although the specific tasks that dogs are called on to perform may vary, the goal is always to provide the assistance needed to enable the disabled person to lead a more independent life. Dogs often can eliminate the necessity of continuous home care assistance, thus dramatically cutting the cost of living for disabled individuals.

Dogs have also been used to help with psychological therapy. Freud, for example, included his favorite chow chow, Jo-Fi, in all his therapy sessions. He not only believed that the presence of dogs had a calming effect on patients (especially children), but also that they possessed a special sense allowing them to judge a person's character accurately. Freud admitted that he often depended on Jo-Fi for an assessment of the patient's mental state. More recent studies have shown that Freud was at least partially correct.[29] Petting a calm and friendly dog reduces muscle tension, stimulates more regular breathing, and slows heart rate—all signs of decreased stress. There is even evidence that people who own dogs are likely to live longer and require less medical attention.

Today, there are special programs designed to train therapy dogs.[30] These dogs are often used to visit the elderly and young children in hospitals. They are trained to approach patients in a gentle, slow, and friendly manner and to stay close to patients, thus providing opportunities for social interactions. As a result of contact with these dogs, patients who had isolated themselves from the social world sometimes begin to make social contacts again. I was present at one such occasion.

Sarah, a sixty-seven-year-old woman, had been hospitalized for five months following a tragic car accident in which she was the sole survivor; her husband, only son, daughter-in-law, and grandchild were all killed. Since being told of the deaths two days after the accident, she had spoken to no one. Neither drugs nor traditional psychotherapy seemed to improve her depression and psychological shock. But a golden retriever, who happened to be visiting the ward, noticed Sarah sitting and staring listlessly out of the window. The dog approached Sarah quietly and nosed at her hand. Sarah looked down, and then the dog slipped her big head under Sarah's palm and nuzzled at her side. Sarah began to stroke the dog gently and allowed the dog to lick her face. She began to cry and spoke her first words in five months: "You're so much like Blondie. Oh, how I loved Blondie." After several more visits from the dog and more psychotherapy, Sarah was able to leave the hospital. As she left, she carried a small spaniel that had been "prescribed" by her psychologist.

Perhaps one of the most unusual functions for which dogs are trained is to alert their human to the imminent appearance of a seizure. Amazingly, these seizure-alert dogs can sense the onset of a seizure several minutes before the person does and provide a warning that allows the person to get to a safe location or at least stop any activity such as driving, that might be potentially dangerous when the seizure occurs. If the person loses consciousness, the dog is trained to expose the person's medical emergency tags and, in some cases, to use special pull-cords or push buttons that trigger a signal for help from medical personnel. Victoria Doroshenko, whose epilepsy is not adequately controlled by medication, says of her seizure-alert golden retriever, "Before I got my dog I was afraid and housebound. Harley gave me my life back."[31] The Seizure Dog Alert Association trains these animals, and their success has been phenomenal.

THE IMPACT OF PSYCHOLOGICAL RESEARCH ON ANIMAL TRAINING

Changes in the way psychologists view animal cognition have brought corresponding changes in animal training procedures. For example, early writings on animal training emphasized Thorndike's law of exercise, which means simply relying on repetition to help an animal learn a new task.[32] Accordingly, animals were forced to perform the to-be-learned action, often by being physically manipulated into the positions required. A dog was trained to sit by being given a "sit" command while being pushed into a sitting position. Repetition of this sequence eventually led the dog to associate the "sit" command and the sitting response; if it did not, the animal would be subjected to greater force, using specially designed collars that choke the dog, pinch its neck, or even deliver electric shock.

Later, with a greater emphasis on Thorndike's law of effect, animal trainers began to focus on building desirable behaviors through reward. In dog training, the most common reward was once a pat on the head and an enthusiastic "Good dog!" but today you are most likely to see food used to reward desired actions. The animal may still be manipulated into the target behavior, but once having completed the behavior, a reward follows immediately. For some animals, the reward is not food but a chance to play. For example, some labrador retrievers trained to detect narcotics are rewarded by the chance to chase, catch, and briefly play with a thrown rubber toy.

The most recent incarnation of the use of reward is called *click training*,[33] a method that allows the trainer to give animals immediate reward for a correct response, even when the animals are not close by. The first step in click training is to associate a tidbit of food (or the opportunity to play) with a click or other specific sound. Eventually the click becomes a *secondary reinforcer,* meaning that it not only signals a reward but becomes a reward in its own right. The click becomes a secondary reinforcer for animals in much the same way that money, grades, or a "Good job!" become secondary reinforcers for people: providing good feelings that help sustain and strengthen ongoing behaviors.

Most recently, animal training is being affected by psychologists' explorations of animal cognition. If, as pet owners have long suspected, animals are capable of reasoning and problem solving, perhaps these cognitive mechanisms and abilities can be used to train animals better and faster. For instance, it has become quite clear that, like humans, some animals can learn by observing actions and imitating them. A monkey who sees another opening a drawer and finding food may well learn to open drawers too. Because this kind of learning implies the existence of animal consciousness and because many people, including some psychologists, are still somewhat encumbered by Descartes's contention that animals lack consciousness, there has been a tendency to downplay observational learning in animals. Recent laboratory studies, however, suggest that learning by observation and imitation is a rather widespread phenomenon.[34] Thus, after watching fellow rats press a bar for food, observer rats will learn to press the bar much more quickly than rats who did not see an exemplar.[35] Similarly, pigeons who observe other pigeons making the correct choice in a visual discrimination task learn to make that same discrimination much more quickly than birds who had no vicarious exposure to it.[36] These results suggest that animals might be more quickly and efficiently trained if they are first exposed to the training situation and watch other animals performing the target activities that they will be required to learn.

The usefulness of observational learning techniques for animal training has not yet been proved in the laboratory, but there are some indications that they do have practical value. Consider the case of Saint Bernard rescue dogs, who seem to work best in teams of three or more. Sent out on patrols following storms in the Swiss Alps, these dogs wander the trails together, looking for lost or stranded hikers. If they come on an unconscious victim, they engage in a complex set of behaviors. Two dogs lie down beside the person to give warmth (one of them also licks the victim's face to awaken him or her), while the third goes back to the St. Bernard Hospice to guide human rescuers to the scene. Perhaps the most remarkable aspect of these dogs' complex and cooperative rescue work is that the animals need no training to do it. They appear to develop their skills entirely on the basis of observational learning and imitation. Young dogs are simply allowed to run with the older dogs on patrol and, in the process of watching their elders, seem to learn what is expected of them. Moreover, each dog appears to decide for itself whether its job will eventually be to lie with victims or to go for help; once this decision is made, the animal continues to perform that task, and only that task, for the rest of its career.

Observational learning is also important in other aspects of animal training. For example, when dogs are being taught to herd sheep, guard facilities, or pull sleds, often the best way to start is to let "student" dogs watch animals that already know the to-be-learned task. Watching student dogs in such situations, one can almost see them trying to figure out the cues and signals to which the other dogs are responding. If nothing else, dogs who receive this type of observational learning experience seem to learn their jobs more quickly and appear to be more confident and competent workers than those not given this opportunity.

CONCLUSION

In our highly technological and industrialized society, it is tempting to think that animal training does not have much impact on people's lives. This is not the case. In agricultural settings, herding animals are still economically vital, and guard dogs help to ensure our personal safety and keep our property secure. Drug detection dogs have had a massive impact on narcotics-related crime, and search and rescue dogs have saved countless thousands of lives. The social and personal importance of dogs that assist the blind, the deaf, and the physically disabled is immeasurable, and I have not had the space here to give more than a passing mention to dogs used for hunting, sports, and recreation. None of these functions would be possible without the training necessary to bring animal behavior reliably under human control, and it is in relation to this training that psychologists' theories and research results have made a significant contribution.

Animal training, and the efficient application of psychologists' research on learning in the context of such training, is important for other reasons as well. About one out of every four people in North America lives with a dog, but the sad fact is that approximately 40 percent of all puppies acquired as pets are killed, abandoned, or left to an uncertain fate in animal shelters before they are a year old.[37] In almost every case, the reasons have to do with problems in training and control. Typical complaints are that the dog cannot be housebroken, is not responding to commands, or is not "acting civilized." All of these problems are ultimately traceable to a lack of knowledge about how to train animals. Remarkably, only 24 percent of people ever give their dogs any formal obedience instruction in the form of classes, and of those who do, a third report that their pet either "flunked out" or that they stopped the training because they saw too little progress.[38] Obviously, information on how to train dogs and other animals efficiently to be companions has not yet fully filtered down to the general public, even though such data are being well used by professional animal trainers to develop the working and assistance skills reviewed here. Indeed, for those who use available psychological knowledge about animal learning to turn animals into working partners and companions, the rewards can be great. Still, psychologists have a long way to go in disseminating what they have learned about learning so that it can be of maximum benefit to the maximum number of people and animals.

SUGGESTIONS FOR FURTHER READING

Bauman, D. L. (1991). *Beyond basic dog training.* New York: Howell Book House.

Pearce, J. M. (1997). *Animal learning and cognition: An introduction.* Hove, East Sussex: Psychology Press.

Pryor, K. (1984). *Don't shoot the dog!* New York: Simon & Schuster.

PSYCHOLOGY AND THE PARANORMAL

Stuart A. Vyse

Jason was worried about his organic chemistry exam. As long as he could remember, he had dreamed of being a doctor, but now he was struggling with the reality of pre-med courses. He had gotten only a 75 on the first hourly exam, and he really wanted to get an A in this course, or at least a B+. Today was the midterm, and it was worth 25 percent of his course grade. For the past week, he had spent three hours a night poring over his notes and rereading the text. He had even participated in a study group with three other members of his class, and he seemed to know the material as well as any of them. He felt well prepared, but Jason was still worried. A bad score on this exam would kill his chances for a good grade in the course, and Professor Winston was unpredictable. Jason had not studied as hard as he should have for the first exam, but the professor had asked some questions that were really out of the blue. The material didn't come from the book, and if it came from lecture, Jason had somehow missed it. And he had never missed a class. He thought he would do well on the exam, but he wasn't sure.

So when he woke up on the day of the exam, Jason wanted to do everything he could to ensure a good grade. Some of the guys who sat in the last row of his class would wear baseball hats, usually backward, but Jason sat near the front. He never wore a hat to class because he was afraid of what Professor Winston would think. But today he decided to wear his green hat. It had been his lucky hat since the first time he put it on and went four-for-four in a high school baseball game, winning the game with a triple in the bottom of the ninth inning. He hadn't gone four-for-four every time he wore the hat, but he always felt more confident wearing it. Somehow it helped. And today he needed all the help he could get. He would wear the hat no matter what Winston thought.

Sally didn't really want to go to the palm reader. She didn't believe in this stuff, but her friend Diane was insistent. Diane had gone to this palm reader several times before, and she said her readings were amazingly accurate. Sally was going along with it mostly to satisfy Diane, but underneath her skepticism was the faint hope that the palmist's reading would produce something interesting. Sally's job at the insurance agency seemed to be going nowhere, and she hadn't met any interesting men in months. As unlikely as it seemed, it would be great if this palm reader gave some hint of a brighter future.

The sitting room in the palm reader's house was nicely decorated and quite comfortable. They sat across a small circular table in high-backed chairs with deep, soft cushions. Silvia, the palm reader, was a friendly middle-aged woman who began almost immediately. Laying Sally's flattened hand in her own, the woman peered at the palm intently. "You have had a life filled with much happiness and some sorrow, but now something is troubling you. You are longing for something." As the reading progressed, Sally found herself becoming convinced. Silvia said a few things that did not make sense, but she seemed to have remarkable knowledge of Sally's life. She had said, "Someone close to you has a serious illness," and indeed her mother was suffering from emphysema. She knew Sally had a brother and that she was not particularly happy in her job. Having sat down a skeptic, Sally soon found herself thinking there might be something to this palm-reading business. Silvia seemed to have a sixth sense—a special intuition about people. When it came time to ask questions about the future, Silvia said she saw a romantic relationship with a dark-haired man with whom she shared similar interests. She also saw new friends coming into her life and a better job. Things would not be perfect, but there would be great joy.

At the end of the appointment, Sally was in a wonderful mood. It had all been so interesting, and although she realized Silvia's predictions might not come true, she really hoped they would. She thanked Silvia and told her she would be back again. And she would. As skeptical as she had been, Sally thought Silvia's reading was so good that there must be something to it. She couldn't explain it, but whatever it was seemed real.

Jason and Sally's stories demonstrate common forms of paranormal belief. Any belief that is in conflict with accepted principles of science and logic is *paranormal*.* Superstitions, such as the one involving Jason's lucky hat, have the additional quality that they are pragmatic: the person takes some action or holds some belief because it will bring good luck or stave off bad.[1] Despite their apparent intellectual and technological sophistication, many people endorse a wide variety of paranormal phenomena. In a Gallup Poll conducted in 1996, only 47 percent of adult Americans reported being not at all superstitious. Table 1 shows the percentage of respondents who reported belief in various specific paranormal phenomena. Each of these beliefs stands in opposition to our current understanding of nature, yet many people accept them as true.

Astrology is an interesting example. This system of belief began three thousand years ago in ancient Babylonia and soon spread to India, Greece, and, eventually,

---

Paranormal is a more comprehensive term than *psychic*. The word *psychic* tends to refer to presumed abilities of an individual to make predictions, to have extra sensory perception, or to levitate objects, for example. *Paranormal* covers all these things, plus experiences such as seeing a ghost or having an out-of-body experience.

TABLE 13.1 Results of a 1996 Gallup Poll of Paranormal Belief Among American Adults

Item	Believe	Not sure	Don't believe	No opinion
Extrasensory perception	48	22	27	3
Possession by the devil	42	13	43	2
Mental telepathy	35	24	39	2
Haunted houses	33	19	47	1
Clairvoyance	27	25	46	2
Astrology	25	22	52	1
Ghosts	30	19	50	1
Reincarnation	22	22	55	1
Communication with the dead	20	22	56	2
Psychokinesis (moving objects with mental energy)	17	26	55	2
Channeling (temporary control of one's body by a "spirit being")	12	21	64	1

Note: Based on a survey of one thousand adults conducted September 3–5, 1996.

throughout the world. Despite its ancient beginnings, astrology retains an air of plausibility because we know that stars and planets have gravitational forces that act on each other. Might it be that these forces, present at the time of our birth, somehow permanently affected our personalities, and thus our fates? It is not likely. The gravitational forces of the stars and planets are far less than those of the hospital delivery room walls, and statistical studies of the relationship between astrological signs and personality dimensions have failed to demonstrate the validity of astrology.[2] Yet millions read their horoscopes in newspapers and magazines, and many pay professional astrologers for personal readings. Why? This question and others about paranormal belief have been the concern of a small group of psychologists since the discipline's early beginnings.

STUDYING THE PARANORMAL

It is not surprising that psychologists are concerned with the paranormal. Although the sciences of astronomy, physics, and chemistry are summoned to examine the mechanisms of the paranormal, such as the possibility of planetary influences, many paranormal phenomena boil down to psychological issues such as unusual examples of perception (e.g., extrasensory perception, or ESP and clairvoyance), behavior (e.g., mental telepathy, telekinesis), or belief (e.g., demonic possession, reincarnation). Indeed, a number of the most famous figures in the history of psychology have, at one time or another, been fascinated with paranormal phenomena.

No less than the founder of American psychology, William James, attended hundreds of seances, and although he denounced several mediums as charlatans, he believed that the trances of at least one, a Mrs. Leonora Piper, were genuine.[3] He also founded, and was an active member of, the American Society for Psychical Research. Carl Jung, perhaps Sigmund Freud's most famous follower, endorsed a number of mystical beliefs, such as the existence of the *collective unconscious,* a memory within us all of many important experiences of our species. Jung also studied astrology and wrote an entire book on belief in flying saucers.[4] Finally, B. F. Skinner, the noted behavioral psychologist, made an important contribution to the study of superstition with the publication of an article about superstition in pigeons.[5]

Nevertheless, the study of the paranormal has existed somewhat apart from the mainstream of psychological research. Investigators in this field can be loosely divided into believers and skeptics. Because the skeptics enjoy greater support in the academic community, most skeptical researchers work in the psychology departments of colleges and universities. The believers, many of whom also hold Ph.D.s in psychology, and are known as "parapsychologists," more often work in private laboratories and foundations. (One exception is the University of Edinburgh, which operates a non-degree-granting program in parapsychology.) The research of each group tends to be published in different places. Skeptics publish their research in traditional psychological journals, while believers publish their work in their own specialized journals.*

In some cases, researchers begin in one camp and end up in another. For example, British psychologist Susan Blackmore began her career as a believer, but after years of research, she failed to find any reliable evidence of psychic phenomena. She is now a skeptical researcher.[6] Following the opposite path, Cornell University social psychologist Daryl Bem recently took a controversial stand by publishing an article in the prestigious journal *Psychological Bulletin,* in which he supported the validity of the Ganzfeld effect, a form of mental telepathy in which a "sender" or "agent" looks at a visual stimulus in one room while a "receiver" in another room attempts to determine which of several stimuli is being sent.[7] In general, then, research on the paranormal tends to come either from parapsychologists who are attempting to demonstrate the validity of paranormal phenomena or from psychologists in the social, personality, cognitive, and clinical areas who are interested in the nature of belief in the paranormal.

The History of Parapsychology

The first systematic investigations of the paranormal began with the establishment of the Society for Psychical Research in London in 1882. Members of the society attended seances in order to investigate the claims of the popular mediums

---

*Note that traditional psychological journals are more likely than specialized journals to require that information be reviewed and criticized by other scientists before it is published. Consequently, the research in the traditional journals tends to meet higher methodological standards.

and spiritualists of the day. In one celebrated case, it denounced as an impostor Madame Blavatsky, a famous American spiritualist and founder of the Theosophical Society.[8]

The first laboratory investigations of paranormal phenomena were conducted by J. B. and Louisa Rhine. Trained as botanists, the Rhines became interested in parapsychology in the early 1920s, and in 1927, they accepted the invitation of social psychologist William McDougall to conduct research in the Department of Psychology at Duke University. With the founding of the Duke University laboratory, the statistical and experimental methods of scientific psychology were applied to the investigation of paranormal phenomena for the first time. Collaborating with a colleague, Karl Zener, J. B. Rhine popularized the use of "Zener" cards for studies of ESP. Each card showed a star, a circle, or other pattern. In a typical experiment a sender would look at one of the Zener cards, and a receiver, usually seated in the same room, would try to guess which of the five cards the sender was looking at. Rhine also established the *Journal of Parapsychology*. In subsequent decades, parapsychological research began to spread to other laboratories in the United States and Britain, reaching its pinnacle of professional acceptance in 1969, when the Parapsychological Association was voted a member organization of the prestigious American Association for the Advancement of Science.[9]

For over thirty years, the Rhines conducted ESP research at Duke University. In 1935, the Parapsychology Laboratory was separated from the Department of Psychology, and when J. B. Rhine retired in 1965, the laboratory became a private entity, apart from Duke University. It survives today as the Institute for Parapsychology in Durham, North Carolina.

Despite its extensive laboratory history, parapsychology and parapsychological research remain controversial. Many psychologists believe that parapsychologists have failed to demonstrate a single reliable paranormal phenomenon. They criticize parapsychological researchers for using what they see as inadequate experimental methods and controls, inappropriate statistical techniques, biased participant selection techniques, and selective publication of results.[10] For example, parapsychological researchers have used random number generators to produce sequences that, on subsequent examination, were not random at all; they have not always reported on the results of participants who became discouraged and dropped out of the investigations; and some have published only the results of experiments that showed evidence of psychic ability, not those with negative results. However, many skeptics and believers agree that some phenomena, such as the Ganzfeld effect, are worthy of further study.[11]

Psychological Study of the Paranormal

Some research psychologists have concentrated on the investigation of paranormal beliefs, superstitious behavior, and perceptual illusions. Psychologists in this field, sometimes called *anomalistic psychology*[12] because it studies what is irregular or abnormal, have explored the effects of conditioning on superstition,[13] the relationship of personality traits to paranormal belief,[14] the role of reasoning errors in paranormal belief,[15] and the causes of various perceptual illusions.[16] Their research has helped us to understand paranormal beliefs better by applying current cognitive psychological research methods to the many fallacies, short-cuts, and biases inherent in human thought processes.[17]

Psychologists who study paranormal beliefs have performed two important functions. First, they have broadened our understanding of human behavior. By investigating basic questions of personality, learning, and cognition and, by applying these findings to the paranormal, they have begun to unravel the paradox of how so many members of a such a technologically advanced society can subscribe to the beliefs listed in Table 1. Second, by enumerating the psychological sources for paranormal belief, they have revealed limitations on people's objectivity and dramatized the need for critical thinking in the examination of the paranormal phenomena of everyday life. In an attempt to promote a greater understanding of the psychology of the paranormal, a number of psychologists have written books and articles aimed at a general audience,[18] and others have studied the effects of instruction in critical thinking and science on paranormal belief.[19]

APPLIED PSYCHOLOGY AND THE PARANORMAL

The most important activities of psychologists in relation to the paranormal fall into three broad categories: (1) conducting research on paranormal belief, superstition, and anomalous experience; (2) serving as experts, for both the government and the media; and (3) teaching critical thinking.

Research on Paranormal Belief, Superstition, and Anomalous Experience

Throughout its history, psychological research has shown that normal people are prone to many perceptual illusions, reasoning errors, and irrational quirks of behavior. In the early decades of the twentieth century, Gestalt psychologists discovered a number of perceptual illusions and proposed psychological principles to explain them. For example, in 1910 Max Wertheimer identified the *phi phenomenon,* which creates the perception of smooth motion when two adjacent lights are flashed on and off in rapid succession. It is the phi phenomenon that makes blinking lights appear to race each other around the edges of a movie marquee and the flashing images on the screen inside the theater appear to move like objects in the real world outside.[20] More recently, cognitive psychologists have discovered a variety of common, and potentially correctable, reasoning errors and mental biases that are analogous to the perceptual illusions studied by the Gestalt psychologists. Such errors and biases produce skewed judgment and faulty decision making.[21] (Some of these errors and biases are described in Chapter 5.) These historical trends have led quite naturally to basic and applied research on paranormal belief.

Some researchers have used situations involving paranormal belief as a mechanism for basic research on psychological theories. In such cases, paranormal beliefs are merely tools for pursuing answers to questions about nonparanormal theories of psychological functioning. However, by choosing paranormal beliefs as the context for their experiments, these researchers have forged a link to common beliefs found outside the laboratory. Other investigators study paranormal beliefs directly. They apply known principles in personality, cognitive, or clinical psychology to form and test hypotheses about the causes of paranormal belief. Their goals are to understand paranormal belief for its own sake and to make a direct contribution to our understanding of the psychology of everyday life.

Examples of Basic Research on the Paranormal   Cornell University psychologist Thomas Gilovich conducts research on social cognition, that is, on how people process information about themselves and other people. In a series of experiments published in 1993, he and coauthor Scott Madey studied the well-known tendency for people to recall events that seem to confirm their beliefs and expectations more often than events that do not.[22] They hypothesized that this bias for confirming information would be particularly powerful when the events in question are not tied to a particular moment in time. For example, individuals who are strong supporters of the U.S. president will tend to remember those general aspects of his career that put the president in a favorable light. However, if an event is associated with a particular moment in time, such as a presidential election, they will be forced to attend to the outcome, whether it confirms their beliefs (he wins) or not (he loses). In short, these investigators hypothesized that our bias toward forgetting disconfirming information will be diminished for events that are *temporally focused.*

Gilovich and Madey decided to test their hypothesis on the recall of events that either confirm or do not confirm psychic predictions. Professional psychics usually make predictions that are not fixed in time: "Your luck will change for the better," rather than, "Your luck will change for the better next Tuesday at noon." Or, as in Sally's case, "Someone close to you has a serious illness," not, "Your mother has emphysema and will be hospitalized within the next two months." The researchers reasoned that psychics' unfocused predictions take advantage of humans' bias toward recalling confirming rather than disconfirming information. Accordingly, they designed a situation in which psychic predictions were sometimes tied to a particular date and sometimes not, and were sometimes confirmed and sometimes not.

The Cornell University students who served as research participants read what they were told was the diary of a student who was in an experiment on extrasensory perception. In each case, the diary identified several psychic predictions and subsequent events that sometimes confirmed the predictions and sometimes did not. In one version of the diary, the predictions were tied to a specific day (e.g., "I have a feeling that I will get into an argument with my psychology research group on Friday"), and in the other version they were not (e.g., "I have a feeling I will get into an argument with my psychology research group").[23] In each experiment, Gilovich and Madey's hypothesis was supported. Participants remembered confirming events equally well whether they were temporally focused or not, but disconfirming events that were not tied to a specific day were recalled significantly less often. Thus, psychics who wish to gain a reputation for success would be wise to keep the timing of their predictions vague, like telling Sally that there "would be great joy" in her life.

Giora Keinan of Tel Aviv University used a similar strategy in a study of stress and superstition conducted during the 1991 Gulf War.[24] Keinan's previous research had been on the effects of stress on higher cognitive functions, such as decision making and problem solving.[25] When the threat of SCUD missile attacks presented a new kind of stressor, however, he chose to examine its effects on lower-level functions, specifically superstition, or what he called "magical thinking." Many superstitions about how to avoid being bombed became popular in Israel during the Gulf War. A number of these centered around the special rooms, sealed against the threat of poison gas, in which Israelis hid during missile attacks. Some people believed, for example, that it was important to step into the sealed room with one's right foot. Others believed it was bad luck to allow a neighbor whose house had been hit by a missile into one's sealed room.

To examine the effect of stress on these beliefs, Keinan compared people who lived in cities where missiles regularly landed (e.g., Tel Aviv) with those living in cities that were never attacked (e.g., Jerusalem). He went door to door interviewing people from high- and low-risk cities about their beliefs and about how much stress they felt they were under. In addition, Keinan used a questionnaire to measure his participants' tolerance for ambiguity, a trait that he hypothesized might be important to the emergence of magical thinking. People with low tolerance for ambiguity have a strong need to finish things they begin and have difficulty accepting conflicting ideas or the ambiguity of an unanswered question. People with high tolerance for ambiguity are less troubled by these situations. Keinan discovered that both high stress and lower tolerance for ambiguity encouraged magical thinking. People who lived in more dangerous cities endorsed more superstitious ideas, regardless of their tolerance for ambiguity, and people with lower tolerance for ambiguity were more superstitious, regardless of where they lived. However, people who had low tolerance for ambiguity *and* lived in cities where missile attacks occurred were especially prone to magical thinking. Thus, Keinan had established that both stress and tolerance for ambiguity play an important role in the emergence of superstition.

Keinan's study of stress and magical thinking and the Gilovich and Madey studies of memory for expectancy-confirming and expectancy-disconfirming events had their beginnings in basic research questions not specifically connected with the psychology of paranormal belief. In each case, however, paranormal beliefs were chosen as an example of a particular kind of thinking. In making that choice, the researchers answered a basic scientific question, but they also extended the implications of their research to a common form of behavior found in everyday life. Because it was a field study, conducted in the streets, Keinan's research gains an additional degree of generality, and in both studies the researchers adopted a valuable strategy for gaining insight into the psychology of the paranormal.

Examples of Applied Research on the Paranormal   Other researchers make the paranormal the primary focus of their research. University of Pennsylvania psychologist Paul Rozin has conducted a number of investigations of magical thinking. He was motivated partly by his reading of *The Golden Bough,* a multivolume work in which the Scottish classicist Sir James Frazer had argued that belief in magic is limited to "primitive" cultures. Rozin set out to prove Frazer wrong. In a series of studies, he demonstrated that University of Pennsylvania college students and other members of "nonprimitive" cultures were prone to both the law of contagious magic, which holds that there is a lasting connection between things that were once in contact, and homeopathic magic, the law of similarity that says "like produces like."[26]

Much of Rozin's research on magical thinking has examined how disgust, aversion, and other negative attitudes can be produced by homeopathic or contagious magic. For example, in a study conducted with collaborators Maureen Markwith and Carol Nemeroff, Rozin showed that people believe that the danger of acquired immunodeficiency disorder (AIDS) can be magically transferred to objects touched by a person with AIDS.[27] The authors asked University of Pennsylvania and Arizona State University students to respond to questionnaires in which they rated their attitudes toward using a fork, or wearing a sweater, that had been used by someone else but then washed. Sometimes the students were told the fork or sweater had been used by a man with AIDS and sometimes by a man not identified as having AIDS. Rozin, Marwith, and Nemeroff found that students' attitudes showed a magical AIDS contagion effect. They were significantly more negative about using objects touched by a person with AIDS, and the negative feelings did not diminish when the contact had been minimal or long ago. In addition, the students showed what Rozin and his colleagues called a "backward contagion" effect. When asked how they felt about staying in a San Francisco hotel room that "will become a hospital for AIDS patients," the students' attitudes were significantly more negative than toward a hotel that was not described in this way.

In other studies, Rozin and his colleagues have shown that college students are also susceptible to homeopathic magic. For example, students were significantly more reluctant to eat sugar when it had been labeled "sodium cyanide" than when it had been labeled correctly as "sugar," even when they had watched the sugar being poured from a new box into two clean containers and had arbitrarily decided themselves which container should get which label.[28]

Another line of research has made a connection between superstitious behavior in animals and humans. In 1948, B. F. Skinner demonstrated that when hungry pigeons were placed in a cage and given a small amount of food every fifteen seconds, regardless of what they might be doing at the time, the birds soon developed odd, idiosyncratic movements (e.g., bobbing their heads or pecking at the chamber floor) that Skinner referred to as "superstitious."[29] The pigeons appeared to behave as though they believed their actions produced the food. This classic study was one of Skinner's most famous publications, but for many years, no one ventured to extend his findings to the analysis of human superstitious behavior. Finally, in 1987, University of Kansas psychologist Edward Morris and his colleague Gregory Wagner attempted to replicate Skinner's experiment with children.[30] Morris and Wagner brought three- to six-year-old children into a small observation room where a plastic clown named Bobo had been mounted on the wall. The children were told that from time to time a marble would come out of Bobo's mouth and that the marbles they collected could be exchanged later for a toy of their choosing. As in Skinner's experiment, the arrival of the marbles was controlled by a clock and had nothing to do with anything the children did. Nevertheless, most of the children developed distinctive superstitious responses similar to those of the pigeons. Some wiggled their hips, others touched Bobo's nose, and still others grimaced at him. In a later study, Morris and his colleagues showed that children can acquire these simple superstitions by imitating a videotaped model,[31] and other researchers went on to show how superstitions can be conditioned in adults.[32]

The distinctions between basic and applied research on the paranormal are somewhat arbitrary. For example, although the research conducted by Rozin, Morris, and their colleagues was aimed at understanding magical thinking and superstitious behavior, Rozin's research contributes to our general understanding of cognition, attitudes, and belief, and Morris's research extends the literature on basic reinforcement processes by demonstrating that the superstitious conditioning observed in pigeons also occurs in children. Similarly, the studies by Gilovich and Madey and by Keinan were designed to answer questions about social cognition and cognition and stress, but the investigators' choices of psychic predictions and superstitions as the subjects of their research add to our understanding of everyday paranormal belief.

PSYCHOLOGISTS AS EXPERTS ON THE PARANORMAL

Powerful images of the paranormal and otherworldly things surround us. Indeed, some of our most popular motion picture dramas have portrayed alien beings who visit earth (*ET, Close Encounters of the Third Kind*),* ghosts (*Ghost*), demonic possession (*The Exorcist*), and people with psychic and psychokinetic powers (*Phenomenon, Powder*). Television programs explore the predictions of the sixteenth-century physician Nostradamus who, some believe, foretold many modern events. On countless talk shows, performers use "psychic powers" to bend spoons and keys. In recent years, "infomercials" and other advertisements for telephone "psychic" services have yielded hundreds of millions of dollars in charges from people who pay an average of forty dollars per call for advice and clues about their future.

---

*It should be noted that belief in alien beings is not necessarily paranormal. Most astronomers and biologists believe there is life beyond our planet based on the simple mathematical likelihood that conditions like those on Earth exist or have existed somewhere else in the vastness of space (Sagan, 1996). However, very few scientists believe there is sufficient evidence that beings from another world, or their space craft, have actually visited Earth. In contrast, according to a Gallup poll conducted in September of 1996, 45 percent of American adults do believe UFOs have visited the Earth. In many cases, people who say they have had contact with aliens report that these beings have a variety of psychic abilities, such as telepathic communication or psychokinesis—the ability to move objects with mental energy.

Psychologists as Experts in the Media

In the face of all this uncritical presentation of things paranormal, psychologists have teamed up with other scientists to present a more reasoned view. Unfortunately, those whose perspectives might provide a degree of balance to the discussion of the paranormal are not usually invited to appear on television or radio programs. As a result, organizations like the Committee for the Scientific Investigation of Claims of the Paranormal (CSICOP) and the Skeptic Society have taken activist positions and voluntarily undertake the study of incidents in which people report having paranormal experiences. Members of these groups publish the results of their investigations in journals such as the *Skeptical Inquirer* and *Skeptic Magazine.*

When psychologists are invited to appear on television or radio programs to talk about the paranormal, they often explain how alleged paranormal events might be the result of perceptual illusions or errors in reasoning. For example, in an unusually balanced presentation of the alleged alien abduction phenomenon, the producers of a 1996 *Nova* program, "Kidnapped by UFOs?" interviewed both supporters of the alien abduction movement and skeptical psychologists. The supporters included Harvard University psychiatrist John Mack, who has written about patients who believe they were abducted[33] and Budd Hopkins, an artist and author who is a major figure in the alien abduction movement. Both men talked about "abductees" they knew, and scenes were presented from one of the support group meetings that Hopkins conducts for those who believe they have had encounters with alien beings.

As a counterpoint, several psychologists gave alternative interpretations. They noted that many "encounters with aliens" occur while people are falling asleep or while waking from sleep. University of Kentucky psychologist Robert Baker discussed how altered states of consciousness associated with these hypnogogic and hypnopompic periods (dreamlike states associated with falling asleep and awakening, respectively) can produce hallucinations. University of Washington psychologist and memory researcher Elizabeth Loftus commented on Hopkins's interviews of adults and children with incomplete memories of abduction. She explained that Hopkins's methods of questioning, which often involved subtle suggestions and prodding for greater elaboration, could serve to construct "memories" of events that never happened. Finally, University of California social psychologist Richard Ofshe commented on the workings of Hopkins's support group for abductees and explained that the members helped to solidify each other's memories and lent credibility to their beliefs.

Psychologists have also contributed to the public's understanding of paranormal belief by writing books and articles for general audiences. A notable example is Thomas Gilovich's 1991 book, *How We Know What Isn't So: The Fallibility of Human Reason in Everyday Life.*[34] Written in an entertaining and accessible style, this book explains that reasoning errors and perceptual illusions can encourage our belief in ESP and the effectiveness of scientifically unfounded "alternative" health practices. Gilovich has also written summaries of his research on temporally focused psychic predictions for general interest magazines.[35] Through these efforts, psychologists bring their research findings directly to the public, where it is needed most.

Psychologists as Expert Commentators on Parapsychology Research

Ever since J. B. and Louisa Rhine began their research at Duke University, parapsychologists have conducted research on an extensive collection of alleged psychic phenomena, and from time to time some claim to have successfully demonstrated them. But because parapsychologists seldom publish their research in traditional psychological journals, their research is rarely reviewed by more skeptical psychologists. To counter this situation, some psychologists have served as methodological experts, publishing criticisms, when justified, of the research methods used by parapsychologists or of the conclusions that parapsychologists draw from their findings. For example, Ray Hyman of the University of Oregon has followed the research on the Ganzfeld effect for many years, and has published his criticisms in parapsychological journals.[36]

On occasion, the methodological debate is carried out in traditional psychological journals. When Daryl Bem and his coauthor, parapsychologist Charles Honorton, published their article on the Ganzfeld effect in the *Psychological Bulletin,* Ray Hyman was invited to write a critique of the article, and Bem was allowed to respond in print to those criticisms.* Bem argued that Honorton's findings were sufficiently strong to support the validity of the Ganzfeld phenomenon; however, Hyman argued that the results were not particularly convincing and that because they had been produced in a single laboratory, they needed to be replicated by other researchers.

Finally, psychologists occasionally evaluate government programs involving the paranormal. Politicians and other government officials are not immune to paranormal belief, and from time to time some have been convinced that research on ESP is of great importance to national security. Indeed, in the 1950s, the U.S. Army sponsored some of J. B. Rhine's parapsychological research. In 1995 the U.S. Central Intelligence Agency revealed a top-secret research program, code-named "Stargate," that had been designed to assess the potential of psychic "remote viewing" (seeing distant locations using ESP) for use in espionage. The agency finally concluded that remote viewing was of no practical value, but not until $20 million had been spent on the project over several years.[37]

That same year, the U.S. Army Research Institute asked the National Research Council to assess a group of New Age techniques for enhancing human performance. Among these were several psychic phenomena, such as remote viewing and psychokinesis. The group assembled to report on these methods, called the Committee on Techniques for the Enhancement of Human Performance, included Ray Hyman and several other noted psychologists. The committee commissioned a number of background reports to aid them in their work, including one by Robert

---

*Honorton died before the article was published.

Rosenthal, a Harvard University psychologist and expert on research methodology, and another by James Alcock, a York University psychologist and expert on parapsychology. Although the committee found that some New Age techniques merited further study (e.g., a self-improvement method called neurolinguistic programming), they concluded that there was "no scientific warrant for the existence of parapsychological phenomena."[38] As a result, the committee recommended that the army not fund any further research in this area and simply monitor the published results of civilian research in parapsychology. Recognizing the need for public education through the dissemination of its findings, the committee publicized its final report in a detailed document and through a press conference. Articles about the committee's findings appeared in major newspapers throughout North America.

PSYCHOLOGISTS AS TEACHERS OF CRITICAL THINKING

Although it is important for psychologists to conduct research on the causes of paranormal belief and to serve as experts who evaluate the methodology used in research on the paranormal, perhaps the most valuable thing they do to combat unwarranted belief in the paranormal is to teach people how to think critically. By equipping their students with the tools needed to test assumptions and evaluate evidence, teachers of psychology at the high school, college, and university level prepare these students to face the many forms of superstition and pseudoscience presented in the media. Critical thinking is basic to the enterprise of science, and psychologists are not the only ones who teach it. Carl Sagan, for example, routinely taught a seminar in critical thinking in the Astronomy Department of Cornell University.[39] However, psychologists' knowledge of human thought and belief make them particularly well suited to teaching this material.[40]

Because of its link to scientific investigation, critical thinking is often taught in the context of a number of courses specifically designed for psychology majors, such as research methods,[41] but it is appropriate to introductory psychology courses as well.[42] In these courses, psychologists use instruction in critical thinking as an introduction to the methods of science, because the principles of critical thinking can be widely applied to everyday life, as in evaluating the claims of advertisers, politicians, social activists, ads for telephone psychics, and even "UFO abductees." Psychologists who teach critical thinking in introductory courses perform an important community service; their students come from a broad range of backgrounds, and many of them will not take any additional psychology courses. Thus, it is in these classes that psychologists can best educate the general public about the importance of critical thinking.

Critical thinking is taught in a number of ways, but at its core it stresses the importance of the quality of evidence and the evaluation of alternative explanations for events in question. Psychologist Carole Wade gives her students the following eight directives for successful critical thinking:[43]

1. *Ask questions.* This means both showing the intellectual curiosity to seek out new information and the willingness to challenge the ideas and explanations that are offered by others.
2. *Define the problem.* Often, questions are not sufficiently narrowed to make them answerable. Psychologists and parapsychologists cannot answer the big questions (e.g., "Is ESP real?") unless they have first posed more specific testable questions (e.g., "Can the Ganzfeld effect be demonstrated under controlled conditions and replicated by other researchers working in a different laboratory?").
3. *Examine the evidence.* Critical thinking requires evidence *and* a careful examination of the quality of that evidence. Individual testimonials are less reliable and less convincing than more objectively gathered information (e.g., "Healing crystals worked for me" versus a double-blind experimental study of the effectiveness of healing crystals).
4. *Analyze biases and assumptions.* This means examining the prejudices and strongly held beliefs that might alter one's evaluation of the facts and acknowledging that we are just as susceptible to this kind of bias as those with whom we disagree.
5. *Avoid emotional reasoning.* Strongly held beliefs are not valid just because they are supported by deep emotion, and much of psychological research suggests our intuition and "gut reactions" can be extremely fallible.
6. *Do not oversimplify.* Simple answers are attractive, but they are often wrong. Human behavior, for example, is usually controlled by a number of variables, and any attempt to explain it by reference to only one or two factors usually obscures rather than reveals the truth.
7. *Consider other interpretations.* True critical thinkers actively seek and evaluate alternative explanations for the events at hand. This principle is particularly important for the assessment of paranormal phenomena because natural, nonmagical explanations are often inadequately explored.
8. *Tolerate uncertainty.* When we have insufficient information to offer a reasonable explanation for some event, there is a strong temptation to fill the void with a speculative theory. We may not know the source of every light in the sky, but the absence of a natural explanation does not make a supernatural one more likely. Nonetheless, it is often difficult simply to say, "We don't know." Living with ambiguous or uncertain circumstances is an uncomfortable proposition for many people, and an important challenge for critical thinkers.

Wade's principles are easily integrated into introductory psychology courses, and many of them are useful recommendations for the assessment of the paranormal and many other events. In everyday life, we often hear unusual claims: that a house is haunted by the ghost of a former inhabitant or that role-playing games like Dungeons and Dragons induce teenagers to commit suicide or murder. When students apply Wade's principles of critical thinking to these propositions, they are prompted to consider other explanations and evaluate the relative likelihood of all the explanations they discover. Rather than automatically adopting the "facts" as they are presented, they learn to be active reasoners who decide for themselves.

In courses devoted entirely to critical thinking, psychologists present additional material. For example, teaching students about classical fallacies in logic prepares them to judge the quality of arguments they encounter. In the fifth and fourth centuries B.C., Greek citizens argued their own cases in court, and at that time a group of teachers known as Sophists traveled from city to city teaching the methods of argument. However, the Sophists were more interested in persuasion than in good reasoning; today, the use of misleading arguments is often called "sophistry." In response to this phenomenon in Greece, Aristotle pointed out that the arguments promoted by the Sophists and others were often based on logical fallacies.[44] For example, the *ad hominem* fallacy involves attacking the person rather than the argument (e.g., "You *would* say that; you're a devout Catholic"). The *slippery slope* fallacy suggests that a single movement in one direction will inexorably lead to complete collapse ("If we do not stop communism in Vietnam, we will soon be fighting communists on the beaches of California"). Sophistry is as common today as it ever has been, so learning about logical fallacies continues to be an important part of some philosophy courses and many courses in critical thinking.[45]

Are the efforts of psychologists and other teachers to promote students' sound reasoning paying off? Are students learning critical thinking skills, and, more important, are they learning to apply them in everyday life? A growing body of research shows that students do learn critical thinking skills and that they can apply them in new situations.[46] Encouraged by such evidence, critical thinking has become an integral part of the curriculum in psychology and many other disciplines.

THE FUTURE OF PSYCHOLOGY AND THE PARANORMAL

Interest in the paranormal appears to be on the upswing. According to Gallup polls, superstition is on the rise.* There may be a number of reasons for this increase. For example, people who are experiencing more stress in an increasingly complex society may find solace in New Age ideas that are a reaction against science, modern medicine, and traditional religion. Whatever the reasons, psychics have profitable businesses, so as the turn of the century draws near, we can expect to see more paranormal images on television, in movie theaters, and in magazines and newspaper articles.

In this atmosphere, there are likely to be many more Jasons and Sallys, people who will put their faith in unsubstantiated systems of belief. It is true that wearing his lucky hat made Jason feel more confident, and going to the palm reader gave Sally some hope for a better future. Furthermore, the only costs incurred were some slight embarrassment for Jason and the palm reader's nominal fee for Sally. Many superstitions and paranormal beliefs have some benefits for the believer and cause little or no harm. But there *is* potential for serious harm to those who choose

---

*The figure of 47 percent who in 1996 said they were not at all superstitious (cited at the beginning of this chapter) was a decrease from 56 percent in 1990.

untested alternative medical remedies over scientifically validated methods, for those who spend large sums of money on psychics, palm readers, and astrologers, and for those whose superstitious beliefs help maintain their gambling problems. Most psychologists would suggest that there are better ways to cope with the uncertainties of life and that, in general, a world based on science and reason is preferable to one based on magic and superstition. As a result, there will be a continuing need for psychologists to answer the challenges that these belief systems pose. More research needs to be done, on both paranormal phenomena such as the Ganzfeld effect and the causes of paranormal belief, but perhaps the most important future roles for psychologists will be as experts on research quality and as educators.

Because government and political initiatives often reflect popular sentiment, the future is likely to bring further government spending on the paranormal and nontraditional therapeutic approaches. For example, in 1992 the National Institutes of Health established the Office of Alternative Medicine (which funds research on alternative medicine techniques), and the Department of Defense recently awarded a large grant for the study of therapeutic touch, a healing technique that involves passing hands over the sick person's body.[47] It is appropriate that we seek out and evaluate new therapeutic techniques, but the ultimate acceptance and use of these methods must be based on scientific evidence that flows from sound experimental research. Therefore, as long as public opinion drives public policy, there will be a need for psychologists to act as experts evaluating governmental and other research on the paranormal and related phenomena.

In the future it will be most important for psychologists to bring their knowledge of the paranormal directly to the general public. Because professional psychics, television and movie producers, and purveyors of alternative medicine techniques are often driven by the profit motive, they have the resources and the resolve to present paranormal and pseudoscientific ideas to a wide audience, and they have little interest in airing opposing viewpoints. To promote a more reasoned view of natural and alleged supernatural events, psychologists will need to put their own scientifically driven ideas before the public. In particular, psychologists and other scientists will continue to encourage the teaching of science, mathematics, and critical thinking at all educational levels.

The National Science Foundation allocates the largest portion of its budget to science education at the elementary and secondary school levels, and this is certainly money well spent.[48] Better science education will undoubtedly lead to greater interest in and appreciation of science, as well as to future advances in science and technology. But psychologists, in cooperation with other educators, could make a valuable contribution to the education of the general public by adapting for use at the elementary, middle, and high school levels the same critical thinking methods that have been used so successfully at the college level. Critical thinking could become an important feature of the elementary school science curricula, and children could be encouraged to apply this mode of thought to events and claims they see and hear outside the classroom.

In the elementary grades, science education typically centers around content areas such as biology, astronomy, and the environment, but as important as it is for children to know what scientists study, it is equally important that they know how scientists think and work. If school children were given the basic tools of critical thinking and taught to apply them to the ideas they hear in their everyday lives, they might avoid unjustified acceptance of pseudoscience and the paranormal. With their extensive experience teaching critical thinking to young adults and their knowledge of human behavior and thought, psychology educators are uniquely qualified to design and promote critical thinking in the elementary and secondary schools. Such an initiative would make an important contribution toward the triumph of science and reason over credulity and unreason.

SUGGESTIONS FOR FURTHER READING

Alcock, J. E. (1981). *Parapsychology: Science or magic?* Oxford: Pergamon Press.

Gilovich, T. (1991). *Why we know what isn't so: The fallibility of human reason in everyday life.* New York: Free Press.

Hines, T. (1988). *Pseudoscience and the paranormal: A critical examination of the evidence.* Buffalo, NY: Prometheus Books.

Sagan, C. (1996). *The demon-haunted world: Science as a candle in the dark.* New York: Random House.

Vyse, S. A. (1997). *Believing in magic: The psychology of superstition.* New York: Oxford University Press.

Zusne, L., & Jones, W. H. (1989). *Anomalistic psychology: A study of magical thinking.* Hillsdale, NJ: Erlbaum.

CHAPTER 14

APPLIED PSYCHOLOGY, TODAY AND TOMORROW

Astrid M. Stec

I hope that after reading the previous twelve chapters, you may realize that hardly a day has gone by when you have not been affected in some way by the applications of psychology. Even though you might not have come face to face with a psychologist for counseling or vocational assessment, you probably have been affected indirectly. The shape of your toothbrush handle, the ads you watch on television, your latest employment interview, the design of your computer, even the training of your pet—all these are likely to have been influenced by the work of applied psychologists. Some of our everyday language, too, is influenced by psychology. Words like *unconscious, IQ, ego, identity crisis, extrovert* or *introvert,* and *positive reinforcement* are all derived from prominent psychological theories. In effect, we have all become more psychologically influenced, and even psychologically minded.

In this chapter, I review two general contributions of applied psychology and then venture to make some predictions about future directions in the application of psychology to everyday life.

A FOCUS ON THE INDIVIDUAL

The twentieth century has seen an increasing emphasis on valuing the individual. For example, one of the most important aspects of our identity, and most important celebrations, is our birthdate; but only a century ago, the birth of an ordinary citizen was not considered important enough to date precisely. We have also witnessed a rise in the number of biographies and autobiographies. On television, talk shows exploring individuals' experiences have become favorite fare.

The popularity of psychology, with its focus on the individual, has been part of this trend. Psychology has intrigued many of us with its explanations of individuals' behavior and insights into the inner world of individuals—the thinking, planning, feeling parts of us. These explanations and insights have been useful not only in understanding and treating psychological disorders, but in making us aware that we often cannot make effective changes or achieve optimal results in many practical situations without taking psychological factors into account. For example, psychological research demonstrates that if we want to develop a successful product, it is not simply a matter of making it efficient and economical, but also a matter of tailoring it to consumers' preferences and expectations. When we advertise a product, we can increase sales by appealing to consumers' emotions and considering the cognitive strategies they use in making purchasing decisions. Ensuring the efficiency of workers, too, is as much a matter of promoting job satisfaction, pride, dedication, and motivation as offering monetary rewards. Similarly, in sports, an athlete's performance can be enhanced by a psychological state that includes moderate arousal, concentration, and confidence. In education, teachers who are enthusiastic, warm, and friendly, as well as knowledgeable, have more involved and attentive students. And the best teaching techniques take into account the learner's motivation and current knowledge, not just the nature and structure of the content to be taught. Even in the design of housing, occupants' sense of control over their space may be just as important to consider as the building's physical structure. Health care professionals, too, now appreciate the close connections between patients' physical state and their emotions and attitudes; individual differences in psychological resourcefulness may not only determine whether they adopt healthy lifestyles but can affect the progress (and recovery from) physical diseases. Furthermore, psychologists understand that psychological factors work in complex ways. For example, in advertising, fear of missing out on a desirable product may convince us to buy the product, but in the area of disease prevention, fear of AIDS won't necessarily increase condom use.

A Focus on the Scientific Approach

The twentieth century has been characterized by a reliance on science to guide our understanding of the world. The findings of scientific research, in psychology as well as in other scientific disciplines, give us more detailed knowledge than has ever been available before. For example, in Chapter 2 we learned about the numerous reasons that can keep people from engaging in healthier lifestyles; in Chapter 4 we covered the intricacies of various teaching techniques; in Chapter 5 we became aware of the mental short-cuts we use in making choices about products; and in Chapters 10 and 11 we discovered the multitude of factors that have to be considered in developing successful consumer products and aviation systems.

The findings of scientific research not only provide us with new information, but stimulate us to question some of our beliefs. For example, in Chapter 6 we learned that the popular technique of relying on unstructured interviews to select potential employees is not as accurate in identifying who will be the best employee as using structured interviews. We also discovered that the "do your best" approach, which so many of us believe to be effective advice, is not as successful in motivating workers as setting specific and difficult, but attainable, short-term goals. In education, teachers have sometimes assumed that understanding context helps students to understand words, when the opposite seems to be true: knowing words helps to derive meaning from context. In the realm of health, we might believe that all we have to do is give people information about how to live healthier and prevent diseases, but information alone is frequently not enough to ensure more healthy behaviors. Doing the "right" thing depends as much, or more, on attitudes about illness and beliefs in one's risk for illness.

Sometimes, of course, scientific research confirms our beliefs. For example, many of us have long had faith in the soothing effect of petting animals, and research described in Chapter 12 shows that it does indeed decrease physiological stress responses.

Finally, the scientific approach, with its reliance on careful, objective examination of information, can encourage us to think more critically about our world. A good example of this is the work reviewed in Chapter 13, which addresses the pervasiveness of belief in paranormal phenomena.

THE FUTURE

It is becoming increasingly important to apply knowledge derived from psychological research to the problems and issues facing the world.[1] Many of these problems and issues cannot be resolved exclusively by the application of psychology, but with its broad focus on understanding people's behaviors, thoughts, and feelings in a variety of situations, psychologists are likely to continue to make significant contributions. Let's consider just one example: aging.

Adjusting to an Aging Society

In the next few decades, the proportion of elderly in the North American population will increase dramatically. In 1900 only 4 percent of the U.S. population was over the age of sixty-five; by 1988 that figure had tripled to 12.4 percent, and by 2030 it will probably reach 22 percent.[2] The biggest increase in this group will occur in its oldest members: by 2010, more than 40 percent of those over sixty-five will be those who are seventy-five and older. These increases mean that almost half the population (including the young and the old) will not be regularly employed, and if the retirement age remains at sixty-five, many people will spend almost a quarter of their lives in retirement.[3]

This "graying of America" will provide challenges and opportunities for psychologists in all the areas of application covered in this book, especially since psychologists still know relatively little about psychological functioning in people over the age of eighty.[4] In the health area, for example, increased longevity will not necessarily be accompanied by an increase in quality of life because the elderly tend to suffer from chronic illness, frailty, poor sleep, and inadequate nutrition.[5] Although psychologists have studied individual differences in younger people's strategies for coping with acute or chronic illness, they still know very little about the coping strategies of the elderly. Therefore, it is not clear how best to motivate the elderly to improve their quality of life by, for example, improving their diets or exercising more. Additionally, although the aged consume the majority of medical services and drug prescriptions, they also have the highest rates of noncompliance with medication.[6] In order to increase compliance, psychologists will have to explore how the aged make their decisions, what kinds of choices are significant for them, and how they process information. Thus, it will be helpful to have the same information in this area that psychologists currently have about consumer decision making.

The elderly not only have to cope with increasing physical difficulties, but also with the loss of companions, mobility, independence, and sometimes, economic security. These life changes may make them more susceptible to psychological disorders. It is estimated that nearly a quarter of hospital costs for older adults are related to the treatment of mental health problems.[7] But many of the elderly do not receive treatment for psychological disorders. Depression, for example, is one of the most common, and usually untreated, disorders of late adulthood. Also, older adults account for approximately one fifth of all suicides, with white males over age eighty having the highest rate of completed suicide.[8] However, clinical psychologists do not yet know how later-life depression or suicidality differs from earlier-life depression and suicidality. Nor are the early warning signs known. This may explain why, although the majority of those who commit suicide had visited their physician within a month beforehand, the doctor may not have been able to predict the suicide.[9] Since the signs, causes, or course of psychological disorders in the aged are not known, psychologists do not yet have clear guidelines for appropriate treatment strategies, or even for determining whether intervention should best focus on the individual, or at the level of the family or community.

In addition to depression and suicidal tendencies, almost half of those over the age of eighty-five suffer some form of dementia: reduced cognitive, behavioral, emotional, and social functioning due to progressive brain disease.[10] Thus, psychologists need to refine assessment procedures so that they not only identify the early onset of dementia, but distinguish between symptoms caused by dementia and the similar symptoms caused by treatable factors such as overmedication, depression, or anxiety. Because of the nature of cognitive deficits, these assessment tools will have to rely more on observational techniques than on the interview procedures described in Chapter 3.

Psychologists in other areas will also be able to apply their expertise to easing daily life for the elderly. The work of environmental psychologists, for example, may increase the quality of life for the aged by improving the design of stairs (a major cause of accidents), ventilation (for those who spend most of their time indoors), and nursing homes so that the cognitive, physical, and social limitations of the elderly are taken into account.[11] The work of psychologists in product design may be useful in designing labels and signs that the elderly can easily understand. Or they can help design elderly-friendly computers that will more easily allow older people to do some of their chores, such as paying bills by computer, as well as to alleviate social isolation by enabling electronic communication with family and friends—or even strangers who share their interests. Sport psychologists may be able to translate what they know about motivating young people in sports to encouraging the elderly to be as physically active as possible. Consumer psychologists may explore the kinds of mental shortcuts the elderly use in deciding whether to purchase a particular product. Forensic psychologists may be dealing with more elderly as courtroom witnesses and will therefore need to know how their cognitive and perceptual capacities influence the recall of crimes. Industrial/organizational psychologists may use their skills to assess and train (or retrain) older adults so that they can remain productive workers for as long as possible. There are likely to be great benefits here because we already know that older adults are among the most reliable and satisfied workers. Not only that, older adults can, given enough training, use their wealth of experience to compensate for deficits in memory and decreases in mental processing speed.[12] Educational psychologists as well may work with schools to help incorporate the skills, wisdom, and experiences of older adults. Even psychologists who are interested in promoting the critical thinking skills described in Chapter 13 may be able to strengthen these skills in older adults so that they can make more informed decisions and therefore be less likely to fall victim to home repair, investment, and other scams aimed at the elderly. Exercises to stimulate critical thinking have proved effective with college students;[13] a version of these exercises may be equally effective with older adults, helping them to adjust to significant changes in their lives and in society as a whole.

EXPANDING THE FOCUS TO UNDERSERVED AND UNDERSTUDIED GROUPS

Much of traditional work in applied psychology has focused on the middle-class urban adult white male. The few exceptions can be seen in the work of industrial/ organizational psychologists in designing nondiscriminatory employee selection procedures, the work of environmental psychologists in creating safer urban housing projects, and the adaptations that human factors psychologists have made to accommodate diverse users of products. Other groups, such as the poor, the elderly, minorities, rural populations, people with disabilities, and women have generally been understudied and underserved by applied psychology. If psychologists are to understand all of human behavior, then psychological theories, research, and applications will have to expand to more specifically include these groups. This expansion will become especially important in light of the fact that most of the oldest of the old in our aging population will be women, and that the number of ethnic minority group members (of all ages) is increasing more rapidly than the rest of the population.[14]

We already have information about some of the differences among various groups, particularly in the areas of physical and psychological health. We know, for example, that women are more likely to suffer from depression, anxiety, and eating disorders, while men are more prone to substance abuse and antisocial personality disorders.[15] We also know that disadvantaged groups suffer from poorer health, are more at risk for psychological disorders, and probably constitute the majority of those who go without treatment. But often we lack explanations for the differences. For example, statistics show that heart disease is two and a half times higher in people with lower-grade occupations.[16] It is likely that aspects of the environment contribute to this phenomenon, but the specific casual factors have not been identified. Is it a result of greater exposure to occupational hazards, chronic domestic or occupational stress, or because of an increased tendency to engage in risky behaviors such as smoking and drug use? We also know that African Americans suffer higher mortality than do European Americans from similar-stage cardiovascular disease, but the psychological and social factors that may contribute to the virulence of the disease process are not known. It is also not clear how much health care professionals' availability, attitudes, and communication styles (described in Chapter 2) influence detection and reporting of diseases. For example, heart disease is more frequently diagnosed in men than in women even though it is a leading killer of women. African American women delay longer than European American women in seeking care for symptoms of breast cancer.[17] Until we know more about how symptoms, diseases, and prevention are perceived and managed by different groups, and how diseases affect their daily lives, we will not know what kind of health-promotion and disease-prevention information or services are required or when it is best to offer those services.

There are also changes in the workplace that will require more knowledge of previously understudied groups. One of the major changes is that the workforce will include more older workers, more women, and more members of minority groups.[18] The increase in older workers means that psychologists will be involved in determining how to build on the wisdom and experience of these workers. The presence of more women workers may require a better understanding of the impact of workplace events on family life. And the rising number of minority members will demand continuing development of nondiscriminatory vocational counseling and assessment procedures.

Expanding the International Focus

The world has become a more interconnected place. Electronic mail allows for almost instant communication around the globe; there are more opportunities for travel, greater sharing of global markets (in terms of both goods and professionals), and increasing concern about worldwide climate changes, energy consumption, resource conservation, health education, and disease prevention. As a result, many disciplines, including psychology, are increasingly focusing on international issues.*

In the past, psychology has been based mostly in North America; most psychology journals and textbooks are published in the United States under the authorship or influence of American psychologists.[19] And although psychologists have helped with postwar stress disorders in developing countries and have contributed to international education programs and health education,[20] the fact remains that psychological theories and research, and the applications of both, have generally focused on North American concerns. For example, the emphasis on the individual and on differences among individuals is characteristic of Western industrialized nations. But other cultures minimize the distinction between self and others. They value self-discipline more than self-expression and prefer to encourage compliance to group norms rather than individual assertiveness.[21] Thus, whereas North Ameri-

---

*For example, in May 1996, the *American Psychologist*, the main journal of the American Psychological Association, devoted an entire issue to international perspectives in psychology.

cans are likely to say, "The squeaky wheel gets the grease," other cultures warn, "The nail that sticks out gets pounded down."

Even reliance on the scientific approach, with its reverence for objectivity, may not be as valued by cultures that emphasize spirituality. Consequently, if psychology is going to benefit other societies as it has benefited North America, psychologists within all areas of application will have to consider how the everyday lives of people in various cultures and countries are different from those of North Americans, and how psychological knowledge and practice can accommodate differing belief systems.

CITATIONS

Chapter 1

1. Wood, Jones, & Benjamin (1986, p. 947).
2. APA, personal communication (September 1997).
3. APS, personal communication (September 1997).
4. Koch & Leary (1992, p. 949).
5. Ebbinghaus (1910).
6. Lapointe (1992).
7. Cited by Kaufmann (1992, p. 919).
8. Capshew (1992, p. 92).
9. Chorover (1992, p. 878).
10. Hilgard (1987).
11. Rosenzweig (1992).
12. Cited by Benjamin (1986, p. 941).
13. Wood, Jones, & Benjamin (1986, p. 950).
14. Miller (1992, pp. 40–41).
15. Leahey (1997).
16. MacLeod (1975, p. 29).
17. Pion et al. (1996).
18. Murray (1996).
19. Leahey (1997, p. 352).
20. Spillmann & Spillmann (1993).
21. Cited by Spillmann & Spillmann (1993, p. 338).
22. Described in Rilling (1996).
23. Cited by Rilling (1996, p. 594).
24. Skinner (1945).
25. See, for example, Goleman (1995); Tannen (1990); Tavris (1989); and Tavris & Wade (1984).
26. Napoli (1981).
27. Described in Benjamin, Rogers, & Rosenbaum (1991).
28. Dudycha (1963).
29. Leahey (1991).
30. Leahey (1997).
31. Cited by Napoli (1981, p. 42).
32. Leahey (1991).
33. Leahey (1991, p. 262).
34. Rogers (1942); Maslow (1943).
35. Watson (1928, pp. 5–6).
36. Watson (1928, pp. 84–85).
37. Watson (1928, pp. 12–13).
38. Watson (1928, p. 9).
39. Fagan (1992, p. 236).
40. Makari (1993).
41. Makari (1993).
42. Napoli (1981).
43. Benjamin (1997).
44. Napoli (1981).
45. Leahey (1991).
46. Dipboye, Smith, & Howell (1994).
47. Napoli (1981).
48. Dudycha (1963).
49. Dudycha (1963).
50. Cited by Buckley (1982, p. 425).
51. Spillmann & Spillmann (1993).
52. Spillmann & Spillmann (1993).
53. Napoli (1981); Samelson (1978).
54. Cited by Napoli (1981, p. 105).
55. Napoli (1981).
56. Leahey (1997).
57. Coon (1992).
58. Coon (1992).
59. See, for example, Parot (1993).
60. See, for example, Taylor (1995).
61. Luchins (1993).
62. Leahey (1997, p. 459).

Chapter 2

1. Adler & Matthews (1994).
2. See American Psychological Association Science Directorate (1995) and Taylor (1995) for reviews.
3. Engel (1977); Friedman & DiMatteo (1989).
4. Brickman, Coates, & Janoff-Bulman (1978).
5. Wortman & Silver (1987).
6. See Wortman & Silver (1987) for a review.
7. Brickman et al. (1978).
8. Janoff-Bulman (1989).
9. Taylor (1983).
10. Taylor (1983, p. 1163).
11. Taylor & Aspinwall (1996).
12. Taylor (1983, p. 1166).
13. See Buunk & Gibbons (1997).
14. Wortman & Silver (1987) call these beliefs the myths of coping with loss.
15. Wortman & Silver (1987).
16. Tait & Silver (1989).
17. Rosenstock (1974); see Janz & Becker (1984) for a review.
18. Quadrel, Fischhoff, & Davis (1993); Weinstein (1987).
19. See Klein, & Weinstein (1997) for a review.
20. Bandura (1986); O'Leary (1985).
21. Weinstein (1988).
22. Fisher, Fisher, Misovich, Kimble, & Malloy (1996); Kelly et al. (1992).
23. Katon & Sullivan (1990); Melamed (1995).

24. Cohen & Rodriguez (1995).
25. Christy (1979).
26. Rutter, Iconomou, & Quine (1996).
27. Roter (1984).
28. Greenfield, Kaplan, Ware, Yano, & Frank (1988).
29. Leventhal (1970).
30. Cummings & Follette (1968).
31. Kobasa (1979); Kobasa, Maddi, & Courington (1981).
32. See Allred & Smith (1989); Taylor & Aspinwall (1996).
33. Peterson, Seligman, & Vaillant (1988).
34. Peterson (1988).
35. Taylor (1995).
36. Segerstrom, Taylor, Kemeny, Reed, & Visscher (1996).
37. Scheier et al. (1989).
38. See Taylor & Aspinwall (1996) for a review.
39. Aspinwall & Brunhart (1996).
40. Greer & Morris (1975) and Dattore, Shontz, & Coyne (1980), respectively.
41. Pennebaker (1993).
42. Esterling, Antoni, Fletcher, Margulies, & Schneiderman (1994).
43. Thoits (1986); Cohen & Wills (1985).
44. See Cohen & Wills (1985), Taylor (1995), and Taylor & Aspinwall (1996) for reviews.
45. Spiegel, Bloom, & Gottheil (1983); Pistrang & Barker (1995).
46. See Dunkel-Schetter & Wortman (1982) and Lehmann, Ellard, & Wortman (1986) for examples and discussion.
47. Jacobs & Goodman (1989).
48. Kaplan (1994).
49. See Taylor & Aspinwall (1990) for a review.
50. Grieco & Long (1984).
51. Jachuck, Brierley, Jachuck, & Willcox (1982).
52. Kaplan (1994).
53. Ryff (1989); Ryff & Keyes (1995).
54. Prochaska & DiClemente (1983).
55. Bryan, Aiken, & West (1996).
56. Catania, Coates, & Kegeles (1994).
57. See Gerrard, Gibbons, & Bushman (1996) for a review.
58. Coates, McKusick, Kuno, & Stites (1989).
59. Gerrard, Gibbons, Warner, & Smith (1993).
60. Alden & Crowley (1995).
61. Leary, Tchividjian, & Kraxberger (1994).
62. Helweg-Larson & Collins (1994).
63. Hammer, Fisher, Fitzgerald, & Fisher (1996); Miller et al. (1993).
64. Sanderson & Cantor (1995).
65. See Amaro (1995) for a review.
66. Pleck, Sonenstein, & Ku (1993).
67. Miller, Bettencourt, DeBro, & Hoffman (1993).
68. Herek & Glunt (1993); Thomas & Quinn (1991).

69. Treichler (1991).
70. See Bryan et al. (1996) and Fisher, Fisher, Misovich, Kimble, & Malloy (1996) for excellent examples of this multifaceted approach.
71. Banks et al. (1995); see Rothman & Salovey (1997) for a review.
72. See Taylor (1995) for a review.
73. Donovan & Blake (1992); Leventhal, Diefenbach, & Leventhal (1992).
74. Leventhal et al. (1992, p. 144).
75. Meyer, Leventhal, & Guttman (1985).

Chapter 3

1. Stapp, Fulcher, & Wicherski (1984).
2. Norcross, Prochaska, & Gallagher (1989b).
3. For a description of interviewing techniques, see, for example, Shipley & Wood (1996).
4. Baekeland & Lundwall (1975).
5. For a complete listing of tests, see Kramer & Conoley (1995).
6. See, for example, Thorndike, Hagen, & Sattler (1986).
7. Costa & McCrae (1992).
8. Olfson, Pincus, & Sabshin (1994).
9. See, for example, DeLeon, Fox, & Graham (1991).
10. See Klopfer & Kelley (1937) or Exner (1993).
11. Harrison (1965).
12. Bankart (1997, p. 21).
13. For an introduction to Freud, see, for example, Gay (1988). For Freud's own work, see, for example, Freud (1938).
14. For more comprehensive coverage, see, for example, Eagle (1984).
15. See, for example, Adler (1927).
16. For an introduction to Jung, see, for example, Jung (1983). For a description of analytical psychology, see Jung (1968/1935).
17. Progoff (1973).
18. Kaufmann (1989, p. 119).
19. Bankart (1997, p. 163).
20. Bankart (1997, p. 172).
21. See, for example, Fairbairn (1952), Winnicott (1965), Klein (1975), or Kohut (1977).
22. For an analysis and critique of traditional therapies, as well as examples of feminist therapy, see, for example, Greenspan (1983).
23. For details of relaxation training, see Bernstein & Borkovec (1973).
24. Bandura (1969).
25. Bandura (1977).
26. Beck, Rush, Shaw, & Emery (1979).
27. Ellis (1973).
28. Rogers (1951).
29. Perls (1969).

30. Seligman (1995).
31. For a fuller discussion of research methods, see, for example, Nietzel, Bernstein, & Milich (1997).
32. See, for example, Stiles, Shapiro, & Elliot (1986) or Smith, Glass, & Miller (1980).
33. See, for example, Shapiro & Shapiro (1982), or Smith, Glass, & Miller (1980).
34. See, for example, Smith, Glass, & Miller (1980).
35. See, for example, Lambert (1989) or Mahoney (1991).
36. Howard et al. (1986).
37. See, for example, Gallagher-Thompson, Hanley-Peterson, & Thompson (1990) or Robinson, Berman, & Neimeyer (1990).
38. See, for example, Austed & Berman (1991) or Bloom (1992).
39. See, for example, I. J. Miller (1996).

Chapter 4

1. Berliner (1992, p. 145).
2. Hilgard (1996).
3. Berliner (1993); Tyack & Hansot (1982).
4. Berliner (1996).
5. Ross (1972).
6. Hilgard (1996).
7. Piaget (1954, 1963, 1970).
8. Skinner (1953).
9. Bruner, Goodnow, & Austin (1956).
10. Ausubel (1977).
11. Corkill (1992); Mayer (1984); Shuell (1981b).
12. Mayer (1983a, 1984).
13. Bloom, Engelhart, Frost, Hill, & Krathwohl (1956).
14. Pring (1971).
15. Greeno, Collins, & Resnick (1996, p. 18).
16. Alexander (1996, p. 31).
17. Prawat (1992, p. 357).
18. Mager (1975).
19. Woolfolk (1998).
20. Bloom (1968); Guskey & Gates (1986).
21. Sherman, Ruskin, & Semb (1982).
22. Guskey & Gates (1986); Kulick, Kulick, & Bangert-Drowns (1990); Shuell (1996).
23. Arlin (1984).
24. Kiewra (1989); DiVesta & Gray (1972).
25. Van Metter, Yokoi, & Pressley (1994).
26. Robinson & Kiewra (1995).
27. Pressley, Levin, & Delaney (1982).
28. Driscoll (1994).
29. Pasch, Sparks-Langer, Gardner, Starko, & Moody (1991, pp. 188–189).
30. Dansereau (1985).
31. Maslow (1968, 1970).
32. Rogers & Freiberg (1994).
33. Deci, Vallerand, Pelletier, & Ryan (1991).
34. Miller, Galanter, & Pribram (1960).
35. Locke & Latham (1990).
36. Ortony, Clore, & Collins (1988).
37. Vroom (1964).
38. Weiner (1992).
39. Brophy (1988, p. 205).
40. Brophy (1988); Johnson & Johnson (1985).
41. Medley (1979).
42. Land (1987).
43. Murray (1983); Ryans (1960); Soar & Soar (1979).
44. Gillett & Gall (1982).
45. Rosenthal & Jacobson (1968).
46. Braun (1976); Brophy (1982); Cooper & Good (1983); Good (1988); Rosenthal (1987).
47. Brophy (1982).
48. Good (1983a); Rosenshine (1986).
49. Brophy & Good (1986); Weinert & Helmke (1995).
50. Brophy & Good (1986); Good (1996); Shuell (1996).
51. Weinert & Helmke (1995).
52. Anderson, Reder, & Simon (1996).
53. Gustafsson & Undheim (1996).
54. Lohman (1989); McNemar (1964).
55. Thurstone (1938); Gardner (1983).
56. See, for example, Gardner (1983, 1993).
57. Sternberg (1985, 1990).
58. Lyman (1986).
59. Smith (1991).
60. James (1899/1983, p. 84).
61. Hilgard (1996).
62. Garmon, Nystrand, Berends, & LePore (1995); Good & Marshall (1984); Slavin (1987, 1990).
63. Gutierrez & Slavin (1992).
64. Goodman (1986, p. 7).
65. Pearson (1989, p. 235).
66. Vellutino (1991).
67. Adams, Trieman, & Pressley (1998); Vellutino (1991); Wharton-McDonald, Pressley, & Mistretta (1996).
68. Graham & Harris (1994); Morrow (1992); Neuman & Roskos (1992).
69. Pressley (1996).

Chapter 5

1. Kahn & McAlister (1997).
2. Pratkanis & Aronson (1992).
3. Kreshel (1990).
4. Watson (1913, p. 168).
5. Tversky & Kahneman (1974), and Kahneman, Slovic, & Tversky (1982).
6. Tversky & Kahneman (1974) and Kahneman, Slovic, & Tversky (1982).
7. Northcraft & Neale (1987).
8. Petty & Cacioppo (1986).

9. Chaiken, Liberman, & Eagly (1989); Eagly & Chaiken (1993); Sanbonmatsu & Kardes (1988).
10. Chaiken, Liberman, & Eagly (1989).
11. Chaiken, Liberman, & Eagly (1989).
12. Chaiken, Liberman, & Eagly (1989).
13. Cialdini (1993).
14. Cialdini, Capioppo, Bassett, & Miller (1978).
15. Freedman & Fraser (1966).
16. Langer (1978, 1989).
17. Cialdini et al. (1976).
18. Comer, Kardes, & Sullivan (1992).
19. Burger (1986).
20. Reingen (1982).
21. Cialdini et al. (1976).
22. Payne, Bettman, & Johnson (1993).
23. Payne et al. (1993).
24. Payne et al. (1993).
25. Borgida & Howard-Pitney (1983); Meyers-Levy & Peracchio (1992).
26. Keller (1987, 1991).
27. Tybout, Calder, & Sternthal (1981).
28. Tybout et al. (1981).
29. Herr (1989).
30. Kardes & Gurumurthy (1992); Kardes & Sanbon-matsu (1993); Sanbonmatsu, Kardes, & Herr (1992); Sanbonmatsu, Kardes, & Sansone (1991).
31. Sanbonmatsu, Kardes, Posavac, & Houghton (1997).
32. Huber, Payne, & Pluto (1982); Simonson (1989).
33. Simonson (1989); Simonson & Tversky (1992).
34. Lehmann & Pan (1994).
35. Levin & Gaeth (1988).
36. Kisielius & Sternthal (1984).
37. Kisielius & Sternthal (1984).
38. Kisielius & Sternthal (1984).
39. Hannah & Sternthal (1984).
40. Tybout & Scott (1983).
41. Tybout, Sternthal, & Calder (1983).
42. Tybout et al. (1983).
43. Feldman & Lynch (1988); Lynch, Marmorstein, & Weingold (1988).
44. See, for example, Herr, Kardes, & Kim (1991).
45. Lynch et al. (1988).
46. Feldman & Lynch (1988); Menon, Raghubir, & Schwartz (1995).
47. Kardes (1988a, 1988b).
48. Feldman & Lynch (1988).
49. Feldman & Lynch (1988).
50. Feldman & Lynch (1988); Kardes (1988b); Lynch et al. (1988).
51. Higgins (1996).
52. Higgins (1996).
53. Higgins (1996).
54. Anderson (1983).
55. Higgins (1996).
56. Broniarczyk & Alba (1994a, 1994b); Sujan (1985); Wyer & Srull (1989).
57. Anderson (1981, 1982); Fishbein & Ajzen (1975).
58. Johar & Simmons (1997).
59. Petty & Wegener (1993); Wegener & Petty (1994); Wilson & Brekke (1994).
60. Kruglanski & Webster (1996, p. 264).
61. Kruglanski & Webster (1996).

Chapter 6

1. Hollingworth (1912).
2. See, for example, Benjamin (1996) and Benjamin, Rogers, & Rosenbaum (1991).
3. Napoli (1981, p. 28).
4. Bryant & Dethloff (1990).
5. Hale (1980).
6. Kuna (1976).
7. Scott (1903, 1908).
8. Buckley (1989).
9. Bregman (1922).
10. Wiggam (1928).
11. Benjamin & Bryant (1997).
12. Taylor (1911).
13. Perloff & Naman (1996).
14. Gies (1991).
15. Viteles (1932, p. 4).
16. Blackford & Newcomb (1914).
17. Katzell & Austin (1992).
18. Borman & Cox (1996).
19. Thayer (1977).
20. Gaugler, Rosenthal, Thornton, & Bentsen (1987).
21. Spychalski, Quinones, Gaugler, & Pohley (1997).
22. Gaugler et al. (1987); Hinrichs (1978).
23. Campbell & Bray (1993).
24. Huck & Bray (1976); Moses & Boehm (1975); Ritchie & Moses (1983).
25. Hoffman & Thornton (1997).
26. Meyer & Zucker (1989).
27. Arthur, Doverspike, & Kuthy (1996).
28. Hartley, Roback, & Abramowitz (1976).
29. Huffcutt & Arthur (1994).
30. Campbell (1990).
31. Borman & Motowidlo (1997); Campbell (1990); Motowildo, Borman, & Schmidt (1997).
32. Smith, Organ, & Near (1983).
33. Borman & Motowidlo (1997); Motowidlo & Van Scotter (1994).
34. Locke (1968); Locke, Shaw, Saati, & Latham (1981).
35. Mento, Steel, & Karren (1987); Wood, Mento, & Locke (1987); Wright (1990).
36. Ordiorne (1979).
37. Hunter & Schmidt (1990).

38. Schmidt, Hunter, Pearlman, & Shane (1979).
39. Hunter & Hunter (1984); Ree & Earles (1992).
40. Adler (1983); Roberts & Boyacigiller (1984).
41. Lefkowitz & Murphy (1992); Dorfman & Howell (1984).
42. Sekimoto (1983).
43. Hofstede (1991, 1993).
44. Adler, Campbell, & Laurent (1989).
45. Arthur, Woehr, Akande, & Strong (1995).
46. Steiner & Gilliland (1996).
47. Hofstede (1991, 1993).
48. For a more detailed discussion of both scientific and legal issues pertaining to banding, see Barrett, Doverspike, & Arthur (1995); Cascio, Outtz, Zedeck, & Goldstein (1991); Gutman & Christiansen (1997); Murphy, Osten, & Myors (1995); Sackett & Roth (1991); Schmidt (1991); and Scientific Affairs Committee (1994).
49. For comprehensive reviews of the current state of personality in research in personnel selection, see Hogan, Hogan, & Roberts (1996).
50. See, for example, Barrick & Mount (1991), or Tett, Jackson, & Rothstein (1991).
51. Goldberg (1993); McRae & Costa (1990); Ozer & Reise (1994); Wiggins & Trapnell (1997).
52. See, for example, Arthur & Graziano (1996); Barrick, Mount, and Strauss (1993); and Hogan, Hogan, & Gregory (1992).
53. Arthur & Graziano (1996).
54. Hogan et al. (1996, p. 471).
55. Morgan et al. (1986, p. 3).
56. Salas, Dickinson, Converse, & Tannenbaum (1992).
57. Kirkman & Shapiro (1997).
58. Cited by Azar (1997).
59. See, for example, Arthur, Young, Jordan, & Shebilske (1996), and Dossett & Hulvershorn (1983).
60. Salas, Bowers, & Cannon-Bowers (1995).
61. See, for example, Bohlander & McCarthy (1996) and Salas et al. (1992).
62. See, for example, Swezey & Salas (1992).
63. American Management Association (1996).
64. See, for example, Furnham & Stringfield (1994) and Nilsen & Campbell (1993).
65. Moses, Hollenbeck, & Sorcher (1993).
66. Chan & Schmitt (1997); Dalessio (1994); Jones & DeCotiis (1986).
67. Arthur (1996).
68. Weekley & Jones (1997, p. 30).
69. Weekley & Jones (1997).
70. Weekley & Jones (1997).
71. Arthur (1996).
72. Chan & Schmitt (1997); Smiderle, Perry, & Cronshaw (1994); Weekley & Jones (1997).

Chapter 7

1. Wiggins (1984).
2. Kroll & Lewis (1970); Wiggins (1984).
3. Williams & Straub (1997).
4. Kroll & Lewis (1970, p. 4).
5. For example, Cratty (1964).
6. McCullagh & Noble (1996).
7. Murphy (1995).
8. Murphy (1995).
9. Williams & Straub (1997).
10. Williams & Straub (1997).
11. Suinn (1985).
12. Gould & Roberts (1989).
13. Roberts & Halliwell (1990).
14. Rotella (1995).
15. Loehr (1994).
16. Murphy (1996).
17. Williams & Straub (1997).
18. See, for example, Murphy (1995), Van Raalte & Brewster (1996), and Williams & Straub (1997).
19. Anderson, Williams, Aldridge, & Taylor (1997).
20. Murphy (1995).
21. Williams & Straub (1997).
22. See, for example, Anshel (1992, 1993); Danish & Hale (1981, 1982); Heyman (1982); Rejeski & Brawley (1988); Silva (1989); or Zaichkowsky & Perna (1992, 1996).
23. APA (1992, Standard 1.04).
24. AAASP (1990).
25. Murphy (1995).
26. Anderson et al. (1997).
27. Whealan & Meyers (1996).
28. APA (1992).
29. See, for example, Petitpas, Brewer, Rivera, & Van Raalte (1994); Sachs (1993); Singer (1993); or Whealan & Meyers (1993, 1996).
30. Singer (1993).
31. Zeigler (1987).
32. Anderson et al. (1997).
33. Anderson et al. (1997).
34. Williams & Straub (1997).
35. LeUnes & Hayward (1990).
36. Murphy (1995).

Chapter 8

1. Stern (1939).
2. Rothgeb (1973).
3. The division publishes its own journal, *Law and Human Behavior,* and APA publishes another journal devoted to psychology and the law, *Psychology, Public Policy, and Law.*

4. Saywitz & Snyder (1996).
5. O'Connor, Sales, & Schuman (1996).
6. These advances are reviewed in journals such as *Law and Human Behavior, Forensic Reports,* or *Psychology, Public Policy, and Law,* and in several textbooks on law and psychology such as those by Bartol & Bartol (1994); Foley (1993); Monahan & Walker (1989); Sales & Schuman (1996); and Wrightsman, Nietzel, & Fortune (1998).
7. Melton, Petrila, Poythress, & Slobogin (1987).
8. Nicholson & Kugler (1991).
9. Poythress, Bonnie, Hoge, Monahan, & Oberlander (1994).
10. Nicholson & Kugler (1991).
11. Steadman (1979).
12. See for example, Roesch & Golding (1980); Nicholson, Briggs, & Robertson (1988); Ustad, Rogers, Sewell, & Guarnaccia (1996); and Siegal & Elwork (1990).
13. Siegal & Elwork (1990).
14. Post (1963, p. 20).
15. Applebaum (1994).
16. Steadman & Braff (1983).
17. Silver (1995).
18. Nicholson et al. (1991).
19. Pasewark, Bieber, Bosten, Kiser, & Steadman (1982).
20. Cohen, Spodak, Silver, & Williams (1989); Melton et al. (1987).
21. Monahan (1992); Link, Cullen, & Andrews (1993).
22. Dawes, Faust, & Meehl (1989); Ziskin & Faust (1988).
23. Sales & Hafemeister (1984).
24. Fulero & Finkel (1991).
25. Elwork, Sales, & Suggs (1981).
26. Arens, Granfield, & Susman (1965); Ogloff (1991).
27. Finkel (1989).
28. Roberts & Golding (1991).
29. Weissman (1985).
30. Hersh & Alexander (1990).
31. Sparr (1995).
32. Applebaum & Grisso (1995).
33. Grisso & Applebaum (1995).
34. Wexler & Winnick (1992).
35. Ogloff & Otto (1993).
36. Ebert (1987).
37. Bray (1991).
38. Keilin & Bloom (1986).
39. Ackerman & Ackerman (1997).
40. Emery, Matthews, & Wyer (1991); Emery, Matthews, & Kitzman (1994).
41. Bonnie & Slobogin (1980); Ennis & Litwack (1974); Morse (1978).
42. Ziskin & Faust (1988).
43. Smith (1989).
44. Faust & Ziskin (1988); Imwrinkelreid (1994).
45. Gless (1995).
46. Richey (1994).

Chapter 9

1. Newman & Frank (1982).
2. Shaw & Gifford (1994).
3. Cisneros (1995).
4. Cisneros (1995).
5. Davis (1971, p. 78).
6. Shaw & Gifford (1994).
7. Gardner & Stern (1996).
8. Hardin (1968).
9. Ophuls (1977).
10. Canter (1985).
11. Wineman (1979).
12. Lewin (1951).
13. Barker (1968).
14. Whyte (1988).
15. Gladwell (1996).
16. Geller (1987).
17. See, for example, Babbie (1998), or Sommer & Sommer (1997).
18. Thiel (1996).
19. Craik & Feimer (1987).
20. Cherulnik (1993).
21. Tart (1990).

Chapter 10

1. Warrick (1947).
2. Hunt (1993).
3. Loewy (1951); Dreyfuss (1955).
4. Diffrient et al. (1974/1981).
5. Dittmar (1992, p. 3).
6. For a summary of other ways in which objects have social significance, see Miller (1996).
7. Whiteley (1993); see also Papanek (1995).
8. See Wickens (1992); Rasmussen (1986); Grandjean (1980); or Pheasant (1986) for books that estimate user psychological, physiological, and cognitive limitations.
9. For further reading on human performance and errors, see Reason (1990).
10. See, for example, Ivergard (1989); Pheasant (1986); and Eastman Kodak Company (1983).

Chapter 11

1. Wickens (1998).
2. Wickens, Gordon, & Liu (1998).

3. See, for example, Sanders & McCormick (1992), or Wickens, Gordon, & Liu (1998).
4. Mackworth (1961).
5. Fitts, Jones, & Milton (1950).
6. Parasuraman, Davies, & Beatty (1984).
7. Roscoe (1968).
8. Fitts & Jones (1947).
9. Reason (1990).
10. Williams & Flexman (1949).
11. Wiener (1948).
12. See, for example, Birmingham & Taylor (1954), or McRuer & Jex (1967).
13. See, for example, Williges & Wierwille (1979), or Moray (1969).
14. Haskell & Wickens (1993); Theunissen (1996).
15. Norman (1991).
16. Sarter & Woods (1995, 1997); Billings (1996).
17. Sarter & Woods (1995, 1997); Billings (1996).
18. Sarter & Woods (1997).
19. Parasuraman & Riley (1997).
20. Parasuraman, Molloy, & Singh (1993).
21. Parasuraman & Riley (1997); Wickens, Mavor, Parasuraman, & McGee (1998).
22. Billings (1996); Wickens et al. (1998).
23. Norman (1988).
24. Endsley (1995); Adams, Tenney, & Pew (1995).
25. For example, Flach (1995), Goettl (1997), or Andre & Hancock (1996).
26. Wickens (1995).
27. Gopher, Weil, & Baraket (1994).
28. Kintch & Ericcson (1995).
29. Smith & Hancock (1995).
30. Wiener, Kanki, & Helmreich (1993).
31. Cooper, White, & Lauber (1979).
32. Jensen & Biegelski (1989).
33. Wickens (1992).
34. Vlek (1984).
35. Kahneman, Slovic, & Tversky (1982).
36. Klein (1989); Orasanu & Fischer (1997).
37. Orasanu (1994).
38. Ree & Caretta (1996).
39. Gopher et al. (1994).
40. Hopkin (1995); Wickens et al. (1997, 1998).
41. Shepard & Johnson (1995).
42. Reason (1990).
43. Foyle, McCann, & Shelden (1995); Foyle, Sanford, & McCann (1991).
44. Foyle et al. (1996); Wickens & Long (1995).
45. Planzer & Jenny (1995); Wickens, Mavor, Parasuraman, & McGee (1998).
46. Stark (1989).
47. Hutchins (1995).
48. See, for example, Kaempf, Klein, Thordsen, & Wolf (1996).
49. Planzer & Jenny (1995); Wickens et al. (1998).
50. Wickens et al. (1998).

Chapter 12

1. Vila et al. (1997).
2. Zeuner (1963).
3. Coren (1995).
4. Lorenz (1954).
5. Wedin (1988).
6. Aertsen (1988).
7. Descartes (1960/1937).
8. Carter (1983).
9. Darwin (1859).
10. Darwin (1965/1872).
11. Romanes (1883).
12. Thorndike (1905).
13. Thorndike (1905, p. 203).
14. Watson (1930).
15. Guthrie (1952).
16. Skinner (1938).
17. Plomin, DeFries, McClearn, & Rutter (1997).
18. Fiennes & Fiennes (1968).
19. Coren (1995).
20. Breland & Breland (1961).
21. U.S. Department of Justice (1990).
22. Ritchie (1981).
23. Gray (1989).
24. Iverson (1995).
25. Yale & Yale (1980).
26. Scott & Fuller (1965).
27. Pfaffenberger (1963).
28. Eames & Eames (1997).
29. Coren (1995).
30. Davis (1992).
31. Coren & Walker (1997).
32. Eipper (1931).
33. Pryor (1984).
34. Moore (1996).
35. Zentall (1988).
36. Hogan (1988).
37. Coren (1998).

Chapter 13

1. Hines (1988); Vyse (1997).
2. Carlson (1985); Zusne & Jones (1989).
3. Gardner (1996).
4. Jung (1978/1958).
5. Skinner (1948b).
6. Blackmore (1986).
7. Bem and Honorton (1994).
8. Broughton (1991).
9. Alcock (1981).

10. Alcock (1981); Hines (1988).
11. Bem & Honorton (1994); Blackmore (1994).
12. Reed (1974); Zusne & Jones (1989).
13. Wagner & Morris (1987).
14. Tobacyk & Milford (1983).
15. Langer & Roth (1975).
16. Wolf (1996).
17. Kahneman, Slovic, & Tversky (1982); Baron (1994).
18. Gilovich (1997, 1991); Vyse (1997).
19. Gray (1987).
20. Hilgard (1987).
21. Kahneman et al. (1982).
22. Madey & Gilovich (1993).
23. The example described here comes from Madey & Gilovich (1993), Experiment 2.
24. Keinan (1994).
25. Keinan (1987); Keinan, Friedland, & Arad (1991).
26. Frazer (1922).
27. Rozin, Markwith, & Nemeroff (1992).
28. Rozin, Millman, & Nemeroff (1986); Rozin, Markwith, & Ross (1990).
29. Skinner (1948).
30. Wagner and Morris (1987).
31. Higgins, Morris, & Johnson (1989).
32. Heltzer & Vyse (1994); Ono (1987); & Vyse (1991).
33. Mack (1995).
34. Gilovich (1991).
35. Gilovich & Savitsky (1996); Gilovich (1997).
36. Hyman (1985); Hyman & Honorton (1986).
37. Gardner (1996); Swets & Bjork (1990).
38. Swets & Bjork (1990, p. 92).
39. Sagan (1996).
40. Nummedal & Halpern (1995).
41. Vyse (1997).
42. Bernstein (1997).
43. Wade (1995, 1997).
44. Baron (1994). Sagan's (1996) chapter entitled, "The Fine Art of Baloney Detection," gives a good introduction to the fallacies and other features of his course in critical thinking.
45. Sagan (1996). For an interactive introduction to the fallacies, see the Fallacy Tutorial Pro program for Macintosh computers (LaBossiere, 1996).
46. Halpern & Nummedal (1995); Herrnstein, Nickerson, de Sanchez, & Swets (1986).
47. Scheiber & Selby (1997).
48. Zurer (1994).

Chapter 14

1. For a review of the issues that face the nation, see the Human Capital Initiative Reports. These reports address six research priority areas: productivity in the workplace, schooling and literacy, the aging society, drug and alcohol abuse, health, and violence in America. They are available from the American Psychological Society, 1010 Vermont Ave. NW, Suite 1100, Washington, DC, 20005-4907.
2. Stokols (1995).
3. Pawlik & d'Ydewall (1996).
4. *APS Observer* (1993b).
5. *APS Observer* (1993b).
6. *APS Observer* (1993b).
7. *APS Observer* (1993b).
8. *APS Observer* (1993b).
9. *APS Observer* (1993b).
10. *APS Observer* (1993b).
11. Stokols (1995).
12. Stokols (1995).
13. Halpern (1998).
14. *APS Observer* (1993b)
15. *APS Observer* (1996a).
16. *APS Observer* (1996b).
17. *APS Observer* (1996b).
18. *APS Observer* (1993a).
19. Lunt & Poortinga (1996).
20. Pawlik & d'Ydewall (1996).
21. Brennan (1994).

REFERENCES

Abell, G. O. (1981). Astrology. In G. O. Abell & B. Singer (Eds.), *Science and the paranormal: Probing the existence of the supernatural* (pp. 70–94). New York: Scribners.

Ackerman, M. J., & Ackerman, M. C. (1997). Custody evaluation practices: A survey of experienced professionals (revisited). *Professional Psychology: Research and Practice, 28,* 137–145.

Adams, M. J., Tenney, Y. J., & Pew, R. W. (1995). Situation awareness and the cognitive management of complex systems. *Human Factors, 37*(1), 85–104.

Adams, M. J., Treiman, R., & Pressley, M. (1998). Reading, writing, and literacy. In I. Sigel & A. Renninger (Eds.), *Handbook of child psychology.* New York: Wiley.

Adler, A. (1927). *Understanding human nature.* Garden City, NY: Garden City Publishing.

Adler, N. J. (1983). Cross-cultural management research: The ostrich and the trend. *Academy of Management Review, 8,* 226–232.

Adler, N. J., Campbell, N., & Laurent, A. (1989). In search of appropriate methodology: From outside the People's Republic of China, looking in. *Journal of International Business Studies, 20,* 61–74.

Adler, N., & Matthews, K. (1994). Health psychology: Why do some people get sick and some stay well? *Annual Review of Psychology, 45,* 229–259.

Aertsen, J. (1988). *Nature and creature: Thomas Aquinas's way of thought.* New York: E. J. Brill.

Alcock, J. E. (1981). *Parapsychology: Science or magic?* Oxford: Pergamon Press.

Alden, D. L., & Crowley, A. E. (1995). Sex guilt and receptivity to condom advertising. *Journal of Applied Social Psychology, 25,* 1446–1463.

Alexander, P. A. (1996). The past, present, and future of knowledge research: A reexamination of the role of knowledge in learning and instruction. *Educational Psychologist, 31,* 89–92.

Allred, K. D., & Smith, T. W. (1989). The hardy personality: Cognitive and physiological responses to evaluative threat. *Journal of Personality and Social Psychology, 56,* 257–266.

Amaro, H. (1995). Love, sex, and power: Considering women's realities in HIV prevention. *American Psychologist, 50,* 437–447.

American Management Association. (1996, March). *Performance appraisal systems* (survey by fax). New York: AMA.

American Psychological Association. (1992). Ethical principles of psychologists and code of conduct. *American Psychologist, 47,* 1597–1611.

American Psychological Association Science Directorate. (1995). *Doing the right thing: A research plan for healthy living. A Human Capital Initiative report.* Washington, DC: APA.

Andersen, M. B., Williams, J., Aldridge, T., & Taylor, J. (1997). Tracking the training and careers of advanced degree programs in sport psychology, 1989–1994. *Sport Psychologist, 11,* 326–345.

Anderson, J. R. (1983). *The architecture of cognition.* Cambridge, MA: Harvard University Press.

Anderson, J. R., Reder, L. M., & Simon, H. A. (1996). Situated learning and education. *Educational Researcher, 25,* 5–11.

Anderson, N. H. (1981). *Foundations of information integration theory.* New York: Academic Press.

Anderson, N. H. (1982). *Methods of information integration theory.* New York: Academic Press.

Andre, A. D., & Hancock, P. A. (1996). When situations demand awareness: An operator or researcher's dilemma? In *Proceedings of the Human Factors and Ergonomics Society 40th Annual Meeting.* Santa Monica: HFES.

Anshel, M. H. (1992). The case against the certification of sport psychologists: In search of the phantom expert. *Sport Psychologist, 6,* 265–286.

Anshel, M. H. (1993). Against the certification of sport psychology consultants: A response to Zaichkowsky and Perna. *Sport Psychologist, 7,* 344–353.

Appelbaum, P. (1994). *Almost a revolution: Mental health law and the limits of change.* New York: Oxford University Press.

Appelbaum, P. S., & Grisso, T. (1995). The MacArthur Treatment Competence Study. I: Mental illness and competence to consent to treatment. *Law and Human Behavior, 19,* 105–126.

APS Observer: (October 1993). Report 1. Human Capital Initiative: The changing nature of work [Special issue].

APS Observer. (December 1993). Report 2. Human Capital Initiative: Vitality for life: Psychological research for productive aging [Special issue].

APS Observer. (February 1996). Report 3. Human Capital Initiative: Reducing mental disorders: A behavioral science research plan for psychopathology [Special issue].

APS Observer. (April 1996). Report 4. Human Capital Initiative: Doing the right thing: A research plan for healthy living [Special issue].

Arens, R., Granfield, D. D., & Susman, J. (1965). Jurors, jury charges, and insanity. *Catholic University Law Review, 14,* 1–29.

Arlin, M. (1984). Time, equality, and mastery learning. *Review of Educational Research, 54,* 65–86.

Arthur, W., Jr. (1996). *Review and summary of the use and status of simulations in testing for selection and promotion* (Tech. Rep. No. 36). College Station, TX: Winfred Arthur, Jr., Consulting.

Arthur, W., Jr., Doverspike, D., & Kuthy, J. E. (1996). Striking gold through a deep-level organizational intervention in Ghana's mining industry. *International Journal of Organizational Analysis, 4,* 175–186.

Arthur, W., Jr., & Graziano, W. G. (1996). The five-factor model, conscientiousness, and driving accident involvement. *Journal of Personality, 64,* 593–618.

Arthur, W., Jr., Woehr, D. J., Akande, D., & Strong, M. H. (1995). Human resource management in West Africa: Practices and perceptions. *Human Resource Management, 6,* 347–367.

Arthur, W., Jr., Young, B., Jordan, J. A., & Shebilske, W. L. (1996). Effectiveness of dyadic training protocols: The influence of trainee interaction anxiety. *Human Factors, 38,* 79–86.

Association for the Advancement of Applied Sport Psychology, AAASP Passes Certification Criteria (1990). *AAASP Newsletter, 6* (1), 3–4.

Aspinwall, L. G., & Brunhart, S. M. (1996). Distinguishing optimism from denial: Optimistic beliefs predict attention to health threats. *Personality and Social Psychology Bulletin, 22,* 993–1003.

Austed, C. S., & Berman, W. H. (1991). Managed health care and the evolution of psychotherapy. In C. S. Austed & W. H. Berman (Eds.), *Psychotherapy in managed health care: The optimal use of time and resources.* Washington, DC: American Psychological Association.

Ausubel, D. P. (1977). The facilitation of meaningful verbal learning in the classroom. *Educational Psychologist, 12,* 162–178.

Azar, B. (1997). Team building isn't enough: Workers need training, too. *APA Monitor, 28,* 14–15.

Babbie, E. (1998). *The practice of social research* (8th ed.). Belmont, CA: Wadsworth.

Baekeland, F., & Lundwall, L. (1975). Dropping out of treatment: A critical review. *Psychological Bulletin, 82,* 738–783.

Balague, G. (1997, September). *Preparing for consulting with elite level athletes. Intervention/performance enhancement.* Keynote address at the AAASP annual meeting, San Diego, CA.

Bandura, A. (1969). *Principles of behavior modification.* New York: Holt, Rinehart & Winston.

Bandura, A. (1977). Self-efficacy: Toward a unifying theory of behavioral change. *Psychological Review, 84,* 191–215.

Bandura, A. (1986). *Social foundations of thought and action: A social cognitive theory.* Englewood Cliffs, NJ: Prentice Hall.

Bankart, C. P. (1997). *Talking cures: A history of Western and Eastern psychotherapies.* New York: Brooks/Cole.

Banks, S. M., Salovey, P., Greener, S., Rothman, A. J., Moyer, A., Beauvais, J., & Epel, E. (1995). The effects of message framing on mammography utilization. *Health Psychology, 14,* 178–184.

Barker, R. G. (1968). *Ecological Psychology.* Stanford, CA: Stanford University Press.

Baron, J. (1994). *Thinking and deciding* (2nd ed.). New York: Cambridge University Press.

Barrett, G. V., Doverspike, D., & Arthur, W., Jr. (1995). The current status of the judicial review of banding: A clarification of the meaning of recent court cases. *Industrial-Organizational Psychologist, 33* (1), 39–41.

Barrick, M. R., & Mount, M. K. (1991). The Big-Five personality dimensions in job performance: A meta-analysis. *Personnel Psychology, 44,* 1–26.

Barrick, M. R., Mount, M. K., & Strauss, J. P. (1993). Conscientiousness and performance of sales representatives: Test of the mediating effects of goal setting. *Journal of Applied Psychology, 78,* 111–118.

Bartol, C. R., & Bartol, A. M. (1994). *Psychology and law: Research and application.* Pacific Grove, CA: Brooks/Cole.

Beck, A. T., Rush, A. J., Shaw, B. F., & Emery, G. (1979). *Cognitive therapy of depression.* New York: Guilford Press.

Becker, F., & Steele, F. (1994). *Workplace by design.* San Francisco: Jossey Bass.

Bell, P. A., Greene, T. C., Fisher, J. D., and Baum, A. (1996). *Environmental psychology* (4th ed.). Fort Worth, TX: Harcourt Brace.

Bem, D. J. (1994). Response to Hyman. *Psychological Bulletin, 115,* 25–27.

Bem, D. J., & Honorton, C. (1994). Does psi exist? Replicable evidence for an anomalous process of information transfer. *Psychological Bulletin, 1994,* 4–18.

Benjamin, L. T., Jr. (1996). Harry Hollingworth: Portrait of a generalist. In G. A. Kimble, C. A. Boneau, & M. Wertheimer (Eds.), *Portraits of pioneers in psychology* (Vol. 2, pp. 119–135). Washington, DC: American Psychological Association.

Benjamin, L. T., Jr. (1986). Why don't they understand us? A history of psychology's public image. *American Psychologist, 41,* 941–946.

Benjamin, L. T., Jr. (1997). *A history of psychology: Original sources and contemporary research.* New York: McGraw-Hill.

Benjamin, L. T., Jr., & Bryant, W. H. M. (1997). A history of popular psychology magazines in America. In W. G. Bringmann, H. E. Lück, R. Miller, & C. E. Early (Eds.), *A pictorial history of psychology* (pp. 585–593). Carol Stream, IL: Quintessence.

Benjamin, L. T., Rogers, A. M., & Rosenbaum, A. (1991). Coca-Cola, caffeine, and mental deficiency: Harry Hollingworth and the Chattanooga Trial of 1911. *Journal of the History of the Behavioral Sciences, 27,* 42–55.

Berliner, D. (1992).Telling the stories of educational psychology. *Educational Psychologist, 27,* 143–152.

Berliner, D. C. (1993). The 100-year journey of educational psychology: From interest, to disdain, to respect for practice. In T. Fagan & G. VandenBos (Eds.), *Exploring applied psychology: Origins and critical analyses.* Washington, DC: American Psychological Association.

Berliner, D. C. (1996, August). *Educational psychology meets the Christian right: Different views of childhood, learning, teaching, and schooling.* Paper presented at the American Psychological Association meeting, Toronto.

Bernstein, D. A. (1997). Reflections on teaching introductory psychology. In R. J. Sternberg (Ed.), *Teaching introductory psychology* (pp. 35–47). Washington, DC: American Psychological Association.

Bernstein, D. A., & Borkovec, T. D. (1973). *Progressive relaxation training.* Champaign, IL: Research Press.

Billings, C. (1996). *Aviation automation: The search for a human centered approach.* Hillside, NJ: Erlbaum

Birmingham, H. P., & Taylor, F. V. (1954). A design philosophy for man-machine systems. *Proceedings of the I.R.E., 42,* 1748–1758.

Blackford, K. M. H., & Newcomb, A. (1914). *The job, the man, the boss.* New York: Doubleday & Page.

Blackmore, S. J. (1986). *Adventures of a parapsychologist.* Buffalo, NY: Prometheus Books.

Blackmore, S. (1994). Psi in psychology. *Skeptical Inquirer, 18,* 351–355.

Bloom, B. L. (1992). *Planned short-term psychotherapy: A clinical handbook.* Boston: Allyn & Bacon.

Bloom, B. S. (1968). Learning for mastery. Evaluation *Comment, 1*(2). Los Angeles: University of California, Center for the Study of Evaluation of Instructional Programs.

Bloom, B. S., Engelhart, M. D., Frost, E. J., Hill, W. H., & Krathwohl, D. R. (1956). *Taxonomy of educational objectives. Handbook I: Cognitive domain.* New York: David McKay.

Bohlander, G. W., & McCarthy, K. (1996). How to get the most from team training. *National Productivity Review, 15,* 25–35.

Bonnie, R., & Slobogin, C. (1980). The role of mental health professionals in the criminal process: The case for informed speculation. *Virginia Law Review, 66,* 427–522.

Borgida, E., & Howard-Pitney, B. (1983). Personal involvement and the robustness of perceptual salience effects. *Journal of Personality and Social Psychology, 45,* 560–570.

Borman, W. C., & Cox, G. L. (1996). Who's doing what: Patterns in the practice of I/O psychology. *Industrial-Organizational Psychologist, 33* (4), 21–29.

Borman, W. C., & Motowidlo, S. J. (1997). Task performance and contextual performance: The meaning for personnel selection research. *Human Performance, 10,* 99–109.

Braginsky, D. D. (1992). Psychology: Handmaiden to society. In S. Koch & D. E. Leary (Eds.), *A century of psychology as science.* Washington, DC: American Psychological Association.

Braun, C. (1976). Teacher expectation: Sociopsychological dynamics. *Review of Educational Research, 46* (2), 185–212.

Bray, J. H. (1991). Psychological factors affecting custodial and visitation arrangements. *Behavioral Sciences and the Law, 9,* 419–437.

Bregman, E. O. (1922, June). A scientific plan for sizing up employees. *System,* pp. 696–698, 762–763.

Breland, K., & Breland, M. (1961). The misbehavior of organisms. *American Psychologist, 16,* 681–684.

Brennan, J. F. (1994). *History and systems of psychology* (4th ed.). Englewood Cliffs, NJ: Prentice Hall.

Brickman, P., Coates, D., & Janoff-Bulman, R. (1978). Lottery winners and accident victims: Is happiness relative? *Journal of Personality and Social Psychology, 36,* 917–927.

Broniarczyk, S. M., & Alba, J. W. (1994a). The role of consumers' intuitions in inference making. *Journal of Consumer Research, 21,* 117–139.

Broniarczyk, S. M., & Alba, J. W. (1994b). Theory versus data in prediction and correlation tables. *Organizational Behavior and Human Decision Processes, 57,* 117–139.

Brophy, J. E. (1982, March). *Research on the self-fulfilling prophecy and teacher expectations.* Paper presented at the annual meeting of the American Educational Research Association, New York.

Brophy, J. E. (1988). On motivating students. In D. Berliner & B. Rosenshine (Eds.), *Talks to teachers* (pp. 201–245). New York: Random House.

Brophy, J. E., & Good, T. (1986). Teacher behavior and student achievement. In M. Wittrock (Ed.), *Handbook of research on teaching* (3rd ed.) (pp. 328–375). New York: Macmillan.

Broughton, R. (1991). *Parapsychology: The controversial science.* New York: Ballentine.

Brown, J. M., Berrien, F. K., & Russell, D. L. (1966). *Applied psychology.* New York: Macmillan.

Bruner, J. S., Goodnow, J. J., & Austin, G. A. (1956). *A study of thinking.* New York: Wiley.

Bryan, A. D., Aiken, L. S., & West, S. G. (1996). Increasing condom use: Evaluation of a theory-based intervention to prevent sexually transmitted diseases in young women. *Health Psychology, 15,* 371–382.

Bryant, K. L., Jr., & Dethloff, H. C. (1990). *A history of American business* (2nd ed.). Englewood Cliffs, NJ: Prentice Hall.

Buckley, K. W. (1982) The selling of a psychologist: John Broadus Watson and the application of behavioral techniques to advertising. In L. T. Benjamin, Jr., *A history of psychology: Original sources and contemporary research* (2nd ed.). New York: McGraw-Hill.

Buckley, K. W. (1989). *Mechanical man: John Broadus Watson and the beginnings of behaviorism.* New York: Guilford Press.

Burger, J. M. (1986). Increasing compliance by improving the deal: The that's-not-all technique. *Journal of Personality and Social Psychology, 51,* 277–283.

Buunk, B. P., & Gibbons, F. X. (1997). *Health and coping: Perspectives from social comparison theory.* Hillsdale, NJ: Erlbaum.

Campbell, D. T., & Bray, D. W. (1993). Use of an assessment center as an aid in managerial selection. *Personnel Psychology, 46,* 691–699.

Campbell, J. P. (1990). Modeling the performance prediction problem in industrial and organizational psychology. In M. D. Dunnette & L. M. Hough (Eds.), *Handbook of industrial and organizational psychology* (2nd ed.) (Vol. 1, pp. 687–732). Palo Alto, CA: Consulting Psychologists Press.

Canter, D. (1985, May 1). *Applying psychology.* Inaugural lecture presented at the University of Surrey, U.K.

Capshew, J. H. (1992). Psychologists on site: A reconnaissance of the historiography of the laboratory. *American Psychologist, 47* (2), 132–142.

Carlson, S. (1985). A double-blind test of astrology. *Nature, 318,* 419–425.

Carter, R. B. (1983). *Descartes' medical philosophy: The organic solution to the mind-body problem.* Baltimore: Johns Hopkins University Press.

Cascio, W. F., Outtz, J., Zedeck, S., & Goldstein I. L. (1991). Statistical implications of six methods of test score use in personnel selection. *Human Performance, 4,* 233–264.

Catania, J. A., Coates, T. J., & Kegeles, S. (1994). A test of the AIDS Risk Reduction Model: Psychosocial correlates of condom use in the AMEN cohort survey. *Health Psychology, 13,* 548–555.

Chaiken, S., Liberman, A., & Eagly, A. H. (1989). Heuristic and systematic processing within and beyond the persuasion context. In J. S. Uleman & J. A. Bargh (Eds.), *Unintended thought* (pp. 212–252). New York: Guilford Press.

Chan, D., & Schmitt, N. (1997). Video-based versus paper-and-pencil method of assessment in situational judgment tests: Subgroup differences in test performance and face validity perceptions. *Journal of Applied Psychology, 82,* 143–159.

Cherulnik, P. D. (1993). *Applications of environment behavior research.* New York: Cambridge University Press.

Chorover, S. L. (1992) Psychology in cultural context: The division of labor and the fragmentation of experience.

In S. Koch & D. E. Leary (Eds.), *A century of psychology as a science.* Washington, DC: American Psychological Association.

Christy, N. P. (1979). English is our second language. *New England Journal of Medicine, 300,* 979–981.

Cialdini, R. B. (1993). *Influence: Science and practice.* New York: HarperCollins.

Cialdini, R. B., Borden, R. J., Thorne, A., Walker, M. R., Freeman, S., & Sloan, L. R. (1976). Basking in reflected glory: Three (football) field studies. *Journal of Personality and Social Psychology, 34,* 366–375.

Cialdini, R. B., Cacioppo, J. T., Bassett, R., & Miller, J. A. (1978). Low-ball procedure for producing compliance: Commitment then cost. *Journal of Personality and Social Psychology, 36,* 463–476.

Cisneros, H. G. (1995). *Defensible space: Deterring crime and building community.* Washington DC: Department of Housing and Urban Development.

Coates, T. J., McKuisck, L., Kuno, R., & Stites, D. P. (1989). Stress reduction training changed number of sexual partners but not immune function in men with HIV. *American Journal of Public Health, 79,* 885–887.

Cohen, M. I., Spodak, M. K., Silver, S. B., & Williams, K. (1989). Predicting outcome of insanity acquittees released to the community. *Behavioral Sciences and the Law, 6,* 515–530.

Cohen, S., & Rodriguez, M. S. (1995). Pathways linking affective disturbances and physical disorders. *Health Psychology, 14,* 374–380.

Cohen, S., & Wills, T. A. (1985). Stress, social support, and the buffering hypothesis. *Psychological Bulletin, 98,* 310–357.

Comer, J. M., Kardes, F. R., & Sullivan, A. K. (1992). Multiple deescalating requests, statistical information, and compliance: A field experiment. *Journal of Applied Social Psychology, 22,* 1199–1207.

Conway, J. B. (1992). A world of differences among psychologists. *Canadian Psychology, 33,* 1–22.

Coon, D. J. (1992). Testing the limits of sense and science: American experimental psychologists combat spiritualism, 1880–1920. *American Psychologist, 47,* 143–151.

Cooper, G. E., White, M. D., & Lauber, J. K. (Eds.). (1979). *Resource management in the cockpit* (NASA Conference Publication 2120). Moffett Field, CA: NASA Ames Research Center.

Cooper, H. M., & Good, T. (1983). *Pygmalion grows up: Studies in the expectation communication process.* New York: Longman.

Coren, S. (1995). *The intelligence of dogs: Canine consciousness and capabilities.* New York: Bantam Books.

Coren, S. (1998). *Why we love the dogs we do.* New York: Free Press.

Coren, S., & Walker, J. (1997). *What do dogs know?* New York: Free Press.

Corkill, A. J. (1992). Advance organizers: Facilitators of recall. *Educational Psychology Review, 4,* 33–67.

Costa, P. T., & McCrae, R. (1992). *Manual for the Revised NEO Personality Inventory (NEO-PIR) and the NEO Five-Factor Inventory (BEO-FFI).* Odessa, FL: Psychological Assessment Resources.

Craik, K. H., & Feimer, N. H. (1987). Environmental assessment. In D. Stokols & I. Altman (Eds.), *Handbook of environmental psychology* (pp. 891–918). New York: Wiley.

Cratty, B. J. (1964). *Movement behavior and motor learning.* Philadelphia: Lea & Feibiger.

Crosbie-Burnett, M. (1991). Impact of joint versus sole custody and quality of co-parental relationship on adjustment of adolescents in remarried families. *Behavioral Sciences and the Law, 9,* 439–449.

Cummings, N. A., & Follette, W. T. (1968). Psychiatric services and medical utilization in a prepaid healthplan setting: Part II, *Medical Care, 6,* 31–41.

Dalessio, A. T. (1994). Predicting insurance agent turnover using a video-based situational judgment test. *Journal of Business and Psychology, 9,* 23–32.

Danish, S. J., & Hale, B. D. (1981). Toward an understanding of the practice of sport psychology. *Journal of Sport Psychology, 3,* 90–99.

Danish, S. J., & Hale, B. D. (1982). Further considerations on the practice of sport psychology. *Journal of Sport Psychology, 4,* 10–12.

Dansereau, D. F. (1985). Learning strategy research. In J. Segal, S. Chipman, & R. Glaser (Eds.), *Thinking and learning skills: Vol. 1. Relating instruction to research.* Hillsdale, NJ: Erlbaum.

Danziger, K. (1990). *Constructing the subject: Historical origins of psychological research.* Cambridge, MA: Cambridge University Press.

Darwin, C. (1859). *The origin of species.* London: John Murray.

Darwin, C. (1965/1872). *The expression of the emotions in man and animals.* Chicago: University of Chicago Press.

Dattore, P. J., Shontz, F. C., & Coyne, L. (1980). Premorbid personality differentiation of cancer and noncancer groups: A test of the hypothesis of cancer proneness. *Journal of Consulting and Clinical Psychology, 48,* 388–394.

Davis, D. (1971, April 19). New architecture. *Newsweek,* p. 78.

Davis, K. D. (1992). *Therapy dogs.* New York: Howell Book House.

Dawes, R. M., Faust, D., & Meehl, P. E. (1989). Clinical versus actuarial judgment. *Science, 243,* 1668–1674.

Deci, E., Vallerand, R. J., Pelletier, L. G., & Ryan, R. M. (1991). Motivation and education: The self-determination perspective. *Educational Psychologist, 26,* 325–346.

DeLeon, P. H., Fox, R. E., & Graham, S. R. (1991). Prescription privileges: Psychology's next frontier. *American Psychologist, 46,* 384–393.

Descartes, R. (1960/1637). *Discourse on method, and meditations.* Indianapolis: Bobbs-Merrill.

Diffrient, N., Tilley, A. R., & Bardagjy, J. C. (1974). *Humanscale 1/2/3.* Cambridge, MA: MIT Press.

Diffrient, N., Tilley, A.R., & Harman, D. (1981). *Humanscale 7/8/9.* Cambridge, MA: MIT Press.

Dipboye, R. L., Smith, C. S., & Howell, W. C. (1994). *Understanding industrial and organizational psychology: An integrated approach.* Fort Worth, TX: Harcourt Brace.

Dittmar, H. (1992). *The social psychology of material possessions: To have is to be.* Hemel Hemstead, U.K.: Harvester-Wheatsheaf.

DiVesta, F. J., & Gray, G. S. (1972). Listening and notetaking. *Journal of Educational Psychology, 63,* 8–14.

Donovan, J. L., & Blake, D. R. (1992). Patient noncompliance: Deviance or reasoned decision-making. *Social Science and Medicine, 34,* 507–513.

Dorfman, P. W., & Howell, J. P. (1984). Production sharing in the Mexican Maquiladora industry: A challenge for I/O psychology. *Industrial-Organizational Psychologist, 22* (1), 20–26.

Dossett, D. L., & Hulvershorn, P. (1983). Increasing technical training efficiency: Peer training via computer-assisted instruction. *Journal of Applied Psychology, 68,* 552–558.

Dreyfuss, H. (1955). *Designing for people.* New York: Simon & Schuster.

Driscoll, M. P. (1994). *Psychology of learning for instruction.* Boston: Allyn & Bacon.

Dudycha, G. J. (1963). *Applied psychology.* New York: Ronald Press.

Dunkel-Schetter, C., & Wortman, C. B. (1982). The interpersonal dynamics of cancer: Problems in social relationships and their impact on the patient. In H. S. Friedman & M. R. DiMatteo (Eds.), *Interpersonal issues in health care* (pp. 69–100). New York: Academic Press.

Eagle, M. N. (1984). *Recent developments in psychoanalysis: A critical evaluation.* Cambridge, MA: Harvard University Press.

Eagly, A. H., & Chaiken, S. (1993). *The psychology of attitudes.* Fort Worth, TX: Harcourt Brace Jovanovich.

Eames, E., & Eames T. (1997). *Partners in independence: A success story of dogs and the disabled.* New York: Howell Book House.

Eastman Kodak Company. (1983). *Ergonomic design for people at work* (Vols. 1, 2). New York: Van Nostrand Reinhold.

Ebbinghaus, H. (1910). *Abriss der Psychologie* (Summary of psychology). Leipzig: Veit.

Ebert, B. W. (1987). Guide to conducting a psychological autopsy. *Professional Psychology: Research and Practice, 18,* 52–56.

Eipper, P. (1931). *Circus: Men, beasts, and joys of the road.* New York: Viking Press.

Ellis, A. (1973). Rational-emotive therapy. In R. Corsini (Ed.), *Current psychotherapies* (pp. 167–206). Itasca, IL: F. E. Peacock.

Elwork, A., Sales, B. D., and Suggs, D. (1981). The trial: A research review. In B. D. Sales (Ed.), *The trial process* (pp. 1–68). New York: Plenum.

Emery, R. E., Matthews, S. G., & Kitzman, K. M. (1994). Child custody mediation and litigation: Parents' satisfaction and functioning one year after settlement. *Journal of Consulting and Clinical Psychology, 62,* 124–129.

Emery, R. E., Matthews, S. G., & Wyer, M. M. (1991). Child custody mediation and litigation: Further evidence on the differing views of mothers and fathers. *Journal of Consulting and Clinical Psychology, 59,* 410–418.

Endsley, M. R. (1995). Toward a theory of situation awareness in dynamic systems. *Human Factors, 37,* 32–64.

Engel, G. L. (1977). The need for a new medical model: A challenge for biomedicine. *Science, 196,* 126–129.

Ennis, B. J., & Litwack, T. R. (1974). Psychiatry and the presumption of expertise: Flipping coins in the courtroom. *California Law Review, 62,* 693–752.

Equal Employment Opportunity Commission et al. (1979). Interpretation and clarification of the Uniform Employee Selection Guidelines. *Federal Register, 44,* 11996–12209.

Esterling, B. A., Antoni, M. H., Fletcher, M. A., Margulies, S., & Schneiderman, N. (1994). Emotional disclosure through writing or speaking modulates latent Epstein-Barr virus antibody titers. *Journal of Consulting and Clinical Psychology, 62,* 130–140.

Estes, W. K. (1944). An experimental study of punishment [Whole issue No. 263]. *Psychological Monographs, 57* (3).

Evans, G. W. (Ed.). (1982). *Environmental stress.* New York: Cambridge University Press.

Exner, J. E. (1993). *The Rorschach: A comprehensive system: Vol. 1. Basic foundations* (3rd ed.). New York: Wiley.

Fagan, T. K. (1992). Compulsory schooling, child study, clinical psychology, and special education: Origins of school psychology. *American Psychologist, 47,* 236–243.

Fairbairn, W. R. D. (1952). *Psychoanalytic studies of the personality.* London: Tavistock Publications/Routledge & Kegan Paul.

Faust, D., & Ziskin, J. (1988). The expert witness in psychology and psychiatry. *Sciences, 242,* 31–35.

Federoff, N. E., & Nowak, R. M. (1997). Man and his dog. *Science, 278,* 205.

Feldman, J. M., & Lynch, J. G. (1988). Self-generated validity and other effects of measurement on belief, attitude, intention, and behavior. *Journal of Applied Psychology, 73,* 421–435.

Fiennes, R., & Fiennes, A. (1968). *The natural history of dogs.* London: Weidenfeld & Nicolson.

Finkel, N. J. (1989). The Insanity Defense Reform Act of 1984: Much ado about nothing. *Behavioral Sciences and the Law, 7,* 403–419.

Fishbein, M., & Ajzen, I. (1975). *Belief, attitude, intention, and behavior: An introduction to theory and research.* Reading, MA: Addison-Wesley.

Fisher, J. D., Fisher, W. A., Misovich, S. J., Kimble, D. L., & Malloy, T. E. (1996). Changing AIDS risk behavior: Effects of an intervention emphasizing AIDS risk reduction information, motivation, and behavioral skills in a college population. *Health Psychology, 15,* 114–123.

Fitts, P. M., & Jones, R. E., (1947) Analysis of factors contributing to 460 "pilot error" experiences in operating aircraft controls (AMC memorandum Rep. TSEAA-694-12). In W. Sinaiko (Ed) (1961). *Selected applications of human factors in the design and use of control systems.* New York: Dover.

Fitts, P., Jones, R. E., & Milton, E. (1950). Eye movements of aircraft pilots during instrument landing approaches. *Aeronautical Engineering Review, 9,* 24–29.

Flach, J. M. (1995). Situation awareness: Proceed with caution. *Human Factors, 37,* 149–157.

Foley, L. A. (1993). *A psychological view of the legal system.* Madison, WI: Brown & Benchmark.

Foyle, D. C., Andre, A. D., McCann, R. S., Wenzel, E., Begault, D. & Battiste, V. (1996). Taxiway Navigation and Situation Awareness (T-NASA) System: Problem, design philosophy and description of an integrated display suite for low-visibility airport surface operations. *SAE Transactions: Journal of Aerospace, 105,* 1411–1418.

Foyle, D. C., McCann, R. S., & Shelden, S. G. (1995). Attentional issues with superimposed symbology: Formats for scene-linked displays. In R. S. Jensen & L. A. Rakovan (Eds.). *Proceedings of the Eighth International Symposium on Aviation Psychology* (pp. 98–103). Columbus, OH: OSU.

Foyle, D. C., Sanford, B., & McCann, R. S. (1991). Attentional issues in superimposed flight symbology. In R. S. Jensen (Ed.), *Proceedings of the Sixth International Symposium on Aviation Psychology* (pp. 577–582). Columbus, OH: OSU.

Frazer, J. G. (1922). *The golden bough.* London: Macmillan.

Freedman, J. L., & Fraser, S. C. (1966). Compliance without pressure: The foot-in-the-door technique. *Journal of Personality and Social Psychology, 4,* 195–203.

Freud, S. (1938). *The basic writings of Sigmund Freud.* New York: Modern Library.

Friedman, H. S., & DiMatteo, M. R. (1989). *Health psychology.* Englewood Cliffs, NJ: Prentice Hall.

Fulero, S. M., & Finkel, N. J. (1991). Barring ultimate issue testimony: An "insane" rule? *Law and Human Behavior, 15,* 495–508.

Furnham, A., & Stringfield, P. (1994). Congruence of self and subordinate ratings of managerial practices as a correlate of supervisor evaluation. *Journal of Occupational and Organizational Psychology, 67,* 57–67.

Gallagher-Thompson, D., Hanley-Peterson, P., & Thompson, L. W. (1990). Maintenance of gains versus relapse following brief psychotherapy for depression. *Journal of Consulting and Clinical Psychology, 58,* 371–374.

Gardner, G. T., & Stern, P. T. (1996). *Environmental problems and human behavior.* Boston: Allyn and Bacon.

Gardner, H. (1983). *Frames of mind: The theory of multiple intelligences.* New York: Basic Books.

Gardner, H. (1993). *Multiple intelligences: The theory in practice.* New York: Basic Books.

Garmon, A., Nystrand, M., Berends, M., & LePore. P. C. (1995). An organizational analysis of the effects of ability grouping. *American Educational Research Journal, 32,* 687–715.

Gaugler, B. B., Rosenthal, D. B., Thornton, G. C., & Bentsen, C. (1987). Meta-analysis of assessment center validity. *Journal of Applied Psychology, 72,* 493–511.

Gay, P. (1988). *Freud: A life for our time.* New York: Norton.

Geller, E. S. (1987). Environmental psychology and applied behavior analysis. In D. Stokols & I. Altman (Eds.), *Handbook of environmental psychology* (Vol. 1, pp. 361–388). New York: Wiley.

Gergen, K. J., Gulerce, A., Lock, A., & Misra, G. (1996). Psychological science in cultural context. *American Psychologist, 51,* 496–503.

Gerrard, M., Gibbons, F. X., & Bushman, B. J. (1996). Relation between perceived vulnerability to HIV and precautionary sexual behavior. *Psychological Bulletin, 119,* 390–409.

Gerrard, M., Gibbons, F. X., Warner, T. D., & Smith, G. E. (1993). Perceived vulnerability to HIV infection and AIDS preventive behavior: A critical review of the evidence. In J. B. Pryor & G. D. Reeder (Eds.), *The social psychology of HIV infection* (pp. 59–84). Hillsdale, NJ: Erlbaum.

Gies, J. (1991, Winter). Automating the worker. *Invention and Technology,* pp. 56–63.

Gifford, R. (1997). *Environmental psychology* (2nd ed.). Boston: Allyn and Bacon.

Gilovich, T. (1991). *How we know what isn't so: The fallibility of human reason in everyday life.* New York: Free Press.

Gilovich, T. (1997). Some systematic biases of everyday judgment. *Skeptical Inquirer, 21,* 31–35.

Gilovich, T., & Savitsky, K. (1996). Like goes with like: The role of representativeness in erroneous and pseudoscientific beliefs. *Skeptical Inquirer, 20* (2), 34–40.

Gillett, M., & Gall, M. (1982, March). *The effects of teacher enthusiasm on the at-task behavior of students in the elementary grades.* Paper presented at the annual meeting of the American Educational Research Association, New York.

Gladwell, M. (1996, November 4). The science of shopping. *New Yorker,* pp. 66–75.

Gless, A. G. (1995). Some post-Daubert trial tribulations of a simple country justice: Behavioral science evidence in trial courts. *Behavioral Sciences and the Law, 13,* 261–292.

Goettl, B. P. (1997). Situation awareness and executive control processes: Quot homines, tot sententiae. In *Proceedings of the Human Factors and Ergonomics Society 41st Annual Meeting.* Santa Monica: HFES.

Goldberg, L. R. (1993). The structure of phenotypic personality traits. *American Psychologist, 48,* 26–34.

Goleman, D. (1995). *Emotional intelligence.* New York: Bantam.

Good, T. L. (1988). Teacher expectations. In D. Berliner & B. Rosenshine (Eds.), *Talks to teachers* (pp. 159–200). New York: Random House.

Good, T. (1996) Teaching effects and teacher evaluation. In J. Sikula (Ed.) *Handbook of research on teacher education* (pp. 617–665). New York: Macmillan.

Good, T. L., & Marshall, S. (1984). Do students learn more in heterogeneous or homogeneous groups? In P. Peterson, L. C. Wilkerson, & M. Hallinan (Eds.), *The social context of instruction: Group organization and group processes* (pp. 15–38). Orlando, FL: Academic Press.

Goodman, K. S. (1986). *What's whole in whole language: A parent-teacher guide.* Portsmouth, NH: Heinemann.

Gopher, D., Weil, M., & Baraket T. (1994). Transfer of skill from a computer game trainer to flight. *Human Factors, 36,* 387–405.

Gould, D., & Roberts, G. C. (Eds.) (1989). Delivering sport psychology services to the 1998 Olympic athletes. *Sport Psychologist* (Special issue), *3* (4).

Graham, S., & Harris, K. R. (1994). The effects of whole language on children's writing: A review of the literature. *Educational Psychologist, 29,* 187–192.

Grandjean, E. (1980). *Fitting the task to the man.* London: Taylor and Francis.

Gray, E. A. (1989). *Dogs of war.* London: Hale.

Gray, T. (1987). Educational experience and belief in paranormal phenomena. In F. B. Harrold & R..A. Eve (Eds.), *Cult archaeology and creationism: Understanding pseudoscientific beliefs about the past* (pp. 21–33). Iowa City: University of Iowa Press.

Greenfield, S., Kaplan, S. H., Ware, J. E., Yano, E. M., & Frank, H. J. L. (1988). Patients' participation in medical care: Effects on blood sugar control and quality of life in diabetes. *Journal of General Internal Medicine, 3,* 448–457.

Greeno, J. G., Collins, A. M., & Resnick, L. B. (1996). Cognition and learning. In D. Berliner & R. Calfee (Eds.), *Handbook of educational psychology* (pp. 15–46). New York: Macmillan.

Greenspan, M. (1983). *A new approach to women and therapy.* New York: McGraw-Hill.

Greer, S., & Morris, T. (1975). Psychological attributes of women who develop breast cancer: A controlled study. *Journal of Psychosomatic Research, 19,* 147–153.

Grieco, A., & Long, C. J. (1984). Investigation of the Karnofsky Performance Status as a measure of quality of life. *Health Psychology, 3,* 129-142.

Griffith, C. R. (1926). *Psychology of coaching.* New York: Scribners.

Griffith, C. R. (1928). *Psychology of athletics.* New York: Scribners.

Grisso, T., & Appelbaum, P. S. (1995). The MacArthur Treatment Competence Study. III: Abilities of patients to consent to psychiatric and medical treatments. *Law and Human Behavior, 19,* 149–174.

Guitierrez, R., & Slavin, R. E. (1992). Achievement effects of the nongraded elementary school: A best evidence synthesis. *Review of Educational Research, 62,* 333–376.

Guskey, T. R., & Gates, S. L. (1986). Synthesis of research on mastery learning. *Education Leadership, 43,* 73–81.

Gustafsson, J-E., & Undheim, J. O. (1996) Individual differences in cognitive functioning. In D. Berliner & R. Calfee (Eds.), *Handbook of educational psychology* (pp. 186–242). New York: Macmillan.

Guthrie, E. R. (1952). *The psychology of learning* (rev. ed.) New York: Harper.

Gutman, A., & Christiansen, N. (1997). Further clarification of the judicial status of banding. *Industrial-Organizational Psychologist, 35* (1), 75–81.

Hale, N., Jr. (1980). *Human science and social order: Hugo Münsterberg and the origins of applied psychology.* Philadelphia: Temple University Press.

Halpern, D. E. (1998). Teaching critical thinking for transfer across domains: Dispositions, skills, structure training, and metacognitive monitoring. *American Psychologist, 53,* 449–455.

Halpern, D. F., & Nummedal, S. G. (1995). Closing thoughts about helping students improve how they think. *Teaching of Psychology, 22,* 82–83.

Hammer, J. C., Fisher, J. D., Fitzgerald, P., & Fisher, W. A. (1996). When two heads aren't better than one: AIDS risk behavior in college-age couples. *Journal of Applied Social Psychology, 26,* 375–397.

Hannah, D., & Sternthal, B. (1984). Detecting and explaining the sleeper effect. *Journal of Consumer Research, 11,* 632–642.

Hardin, G. (1968). The tragedy of the commons. *Science, 162,* 1243–1248.

Harrison, R. (1965). Thematic apperceptive methods. In B. B. Wolman (Ed.), *Handbook of clinical psychology* (pp. 562–620). New York: McGraw-Hill.

Hartley, D., Roback, H., & Abramowitz, S. (1976). Deterioration effects in encounter groups. *American Psychologist, 31,* 247–255.

Haskell, I. D., & Wickens, C. D. (1993). Two- and three-dimensional displays for aviation. *International Journal of Aviation Psychology, 3,* 87–109.

Hawkins, F., & Orlady, H. (1993). *Human factors in flight.* Hampshire, England: Avebury Aviation.

Hearnshaw, L. S. (1964). *A short history of British psychology, 1840–1940.* New York: Barnes & Noble.

Helweg-Larson, M., & Collins, B. E. (1994). The UCLA Multidimensional Condom Attitudes Scale: Documenting the complex determinants of condom use in college students. *Health Psychology, 13,* 224–237.

Heltzer, R. A., & Vyse, S. A. (1994). Problem solving and intermittent consequences: The experimental control of superstitious beliefs. *Psychological Record, 44,* 155–169.

Herek, G. M., & Glunt, E. K. (1993). Public attitudes toward AIDS-related issues in the United States. In J. B. Pryor & G. D. Reeder (Eds.), *The social psychology of HIV infection* (pp. 229–261). Hillsdale, NJ: Erlbaum.

Herr, P. M. (1989). Priming price: Prior knowledge and context effects. *Journal of Consumer Research, 16,* 67–75.

Herr, P. M., Kardes, F. R., & Kim, J. (1991). Effects of word-of-mouth and product-attribute information on persuasion: An accessibility-diagnosticity perspective. *Journal of Consumer Research, 17,* 454–462.

Herrnstein, R. J., Nickerson, R. S., de Sánchez, M., & Swets, J. A. (1986). Teaching thinking skills. *American Psychologist, 41,* 1279–1289.

Hersh, P. D., & Alexander, R. W. (1990). MMPI profile patterns of emotional disability claimants. *Journal of Clinical Psychology, 46,* 795–799.

Heyman, S. R. (1982). A reaction to Danish and Hale: A minority report. *Journal of Sport Psychology, 4,* 7–9.

Higgins, E. T. (1996). Knowledge activation: Accessibility, applicability, and salience. In E. T. Higgins & A. W. Kruglanski (Eds.), *Social psychology: Handbook of basic principles* (pp. 133–168). New York: Guilford.

Higgins, S. T., Morris, E. K., & Johnson, L. M. (1989). Social transmission of superstitious behavior in preschool children. *Psychological Record, 39,* 307–323.

Hilgard, E. R. (1987). *Psychology in America: A historical survey.* San Diego, CA: Harcourt Brace Jovanovich.

Hilgard, E. R. (1996). History of educational psychology. In D. Berliner & R. Calfee (Eds.), *Handbook of educational psychology* (pp. 990–1004). New York: Macmillan.

Hines, T. (1988). *Pseudoscience and the paranormal.* Buffalo: Prometheus Books.

Hinrichs, J. R. (1978). An eight-year follow-up of a management assessment center. *Journal of Applied Psychology, 63,* 596–601.

Hoffman, C. C., & Thornton, G. C. (1997). Examining selection utility where competing predictors differ in adverse impact. *Personnel Psychology, 50,* 455–470.

Hofstede, G. (1991). *Cultures and organizations: Software of the mind.* London: McGraw-Hill.

Hofstede, G. (1993). Cultural constraints in management theories. *Academy of Management Executive, 7,* 81–94.

Hogan, D. E. (1988). Learned imitation by pigeons. In T. R. Zentall & B. G. Galef, Jr. (Eds.), *Social learning: Psychological and biological perspectives* (pp. 239–253). Hillsdale, NJ: Erlbaum.

Hogan, J., Hogan, R., & Gregory, S. (1992). Validation of a sales representative selection inventory. *Journal of Business and Psychology, 7,* 161–171.

Hogan, R., Hogan, J., & Roberts, B. W. (1996). Personality measurement and employment decisions. *American Psychologist, 51,* 469–477.

Hollingworth, H. L. (1912). The influence of caffein on mental and motor efficiency. *Archives of Psychology,* no. 22, 1–166.

Hollingworth, H. L. (1913). *Advertising and selling.* New York: D. Appleton.

Hopkin, D. V. (1995). *Human factors of air traffic control.* London: Taylor & Francis.

Howard, A., Pion, G. M., Gottfriedson, G. D., Flattau, P. E., Oskamp, S., Pfafflin, S. M., & Bray, D. W. (1986). The changing face of American psychology: A report from the Committee on Employment and Human Resources. *American Psychologist, 41,* 1311–1327.

Huber, J., Payne, J. W., & Puto, C. (1982). Adding asymmetrically dominated alternatives: Violations of regularity and the similarity hypothesis. *Journal of Consumer Research, 9,* 90–98.

Huck, J. R., & Bray, D. W. (1976). Management assessment center evaluations and subsequent job performance of black and white females. *Personnel Psychology, 29,* 13–30.

Huffcutt, A. I., & Arthur, W., Jr. (1994). Hunter and Hunter (1984) revisited: Interview validity for entry-level jobs. *Journal of Applied Psychology, 79,* 184–190.

Hunt, M. (1993). *The story of psychology.* New York: Doubleday.

Hunter, J. E., & Hunter, R. F. (1984). Validity and utility of alternative predictors of job performance. *Psychological Bulletin, 96,* 72–98.

Hunter, J. E., & Schmidt, F. L. (1990). *Methods of meta-analysis: Correcting error and bias in research findings.* Beverly Hills, CA: Sage.

Hutchins, E. (1995). *Cognition in the wild.* Cambridge, MA: MIT Press

Hyman, R. (1985). The Ganzfeld psi experiment: A critical appraisal. *Journal of Parapsychology, 49,* 3–49.

Hyman, R. (1994). Anomaly or artifact? Comments on Bem and Honorton. *Psychological Bulletin, 115,* 19–24.

Hyman, R., & Honorton, C. (1986). A joint communique: The psi Ganzfeld controversy. *Journal of Parapsychology, 50,* 351–364.

Imwrinkelreid, E. J. (1994). The next step after Daubert: Developing a similarly epistemological approach to ensuring the reliability of nonscientific expert testimony. *Cardozo Law Review, 15,* 2271-2294.

Ivergard, T. (1989). *Handbook of control room design and ergonomics.* London: Taylor and Francis.

Iverson, T. L. (1995). *U.S. Customs Service Canine Enforcement Program.* Invited address at the California Narcotic Canine Association Meetings, Van Nuys, CA.

Jachuck, S. J., Brierley, H., Jachuck, S., & Willcox, P. M. (1982). The effect of hypotensive drugs on the quality of life. *Journal of the Royal College of General Practitioners, 32,* 103–105.

Jacobs, M. K., & Goodman, G. (1989). Psychology and self-help groups: Predictions on a partnership. *American Psychologist, 44,* 536–545.

James, W. (1899). *Talks to teachers on psychology: And to students on some of life's ideals.* New York: Holt.

Janoff-Bulman, R. (1989). Assumptive worlds and the stress of traumatic events: Applications of the schema construct. *Social Cognition, 7,* 113–136

Janz, N. K., & Becker, M. H. (1984). The Health Belief Model: A decade later. *Health Education Quarterly, 11,* 1–47.

Jensen, R. S., & Biegelski, C. S. (1989). Cockpit resource management. In R. Jensen (Ed.), *Aviation psychology.* Brookfield, VT: Gower Technical.

Johar, G. V., & Simmons, C. J. (1997). *Spontaneous inference and deliberate correction: The perseverance of invalid beliefs.* Unpublished manuscript.

Johnson, D., & Johnson, R. (1985). Motivational processes in cooperative, competitive, and individualistic learning situations. In C. Ames & R. Ames (Eds.), *Research on motivation in education. Vol. 2: The classroom milieu* (pp. 249–286). New York: Academic Press.

Jones, C., & DeCotiis, T. (1986, August). Video-based selection of hospitality employees. *Cornell Hotel and Restaurant Administration Quarterly,* pp. 67–73.

Jung, C. G. (1968). *Analytical psychology: Its theory and practice.* Tavistock lectures. New York: Pantheon Books. (Original work published 1935)

Jung, C. G. (1978). *Flying saucers: A modern myth of things seen in the skies.* Princeton, NJ: Princeton University Press.

Jung, C. G. (1983). *The essential Jung* (A. Storr, Ed.). Princeton, NJ: Princeton University Press.

Kaempf, G. L., Klein, G. A., Thordsen, M. L., & Wolf, S. (1996). Decision making in complex naval command-and-control environments. *Human Factors, 38* (2), 220–231.

Kahn, B. E., & McAlister, L. (1997). *Grocery revolution: The new focus on the consumer.* Reading, MA: Addison Wesley Longman.

Kahneman, D., Slovic, P., & Tversky, A. (Eds.). (1982). *Judgment under uncertainty: Heuristics and biases.* Cambridge: Cambridge University Press.

Kaplan, R. M. (1994). The Ziggy Theorem: Toward an outcomes-focused health psychology. *Health Psychology, 13,* 451–460.

Kaplan, R., & Kaplan, S. (1989). *The experience of nature.* New York: Cambridge University Press.

Kardes, F. R. (1988a). A nonreactive measure of inferential beliefs. *Psychology and Marketing, 5,* 273–286.

Kardes, F. R. (1988b). Spontaneous inference processes in advertising: The effects of conclusion omission and involvement on persuasion. *Journal of Consumer Research, 15,* 225–233.

Kardes, F. R., & Gurumurthy, K. (1992). Order-of-entry effects on consumer memory and judgment: An information integration perspective. *Journal of Marketing Research, 29,* 343–357.

Kardes, F. R., & Sanbonmatsu, D. M. (1993). Direction of comparison, expected feature correlation, and the set-size effect in preference judgment. *Journal of Consumer Psychology, 2,* 39–54.

Katon, W., & Sullivan, M. (1990). Depression and chronic medical illness. *Journal of Clinical Psychology, 6,* 3–11.

Katzell, R. A., & Austin, J. T. (1992). From then to now: The development of industrial-organizational psychology in the United States. *Journal of Applied Psychology, 77,* 803–835.

Kaufmann, W. (1992) Nietzsche as the first great (depth) psychologist. In S. Koch & D. E. Leary (Eds.), *A century of psychology as a science.* Washington, DC: American Psychological Association.

Kaufmann, Y. (1989). Analytical psychotherapy. In R. J. Corsini & D. Wedding (Eds.), *Current psychotherapies* (4th ed.). Itasca, IL: F. E. Peacock.

Keilin, W. B., & Bloom, L. J. (1986). Child custody evaluation practices: A survey of experienced professionals. *Professional Psychology: Research and Practice, 17,* 338–346.

Keinan, G. (1987). Decision making under stress: Scanning of alternatives under controllable and uncontrollable threats. *Journal of Personality and Social Psychology, 52,* 639–644.

Keinan, G. (1994). Effects of stress and tolerance of ambiguity on magical thinking. *Journal of Personality and Social Psychology, 67,* 48–55.

Keinan, G., Friedland, N., & Arad, L. (1991). Chunking and integration: Effects of stress on the structuring of information. *Cognition and Emotion, 5,* 133–145.

Keller, K. L. (1987). Memory in advertising: The effect of advertising memory cues on brand evaluations. *Journal of Consumer Research, 14,* 316–333.

Keller, K. L. (1991). Memory and evaluation effects in competitive advertising environments. *Journal of Consumer Research, 16,* 436–476.

Kelly, J. A., St. Lawrence, J. S., Stevenson, L. Y., Hauth, A. C., Kalichman, S. C., Diaz, Y. E., Brasfield, T. L., Koob, J. J., & Morgan, M. G. (1992). Community AIDS/HIV risk reduction: The effects of endorsements by popular people in three cities. *American Journal of Public Health, 82,* 1483–1489.

Kiewra, K. A. (1989). A review of note-taking: The encoding storage paradigm and beyond. *Educational Psychology Review, 1,* 147–172.

Kintch, W., & Ericcsen, K. A. (1995). Long term working memory. *Psychological Review, 102,* 211–245.

Kirkman, B. L., & Shapiro, D. L. (1997). The impact of cultural values on employee resistance to teams: Toward a model of globalized self-managing work team effectiveness. *Academy of Management Review, 22,* 730–757.

Kisielius, J., & Sternthal, B. (1984). Detecting and explaining vividness effects in attitudinal judgments. *Journal of Marketing Research, 21,* 54–64.

Klein, G. A. (1989). Recognition-primed decision. In W. Rouse (Ed.), *Advances in man-machine systems research* (Vol. 5, pp. 47–92). Greenwich, CT: JAI Press.

Klein, M. (1975). *The writings of Melanie Klein* (Vol. 3). London: Hogarth Press.

Klein, W. M., & Weinstein, N. D. (1997). Social comparison and unrealistic optimism about personal risk. In B. P. Buunk & F. Gibbons (Eds.), *Health and coping: Perspectives from social comparison theory* (pp. 25–61). Hillsdale, N. J.: Erlbaum.

Klopfer, B., & Kelley, D. M. (1937). The techniques of the Rorschach performance. *Rorschach Research Exchange, 2,* 1–14.

Kobasa, S. C. (1979). Stressful life events and health: An inquiry into hardiness. *Journal of Personality and Social Psychology, 37,* 1–11.

Kobasa, S. C., Maddi, S. R., & Courington, S. (1981). Personality and constitution as mediators in the stress-illness relationship. *Journal of Health and Social Behavior, 22,* 368–378.

Koch, S., & Leary, D. E. (Eds.). (1992). *A century of psychology as a science.* Washington, DC: American Psychological Association.

Kohut, H. (1997). *The restoration of self.* New York: International Universities Press.

Koocher, G. P. (1994). APA and the FTC: New adventures in consumer protection. *American Psychologist, 49,* 322–328.

Kramer, J. J., & Conoley, J. C. (Eds.). *The twelfth mental measurements yearbook.* Lincoln, NE: Buros Institute of Mental Measurements.

Kreshel, P. J. (1990). John B. Watson at J. Walter Thompson: The legitimation of "science" in advertising. *Journal of Advertising, 19,* 49–59.

Kroll, W., & Lewis, G. (1970). America's first sport psychologists. *Quest, 13,* 1–4.

Kruglanski, A. W., & Webster, D. M. (1996). Motivated closing of the mind: "Seizing" and "freezing." *Psychological Review, 103,* 263–283.

Kulik, C. L., Kulik, J. A., & Bangert-Drowns, R. L. (1990). Effectiveness of mastery learning programs: A meta-analysis. *Review of Educational Research, 60,* 265–299.

Kuna, D. P. (1976). The concept of suggestion in the early history of advertising psychology. *Journal of the History of the Behavioral Sciences, 12,* 347–353.

LaBossiere, M. (1996). *Fallacy Tutorial Pro 3.1.* Allegiant Technologies.

Lambert, M. J. (1989). The individual therapists' contribution to psychotherapy process and outcome. *Clinical Psychology Review, 9,* 469–485.

Land, M. L. (1987). Vagueness and clarity: In M. Dunkin (Ed.), *The international encyclopedia of teaching and teacher education* (pp. 392–397). New York: Pergamon.

Langer, E. J. (1978). Rethinking the role of thought in social interaction. In J. H. Harvey, W. J. Ickes, & R. F. Kidd (Eds.), *New directions in attribution research* (Vol. 2). Hillsdale, NJ: Erlbaum.

Langer, E. J. (1989). Minding matters. In L. Berkowitz (Ed.), *Advances in experimental social psychology* (Vol. 22). New York: Academic Press.

Langer, E. J., & Roth, J. (1975). Heads I win, tails it's chance: The illusion of control as a function of sequences in a purely chance task. *Journal of Personality and Social Psychology, 32,* 951–955.

Lapointe, F. H. (1992). Who originated the term "psychology"? *Journal of the History of the Behavioral Sciences, 8,* 328–335.

Leahey, T. H. (1991). *A history of modern psychology.* Englewood Cliffs, NJ: Prentice Hall.

Leahey, T. H. (1997). *A history of psychology: Main currents in psychological thought* (4th ed.). Upper Saddle River, NJ: Prentice Hall.

Leary, M. R., Tchividjian, L. R., & Kraxberger, B. E. (1994). Self-presentation can be hazardous to your health: Impression management and health risk. *Health Psychology, 13,* 461–470.

Lefkowitz, J., & Murphy, K. (1992). Psychology in the People's Republic of China. *Industrial-Organizational Psychologist, 29 (4),* 33–34.

Lehmann, D. R., Ellard, J. H., & Wortman, C. B. (1986). Social support for the bereaved: Recipients' and providers' perspectives on what is helpful. *Journal of Consulting and Clinical Psychology, 54,* 438–446.

Lehmann, D. R., & Pan, Y. (1994). Context effects, new brand entry, and consideration sets. *Journal of Marketing Research, 31,* 364–374.

LeUnes, A., & Hayward, S. A. (1990). Sports psychology as viewed by chairpersons of APA-approved clinical psychology programs. *Sport Psychologist, 4,* 18–24.,

Leventhal, H. (1970). Findings and theory in the study of fear communications. *Advances in Experimental Social Psychology, 5,* 119–186.

Leventhal, H., Diefenbach, M., & Leventhal, E.A. (1992). Illness cognition: Using common sense to understand treatment adherence and affect cognition interactions. *Cognitive Therapy and Research, 16,* 143–163.

Levin, I. P., & Gaeth, G. J. (1988). How consumers are affected by the framing of attribute information before and after consuming the product. *Journal of Consumer Research, 15,* 374–378.

Levinson, H. (1994). Why the behemoths fell: Psychological roots of corporate failure. *American Psychologist, 49,* 428–436.

Lewin, K. (1951). *Field theory in social science.* New York: Harper & Row.

Link, B., Cullen, F., & Andrews, H. (1993). Reconsidering the violent and illegal behavior of mental patients. *American Sociological Review, 57,* 1229–1236.

Locke, E. A. (1968). Toward a theory of task motivation and incentives. *Organizational Behavior and Human Performance, 3,* 157–189.

Locke, E. A., & Latham, G. P. (1990). *A theory of goal setting and task performance.* Englewood Cliffs, NJ: Prentice Hall.

Locke, E. A., Shaw, K., Saari, L., & Latham, G. (1981). Goal setting and task performance: 1969–1980. *Psychological Bulletin, 90,* 125–152.

Loehr, J. E. (1994). *The new toughness training for sports.* New York: Penguin.

Loewy, R. (1951). *Never leave well enough alone.* New York: Simon & Schuster.

Lohman, D. L. (1989). Human intelligence: An introduction to advances in theory and research. *Review of Educational Research, 59,* 333–374.

Lorenz, K. (1954). *Man meets dog.* London: Methuen.

Luchins, A. S. (1993). Social control doctrines of mental illness and the medical profession in nineteenth-century America. *Journal of the History of the Behavioral Sciences, 29,* 29–47.

Lunt, I. R., & Poortinga, Y. H. (1996). Internationalizing psychology: The case of Europe. *American Psychologist, 51,* 504–508.

Lyman, H. B. (1986). *Test scores and what they mean.* Englewood Cliffs, NJ: Prentice Hall.

Lynch, J. G., Marmorstein, H., & Weigold, M. F. (1988). Choices from sets including remembered brands: Use of recalled attributes and prior overall evaluations. *Journal of Consumer Research, 15,* 169-184.

Macintyre, A. (1992). How psychology makes itself true—or false. In S. Koch & D. E. Leary (Eds.), *A century of psychology as a science.* Washington, DC: American Psychological Association.

Mack, J. (1995). *Abduction : Human encounters with aliens.* New York: Ballantine.

Mackworth, N. (1961). Researches on the measurement of human performance. In H. W. Sinaiko (Ed.), *Selected papers on human factors in the design and use of control systems.* New York: Dover.

MacLeod, R. B. (1975). *The persistent problems of psychology.* Pittsburgh, PA: Duquesne University Press.

Madey, S. F., & Gilovich, T. (1993). Effect of temporal focus on the recall of expectancy-consistent and expectancy-inconsistent information. *Journal of Personality and Social Psychology, 65,* 458–468.

Mager, R. (1975). *Preparing instructional objectives* (2nd ed.). Palo Alto, CA: Fearon.

Mahoney, M. J. (1991). *Human change processes: The scientific foundations of psychotherapy.* New York: Basic Books.

Makari, G. (1993) Educated insane: A nineteenth-century psychiatric paradigm. *Journal of the History of the Behavioral Sciences, 29,* 8–21.

Martens, R. (1979). About smocks and jocks. *Journal of Sport Psychology, 1,* 94-99.

Maslow, A. H. (1943). A theory of human motivation. *Psychological Review, 50,* 370–396.

Maslow, A. H. (1968). *Toward a psychology of being* (2nd ed.). New York: Van Nostrand.

Maslow, A. H. (1970). *Motivation and personality* (2nd ed.). New York: Harper and Row.

Mayer, R. E. (1984). Twenty-five years of research on advance organizers. *Instructional Science, 8,* 133–169.

McCrae, R. R., & Costa, P. (1990). *Personality in adulthood.* New York: Guilford.

McCullagh, P., & Noble, J. M. (1996). Education and training in sport and exercise psychology. In J. L. Van Raalte & B. W. Brewer (Eds.), *Exploring sport and exercise psychology* (pp. 377–394). Washington, DC: American Psychological Association.

McNemar, Q. (1964). Lost: Our intelligence? Why? *American Psychologist, 19,* 871-882.

McRuer, D., & Jex, H. (1967) A review of quasi linear pilot models. *IEEE Transactions on Human Factors in Electronics, HFE-8,* 231–249.

Medley, D. M. (1979). The effectiveness of teachers. In P. Peterson & H. Walberg (Eds.), *Research on teaching:*

Concepts, findings, and implications (pp. 11–27). Berkeley, CA: McCutchan.

Melamed, B. G. (1995). The neglected psychological-physical interface. *Health Psychology, 14,* 371–373.

Melton, G. B., Petrila, J., Poythress, N. G., & Slobogin, C. (1987). *Psychological evaluations for the courts.* New York: Guilford Press.

Menon, G., Raghubir, P., & Schwartz, N. (1995). Behavioral frequency judgments: An accessibility-diagnosticity framework. *Journal of Consumer Research, 22,* 212–228.

Mento, A., Steel, R., & Karren, R. (1987). A meta-analytic study of the effects of goal setting on task performance: 1966–1984. *Organizational Behavior and Human Decision Processes, 39,* 52–83.

Meyer, D., Leventhal, H., & Guttman, M. (1985). Common-sense models of illness: The example of hypertension. *Health Psychology, 4,* 115–135.

Meyer, M., & Zucker, L. (1989). *Permanently failing organizations.* Newbury Park, CA: Sage.

Meyers-Levy, J., & Peracchio, L. A. (1992). Getting an angle in advertising: The effects of camera angle on product evaluations. *Journal of Marketing Research, 29,* 454–461.

Milgram, S. (1963). Behavioral study of obedience. *Journal of Abnormal and Social Psychology. 67,* 371–378.

Miller, G. A. (1969). Psychology as a means of promoting human welfare. *American Psychologist, 24,* 1063–1075.

Miller, G. A. (1992). The constitutive problem of psychology. In S. Koch & D. E. Leary (Eds.), *A century of psychology as a science.* Washington, DC: American Psychological Association.

Miller, G. A., Galanter, E., & Pribram, K. H. (1960). *Plans and the structure of behavior.* New York: Holt, Rinehart & Winston.

Miller, H. (1996). *The social psychology of objects.* Huddersfield, U.K. Paper presented at Understanding the Social World Conference.

Miller, I. J. (1996). Time-limited brief therapy has gone too far: The result is invisible rationing. *Professional Psychology: Research and Practice, 27,* 567–576.

Miller, L. C., Bettencourt, B. A., DeBro, S. C., & Hoffman, V. (1993). Negotiating safer sex: Interpersonal dynamics. In J. B. Pryor & G. D. Reeder (Eds.), *The social psychology of HIV infection* (pp. 85–123). Hillsdale, NJ: Erlbaum.

Monahan, J. (1992). Mental disorder and violent behavior: Perceptions and evidence. *American Psychologist, 47,* 511–521.

Monahan, J., & Walker, L. (1990). *Social sciences in law: Cases and materials* (2nd ed.). Westbury, NY: Foundation Press.

Moore, B. R. (1996). The evolution of imitative learning. In C. M. Heyes & B. G. Galef, Jr. (Eds.), *Social learning in animals: The roots of culture* (pp. 245–264). San Diego: Academic Press.

Moray, N. P. (1969). *Attention: Selective processes in vision and hearing.* London: Hutchinson.

Morgan, B. B., Glickman, A. S., Woodward, E. A., Blaiwes, A. S., & Salas, E. (1986). *Measurement of team behaviors in a navy environment* (Tech. Rep. No. TR-86-014). Orlando, FL: Naval Training Systems Center, Human Factors Division.

Morrow, L. M. (1992). The impact of a literature-based program on literacy achievement, use of literature, and attitudes of children from minority backgrounds. *Reading Research Quarterly, 27,* 251–275.

Morrow-Bradley, C., & Elliott, R. (1986). Utilization of psychotherapy research by practicing psychotherapists. *American Psychologist, 41,* 188–197.

Morse, S. J. (1978). Law and mental health professionals: The limits of expertise. *Professional Psychology, 9,* 389–399.

Moses, J. L., & Boehm, V. R. (1975). Relationship of assessment center performance to management progress of women. *Journal of Applied Psychology, 60,* 527–529.

Moses, J., Hollenbeck, G. P., & Sorcher, M. (1993). Other people's expectations. *Human Resource Management, 32,* 283–297.

Motowidlo, S. J., Borman, W. C., & Schmit, M. J. (1997). A theory of individual differences in task and contextual performance. *Human Performance, 10,* 71–83.

Motowidlo, S. J., & Van Scotter, J. R. (1994). Evidence that task performance should be distinguished from contextual performance. *Journal of Applied Psychology, 79,* 475–480.

Münsterberg, H. (1913). *Psychology and industrial efficiency.* Boston: Houghton Mifflin.

Murphy, K. R., Osten, K., & Myors, B. (1995). Modeling the effects of banding in personnel selection. *Personnel Psychology, 48,* 61-84.

Murphy, S. M. (Ed.). (1995). *Sport psychology interventions.* Champaign, IL: Human Kinetics.

Murphy, S. M. (1996). *The achievement zone.* New York: Berkeley.

Murray, B. (1996). Psychology remains top college major. *The APA Monitor, Feb,* pp. 1, 42.

Murray, H. G. (1983). Low inference classroom teaching behavior and student ratings of college teaching. *Journal of Educational Psychology, 75,* 138–149.

Napoli, D. S. (1981). *Architects of adjustment: The history of the psychological profession in the United States.* Port Washington, NY: Kennikat Press.

Neuman, S. B., & Roskos, K. (1992). Literacy objects as cultural tools: Effects on children's literacy behaviors in play. *Reading Research Quarterly, 27,* 255–275.

Newburg, D. (1992). Performance enhancement: Toward a working definition. *Contemporary Thought on Performance Enhancement, 1,* 10–15.

Newman, O., & Frank, K., (1982). The effects of building size on personal crime and fear of crime. *Population and environment, 5,* 20-3-220.

Newman, R. (1995). *Head-up displays: Designing the way ahead.* Hampshire, England: Avebury Aviation.

Nicholson, R. A., Briggs, S. R., & Robertson, H. C. (1988). Instruments for assessing competency to stand trial: How do they work? *Professional Psychology: Research and Practice, 19,* 383–394.

Nicholson, R. A., & Kugler, K. E. (1991). Competent and incompetent criminal defendants: A quantitative review of comparative research. *Psychological Bulletin, 109,* 355–370.

Nietzel, M. T., Bernstein, D. A., & Milich, R. (1998). *Introduction to clinical psychology* (5th ed.). Englewood Cliffs, NJ: Prentice Hall.

Nilsen, D., & Campbell, D. P. (1993). Self-observer rating discrepancies: Once an overrater, always an overrater? *Human Resource Management, 32,* 265–281.

Norcross, J. C., Prochaska, J. O., & Gallagher, K. M. (1989). Clinical psychologists in the 1980s: II. Theory, research, and practice. *Clinical Psychologist, 42,* 45–53.

Nordheim, B. (1995). *Aviation Week and Space Technology.*

Norman, D. A. (1988). *The psychology of everyday things.* New York: Harper Collins.

Norman, K. (1991). *The psychology of menu selection.* Hillsdale, NJ: Erlbaum.

Northcraft, G. B., & Neale, M. A. (1987). Experts, amateurs and real estate: An anchoring and adjustment perspective on property pricing decisions. *Organizational Behavior and Human Decision Processes, 39,* 84–97.

Nummedal, S. G., & Halpern, D. F. (1995). Introduction: Making the case for "Psychologists teach critical thinking." *Teaching of Psychology, 22,* 4–5.

O'Connor, M., Sales, B. D., & Schuman, D. (1996). Mental health professional expertise in the courtroom. In B. D. Sales & D. W. Shuman (Eds.), *Law, mental health, and mental disorder.* Pacific Grove, CA: Brooks/Cole.

Ogloff, J. R. P. (1991). A comparison of insanity defense standards on juror decision making. *Law and Human Behavior, 15,* 509–532.

Ogloff, J. R. P., & Otto, R. (1993). Psychological autopsy: Clinical and legal perspectives. *Saint Louis University Law Journal, 37,* 607–646.

O'Leary, A. (1985). Self-efficacy and health. *Behavior Research and Therapy, 23,* 437–451.

Olfson, M., Pincus, H., & Sabshin, M. (1994). Pharmacotherapy in outpatient psychiatric practice. *American Journal of Psychiatry, 151,* 580–585.

Ono, K. (1987). Superstitious behavior in humans. *Journal of the Experimental Analysis of Behavior, 47,* 261–271.

Ophuls, W. (1977). *Ecology and the politics of scarcity.* San Francisco: Freeman.

Orasanu, J. (1994). Shared problem models and flight crew performance. In N. Johnston, N. McDonald, & R. Fuller (Eds.), *Aviation psychology in practice:* Avebury Technical.

Orasanu, J., & Fischer, U. (1997) Finding decisions in natural environments: The view from the cockpit. In C. E. Zsambok & G. Klein (Eds.), *Naturalistic decision making.* Hillsadale, NJ: Erlbaum.

Ordione, G. S. (1979). *Management by objectives II.* Belmont, CA: Davis S. Lake.

Ortony, A., Clore, G. L., & Collins, A. (1988). *The cognitive structure of emotions.* Cambridge: Cambridge University Press.

Otto, R., Poythress, N., Starr, K., & Darkes, J. (1993). An empirical study of the reports of APA's peer review panel in the congressional review of the *USS Iowa* incident. *Journal of Personality Assessment, 61,* 425–442.

Ozer, D. J., & Reise, S. P. (1994). Personality assessment. *Annual Review of Psychology, 45,* 357-388.

Papanek, V. (1995). *The green imperative.* New York: Thames and Hudson.

Parasuraman, R., Davies, R., & Beatty, J. (Eds.). (1984). *Varieties of attention.* New York: Academic Press.

Parasuraman, R., Molloy, R., & Singh, I. L. (1993). Performance consequences of automation-induced complacency. *International Journal of Aviation Psychology, 3*(1), 1–23.

Parasuraman, R., & Riley, V. (1997). Humans and automation: Use, misuse, disuse, abuse. *Human Factors, 39,* 230–253.

Parot, F. (1993). Psychology experiments: Spiritism at the Sorbonne. *Journal of the History of the Behavioral Sciences, 29,* 22-28.

Pasch, M., Sparks-Langer, G., Gardner, T. G., Starko, A. J., & Moody, C. D. (1991). *Teaching as decision making: Instructional practices for the successful teacher.* New York: Longman.

Pasewark, R. A., Bieber, S., Bosten, K. J., Kiser, M., & Steadman, H. J. (1982). Criminal recidivism among insanity acquittees. *International Journal of Law and Psychiatry, 5,* 365–374.

Pawlik, K., & d'Ydewall, G. (1996). Psychology and the global commons. *American Psychologist, 51,* 488–495.

Payne, J. W., Bettman, J. R., & Johnson, E. J. (1993). *The adaptive decision maker.* Cambridge, England: Cambridge University Press.

Pearson, P. D. (1989). Commentary: Reading the whole language movement. *Elementary School Journal, 90,* 231–241.

Pennebaker, J. W. (1993). Putting stress into words: Health, linguistic, and therapeutic implications. *Behavior Research and Therapy, 31,* 539-548.

Perloff, R., & Naman, J. L. (1996). Lillian Gilbreth: Tireless advocate for a general psychology. In G. A. Kimble, C. A. Boneau, & M. Wertheimer (Eds.), *Portraits of pioneers in psychology* (Vol. 2, pp. 107–116). Washington, DC: American Psychological Association.

Perls, F. S. (1969). *Gestalt therapy verbatim.* Lafayette, CA: Real People Press.

Peterson, C. (1988). Explanatory style as a risk factor for illness. *Cognitive Therapy and Research, 12,* 119–132.

Peterson, C., Seligman, M. E. P., & Vaillant, G. E. (1988). Pessimistic explanatory style is a risk factor for physical illness: A thirty-five-year longitudinal study. *Journal of Personality and Social Psychology, 55,* 23–27.

Petitpas, A., Brewer, B., Rivera, P., & Van Raalte, J. (1994). Ethical beliefs and behaviors in applied sport psychology: The AAASP ethics survey. *Journal of Applied Sport Psychology, 6,* 135–151.

Petty, R. E., & Cacioppo, J. T. (1986). The elaboration likelihood model of persuasion. In L. Berkowitz (Ed.), *Advances in experimental social psychology* (Vol. 19, pp. 123–205). San Diego, CA: Academic Press.

Petty, R. E., & Wegener, D. T. (1993). Flexible correction processes in social judgment: Correcting for context-induced contrast. *Journal of Experimental Social Psychology, 29,* 137–165.

Pfaffenberger, C. (1963). *The new knowledge of dog behavior.* New York: Howell Book House.

Pheasant, S. T. (1986). *Bodyspace: Anthropometry, ergonomics and design.* London: Taylor and Francis.

Philipson, I. J. (1993). *On the shoulders of women: The feminization of psychotherapy.* New York: Guilford Press.

Piaget, J. (1954). *The construction of reality in the child* (M. Cook, Trans.). New York: Basic Books.

Piaget, J. (1963). *Origins of intelligence in children.* New York: Norton.

Piaget, J. (1970). Piaget's theory. In P. Mussen (Ed.), *Handbook of child psychology* (3rd ed.). New York: Wiley.

Pion, G. M., Mednick, M. T., Astin, H. S., Iijima Hall, C. C., Kenkel, M. B., Keita, G. P., Kohout, J. L., & Kelleher, J. C. (1996). The shifting gender composition of psychology: Trends and implications for the discipline. *American Psychologist, 51,* 509–528.

Pistrang, N., & Barker, C. (1995). The partner relationship in psychosocial responses to breast cancer. *Social Science and Medicine, 40,* 789–797.

Pitariu, H. D. (1992). I/O psychology in Romania: Past, present, and intentions. *Industrial-Organizational Psychologist, 29* (4), 29–33.

Planzer, N., & Jenny, M. T. (1995, January–March) Managing the evolution to free flight. *Journal of Air Traffic Control,* pp. 18–20.

Pleck, J. H., Sonenstein, F. L., & Ku, L. C. (1993). Masculinity ideology: Its impact on adolescent males' heterosexual relationships. *Journal of Social Issues, 49*(3), 11–19.

Plomin, R., DeFries, J. C., McClearn, G. E., & Rutter, M. (1997). *Behavioral genetics* (3rd ed.). San Francisco: Freeman.

Post, C. G. (1963). *An introduction to the law.* Englewood Cliffs, NJ: Prentice Hall.

Poythress, N. G., Bonnie, R. J., Hoge, S. K., Monahan, J., & Oberlander, L. B. (1994). Client abilities to assist counsel and make decisions in criminal cases: Findings from three studies. *Law and Human Behavior, 18,* 437–452.

Pratkanis, A., & Aronson, E. (1992). *Age of propaganda: The everyday use and abuse of persuasion.* New York: Freeman.

Prawat, R. S. (1992). Teachers' beliefs about teaching and learning: A constructivist perspective. *American Journal of Education, 100,* 354–395.

Pressley, M. (1996, August). *Getting beyond whole language: Elementary reading instruction that makes sense in light of recent psychological research.* Paper presented at the annual meeting of the American Psychological Association, Toronto.

Pressley, M., Levin, J., & Delaney, H. D. (1982). The mnemonic keyword method. *Review of Research in Education, 52,* 61–91.

Pring, R. (1971). Bloom's taxonomy: A philosophical critique. *Cambridge Journal of Education, 1,* 83–91.

Prochaska, J. O., & DiClemente, C.C. (1983). Stages and processes of self-change of smoking: Toward an integrative model of change. *Journal of Consulting and Clinical Psychology, 51,* 390–395.

Progoff, I. (1973). *Jung, synchronicity, and human destiny: Non-causal dimensions of human experience.* New York: Julian Press.

Pryor, K. (1984). *Don't shoot the dog: How to improve yourself and others through behavioral training.* New York: Simon & Schuster.

Quadrel, M. J., Fischhoff, B., & Davis, W. (1993). Adolescent (In)vulnerability. *American Psychologist, 48,* 102–116.

Rasmussen, J. (1986). *Information processing and human machine interaction.* New York: Elsevier.

Reason, J. (1990). *Human error.* New York: Cambridge University Press.

Ree, M. J., & Caretta, T. R. (1996). Central role of g in military pilot selection. *International Journal of Aviation Psychology, 6,* 111–124.

Ree, M. J., & Earles, J. A. (1992). Intelligence is the best predictor of job performance. *Current Directions in Psychological Science, 1,* 86–89.

Reed, G. (1974). *The psychology of anomalous experience: A cognitive approach.* Boston: Houghton Mifflin.

Reingen, P. H. (1982). Test of a list procedure for inducing compliance with a request to donate money. *Journal of Applied Psychology, 67,* 110–118.

Rejeski, W. R., & Brawley, L. R. (1988). Defining the boundaries of sport psychology. *Sport Psychologist, 2,* 231–242.

Resnick, R. J. (1997). A brief history of practice—expanded. *American Psychologist, 52,* 463–468.

Richey, C. R. (1994). Proposals to eliminate the prejudicial effect of the use of the word "expert" under the federal rules of evidence in civil and criminal jury trials. *Federal Rules Decisions, 154,* 537–562.

Rilling, M. (1996). The mystery of the vanished citations: James McConnell's forgotten 1960's quest for planarian learning, a biochemical engram, and a celebrity. *American Psychologist, 51,* 589–598.

Ritchie, C. I. A. (1981). *The British dog.* London: Hale.

Ritchie, R. J., & Moses, J. L. (1983). Assessment center correlates of women's advancement into middle management: A 7-year longitudinal analysis. *Journal of Applied Psychology, 68,* 227–231.

Roberts, C. G., & Golding, S. L. (1991). The social construction of criminal responsibility and insanity. *Law and Human Behavior, 15,* 349–376.

Roberts, G. C., & Halliwell, W. (1990). *Sport Psychologist, 4* (4).

Roberts, K. H., & Boyacigiller, N. A. (1984). Cross-national organizational research: The grasp of the blind men. *Research in Organizational Behavior, 6,* 423–475.

Robinson, D. H., & Kiewra, K. A. (1995). Visual arguments: Graphic outlines are superior to outlines in improving learning from text. *Journal of Educational Psychology, 87,* 455–467.

Robinson, L. A., Berman, J. S., & Neimeyer, R. A. (1990). Psychotherapy for the treatment of depression: A comprehensive review of controlled outcome research. *Psychological Bulletin, 108,* 30–49.

Roesch, R., & Golding, S. L. (1980). *Competency to stand trial.* Urbana, IL: University of Illinois Press.

Rogers, C. R. (1942) *Counseling and psychotherapy.* Boston: Houghton Mifflin.

Rogers, C. R. (1951). *Client-centered therapy.* Boston: Houghton Mifflin.

Rogers, C. R., & Freiberg, H. J. (1994). *Freedom to learn* (3rd ed.). Columbus, OH: Charles E. Merrill.

Romanes, G. J. (1883). *Animal intelligence.* London: Routledge & Kegan Paul.

Roscoe, S. N. (1968). Airborne displays for flight and navigation. *Human Factors, 10,* 321-332.

Rosenshine, B. (1986). Synthesis of research on explicit teaching. *Educational Leadership, 43* (7), 60–69.

Rosenstock, I. M. (1974). Historical origins of the health belief model. *Health Education Monographs, 2,* 1–8.

Rosenthal, R. (1987). Pygmalion effects: Existence, magnitude and social importance. A reply to Wineburg. *Educational Researcher, 16,* 37–41.

Rosenthal, R., & Jacobson, L. (1968). *Pygmalion in the classroom.* New York: Holt, Rinehart, and Winston.

Rosenzweig, M. R. (1992). Psychological science around the world. *American Psychologist, 47,* 718–722.

Ross, D. (1972). *G. Stanley Hall: The psychologist as prophet.* Chicago: University of Chicago Press.

Roter, D. L. (1984). Patient question asking in physician-patient interaction. *Health Psychology, 3,* 395–409.

Rotella, R. (1995). *Golf is not a game less perfect.* New York: Simon and Schuster.

Rothgeb, C. L. (Ed.). (1973). *Abstracts of the standard edition of the complete psychological works of Sigmund Freud.* New York: International Universities Press.

Rothman, A. J., Klein, W. M., & Weinstein, N. D. (1996). Absolute and relative biases in estimations of personal risk. *Journal of Applied Social Psychology, 26,* 1213–1236.

Rothman, A. J., & Salovey, P. (1997). Shaping perceptions to motivate healthy behavior: The role of message framing. *Psychological Bulletin, 121,* 3–19.

Rozin, P., Markwith, M., & Nemeroff, C. (1992). Magical contagion beliefs and fear of AIDS. *Journal of Applied Social Psychology, 22,* 1081–1092.

Rozin, P., Markwith, M., & Ross, B. (1990). The sympathetic magical law of similarity, nominal realism and neglect of negatives in response to negative labels. *Psychological Science, 1,* 383–384.

Rozin, P., Millman, L., & Nemeroff, C. (1986). Operation of the laws of sympathetic magic in disgust and other domains. *Journal of Personality and Social Psychology, 50,* 703–712.

Rutter, D. R., Iconomou, G., & Quine, L. (1996). Doctor-patient communication and outcome in cancer patients: An intervention. *Psychology and Health, 12,* 57-71.

Ryans, D. G. (1960). *Characteristics of effective teachers, their descriptions, comparisons and appraisal: A research study.* Washington, DC: American Council on Education.

Ryff, C. D. (1989). Happiness is everything, or is it? Explorations on the meaning of psychological well-being. *Journal of Personality and Social Psychology, 57,* 1069–1081.

Ryff, C. D., & Keyes, C. L. M. (1995). The structure of psychological well-being revisited. *Journal of Personality and Social Psychology, 69,* 719–727.

Sachs, M. (1993). Professional ethics in sport psychology. In R. N. Singer, M. Murphey, & L. K. Tennant (Eds.), *Handbook of research on sport psychology* (pp. 921–932). New York: Macmillan.

Sackett, P. R., & Roth, L. (1991). A Monte Carlo examination of banding and rank order methods of test scores used in personnel selection. *Human Performance, 4,* 279–295.

Sagan, C. (1996). *The demon-haunted world: Science as a candle in the dark.* New York: Random House.

Salas, E., Bowers, C., & Cannon-Bowers, J. A. (1995). Military team research: 10 years of progress. *Military Psychology, 7,* 55–75.

Salas, E., Dickinson, T. L., Converse, S. A., & Tannenbaum, S. I. (1992). Toward an understanding of team performance and training. In R. W. Swezey & E. Salas (Eds.), *Teams: Their training and performance* (pp. 3–29). Norwood, NJ: Ablex.

Sales, B. D., & Hafemeister, T. (1984). Empiricism and legal policy on the insanity defense. In L. A. Teplin (Ed.), *Mental health and criminal justice* (pp. 253–278). Newbury Park, CA: Sage.

Sales, B. D., & Shuman, D. W. (1996). *Law, mental health, and mental disorder.* Pacific Grove, CA: Brooks/Cole.

Samelson, F. (1977). World War I intelligence testing and the development of psychology. *Journal of the History of the Behavioral Sciences, 13,* 274–282.

Samelson, F. (1978). From "race psychology" to "studies in prejudice": Some observations on the thematic reversal in social psychology. In L. T. Benjamin, Jr. (Ed.), *A history of psychology: Original sources and contemporary research* (2nd ed.). New York: McGraw-Hill.

Sanbonmatsu, D. M., & Kardes, F. R. (1988). The effects of physiological arousal on information processing and persuasion. *Journal of Consumer Research, 15,* 379–385.

Sanbonmatsu, D. M., Kardes, F. R., & Herr, P. M. (1992). The role of prior knowledge and missing information in multiattribute evaluation. *Organizational Behavior and Human Decision Processes, 51,* 76–91.

Sanbonmatsu, D. M., Kardes, F. R., Posavac, S. S., & Houghton, D. C. (1997). Contextual influences on judgment based on limited information. *Organizational Behavior and Human Decision Processes, 69,* 251–264.

Sanbonmatsu, D. M., Kardes, F. R., & Sansone, C. (1991). Remembering less and inferring more: The effects of the timing of judgment on inferences about unknown attributes. *Journal of Personality and Social Psychology, 61,* 546–554.

Sanders, M. S., & McCormick, E. J. (1992). *Human factors in engineering and design.* New York: McGraw-Hill.

Sanderson, C. A., & Cantor, N. (1995). Social dating goals in late adolescence: Implications for safer sexual activity. *Journal of Personality and Social Psychology, 68,* 1121–1134.

Sarter, N. B., & Woods, D. D. (1995). How in the world did we ever get into that mode? Mode error and awareness in supervisory control. *Human Factors, 37,* 5–19.

Sarter, N. B., & Woods, D. D. (1997). Team play with a powerful and independent agent: Operational experiences and automation surprises on the Airbus A-320. *Human Factors, 39,* 553–569.

Saywitz, K. J., & Snyder, L. (1996). Narrative elaboration: Test of a new procedure for interviewing children. *Journal of Consulting and Clinical Psychology, 64,* 1347–1357.

Scheiber, B., & Selby, C. (1997). UAB final report of therapeutic touch—an appraisal. *Skeptical Inquirer, 21,* 55–56.

Scheier, M. F., Matthews, K. A., Owens, J., Magovern, G. J., Sr., Lefebvre, R. C., Abbott, R. A., & Carver, C. S. (1989). Dispositional optimism and recovery from coronary artery bypass surgery: The beneficial effects on physical and psychological well-being. *Journal of Personality and Social Psychology, 57,* 1024–1040.

Schmidt, F. L. (1991). Why all banding procedures in personnel selection are logically flawed. *Human Performance, 4,* 265–277.

Schmidt, F. L., Hunter, J. E., Pearlman, K., & Shane, G. S. (1979). Further tests of the Schmidt-Hunter Bayesian Validity Generalization Model. *Personnel Psychology, 32,* 257–281.

Schoenwald, R. L. (Ed.). (1965). *Nineteenth-century thought: The discovery of change.* Englewood Cliffs, NJ: Prentice Hall.

Scientific Affairs Committee. (1994). An evaluation of banding methods in personnel selection. *Industrial-Organizational Psychologist, 32 (1),* 80–86.

Scott, J. P., Eliot, O. S., & Ginsburg, B. E. (1997). Man and his dog. *Science, 278,* 205-206.

Scott, J. P., & Fuller, J. C. (1965). *Genetics and the social behavior for the dog.* Chicago: University of Chicago Press.

Scott, W. D. (1903). *The theory of advertising.* Boston: Small, Maynard & Co.

Scott, W. D. (1908). *The psychology of advertising.* Boston: Small, Maynard & Co.

Segerstrom, S. C., Taylor, S. E., Kemeny, M. E., Reed, G. M., & Visscher, B. R. (1996). Causal attributions predict rate of immune decline in HIV-seropositive gay men. *Health Psychology, 15,* 485–493.

Sekimoto, M. (1983). Performance appraisal in Japan: Past and future. *Industrial-Organizational Psychologist, 20 (4),* 52–58.

Seligman, M. E. P. (1995). The effectiveness of psychotherapy: The *Consumer Reports* Study. *American Psychologist, 59,* 965–974.

Shapiro, D. A., & Shapiro, D. (1982). Meta-analysis of comparative therapy outcome research: A critical appraisal. *Behavioral Psychotherapy, 10,* 4–25.

Shaw, K. T., & Gifford, R. (1994). Resident' and burglars' assessment of risk from defensible space cues. *Journal of Environmental Psychology, 14,* 177–194.

Shepard, W. T., & Johnson, W. B. (1995). Human factors in aviation maintenance and inspection factors in aviation maintenance and inspection. In *Proceedings of the 39th Annual Meeting of the Human Factors and Ergonomics Society.* Santa Monica, CA: Human Factors.

Sherman, J. G., Ruskin, R. S., & Semb, G. B. (Eds.). (1982). *The Personalized System of Instruction: 48 seminal papers.* Lawrence, KS: TRI Publications.

Shields, S. A. (1975). Functionalism, Darwinism, and the psychology of women: A study in social myth. In L. T.

Benjamin, Jr. (Ed.), *A history of psychology: Original sources and contemporary research* (2nd ed.). New York: McGraw-Hill.

Shiller, V. (1986). Loyalty conflicts and family relationships in latency age boys: A comparison of joint and maternal custody. *Journal of Divorce, 9,* 17-38.

Shipley, K. G., & Wood, J. M. (1996). *The elements of interviewing.* San Diego, CA: Singular Publishing.

Shuell, T. J. (1981, April). *Toward a model of learning from instruction.* Paper presented at a meeting of the American Educational Research Association, Los Angeles.

Shuell, T. (1996). Teaching and learning in a classroom context. In D. Berliner & R. Calfee (Eds.), *Handbook of educational psychology* (pp. 726–764). New York: Macmillan.

Siegal, A. M., & Elwork, A. (1990). Treating incompetence to stand trial. *Law and Human Behavior, 14,* 57–65.

Singer, M., Murphey, M., & L. K, Tennant (Eds.), *Handbook of research on sport psychology* (pp. 921–932). New York: Macmillan.

Singer, R. N. (1993). Ethical issues in clinical services. *Quest, 45,* 88–145.

Silva, J. M. (1989). Toward the professionalization of sport psychology. *Sport Psychologist, 3,* 265–273.

Silver, E. (1995). Punishment or treatment? Comparing the lengths of confinement of successful and unsuccessful insanity defendants. *Law and Human Behavior, 19,* 375–388.

Simonson, I. (1989). Choice based on reasons: The case of attraction and compromise effects. *Journal of Consumer Research, 16,* 158–174.

Simonson, I., & Tversky, A. (1992). Choice in context: Tradeoff contrast and extremeness aversion. *Journal of Marketing Research, 29,* 281–295.

Skinner, B. F. (1938). *The behavior of organisms: An experimental analysis.* New York: Appleton.

Skinner, B. F. (1945, October). Baby in a box. *Ladies Home Journal.*

Skinner, B. F. (1948a). *Walden Two.* New York: Macmillan.

Skinner, B. F. (1948b). "Superstition" in the pigeon. *Journal of Experimental Psychology, 38,* 168–172.

Skinner, B. F. (1953). *Science and human behavior.* New York: Macmillan.

Slavin, R. E. (1987). Ability grouping and student achievement in elementary schools: A best-evidence synthesis. *Review of Educational Research, 57,* 293–336.

Slavin, R. E. (1990). Achievement effects of ability grouping in secondary schools: A best-evidence synthesis. *Review of Educational Research, 60,* 471–500.

Smiderle, D., Perry, B. A., & Cronshaw, S. F. (1994). Evaluation of video-based assessment in transit operator selection. *Journal of Business and Psychology, 9,* 3–22.

Smith, C. A., Organ, D. W., & Near, J. P. (1983). Organizational citizenship behavior: Its nature and antecedents. *Journal of Applied Psychology, 68,* 653–663.

Smith, K., & Hancock, P. A. (1995). Situation awareness is adaptive, externally directed consciousness. *Human Factors, 37,* 137–148.

Smith, M. L. (1991). Put to the test: The effects of external testing on teachers. *Educational Researcher, 20* (5), 8–11.

Smith, M. L., Glass, G. V., & Miller, T. I. (1980). *The benefits of psychotherapy.* Baltimore, MD: Johns Hopkins University Press.

Smith, S. (1983). *Ideas of the great psychologists.* New York: Harper & Row.

Smith, S. (1989). Mental health expert witnesses: Of science and crystal balls. *Behavioral Sciences and the Law, 7,* 145–180.

Soar, R. S., & Soar, R. M. (1979). Emotional climate and management. In P. Peterson & H. Walberg (Eds.), *Research on teaching: Concepts, findings, and implications.* Berkeley, CA: McCutchan.

Sommer, B., & Sommer, R. (1997). A practical guide to behavioral research (4th ed.). New York: Oxford University Press.

Sparr, L. (1995). Post-traumatic stress disorder. *Neurologic Clinics, 13,* 413–429.

Spiegel, D., Bloom, J. R., & Gottheil, E. (1983). Family environment as a predictor of adjustment to metastatic breast carcinoma. *Journal of Psychosocial Oncology, 1,* 33–44.

Spillmann, J., & Spillmann, L. (1993). The rise and fall of Hugo Münsterberg. *Journal of the History of the Behavioral Sciences, 29,* 322–338.

Spychalski, A. C., Quinones, M. A., Gaugler, B. B., & Pohley, K. (1997). A survey of assessment center practices in organizations in the United States. *Personnel Psychology, 50,* 71-90.

Stapp, J., Fulcher, R., & Wicherski, M. (1984). The employment of 1981 and 1982 doctorate recipients in psychology. *American Psychologist, 39,* 1408–1423.

Stark, E. A. (1989). Simulation. In R. Jensen (Ed.), *Aviation psychology* (pp. 109–153), Brookfield, VT: Gower Technical.

Steadman, H. J. (1979). *Beating a rap? Defendants found incompetent to stand trial.* Chicago: University of Chicago Press.

Steadman, H. J., & Braff, J. (1983). Defendants not guilty by reason of insanity. In J. Monahan & H. J. Steadman (Eds.), *Mentally disordered offenders: Perspectives from law and social science.* New York: Plenum.

Stehr, N. (1996). The ubiquity of nature: Climate and culture. *Journal of the History of the Behavioral Sciences, 32,* 151–159.

Steiner, D. D., & Gilliland, S. W. (1996). Fairness reactions to personnel selection techniques in France and the United States. *Journal of Applied Psychology, 81,* 134–141.

Stern, W. (1939). The psychology of testimony. *Journal of Abnormal and Social Psychology, 34,* 3–20.

Sternberg, R. (1985). *Beyond IQ: A triarchic theory of human intelligence.* New York: Cambridge University Press.

Sternberg, R. (1990). *Metaphors of mind: Conceptions of the nature of intelligence.* New York: Cambridge University Press.

Stiles, W. A., Shapiro, D. A., & Elliot, R. (1986). Are all psychotherapies equivalent? *American Psychologist, 41,* 165–180.

Stokols, D. (1995). The paradox of environmental psychology. *American Psychologist, 50,* 821–837.

Stokols, D., & Altman, I. (Eds.). (1987). *Handbook of environmental psychology.* New York: Wiley.

Suinn, R. M. (1985). The 1984 Olympics and sport psychology. *Journal of Sport Psychology, 7,* 321–329.

Sujan, M. (1985). Consumer knowledge: Effects on evaluation strategies mediating consumer judgments. *Journal of Consumer Research, 12,* 31–46.

Swets, J. A., & Bjork, R. A. (1990). Enhancing human performance: An evaluation of "new age" techniques considered by the U.S. Army. *Psychological Science, 1,* 85–96.

Swezey, R. W., & Salas, E. (1992). Guidelines for use in team training development. In R. W. Swezey & E. Salas (Eds.), *Teams: Their training and performance* (pp. 219–245). Norwood, NJ: Ablex.

Tait, R., & Silver, R.C. (1989). Coming to terms with major negative life events. In J. S. Uleman & J. A. Bargh (Eds.), *Unintended thought* (pp. 351–382). New York: Guilford.

Tannen, D. (1990). *You just don't understand: Women and men in conversation.* New York: Ballantine.

Tart, C. T. (1990). Multiple personality, altered states, and virtual reality. *Dissociation, 3,* 222–233.

Tavris, C. (1989). *Anger: The misunderstood emotion.* New York: Touchstone.

Tavris, C., & Wade, C. (1984). *The longest war: Sex differences in perspective* (2nd ed.). San Diego: Harcourt Brace Jovanovich.

Taylor, F. W. (1911). *The principles of scientific management.* New York: Harper & Row.

Taylor, S. E. (1983). Adjustment to threatening events: A theory of cognitive adaptation. *American Psychologist, 38,* 1163–1173.

Taylor, S. E. (1995). *Health psychology* (3rd ed.). New York: McGraw-Hill.

Taylor, S. E., & Aspinwall, L.G. (1990). Psychosocial aspects of chronic illness. In P. T. Costa, Jr., & G. R. VandenBos (Eds.), *Psychological aspects of serious illness: Chronic conditions, fatal disease, and clinical care* (pp. 3–60). Washington, DC: American Psychological Association.

Taylor, S. E., & Aspinwall, L. G. (1996). Mediating and moderating processes in psychosocial stress: Appraisal, coping, resistance and vulnerability. In H. B. Kaplan (Ed.), *Psychosocial stress: Perspectives on structure, theory, life-course, and methods* (pp. 71–110). San Diego: Academic Press.

Terman, L. M., & Merrill, M. A. (1937). *Measuring intelligence.* Boston: Houghton Mifflin.

Tett, R. P., Jackson, D. N., & Rothstein, M. (1991). Personality measures as predictors of job performance: A meta-analytic review. *Personnel Psychology, 44,* 703-742.

Thayer, P. W. (1997). Oh! For the good old days! *Industrial-Organizational Psychologist, 34,* 17–20.

Theunissen, E. (1996). Influence of error gain and position prediction on tracking performance and control activity with perspective flight path displays. *Air Traffic Control Quarterly, 3,* 95–116.

Thiel, P. (1996). *People, paths, and purposes.* Seattle: University of Washington Press.

Thoits, P. A. (1986). Social support as coping assistance. *Journal of Consulting and Clinical Psychology, 54,* 416–423.

Thomas, E. L., & Robinson, H. A. (1972). *Improving reading in every class: A sourcebook for teachers.* Boston: Allyn & Bacon.

Thomas, S. B., & Quinn, S. C. (1991). The Tuskegee Syphilis Study, 1932 to 1972: Implications for HIV education and AIDS risk reduction programs in the black community. *American Journal of Public Health, 11,* 1498-1505.

Thorndike, E. L. (1905). *The elements of psychology.* New York: Seiler.

Thorndike, E. L. (1931). *Human learning.* New York: Appleton.

Thorndike, R. L., Hagen, E. P., & Sattler, J. M. (1986). *What is intelligence? Contemporary viewpoints on its nature and definition.* Chicago: Riverside.

Tobacyk, J., & Milford, G. (1983). Belief in paranormal phenomena: Assessment instrument development and implications for personality functioning. *Journal of Personality and Social Psychology, 44,* 1029–1037.

Tolman, E. C. (1932). *Purposive behavior in animals and men.* New York: Appleton.

Treichler, P. A. (1991). AIDS, homophobia, and biomedical discourse: An epidemic of signification. In D. Crimp (Ed.), *AIDS: Cultural analysis, cultural activism* (pp. 31–70). Cambridge, MA: MIT Press.

Triplett, N. (1897). The dynomogenic factors in pacemaking and competition. *American Journal of Psychology, 9,* 507–553.

Trollip, S., & Jensen, R. (1991). *Human factors in general aviation.* Englewood, CO: Jeppeson Sanders.

Tversky, A., & Kahneman, D. (1974). Judgment under uncertainty: Heuristics and biases. *Science, 185,* 1124–1131.

Tyack, D., & Hansot, E. (1982). *Managers of virtue: Public school leadership in America, 1820–1980.* New York: Basic Books.

Tybout, A. M., Calder, B. J., & Sternthal, B. (1981). Using information processing theory to design marketing strategies. *Journal of Marketing Research, 18,* 73–79.

Tybout, A. M., & Scott, C. A. (1983). Availability of well-defined internal knowledge and the attitude formation process: Information aggregation versus self-perception. *Journal of Personality and Social Psychology, 44,* 474–491.

Tybout, A. M., Sternthal, B., & Calder, B. J. (1983). Information availability as a determinant of multiple request effectiveness. *Journal of Marketing Research, 20,* 280–290.

U.S. Department of Justice (1990). *Uniform Crime Reports for the United States, 1990.* Washington, DC: U.S. Department of Justice.

Ustad, K. L., Rogers, R., Sewell, K. W., & Guarnaccia, C. A. (1996). Restoration of competency to stand trial: Assessment with the Georgia Court Competency Test and the Competency Screening Test. *Law and Human Behavior, 20,* 131–146.

Van Metter, P., Yokoi, L., & Pressley, M. (1994). College students' theory of note-taking derived from their perceptions of note-taking. *Journal of Educational Psychology, 86,* 323–338.

Van Raalte, J. L., & Brewer, B. W. (Eds.). (1996). *Exploring sport and exercise psychology.* Washington, DC: American Psychological Association.

Vellutino, F. R. (1991). Introduction to three studies on reading acquisition: Convergent findings on theoretical foundations of code-oriented versus whole-language approaches to reading instruction. *Journal of Educational Psychology, 83,* 437–443.

Vila, C., Savolainen, P., Maldonado, J. E., Amorim, I. R., Rice, J. E., Honeycutt, R. L., Crandall, K. A., Lundeberg, J., & Wayne, R. K. (1997). Multiple and ancient origins of the domestic dog. *Science, 276,* 1687–1689.

Viteles, M. S. (1932). *Industrial psychology.* New York: Norton.

Vlek, C. (1984). What constitutes "a good decision"? In K. Brocherding et al. (Eds.), *Research perspectives on decision-making under uncertainty.* Amsterdam: North-Holland.

Vroom, V. (1964). *Work and motivation.* New York: Wiley.

Vyse, S. A. (1991). Behavioral variability and rule-generation: General, restricted, and superstitious rule statements. *Psychological Record, 41,* 487–506.

Vyse, S. A. (1997). *Believing in magic: The psychology of superstition.* New York: Oxford University Press.

Wade, C. (1995). Using writing to develop and assess critical thinking. *Teaching of Psychology, 22,* 24–28.

Wade, C. (1997). On thinking critically about introductory psychology. In R. J. Sternberg (Ed.), *Teaching introductory psychology* (pp. 151–162). Washington, DC: American Psychological Association.

Wagner, G. A., & Morris, E. K. (1987). "Supersititious" behavior in children. *Psychological Record, 37,* 471–488.

Wampold, B. E., Mondin, G. W., Moody, M., Stich, F., Benson, K., & Ahn, H. (1997). A meta-analysis of outcome studies comparing bona fide psychotherapies: Empirically, "All must have prizes." *Psychological Bulletin, 122,* 203–215.

Warrick, M. J. (1947). Directions of movement in the use of control knobs to position visual indicators. In P. M. Fitts (Ed.), *Psychological research on equipment design* (Res. Rep. No. 19. Army Air Force, Aviation Psychology Program). Washington, DC: Government Printing Office.

Watson, J. B. (1913). Psychology as a behaviorist views it. *Psychological Review, 20,* 158–177.

Watson, J. B. (1928). *Psychological care of infant and child.* New York: Norton.

Watson, J. B. (1930). *Behaviorism* (rev. ed.). New York: Norton.

Wedin, M. V. (1988). *Mind and imagination in Aristotle.* New Haven: Yale University Press.

Weekley, J. A., & Jones, C. (1997). Video-based situational testing. *Personnel Psychology, 50,* 25–49.

Wegener, D. T., & Petty, R. E. (1994). Flexible correction processes in social judgment: The role of naive theories in corrections for perceived bias. *Journal of Personality and Social Psychology, 68,* 36–51.

Weiner, B. (1992). *Human motivation: Metaphors, theories, and research.* Newbury Park, CA: Sage.

Weinert, F. E., & Helmke, A. (1995). Learning from wise mother nature or big brother instructor: The wrong choice as seen from an educational perspective. *Educational Psychologist, 30,* 135–143.

Weinstein, N. D. (1987). Unrealistic optimism about susceptibility to health problems: Conclusions from a community-wide sample. *Journal of Behavioral Medicine, 10,* 481–500.

Weinstein, N. D. (1988). The precaution adoption process. *Health Psychology, 7,* 355–386.

Weissman, H. N. (1985). Psycholegal standards and the role of psychological assessment in personal injury litigation. *Behavioral Sciences and the Law, 3,* 135–148.

Wexler, D., & Winnick, B. J. (1991). *Essays in therapeutic jurisprudence.* Durham, NC: Carolina Academic Press.

Wharton-McDonald, R. Pressley, M., & Mistretta, J. (1996). *Outstanding literacy instruction in first grade: Teacher practices and student achievement.* Albany, NY: National Reading Research Center.

Whealan, J. P. (1993, Summer). Considering ethics. *AAASP Newsletter, 8,* 24, 27.

Whealan, J. P., & Meyers, A. W. (1996). Ethics in sport and exercise psychology. In J. L. Van Raalte & B. W. Brewer (Eds.), *Exploring sport and exercise psychology* (pp. 431–447). Washington, DC: American Psychological Association.

Whealan, J. P., Meyers, A. W., & Donavan, C. (1995). Interventions with competitive recreational athletes. In S. M. Murphy (Ed.), *Sport psychology interventions* (pp. 71–116). Champaign, IL: Human Kinetics.

Whitely, N. (1993). *Design for society.* London: Reaktion Books.

Whyte, W. H. (1988). *City.* Garden City, NY: Doubleday.

Wickens, C. D. (1992). *Engineering psychology and human performance* (2nd ed.). New York: HarperCollins.

Wickens, C. D. (1995) The tradeoff in the design for routine and unexpected performance: Implications of situation awareness. In D. Garland & M. Endsley (Eds.), *Proceedings of the International Conference on the Experimental Analysis and Measurement of Situation Awareness.* Daytona Beach, FL: Embry Riddle Press.

Wickens, C. D. (1999, in press). Cognitive factors in aviation. In F. T. Durso (Ed.), *Handbook of applied cognitive psychology.*

Wickens, C. D., Gordon, S., & Liu, Y. (1998). *An introduction to human factors engineering.* New York: Addison Wesley Longman.

Wickens, C. D., & Long, J. (1995). Object vs. space-based models of visual attention: Implications for the design of head up displays. *Journal of Experimental Psychology: Applied, 1,* 179–194.

Wickens, C. D., Mavor, A., & McGee, J. (Eds.). (1997). *Flight to the future: The human factors of air traffic control.* Washington, DC: National Academy of Sciences.

Wickens, C. D., Mavor, A. S., Parasuraman, R., & McGee, J. P. (Eds.). (1998). *The future of air traffic control: Human operators and automation.* Washington, DC: National Academy Press.

Wiener, E. L., Kanki, B. G., & Helmreich, R. L. (1993). *Cockpit resource management.* San Diego, CA: Academic Press.

Wiener, E., & Nagel, D. (1989). *Human factors in aviation.* Academic Press; San Diego, CA.

Wiener, N. (1948). *Cybernetics.* New York: Wiley.

Wiggam, A. E. (1928). *Exploring your mind with the psychologists.* New York: Bobbs-Merrill.

Wiggins, D. K. (1984). The history of sport psychology in North America. In J. Silva & R. Weinberg (Eds.), *Psychological foundations of sport* (pp. 9–22). Champaign, IL: Human Kinetics.

Wiggins, J. G., Jr. (1994). Would you want your child to be a psychologist? *American Psychologist, 49,* 485–492.

Wiggins, J. S., & Trapnell, P. D. (1997). Personality structure: The return of the Big Five. In R. Hogan, J. Johnson, & S. Briggs (Eds.), *Handbook of personality psychology.* San Diego, CA: Academic Press.

Williams, A., & Flexman, R. (1949). Evaluation of the school Link as an aid in primary flight instruction. *University of Illinois Bulletin, 46* (71).

Williams, J. M., & Straub, W. F. (1997). Sport psychology: Past, present, and future. In J. Williams (Ed.), *Applied sport psychology* (pp. 1–12). Mountain View, CA: Mayfield.

Williges, R. C., & Wierwille, W. W. (1979). Behavioral measures of aircrew mental workload. *Human Factors, 21,* 549–574.

Wilson, T. D., & Brekke, N. (1994). Mental contamination and mental correction: Unwanted influences on judgments and evaluations. *Psychological Bulletin, 116,* 117–142.

Windt, P. Y., Appleby, P. C., Battin, M. P., Francis, L. P., & Landesman, B. M. (Eds.). (1989). *Ethical issues in the professions.* Englewood Cliffs, NJ: Prentice Hall.

Wineman, J. D. (1979). Color in environmental design. *Proceedings of the Environmental Design Research Association, 10,* 436–439.

Winnicott, D. W. (1965). *The maturational processes and the facilitating environment.* New York: International Universities Press.

Winston, A. S. (1996). "As his name indicates": R. S. Woodworth's letters of reference and employment for Jewish psychologists in the 1930s. *Journal of the History of the Behavioral Sciences, 32,* 30–43.

Wispe, L., Awkard, J., Hoffman, M., Ash, P., Hicks, L. H., & Porter, J. (1969). The Negro psychologist in America. *American Psychologist, 24,* 142–150.

Wolchik, S., Braver, S., & Sandler, I. (1985). Maternal versus joint custody: Children's post-separation experiences and adjustment. *Journal of Child Clinical Psychology, 14,* 5–10.

Wolf, R. (1996). Believing what we see, hear, and touch: The delights and dangers of sensory illusions. *Skeptical Inquirer, 20,* 23–34.

Wood, R., Mento, A., & Locke, E. (1987). Task complexity as a moderator of goal effects: A meta-analysis. *Journal of Applied Psychology, 72,* 416–425.

Wood, W., Jones, M., & Benjamin, L. T. (1986). Surveying psychology's public image. *American Psychologist, 41,* 947–953.

Woolfolk Hoy, A. (1998). *Educational psychology* (7th ed.). Boston: Allyn & Bacon.

Wortman, C. B., & Silver, R. L. (1987). Coping with irrevocable loss. In G. R. VandenBos & B. K. Bryant (Eds.), *Cataclysms, crises, and catastrophes: Psychology in action* (pp. 189–235). Washington, DC: American Psychological Association.

Wright, P. (1990). Operationalization of goal difficulty as a moderator of the goal difficulty-performance relationship. *Journal of Applied Psychology, 75,* 227–234.

Wrightsman, L., Nietzel, M. T., & Fortune, W. (1998). *Psychology and the legal system* (4th ed.). Pacific Grove, CA: Brooks/Cole.

Wyer, R. S., & Srull, T. K. (1989). *Memory and cognition in its social context.* Hillsdale, NJ: Erlbaum.

Yale, M., & Yale, J. (1980). *No dogs allowed.* Toronto: Methuen.

Zaichkowsky, L. D., & Perna, F. M. (1992). Certification of consultants in sport psychology: A rebuttal to Anshel. *Sport Psychologist, 6,* 286–296.

Zaichkowsky, L. D., & Perna, F. M. (1996). Certification in sport and exercise psychology. In J. L. Van Raalte & B. W. Brewer (Eds.), *Exploring sport and exercise psychology* (pp. 395–411). Washington, DC: American Psychological Association.

Zeigler, E. F. (1987). Rationale and suggested dimensions for a code of ethics for sport psychologists. *Sport Psychologist, 1,* 138–150.

Zentall, T. R. (1988). Experimentally manipulated imitative behavior in rats and pigeons. In T. R. Zentall & B. G. Galef, Jr. (Eds.), *Social learning: Psychological and biological perspectives* (pp. 191–206). Hillsdale, NJ: Erlbaum.

Zeuner, F. E. (1963). *A history of domesticated animals.* New York: Harper & Row.

Zimbardo, P. G., Haney, C., & Banks, W. C. (1973, April 8). A pirandellian prison. *New York Times Magazine,* pp. 38–60.

Ziskin, J., & Faust, D. (1988). *Coping with psychiatric and psychological testimony* (4th ed.) (Vols. 1–3). Marina del Rey, CA: Law and Psychology Press.

Zurer, P. S. (1994, August). NSF stakes millions on sweeping reform of science, math education. *Chemical and Engineering News, 72,* 25–31.

Zusne, L., & Jones, W. H. (1989). *Anomalistic psychology: A study of magical thinking.* Hillsdale, NJ: Erlbaum.

NAME INDEX